100 Slow Cooker
& Instant Pot® Recipes

Delicious, easy meals for busy days

Vice President, Content: Stacey C. Rivera
Global Creative Director: Theron Long
Managing Editor: Amy Grippo
Editor at Large: Jill Herzig
Food Editor: Eileen Runyan
Writer and Project Editor: Deborah Mintcheff
Contributing Editor: Lisa Chernick
Copy Editor: Christina Doka
Nutrition Consultant: Laureen Jean Leyden
Recipe Developers: Terry Grieco Kenny, Frank Melodia, Angela Nilsen, Carol Prager
Creative Director: Ed Melnitsky
Designer: Rebecca Kollmer, Arlene Lappen
Production Manager: Alan Biederman
Photo Director: Marybeth Dulany
Photographer: Beatriz da Costa
Food Stylist: Jerrie-Joy Redman-Lloyd
Prop Stylist: Suzie Meyers

© Copyright 2019 WW International, Inc.

Nothing may be reprinted in whole or in part without permission from the publisher. Editorial and art produced by W/W Twentyfirst Corp., 675 Avenue of the Americas, New York, NY 10010.

The WW Coin Logo, SmartPoints, Points, ZeroPoint, and myWW logo are trademarks of WW International, Inc.

SKU #61025
Printed in the USA

Front cover:
Rosemary-garlic pork roast, page 89
Back cover:
Carne guisada with charred tortillas, page 158

WW—Weight Watchers reimagined—is a global wellness company and the world's leading commercial weight-management program. We inspire millions of people to adopt healthy habits for real life. Through our engaging digital experience and face-to-face group Workshops, members follow our livable and sustainable program that encompasses healthy eating, physical activity, and a helpful mindset. With more than five decades of experience in building communities and our deep expertise in behavioral science, we aim to deliver wellness for all. To learn more about the WW approach to healthy living, please visit WW.com. For more information about our global business, visit our corporate website at corporate.ww.com.

Risotto-style barley and peas, page 40

Chicken tacos with pineapple slaw, page 111

Contents

vi	Introduction
viii	Keys to slow cooker success
xii	Instant Pot® know-how
xiv	Air fryer basics
xvi	The best part: leftovers
xviii	About our recipes

1	Chapter 1 **Breakfast & brunch**
23	Chapter 2 **Vegetarian mains**
57	Chapter 3 **Updated classics**
107	Chapter 4 **Global favorites**
149	Chapter 5 **Meals for 2**
171	Bonus chapter **Instant Pot® & air fryer specials**

215	Recipes by SmartPoints® value
217	Index

Introduction

Make life on WW easy (and delicious!)

When you think about slow cooker meals, you probably think of convenience: You can toss in the ingredients before you leave the house, and return hours later to the welcoming smell of dinner—warm, tasty, and miraculously done. Or maybe your mind goes to hearty cold-weather meals: rich stews and chilis. Or to feeding a crowd without the last-minute kitchen frenzy. *100 Slow Cooker & Instant Pot® Recipes* delivers on all those counts *and* puts a new spin on the slow cooker, solidifying it as one of the most important tools in your kitchen.

This book makes it easy to stay on track with your weight and wellness goals, no matter which *myWW™* food plan you're on. Our science-backed SmartPoints® system is at the core of each one—Green, Blue, and Purple—and nudges you toward plenty of fruits, vegetables, lean proteins, and healthy fats. You have a personalized amount of SmartPoints to spend foods you love, along with 100+, 200+, or 300+ ZeroPoint™ foods that you don't have to measure or track.

Your slow cooker is brilliant at prepping meals that keep you on course with your wellness goals. The low-and-slow method coaxes flavor from nutritious ingredients, including loads of ZeroPoint foods. It works wonders with lean proteins, turning out tender dishes without fatty cuts of meat. Beans get creamy, spices meld, veggies caramelize—all without a lot of oil or butter.

When you have people to feed and no time to spare, choose one of the many recipes that let you pile everything into the pot and press a button. On more relaxed days, pick a dish that involves a few minutes of sautéing or browning to add an additional layer of taste. Go Italian, Thai, or maybe Indian. And learn how to brighten it all up with last-minute touches that add flavor and nutrition.

We've also included a bonus chapter on the cool new kids in town—the Instant Pot and air fryer. Your Instant Pot is a do-it-all wonder: an electric pressure cooker that gets dishes on the table in record time, as well as a slow cooker, a rice cooker, and a yogurt maker. Oh, and it can also sauté, simmer, and keep food warm. The air fryer turns out food that's super crisp on the outside outside and tender and juicy on the inside. Hot air does all the work with no oil and no mess, and in practically no time.

So, whether you want to take things slow or speed 'em up, cook for a gang or just for two (check out Chapter 5), we've got you covered with ideas and techniques for your kitchen's most valuable gadgets.

Beef 'n' bean chili, page 82

Slow cooker

Keys to slow cooker success

Today's slow cookers have come a long way, despite having the same basic parts: an outer metal container where the electric coils are housed, a stoneware insert, and a tight-fitting glass lid. The amount of electricity used to heat a slow cooker is still very small (even though the newer models heat up much faster), making it safe to operate while you're at work, running errands, or just relaxing. Here are the three types of slow cookers available in different sizes and at various price points. Choose the one that works best for you:

1 Manual slow cookers

The simplest slow cookers feature three settings (High, Low, and Warm), a stoneware insert that's dishwasher-safe (if removable) and doubles as a serving dish, and a glass lid. They range in size from 1½ quarts to 7 quarts and are priced as low as $9.99 and up to $29.99, depending on the size and features.

2 Programmable slow cookers

These models offer one-touch control with multiple time and temperature settings, a dishwasher-safe stoneware insert, and a glass lid. These cookers automatically shift to the Warm setting when the cooking is finished and can be programmed to cook for as little as 30 minutes or as long as 20 hours. They offer the ability to brown meat or sauté vegetables in the flameproof insert. Two silicone-coated handles make it easy—and safe—to transfer the insert to and from the slow cooker or to the table for serving. They range in size from 4 quarts to 8 quarts and cost from $35 to $150.

3 Programmable cook-and-carry slow cookers

These cookers are perfect for taking food on the road. They boast three settings (High, Low, and Warm), a digital timer that counts down the cooking time, and the ability to program the cook time from 30 minutes up to 20 hours. They also automatically shift to the Warm setting once the cook time is complete. The oval-shaped stoneware insert is both removable and dishwasher-safe, while a glass lid has a hinged lock on either side to help get food where it's going without spills. Most are 6 quarts and priced at about $75.

Easy care

Be sure to allow the slow cooker to cool completely before cleaning. The lid and stoneware insert (if removable) are dishwasher-safe. The insert can also be washed using a sponge and hot, soapy water, but be careful not to immerse the base in water. To remove spots or stains, use a nonabrasive cleanser or white vinegar. The exterior of a slow cooker should be wiped clean with a damp cloth. Check with the manufacturer for full cleaning and care instructions.

Remember these basics

Cut similar foods (hard vegetables, soft vegetables, meat, poultry, and seafood) the same size. This ensures they cook in the same amount of time.

Don't substitute frozen food for fresh unless a recipe calls for it. Frozen food will greatly slow the cooking process and could introduce bacteria (especially fish and poultry) because of the long and slow cooking time.

Brown to bring out flavor. Even if a recipe doesn't call for it, you can opt for first browning meat and sautéing vegetables to help bring out their flavor.

Fill the slow cooker just right. This means filling it at least halfway but no more than two-thirds full to ensure all the food cooks evenly and safely.

Add dairy and seafood last. These ingredients can break down if slow cooked for too long (dairy can curdle and seafood can turn mushy). Seafood is usually added during the last hour of cooking, while dairy is usually added during the last 15 minutes or so.

No peeking or stirring! You might wonder what's going on in your slow cooker, but lifting the lid is not recommended unless a recipe directs you to do so. Every time you remove the lid, you're adding approximately 20 minutes to the total cooking time. The only safe time to peek is around 45 minutes before the end of the cooking.

Rotate the insert. As you become more familiar with your slow cooker, you might notice a hot spot (an area that cooks hotter than the rest of the cooker). If this happens, simply swivel the insert (wear oven mitts) halfway through cooking time to ensure even heating.

Use slow cooker plastic liners. These made-for-slow-cooker liners, available in supermarkets, fit neatly inside the insert of a slow cooker. Some recipes, such as frittatas and cakes, call for these liners to make removal easy. But you can also use them for "dump and cook" recipes to ensure fast cleanup.

Plan ahead! If you're one of those people whose morning routine is hectic, get everything ready for your slow cooker recipe the night before. Chop all the vegetables or herbs, trim any meat or poultry, and prepare any sauces or spice mixes. Store each in a separate container or zip-close plastic bag and refrigerate. In the morning, layer or combine the ingredients in your slow cooker as directed and you're good to go.

End with fresh flavor. Brighten the taste of slow cooker recipes by squeezing some lemon or lime juice on top; sprinkling on fresh herbs; dusting with coarse sea salt or fresh black pepper; or topping with orange, lemon, or lime zest.

Slow cooker fitness test

A properly working slow cooker cooks food slowly enough for it to be unattended yet fast enough to keep food out of the bacteria danger zone, which is 40° to 140°F. Here's how to check yours:

- Fill slow cooker halfway to two-thirds full with water.
- Cover and set it on Low for 8 hours.
- Uncover and immediately insert an instant-read thermometer into the water. The temperature should register 185°F. If the temperature is lower, the slow cooker is not getting hot enough to avoid potential food-safety problems and should be replaced.

Slow cooker

Tailor recipes for slow cooking

Good news! You're not limited to recipes written specifically for the slow cooker. Here's how to convert conventional favorites:

Be choosy
Slow cookers are ideal for soups, stews, chilis, and braises, as well as vegetarian and vegan dishes that include root vegetables like potatoes, parsnips, carrots, and turnips.

Pick the right slow cooker
Note the number of servings your recipe makes. You may need to scale it up or down depending on the size of your cooker. (Oval-shaped slow cookers are best for whole poultry and roasts, while round cookers are ideal for soups, stews, and braises).

Cut vegetables and meat in uniform pieces
This ensures they cook in the same amount of time. Layer hard vegetables on the bottom of the slow cooker, top with meat or poultry, and end with tender vegetables like tomato, bell pepper, mushrooms, onion, or zucchini.

Cut the amount of liquid in half
Since slow cookers remain covered, the cooking liquid doesn't evaporate. It accumulates as condensation. If a recipe doesn't contain any liquid (not including frittatas, cakes, casseroles, etc.), add about ½ cup water or broth to the cooker. Moisture is needed to produce steam so the cooker can reach temperature and to prevent ingredients from sticking to the bottom of the insert.

Season later rather than sooner
Slow cooking tends to heighten the flavor of dried herbs and spices, so add half the amount the recipe calls for and adjust the seasoning toward the end of the cooking time. You may also find that a bit more salt and pepper is needed at the end, as slow cooking can also mellow the flavor of a dish. Fresh herbs should be added toward the end of cooking time to retain their flavor.

Reduce the wine
If a recipe calls for wine, reduce the amount by half or boil it down in a saucepan before adding it to the slow cooker in order to cook off the alcohol.

Add dairy later
Milk, yogurt, sour cream, or cheese should be added around 15 minutes before the end of cooking time to prevent curdling.

Thicken if needed
If a finished dish seems a bit soupy, uncover the slow cooker, turn the pot to High, and cook until the liquid is reduced. Alternatively, transfer the pot liquid to a saucepan and reduce over high heat, then pour it back into the slow cooker.

How long to cook conventional recipes in a slow cooker

CONVENTIONAL COOK TIME	SLOW COOKER TIME
15 to 30 minutes	2 to 3 hours on High or 4 to 6 hours on Low
35 to 45 minutes	3 to 4 hours on High or 6 to 8 hours on Low
50 minutes to 1 hour	4 to 6 hours on High or 8 to 10 hours on Low

Chicken with celery root and apple, page 58

Slow cooker FAQs

Q: Is it really safe to cook food for such a long time at a low temperature?

A: Yes! According to the USDA, bacteria in food are killed at 165°F. As long as the lid is kept on and food is cooked for the amount of time specified in a recipe, it will be safe. If you're not browning larger cuts of meat or poultry first, you can give the cooking process a head start by beginning the cooking on High for 1 or 2 hours before lowering the setting if needed. Or prepare the recipe as directed, but bring the liquid ingredients to a simmer on the stovetop before adding them to the cooker to jumpstart the heating process.

Q: Can I reheat leftovers in a slow cooker?

A: No. Although some slow cookers can keep food warm up to 2 hours, they cannot reheat refrigerated leftovers safely because they take too long to come to the right temperature. The good news is that some slow cooker inserts are microwavable and ovenproof up to 400°F, so you can refrigerate leftovers and reheat them all in the same pot. Check the manufacturer's instructions to make sure your insert holds up to conventional cooking methods.

Q: Can I prep recipe ingredients and refrigerate them overnight in the insert?

A: We don't recommend this. It takes too long for a chilled insert filled with raw or uncooked ingredients to reach the right temperature in the slow cooker. Instead, put the prepared ingredients in separate airtight containers or zip-close plastic bags and refrigerate. Avoid browning meat or poultry ahead because browning partially cooks the food and raises the temperature to a level that might encourage bacteria to grow. Brown meat and poultry right before you assemble the dish for cooking.

Slow cooker

Instant Pot®

Instant Pot® know-how

Whether you're new to the Instant Pot or a long-time user, these handy tips will help you take full advantage of its superpowers. The Instant Pot is several appliances packed into one: an electric pressure cooker that gets dishes on the table in record time as well as a slow cooker, a rice cooker, and a yogurt maker. It also has programs for pressure cooking soups, chilis, multigrains, and beans at the touch of a button, along with the ability to sauté, simmer, and keep food warm.

Getting started

The panel on the front of your Instant Pot has controls for cooking various foods and dishes, cooking at High or Low pressure, regulating the temperature, and setting the cook time. The display also tells you when the Instant Pot is on or off, while a timer counts down the cooking time.

Smart Program keys

There's a Smart Program for whatever you're cooking. Although the Instant Pot has settings for cooking soups, chilis, stews, beans, and meat, most of our recipes use the manual setting and High and Low pressure keys. The Sauté Smart Program is excellent for browning vegetables, meat, or poultry.

Mode and indicators

These lights show which Smart Program you are using and whether you're cooking on High or Low pressure. The Keep Warm Smart Program sets the cooker to the warm setting, while the Cancel key stops the cooking program you selected.

Natural release versus quick release

The Instant Pot's lid can be set to two positions: sealing and venting. When pressure cooking, the steam release handle, quick release button, or quick release switch must be in the sealing (closed) position so the cooker can come up to pressure. When the cooking has completed, there are two options for releasing the pressure: quick or natural. If a recipe says to use the natural release, you don't have to do anything. The cooker will slowly release pressure on its own, which can take 5 to 30 minutes or longer, depending on the amount and type of food cooked. Once the pressure has released, the cooker will automatically default to the Keep Warm Smart Program, which can warm food up to 10 hours. During a natural release, the food will continue to cook. For a quick release, set the steam release to the venting position as soon as the cooking has completed. This will cause a forceful steam plume to escape, releasing all the pressure. If your cooker spatters, move the steam release back to the sealing position and try again after a few minutes. Quick release is best for foods that don't benefit from more cooking time. Recipes also sometimes direct you to let the pressure release naturally for 10 to 15 minutes and then release any remaining pressure.

*Models may vary. Refer to **instantpot.com** for specific cooking steps and venting methods.

xii 100 Slow Cooker & Instant Pot® Recipes

Instant Pot® FAQs

Q: How long does it take for a cooking program to start?

A: Once you select a Smart Program, expect it to take about 10 seconds before the program starts. This lag time allows you to change your mind or adjust the cook time or type of pressure. It will start beeping once the cooking program begins.

Q: How do I adjust the pressure setting or cooking time?

A: To adjust the pressure setting, press the Pressure level key so it toggles between Low and High, and select which setting you want. To set the cooking time, use the + and − keys to adjust the cooking time longer or shorter.*

Q: Why does it take longer for my food to cook than the time selected?

A: When pressure cooking, the timing countdown does not begin until the pot comes up to pressure, which can take anywhere from 5 to 40 minutes, depending on the amount of food and cooking program selected.

Q: Can I cook a chicken or roast without thawing it first?

A: Yes, but you should really thaw it ahead of time. See page xvii for quick-thawing methods.

Q: Why am I having trouble removing the lid?

A: Your Instant Pot will not open until all the pressure has been released. If, however, the cooker is quiet, which indicates that all the pressure has been released and it still won't open, the problem could be that the small float valve in the lid is stuck in the raised position. Try nudging it with the end of a wooden spoon or with a chopstick so it can return to the lowered position.

How to convert slow cooker recipes for the Instant Pot

Follow these pointers to ensure your slow cooker recipe is a good fit for your Instant Pot:

- If a recipe is meat-based and cooks in about 4 hours on High or 8 hours on Low, it will most likely be pressure cooked in around 30 minutes in your Instant Pot. You can also use the program buttons to take the guesswork out of the cooking time.

- Don't fill an Instant Pot past the maximum fill mark. If needed, cut the recipe in half.

- The Instant Pot requires a minimum of 1 cup of liquid to reach pressure. If a recipe calls for less liquid, add enough to equal at least 1 cup. Use water or broth or a combination.

- Avoid adding beer or wine to recipes because the alcohol won't burn off. Instead, if first sautéing vegetables in your Instant Pot, add the beer or wine—you'll only need half the amount of either—and cook it off before adding the rest of the ingredients.

- Thickeners, such as cornstarch and flour, should only be added after pressure cooking.

- Use half the amount of dried herbs called for; pressure cooking intensifies their flavor. You can always sprinkle in a bit more at the end.

Air fryer

Air fryer basics

An air fryer is really just a compact countertop convection oven. It utilizes super-hot circulated air to cook food in a basket, so it gets crispy and brown on the outside, moist and tender on the inside. Unlike deep frying, an air fryer uses a very small amount of oil to work its magic, which keeps the SmartPoints® low. Other benefits? Air-frying is energy efficient and there's no splattering oil to burn you (or mess up your kitchen). Follow these steps to get started:

Place your air fryer on a level, heat-resistant countertop, making sure there are several inches of space behind the air fryer where the exhaust vent is located.

Preheat the air fryer for 2 or 3 minutes.

Spray on oil. It's worthwhile to buy a kitchen spray bottle to spritz oil on food. It's much easier than drizzling or brushing, and you'll use less. Or simply use nonstick spray.

Don't overcrowd the basket, or the food won't crisp and brown evenly. Ideally, spread food in a single layer, or arrange it so air can circulate around.

Turn food over halfway through the cooking time for even browning. Remember to shake the basket a couple of times during cooking to distribute the ingredients. This is especially helpful when air-frying potatoes or vegetables.

Open the air fryer to check for doneness—and do it as often as you like. Peeking won't interfere with the cooking or timing.

Make cleanup easy:
- Remove the air fryer basket from the drawer before removing the food. This will prevent any fat or grease from dripping onto the food.
- Clean the basket and the drawer with hot, soapy water after every use.
- To dry the basket and drawer after washing, put them back into the fryer, and turn it on for a couple of minutes.

Air fryer FAQs

Q: Can I reheat food in my air fryer?
A: Yes. We recommend heating leftovers at 350°F until they reach the safe temperature of 165°F. Use an instant-read thermometer to check.

Q: There's white smoke coming from my air fryer. What's causing that?
A: It is likely that a bit of grease has drained into the drawer and is burning. Simply add some water to the drawer under the basket.

Q: Why isn't my food getting really crispy?
A: Make sure you're not overcrowding the basket and that you're using only a little oil.

Q: I can't turn off my air fryer. What should I do?
A: Some air fryers are built with a delayed shutdown mechanism. Once you press the power button off, the fan will continue to blow hot air for about 20 seconds. Do not press the power button a second time; that will turn the machine back on.

Colombian beef and potato empanadas, page 205

The best part: leftovers

You'll love your slow cooker or Instant Pot® for big-batch cooking, and leftovers like stews, soups, braises, and casseroles are even tastier the second time around. Just keep these tips in mind to make sure you store and freeze like a pro:

Speed the cooling
When storing soups and stews, transfer them to smaller containers, and allow them to stand at room temperature until cooled (but no longer than two hours), then refrigerate or freeze. Faster cooling avoids bacteria growth (yuck!).

Choose the right container
Plastic or glass containers designed especially for freezing are ideal. If wrapping food in plastic wrap, overwrap it in heavy-duty foil or pop it into a plastic freezer bag with the air pressed out before sealing. This will help prevent freezer burn and protect against flavor changes (particularly important for foods stored for more than a week or two).

Consider portions
If you plan on reheating an entire dish for another meal, store it in one large container. But if you'll just be reheating enough to serve one or two, divide it into smaller portions before storing.

Cover and seal
Leave as little air as possible when refrigerating or freezing leftovers, unless you're freezing liquids like soups or stews—it's important to leave space at the top of the container since these foods will expand a bit during freezing (you don't want the lid to pop off). You can also pack stews and braises into zip-close freezer bags, pressing out the air.

Label it
Mark leftovers with the name of the dish, the number of servings, the date, and the SmartPoints® value. This will simplify tracking and help you keep tabs on when to use it by. Use a permanent marker.

Storage times for cooked foods

While frozen foods can remain safe almost indefinitely when stored at 0°F, follow these recommended times to ensure the best texture and flavor.

TYPE OF LEFTOVER	REFRIGERATE	FREEZE
Beef, pork, lamb	3–4 days	2–3 months
Poultry	3–4 days	2–3 months
Seafood	2–3 days	2–3 months
Soups, stews, casseroles	3–4 days	2–3 months
Egg dishes	3–4 days	Not recommended

Super easy three-bean chili, page 27

The right way to defrost

How you defrost food is just as important as how you freeze it.

1 Refrigerator method
Experts agree: From a quality and safety standpoint, it's always best to thaw food in the refrigerator. Plan ahead and transfer food from the freezer to the fridge 1 to 3 days in advance of using. And always place food on a plate or in a bowl to catch any drips.

- 1 pound of frozen food will take about 24 hours to thaw
- 9 x 13-inch casserole will take 1 to 2 days to thaw

2 Microwave method
This is going to be your fastest way. Remove the food from its wrapping and transfer to a microwavable bowl or plate. For most microwaves, the rule is 7 to 10 minutes per pound of food on the defrost setting (which translates to 50 percent power). Or check your microwave's manual for defrosting instructions.

3 Cold-water method
If you find yourself pressed for time, this is a quicker way to safely defrost food (though not as quick as the microwave). Pop the still-wrapped food into a zip-close plastic bag. Squeeze out the air and seal the bag. Set it in a large bowl, pot, or sink of very cold water (never use warm water). Change the water every 30 minutes (set a timer) until the food softens. Each pound of food will take up to 2 hours to thaw.

Leftovers xvii

About our recipes

While losing weight isn't only about what you eat, WW realizes the critical role it plays in your success and overall good health. That's why our philosophy is to offer great-tasting easy recipes that are nutritious as well as delicious. They emphasize the kinds of healthy foods we love: lots of fresh fruits and vegetables, most of which have 0 SmartPoints® value, and lean proteins. We also try to ensure that our recipes fall within the recommendations of the U.S. Dietary Guidelines for Americans—lower in saturated fat and sugar with plenty of fruits and vegetables, lean proteins, and low-fat dairy—so they support a diet that promotes health and reduces the risk for disease. If you have any special dietary needs, consult with your health-care professional for advice on a diet that is best for you. Then adapt these recipes to meet your specific nutritional needs.

Get started, keep going, and enjoy good nutrition

At WW, we believe that eating well makes life better, no matter where you are in your weight-loss journey. These tasty recipes are ideal, whether you're just getting started or have already reached your goals on the SmartPoints system. Unlike other weight-loss programs, which focus solely on calories, the SmartPoints system guides you toward healthier foods that are lower in sugar and saturated fat, and higher in protein. But this isn't a diet—all food is in. Eating well should be fun, energizing, and delicious, so that healthy food choices become second nature. To get maximum satisfaction, keep the following in mind:

- On the *myWW*™ program—whether you're on Green, Blue, or Purple—eating a mix of foods (rather than all-ZeroPoint™ meals) can help keep you from feeling bored or deprived. There's room for all SmartPoints foods in your plan—variety is key to a healthy and livable eating style.

- SmartPoints value is given for each recipe. The SmartPoints value for each ingredient is assigned based on the number of calories and the amount of saturated fat, sugar, and protein in each ingredient. The SmartPoints value for each ingredient is then added together and divided by the number of servings, and the result is rounded.

- Recipes include approximate nutritional information: They are analyzed for Calories (Cal), Total Fat, Saturated Fat (Sat Fat), Sodium (Sod), Total Carbohydrates (Total Carb), Sugar, Dietary Fiber (Fib), and Protein (Prot). The nutritional values are obtained from the WW database, which is maintained by registered dietitians.

- To boost flavor, we often include fresh herbs or a squeeze of citrus instead of increasing the salt. If you don't need to restrict your sodium intake, feel free to add a touch more salt.

- Look for these icons throughout the book to choose recipes that fit best with your dietary needs:

    Vegetarian: Recipes that contain no animal-flesh foods or products made from animal flesh, though they may contain eggs and dairy products.

    Vegan: Recipes that contain no animal-flesh foods, eggs, dairy products, or honey.

    Gluten-free: Recipes that contain no wheat, barley, or rye, or any products made from these ingredients. (Always check the label on ingredients such as broth and spices—they could contain gluten depending on the manufacturer.)

    Dairy-free: Recipes that contain no milk from any animal and no products made from animal milk.

    Nut-free: Recipes that contain no tree nuts or peanuts.

    Note: Recipes conform to the icon designations, but tip and serving suggestions may not.

- Recipe introductory headnote suggestions and tips may increase the recipe's SmartPoints value; be sure to track any additional SmartPoints.
- For information about the WW plan, please visit WW.com/us/m/cms/plan-basics.

Calculations not what you expected?

SmartPoints value for the recipes in this book are calculated without counting the ZeroPoint foods—fruits, most vegetables, and some lean proteins that are part of the plan. However, the nutritional information does include the nutrient content of these ingredients. This means you may notice discrepancies with the SmartPoints value you calculate using the nutrition information provided for the recipe versus the SmartPoints value listed for the recipe. That's because the SmartPoints value for the recipes that contain ZeroPoint ingredients has been adjusted to reflect those ingredients, while the nutrition information provided includes the nutrition for all of the ingredients. For tracking purposes, use the SmartPoints value listed for the recipe.
Also, please note, when fruits and veggies are liquefied or pureed (as in a smoothie), their nutrient content is incorporated into the recipe calculations. These nutrients can increase the SmartPoints.

Alcohol is included in our SmartPoints calculations. Because alcohol information is generally not included on nutrition labels, it's not an option you can include when using the handheld or online SmartPoints calculator or the WW app. But since we include the alcohol information that we get from our database in our recipes, you might notice discrepancies between the SmartPoints you see here in our recipes and the values you get using the calculator. The SmartPoints listed for our recipes are the most accurate values.

The *myWW* program is freeing and flexible for you because it takes your personal needs into account and figures out which option best aligns with your lifestyle.

- **A sizable SmartPoints Budget** to spend on foods you love.
- **A smaller list of foods** that form the basis of healthy eating habits.
- **100+ ZeroPoint foods** including fruits and non-starchy veggies.

- This is our most recent program, **WW Freestyle.**
- **A moderate list of foods** that form the basis of healthy eating habits.
- **200+ ZeroPoint foods** including fruits, veggies, and lean proteins.

- **A modest SmartPoints Budget** to spend on foods you love.
- **A long list of foods** that form the basis of healthy eating habits.
- **300+ ZeroPoint foods** including fruits, veggies, lean proteins, and whole grains.

About our recipes xix

Chapter 1
Breakfast & brunch

Just-like-banana-bread overnight oats 2
Pumpkin and spice oatmeal 5
Multigrain hot cereal with mango 6
Cheese grits with greens and eggs 9
Cheese and chorizo tortilla casserole 10
Egg casserole with hash browns and peppers 13
Parmesan, pasta, and pea frittata 14
Tomato, basil, and ricotta frittata 17
Italian sausage and mozzarella strata 18
Apple-stuffed French toast casserole 21

Just-like-banana-bread overnight oats

Prep 5 min   Cook 3 to 7 hr   Serves 10

Imagine breakfast oatmeal with all the satisfying flavors of banana bread: creamy ripe bananas, ground cinnamon and nutmeg, brown sugar, and of course a little vanilla. Wish granted!

- 7½ cups low-fat (1%) milk
- 2 cups steel-cut oats
- 4 ripe large bananas, well mashed
- 3 tbsp light brown sugar
- 1 tbsp cinnamon
- 1 tsp vanilla extract
- 1 tsp kosher salt
- ¼ tsp ground nutmeg

1 In a 5- or 6-qt slow cooker, stir together milk, oats, bananas, brown sugar, cinnamon, vanilla, salt, and nutmeg until well mixed. Cover and cook until oats are tender, 3 to 4 hours on High or 6 to 7 hours on Low.

2 Divide oatmeal evenly among 10 bowls. (The oats can also be cooled and refrigerated up to several days. Gently reheat in a microwave or on the stovetop, adding a little water to loosen oat mixture.)

Per serving (⅔ cup): 259 Cal, 4 g Total Fat, 1 g Sat Fat, 274 mg Sod, 46 g Total Carb, 19 g Sugar, 5 g Fib, 11 g Prot.

Serving idea
Top each serving with thinly sliced banana and fresh blueberries or blackberries dusted with cinnamon.

Pumpkin and spice oatmeal

Prep 10 min   Cook 8 hr   Serves 8

Pumpkin pie, meet morning oatmeal! Steel-cut oats and pumpkin seeds add great texture, and mild honey lends just enough sweetness. For the freshest flavor, grate your own nutmeg.

3	cups pumpkin puree (not pie filling)
1½	cups steel-cut oats
½	cup honey
1	tsp cinnamon
½	tsp salt
¼	tsp ground nutmeg
4	oranges, segmented
½	cup pumpkin seeds

In a 4- or 5-qt slow cooker, stir together 6 cups water, pumpkin, oats, honey, cinnamon, salt, and nutmeg until well mixed. Cover and cook until oats are tender, about 8 hours on Low; stir well. Divide evenly among 8 bowls. Top each serving with about 3 orange segments and 1 tbsp pumpkin seeds. (The oats can be cooled and refrigerated for several days. Gently reheat in a microwave or on the stovetop, adding a little water to loosen oat mixture.)

Per serving (1 cup oatmeal, 3 orange segments, and 1 tbsp pumpkin seeds): 247 Cal, 6 g Total Fat, 1 g Sat Fat, 153 mg Sod, 45 g Total Carb, 22 g Sugar, 5 g Fib, 7 g Prot.

Multigrain hot cereal with mango

Prep 5 min   Cook 7 hr   Serves 8

Why settle for a one-note hot cereal when you can easily combine three whole grains? The ginger and vanilla infuse flavor while the mixture cooks, and fresh mango adds tropical sweetness.

6	cups plain unsweetened almond milk
1	(2-inch) piece ginger, quartered
2	tsp vanilla extract
¾	tsp salt
¾	cup pearl barley
¾	cup steel-cut oats
½	cup quinoa, rinsed
2	large mangoes, peeled, pitted, and diced
½	cup unsweetened coconut flakes
8	tsp honey

1 In a 5- or 6-qt slow cooker, combine almond milk, 2½ cups water, ginger, vanilla, and salt. Stir in barley, oats, and quinoa. Cover and cook until grains are very tender, about 7 hours on Low.

2 Remove and discard ginger. Divide porridge evenly among 8 bowls and top with mango and coconut; drizzle with honey. (Leftover porridge can be cooled and refrigerated several days. Gently reheat in microwave or on stovetop, adding a little water to loosen.)

Per serving (about 1 cup porridge, ¼ cup mango, 1 tbsp coconut, and 1 tsp honey): 294 Cal, 6 g Total Fat, 2 g Sat Fat, 332 mg Sod, 55 g Total Carb, 21 g Sugar, 8 g Fib, 7 g Prot.

Serving idea
Add fresh raspberries along with the diced mango for a 0 SmartPoints® value.

Cheese grits with greens and eggs

Prep 15 min   Cook 8½ hr   Serves 6

The classic combo of cheese grits and eggs gets a healthy boost when you add kale to the slow cooker toward the end of the cooking time. This recipe works beautifully overnight, so you wake up to the smell of a Southern breakfast.

Nonstick spray
- 1½ cups corn grits
- 1 tsp kosher salt (or to taste), plus more for seasoning
- 4 cups firmly packed baby kale (about 6 oz)
- 1 cup shredded reduced-fat sharp cheddar
- ⅛ tsp black pepper (or to taste), plus more for seasoning
- 1 cup cherry tomatoes, halved
- 3 slices cooked bacon, warmed, crumbled
- 6 large eggs, sunny-side up or poached

1 Spray the insert of a 6-qt slow cooker with nonstick spray.

2 Pour 6 cups water into slow cooker; slowly whisk in grits. Add salt. Cover and cook until grits are tender and creamy, about 8 hours on Low. Stir in kale and cheddar. Cover and cook until kale is wilted, about 30 minutes more; stir in pepper. Season with more salt and pepper, if desired.

3 Spoon grits evenly into 6 large shallow bowls. Sprinkle with tomatoes and bacon; top with eggs.

Per serving (1 cup grits mixture, about 4 tomatoes, and 1 egg): 312 Cal, 12 g Total Fat, 5 g Sat Fat, 611 mg Sod, 34 g Total Carb, 1 g Sugar, 3 g Fib, 17 g Prot.

Serving idea
A sweet finishing touch for any brunch? Cinnamon-dusted cappuccinos made with reduced-fat (2%) milk.

Breakfast & brunch

Cheese and chorizo tortilla casserole

Prep 32 min   Cook 2 to 8 hr   Serves 12

This hearty Tex-Mex egg casserole satisfies with spicy, cheddar-y, sausage-y goodness. You can prep it through step 1 the night before and refrigerate the pepper mixture, then assemble the casserole in minutes the next morning.

Nonstick spray
- 2 large red bell peppers, chopped
- 1 large poblano pepper, chopped
- 2 large red onions, chopped
- 9 oz cooked chorizo chicken sausage, finely chopped
- 1 large garlic clove, minced
- 2 tsp salt, divided
- 1 tsp ground cumin
- 16 (6-inch) corn tortillas
- 2 cups shredded reduced-fat cheddar (8 oz)
- 12 large eggs
- 1 cup low-fat (1%) milk
- 2 tomatoes, diced
- 1 small sweet onion, diced
- 4 scallions, thinly sliced
- ¼ cup chopped cilantro
- 2 small limes, each cut into 6 wedges

1 Spray a large heavy skillet with nonstick spray and set over medium-high heat. Add bell peppers, poblano, and onions and cook, stirring often, until softened, 8 to 10 minutes. Stir in sausage, garlic, 1 tsp salt, and cumin and cook, stirring occasionally, until heated through, about 3 minutes.

2 Spray the insert of a 6-qt slow cooker with nonstick spray. Arrange 4 tortillas in bottom of slow cooker, overlapping as needed. Top with one-third of pepper mixture and ½ cup cheddar. Repeat to make three layers; top with remaining 4 tortillas.

3 In a medium bowl, beat eggs, milk, and remaining 1 tsp salt. Pour over tortilla mixture and sprinkle with remaining ½ cup cheddar. Cover and cook 2 hours on High or 6 to 8 hours on Low. Serve sprinkled with tomatoes, sweet onion, scallions, and cilantro; serve with lime wedges.

Per serving (1 cup casserole and about ⅓ cup tomato-scallion topping): 244 Cal, 10 g Total Fat, 4 g Sat Fat, 720 mg Sod, 23 g Total Carb, 5 g Sugar, 3 g Fib, 17 g Prot.

Egg casserole with hash browns and peppers

Prep 40 min   Cook 4 hr   Serves 12

This egg casserole includes favorite Italian ingredients—garlic, mozzarella, basil—plus hash browns baked right in.

Nonstick spray
- 4 tsp olive oil, divided
- 2 large onions, thinly sliced
- 2 red bell peppers, sliced
- 4 Italian frying peppers (Cubanelles), halved lengthwise and sliced
- 1½ tsp kosher salt, divided
- ½ tsp black pepper, divided
- 1½ pints grape tomatoes, halved
- 3 large garlic cloves, minced
- ¾ tsp dried oregano, divided
- 1 (20-oz) bag frozen shredded hash brown potatoes
- 2 cups shredded part-skim mozzarella (about 8 oz)
- 12 large eggs
- 1½ cups low-fat (1%) milk
- 1 cup basil leaves, thinly sliced, plus more leaves for garnish
- 3 tbsp grated Pecorino Romano
- 12 thin slices whole-grain bread, toasted

1 In a large skillet over medium-high heat, warm 2 tsp oil. Add onions, bell peppers, frying peppers, ½ tsp salt, and ¼ tsp black pepper and cook, stirring often, until onions are light golden, about 10 minutes. Stir in tomatoes, garlic, and ½ tsp oregano and cook, stirring, 1 minute more. Spoon vegetable mixture into a large bowl; set aside.

2 Add remaining 2 tsp oil to skillet. Add hash browns and cook, turning occasionally, until nicely browned, about 6 minutes.

3 Spray the insert of a 6-qt slow cooker with nonstick spray. Place one-third of potatoes in bottom of slow cooker; top with half of vegetable mixture and ⅔ cup mozzarella. Repeat layers with half of remaining potatoes, remaining vegetable mixture, and ⅔ cup mozzarella. Top evenly with remaining potatoes.

4 In a medium bowl, beat eggs, milk, sliced basil, remaining 1 tsp salt, and remaining ¼ tsp black pepper. Pour over potato mixture and sprinkle with remaining ⅔ cup mozzarella, remaining ¼ tsp oregano, and Pecorino Romano. Cover and cook until top is set when gently pressed and edges are golden, 4 to 5 hours on Low. Pour off any liquid in bottom of cooker. Serve over slices of toast and sprinkle with basil leaves.

Per serving (1¼ cups casserole and 1 slice toast): 297 Cal, 12 g Total Fat, 4 g Sat Fat, 834 mg Sod, 31 g Total Carb, 6 g Sugar, 3 g Fib, 16 g Prot.

Parmesan, pasta, and pea frittata

Prep 30 min   Cook 2 hr   Serves 6

Slow cooking breakfast is ideal for the weekends, when your morning routine is more leisurely. This recipe also allows the eggs, pasta, peas, and Parmesan to come together with minimal effort, then cook to tender perfection.

Nonstick spray
- 9   large eggs
- ½   cup grated Parmesan
- ¼   tsp black pepper
- 1   cup frozen peas, thawed
- 5   slices Canadian bacon, thinly sliced and halved crosswise
- ⅓   cup moist-packed sun-dried tomatoes, chopped
- 4   oz cooked whole-wheat spaghetti, drained and cooled
- ⅓   cup shredded part-skim mozzarella
- 1   lemon, cut into 6 wedges

1 In a large bowl, beat eggs, Parmesan, and pepper. Stir in peas, Canadian bacon, and sun-dried tomatoes. Add spaghetti, stirring to combine.

2 Line a 5- or 6-qt slow cooker insert with plastic liner, then generously spray liner with nonstick spray.

3 Pour egg mixture into prepared slow cooker, pressing to ensure pasta is submerged. Sprinkle with mozzarella, leaving a 1-inch border to prevent frittata from sticking to sides. Cover and cook until a knife inserted into center of frittata comes out clean, about 2 hours on High. Carefully remove lid to prevent condensation from dripping onto frittata.

4 Using liner as handles, lift out frittata and set on a work surface; let stand, uncovered, 10 minutes. Cut frittata into 6 equal portions. Serve with lemon wedges.

Per serving (1 portion): 279 Cal, 12 g Total Fat, 5 g Sat Fat, 506 mg Sod, 21 g Total Carb, 4 g Sugar, 3 g Fib, 22 g Prot.

Serving idea

Pair this dish with a salad of thinly sliced fennel and fronds, dressed with a bit of fruity extra-virgin olive oil, red-wine vinegar, salt, and pepper.

Tomato, basil, and ricotta frittata

Prep 30 min   Cook 3 hr   Serves 4

A frittata is basically an omelette, Italian style. Instead of tucking the filling inside an egg envelope (the French way), the eggs, ricotta, tomatoes, and basil all get mixed together. This frittata is just as good for breakfast and brunch as it is for lunch or dinner.

Nonstick spray
- 2 tsp olive oil
- 1 small red onion, thinly sliced
- ½ lb white potatoes, scrubbed and cut into ⅛-inch slices
- 1 tsp kosher salt, divided
- 1¼ cups cherry tomatoes (6 oz), halved or quartered if large
- ⅓ cup thinly sliced basil
- 5 large eggs
- ¼ tsp black pepper
- ⅛ tsp ground nutmeg
- ½ cup part-skim ricotta

1. Line a 4- or 5-qt slow cooker insert with plastic liner. Spray liner with nonstick spray.

2. In a medium heavy nonstick skillet over medium-high heat, warm oil. Add onion and cook, stirring, until beginning to soften and turn golden, about 6 minutes. Add potatoes and sprinkle with ¼ tsp salt; cook, stirring, until potatoes are partially cooked, about 4 minutes, reducing heat to medium if onion browns too quickly.

3. Transfer potato mixture to prepared slow cooker, spreading to form even layer; sprinkle with ¼ tsp salt. Top with tomatoes and basil. In a medium bowl, beat eggs, pepper, nutmeg, and remaining ½ tsp salt; pour over potato mixture. With a fork, gently stir to ensure eggs are mixed throughout. Dollop ricotta on top, spacing evenly. Cover and cook until potatoes are fork-tender and a knife inserted into center of frittata comes out clean, 3 to 3½ hours on Low. Carefully remove lid to prevent condensation from dripping onto frittata.

4. Using liner as handles, lift out frittata and set on a work surface; let stand, uncovered, 5 minutes. Cut frittata into 4 wedges.

Per serving (1 wedge): 214 Cal, 11 g Total Fat, 4 g Sat Fat, 488 mg Sod, 15 g Total Carb, 3 g Sugar, 2 g Fib, 13 g Prot.

Italian sausage and mozzarella strata

Prep 15 min   Cook 3 hr   Serves 6

A strata is really just a savory bread pudding. This one is made by layering sweet Italian sausage, eggs, shredded mozzarella, and peppers with whole-wheat bread.

Nonstick spray

½	lb sweet Italian turkey sausage links, casings removed
2	Italian frying peppers (Cubanelles), diced
1	onion, chopped
1½	tsp dried oregano
5	slices day-old reduced-calorie whole-wheat bread, cubed
1	cup shredded part-skim mozzarella
⅓	cup grated Parmesan
2½	cups low-fat (1%) milk
6	large eggs
¾	tsp kosher salt
¼	tsp black pepper

Oregano leaves, torn (optional)

1 Spray a large skillet with nonstick spray and set over medium heat. Add sausages, frying peppers, and onion and cook, breaking up sausages with a wooden spoon, until no longer pink, about 6 minutes. Stir in dried oregano.

2 Line a 5- or 6-qt slow cooker insert with plastic liner. Spray liner with nonstick spray.

3 Layer half of bread cubes, half of sausage mixture, ½ cup mozzarella, and 3 tbsp Parmesan in prepared slow cooker. Repeat layering with remaining bread, sausage mixture, mozzarella, and Parmesan.

4 In a large bowl, whisk together milk, eggs, salt, and black pepper; pour over bread-sausage mixture. Cover and cook until knife inserted into center of strata comes out clean, 3 to 4 hours on Low.

5 Wearing oven mitts, lift out slow cooker insert and transfer to wire rack; let strata cool about 10 minutes. Using liner as handles, lift out strata and place on a cutting board. Cut into 6 wedges. Sprinkle with oregano leaves, if using.

Per serving (1 wedge): 293 Cal, 14 g Total Fat, 6 g Sat Fat, 862 mg Sod, 18 g Total Carb, 8 g Sugar, 3 g Fib, 25 g Prot.

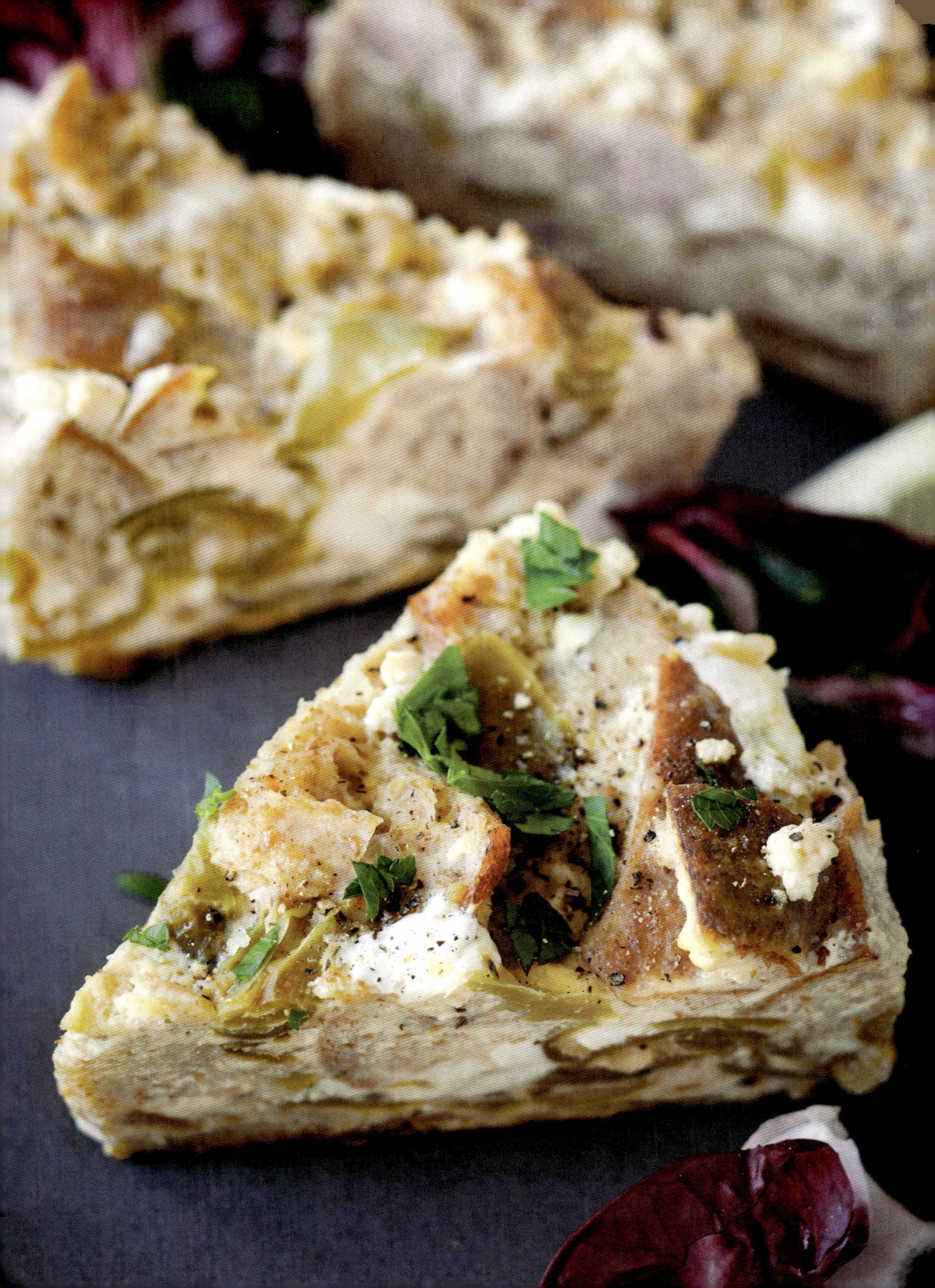

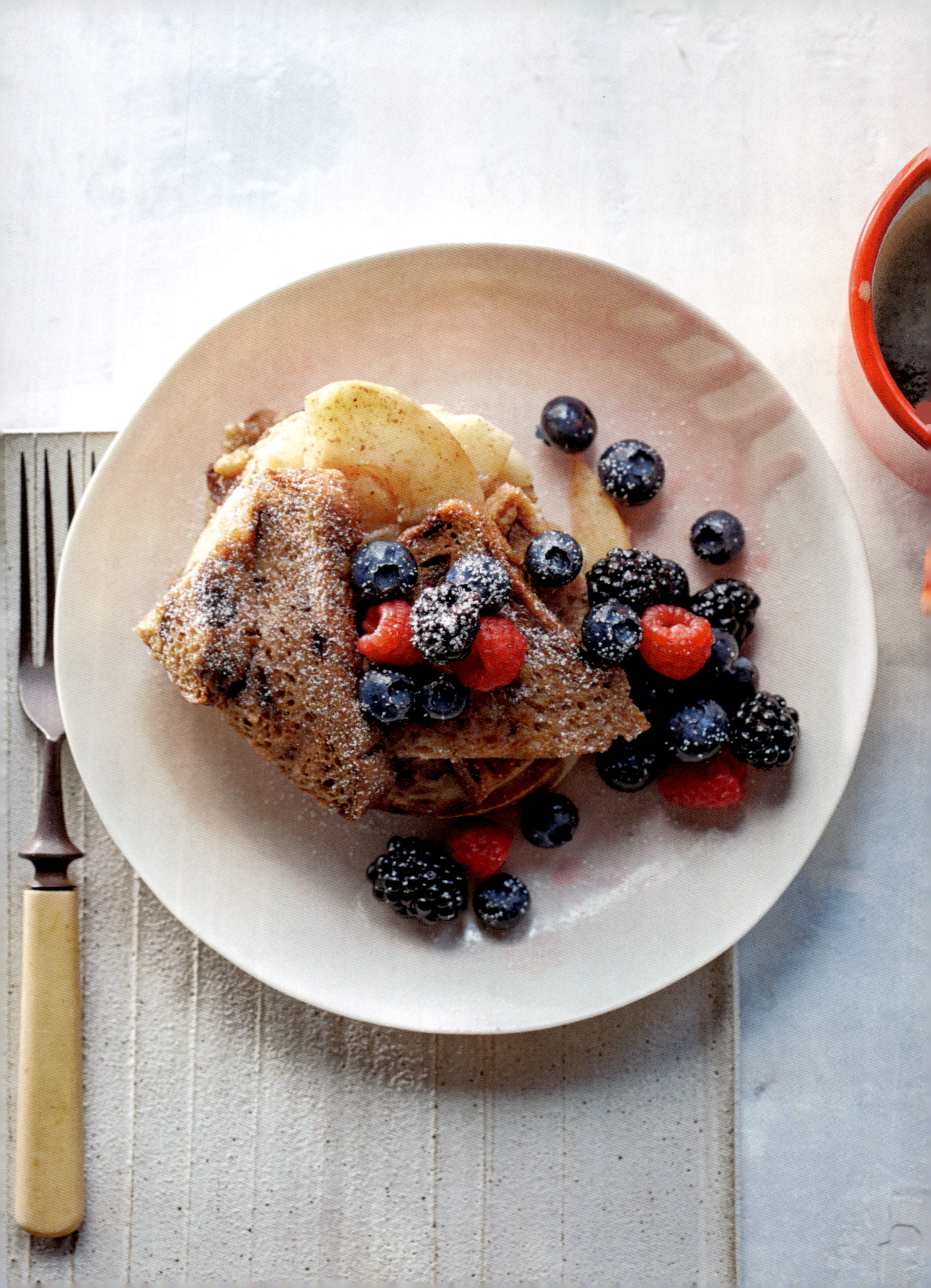

Apple-stuffed French toast casserole

Prep 20 min   Cook 2 hr   Serves 8

This is the easiest way to make French toast for a crowd! Slices of cinnamon-raisin bread soak up a custard-y mixture of eggs, milk, and vanilla. In the middle, there's a sweet layer of apples, brown sugar, and spices.

Nonstick spray
4   large Honeycrisp apples, peeled, cored, and thinly sliced
1   tbsp light brown sugar
1½ tsp cinnamon, divided
Pinch ground nutmeg
Pinch ground allspice
1   tsp lemon juice
5   large eggs
1   cup low-fat (1%) milk
1   tsp vanilla extract
¼   tsp salt
9   slices cinnamon-raisin bread, halved diagonally

1 In a microwavable bowl, combine apples, brown sugar, ½ tsp cinnamon, nutmeg, allspice, and lemon juice. Cover with plate or piece of microwavable plastic wrap folded back on one edge to vent; microwave until apples are softened, about 4 minutes on High.

2 Meanwhile, in a shallow bowl, beat eggs, milk, remaining 1 tsp cinnamon, vanilla, and salt.

3 Spray the insert of a 6-qt slow cooker with nonstick spray. Dip 10 bread halves in egg mixture until well coated on both sides. Arrange in an overlapping circle in bottom of slow cooker. Spoon cooked apples on top to form even layer.

4 Dip remaining 8 bread halves in egg mixture until well coated on both sides; arrange around edge over apples in wreathlike pattern, leaving apple mixture showing in center. On top, evenly pour any egg mixture remaining in bowl. Cover and cook 2 hours on Low.

Per serving (¾ cup): 235 Cal, 5 g Total Fat, 1 g Sat Fat, 263 mg Sod, 40 g Total Carb, 22 g Sugar, 5 g Fib, 8 g Prot.

Serving idea
Top each serving of French toast with ¼ tsp confectioners' sugar and a mix of fresh berries.

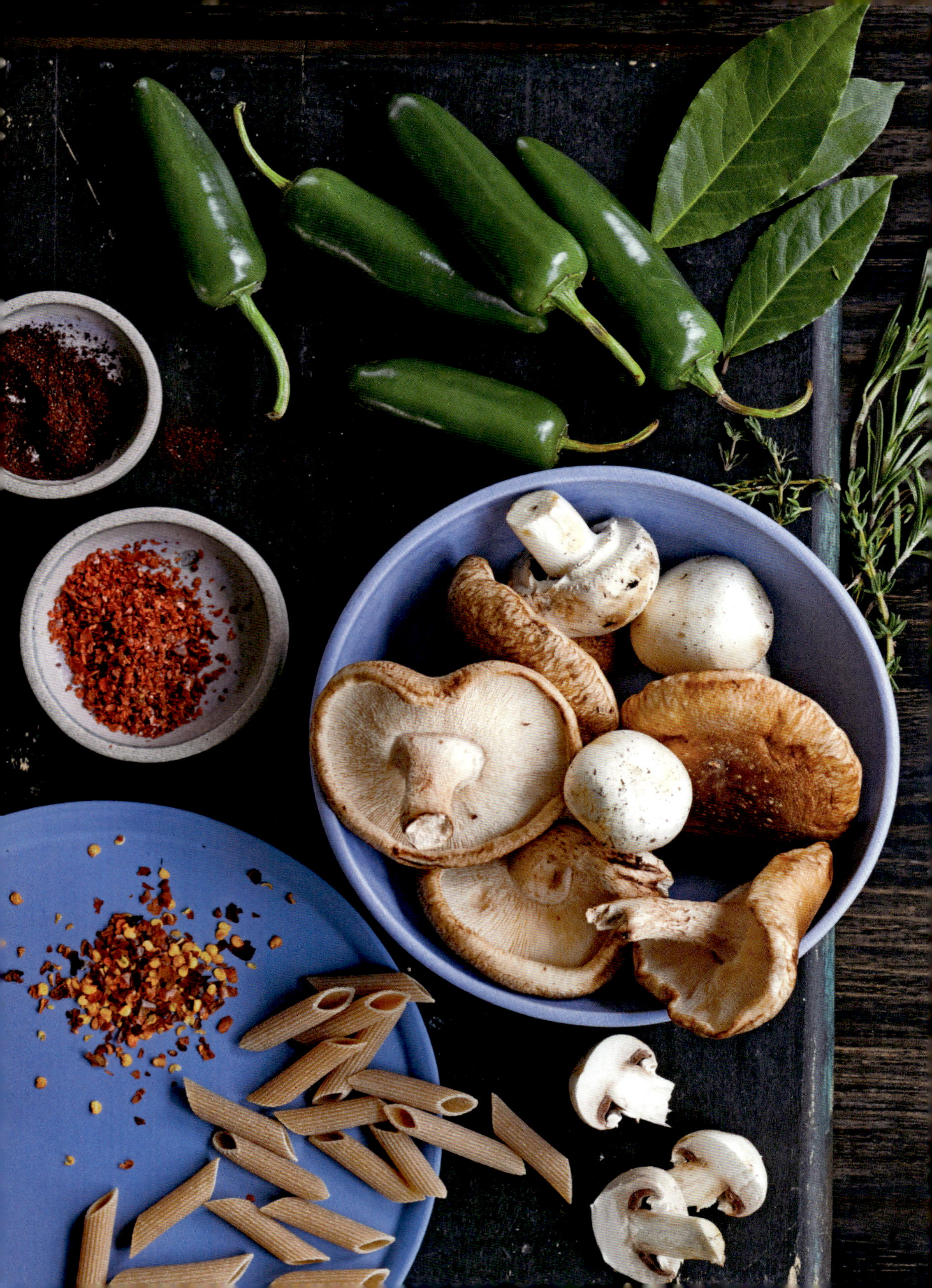

Chapter 2
Vegetarian mains

Butternut squash and chickpea chili 24
Super-easy three-bean chili 27
Portobello mushroom and eggplant chili 28
Rice-and-bean stuffed peppers 31
Italian vegetable-bean stew 32
Tomato-eggplant puttanesca 35
North African lentil-chickpea tagine 36
Farro and double-mushroom pot 39
Risotto-style barley and peas 40
Tortellini with garlicky tomato sauce 43
Ricotta-and-spinach stuffed cabbage 44
Spaghetti with caramelized onions 47
Summer tomato sauce with pasta 48
Indian-spiced potatoes with cauliflower 51
Artichoke and bell pepper paella 52
Scalloped potatoes with thyme 55

Butternut squash and chickpea chili

Prep 25 min   Cook 4 to 10 hr   Serves 6

You won't miss the meat in this vegetarian chili, thanks to high-protein soy crumbles and chickpeas, plus chunks of butternut squash and an ancho chile kick. It's easy enough to prep in the morning so you can come home to an already-done dinner.

- 2 tsp canola oil
- 1 onion, chopped
- 3 garlic cloves, minced
- 1 tbsp ancho chile powder
- 2 tsp ground cumin
- 3 tbsp tomato paste
- 1½ cups vegetable broth (or water)
- 1 (1¼-lb) container cut-up butternut squash, cut into 1-inch chunks
- 1 large red bell pepper, diced
- 2 celery stalks, chopped
- 1 (14½-oz) can diced tomatoes with Italian herbs
- 1 (15½-oz) can chickpeas, rinsed and drained
- ½ tsp salt
- 1 (12-oz) package soy crumbles
- ¾ cup plain fat-free Greek yogurt
- Thinly sliced radishes
- Oregano leaves (optional)
- 1 small lime, cut into 6 wedges

1 In a large skillet over medium-high heat, warm oil. Add onion and cook, stirring, until golden, about 8 minutes. Add garlic, ancho chile powder, and cumin and cook, stirring constantly, until fragrant, about 30 seconds. Add tomato paste and cook, stirring, 30 seconds. Add broth and bring to a boil, scraping up browned bits from bottom of pan.

2 Transfer onion mixture to a 5- or 6-qt slow cooker. Add squash, bell pepper, celery, diced tomatoes, chickpeas, and salt, stirring to combine. With a spoon, gently press vegetables to form even layer. Put soy crumbles in center of vegetable mixture, leaving a border. Cover and cook until squash is fork-tender, 4 to 5 hours on High or 8 to 10 hours on Low.

3 Spoon chili evenly into 6 bowls. Top with yogurt, radishes, and oregano leaves, if using; serve with lime wedges.

Per serving (1½ cups chili and 2 tbsp yogurt): 264 Cal, 5 g Total Fat, 0 g Sat Fat, 983 mg Sod, 37 g Total Carb, 10 g Sugar, 11 g Fib, 20 g Prot.

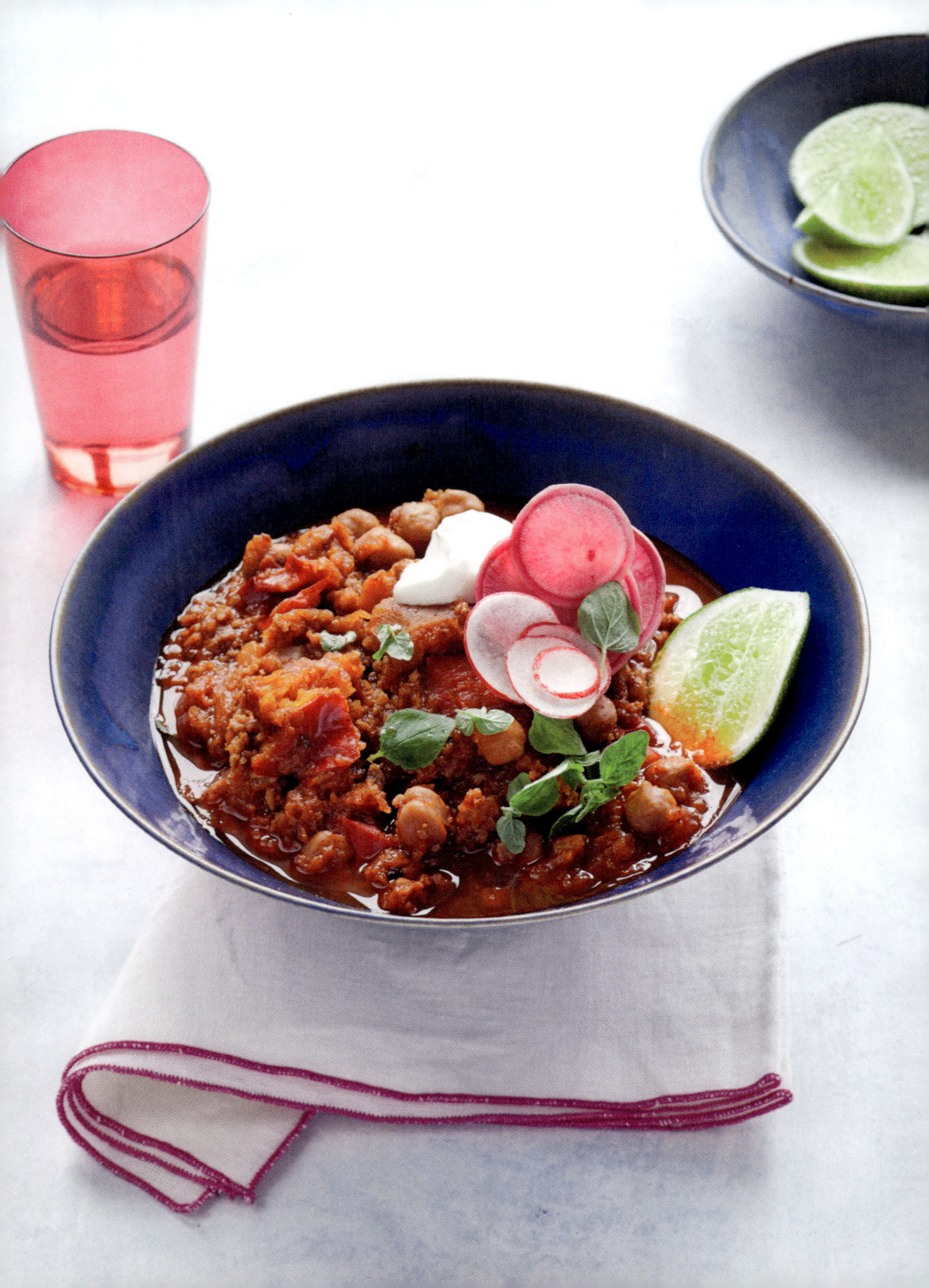

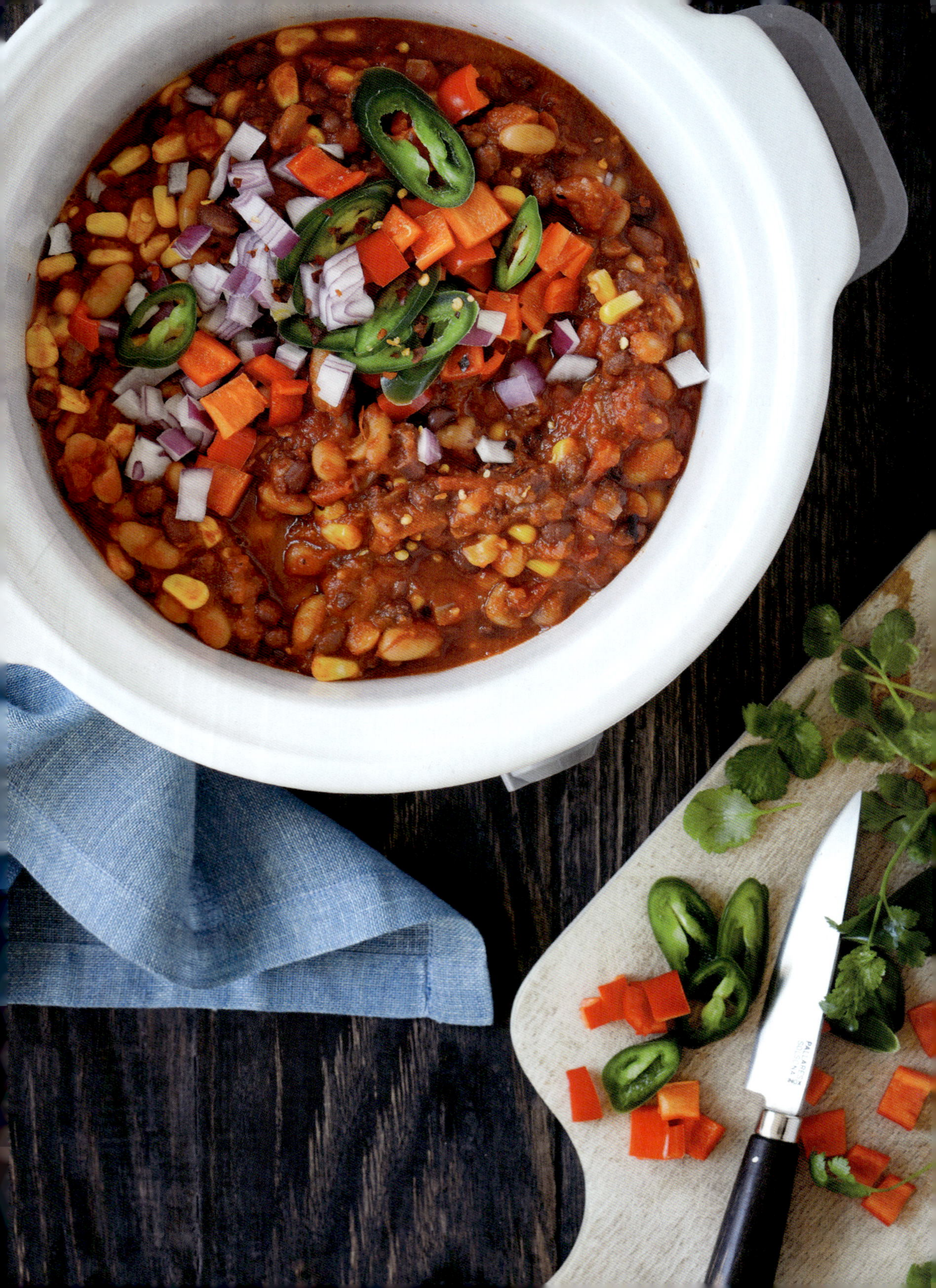

Super-easy three-bean chili

Prep 15 min   Cook 2½ to 6½ hr   Serves 8

Simply combine the ingredients, and the slow cooker does all the work. We like this mix of black, white kidney, and pinto beans, but any others you have on hand would also work great in this chili.

2	(15½-oz) cans no-salt-added black beans, rinsed and drained
2	(15½-oz) cans no-salt-added white kidney (cannellini) beans, rinsed and drained
2	(15½-oz) cans no-salt-added pinto beans, rinsed and drained
2	(14½-oz) cans diced tomatoes with chiles
1	(15-oz) can tomato sauce
1	large onion, chopped
2	large garlic cloves, minced
1	(1.25-oz) package chili seasoning mix
1	(14-oz) package frozen corn kernels, thawed
½	cup chopped cilantro
1	tbsp lime juice (or to taste)

In a 5- or 6-qt slow cooker, combine black beans, kidney beans, pinto beans, diced tomatoes, tomato sauce, onion, garlic, and seasoning mix. Cover and cook 2 to 3 hours on High or 4 to 6 hours on Low. Stir in corn and cook 30 minutes longer. Just before serving, stir in cilantro and lime juice.

Per serving (1½ cups): 315 Cal, 1 g Total Fat, 0 g Sat Fat, 841 mg Sod, 59 g Total Carb, 6 g Sugar, 17 g Fib, 19 g Prot.

Cooking idea
Gussy up this healthy, flavorful chili with fresh veggies: chopped bell pepper, diced red onion, thinly sliced scallion, and thin rings of jalapeño.

Portobello mushroom and eggplant chili

Prep 20 min, plus standing   Cook 4 to 10 hr   Serves 6

This hearty mushroom and eggplant chili isn't vegetarian because Worcestershire sauce contains anchovy, an ingredient that deepens flavor. If you're vegetarian, look for a vegan version like Annie's.

1	(1-lb) eggplant, peeled and diced
1½	tsp kosher salt, divided
1	(14½-oz) can diced tomatoes in sauce
1	(8-oz) can tomato sauce
2½	tbsp chili powder
1½	tsp Worcestershire sauce
1	tsp dried oregano
½	lb portobello mushroom caps, diced
1	large onion, chopped
1	large red bell pepper, diced
1	poblano pepper, diced
1	(15½-oz) can black beans, rinsed and drained
2	tbsp cornmeal
¾	cup plain fat-free Greek yogurt

Diced bell and chile peppers

1 Put eggplant into a colander and sprinkle with 1 tsp salt, tossing to coat evenly. Place a large plate on top of eggplant and weigh it down with one or two large cans. Let stand about 30 minutes. With hands, squeeze out excess liquid from eggplant.

2 In a 5- or 6-qt slow cooker, stir together diced tomatoes, tomato sauce, chili powder, Worcestershire sauce, oregano, and remaining ½ tsp salt. Add portobellos, onion, bell pepper, poblano, and black beans, stirring to mix well. With back of a wooden spoon, gently press vegetable mixture to form an even layer. Put eggplant on top in even layer, leaving a ½-inch border. Cover and cook until vegetables are softened, 4 to 5 hours on High or 8 to 10 hours on Low.

3 About 20 minutes before cooking time is up, slowly stir in cornmeal. Cover and cook until chili thickens, about 15 minutes. Divide chili evenly among 6 bowls and top evenly with yogurt, bell pepper, and chile pepper; sprinkle with additional chili powder, if desired.

Per serving (about 1¼ cups chili and 2 tbsp yogurt): 171 Cal, 1 g Total Fat, 0 g Sat Fat, 1,165 mg Sod, 33 g Total Carb, 10 g Sugar, 11 g Fib, 11 g Prot.

Serving idea

Charred corn tortillas pair well with this chili; tear them into strips and use as garnish or fill them to make a chili taco.

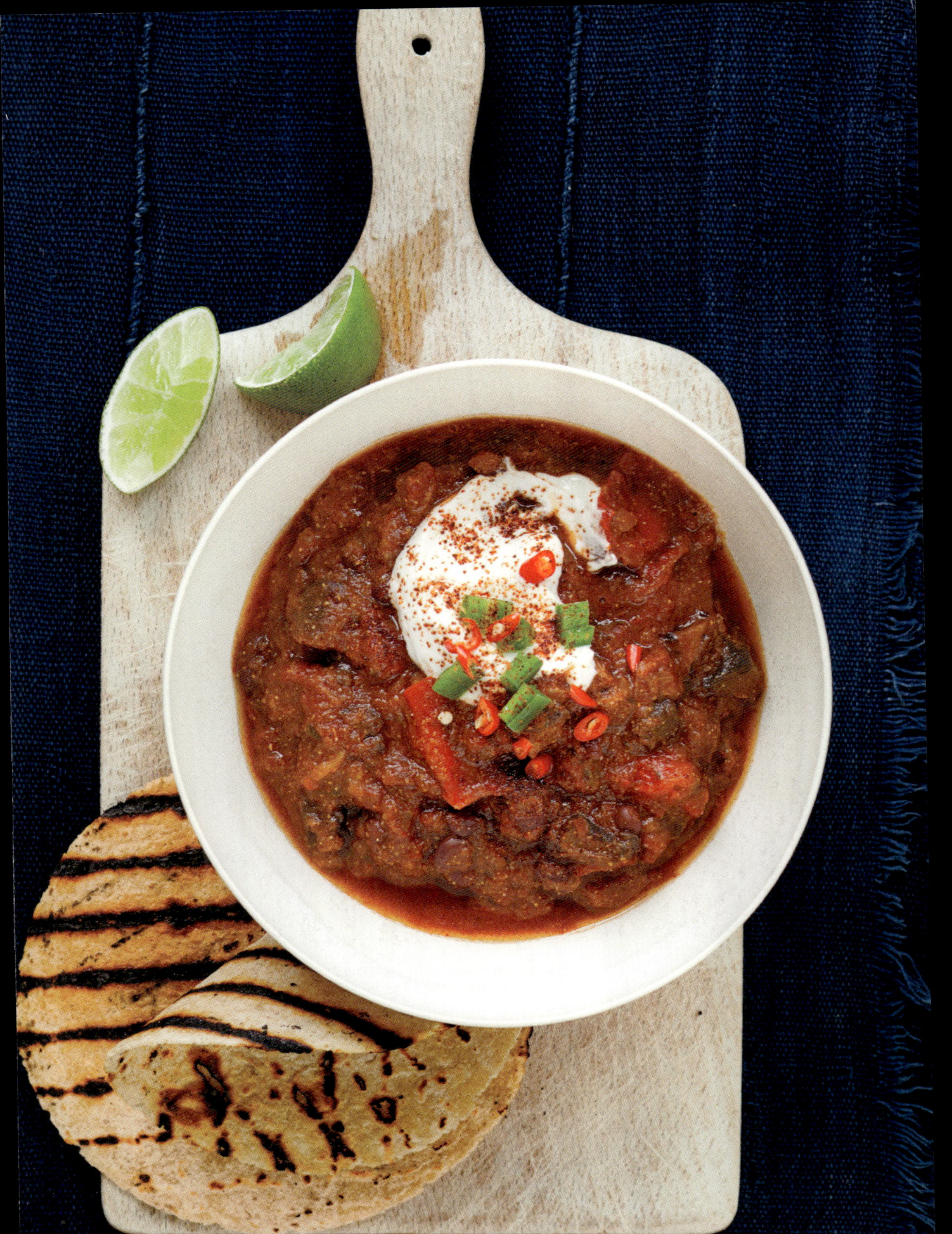

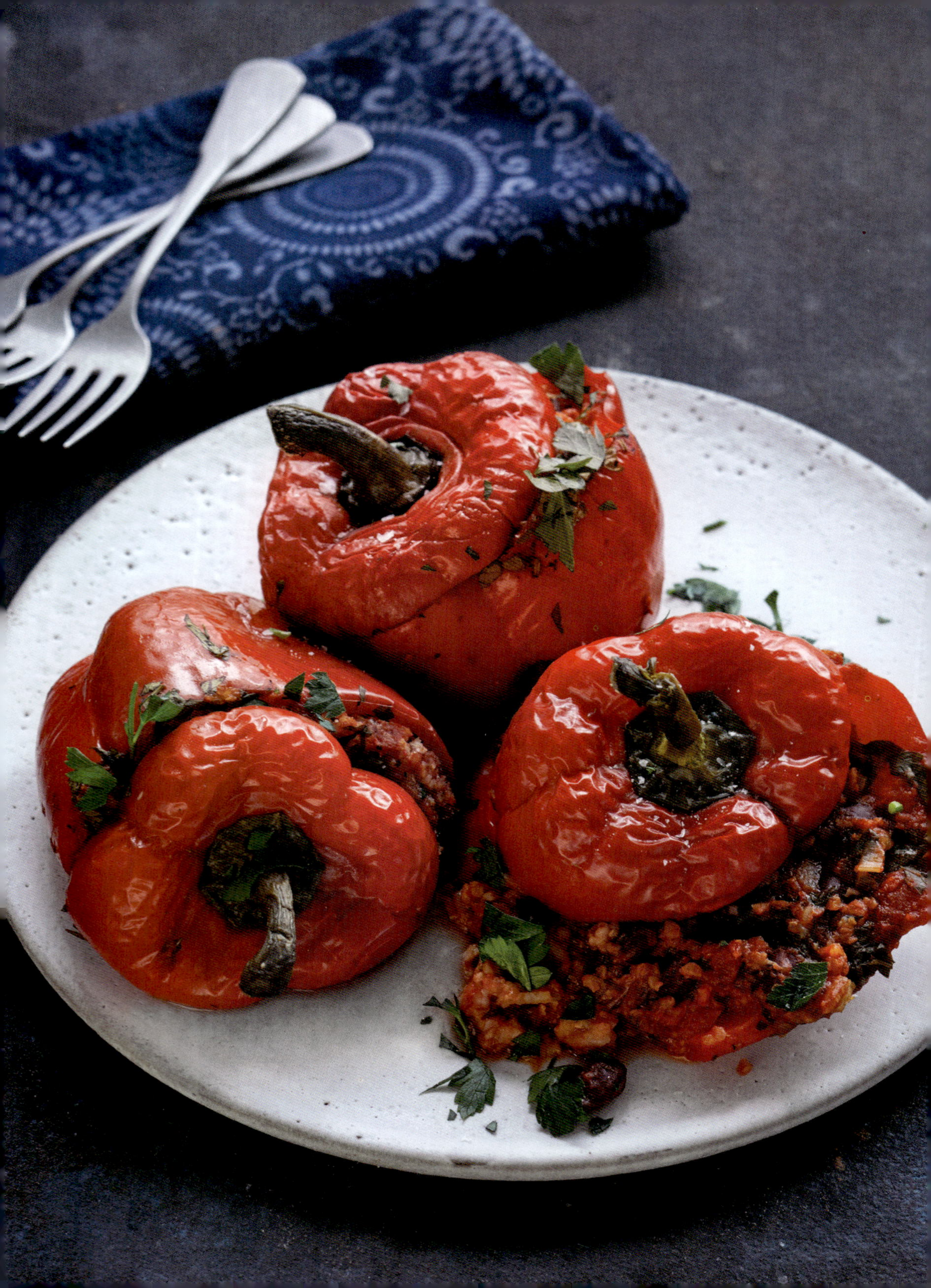

Rice-and-bean stuffed peppers

Prep 10 min   Cook 4 hr   Serves 4

Stuffed peppers have a rustic elegance, but are also super-easy to make. Serve them as a vegetarian main or as a side that frees up your oven (and your time) for roasting something delicious.

1	(15½-oz) can red kidney beans, rinsed and drained
1	(15-oz) can tomato sauce with Italian herbs
1½	cups cooked long-grain white or brown rice
¾	cup grated Pecorino Romano
1	small onion, finely chopped
1	tsp dried Italian seasoning or oregano
¼	tsp black pepper
4	red bell peppers, tops cut off and reserved, seeds removed
2	tbsp chopped flat-leaf parsley

1. In a large bowl, mix together beans, ¼ cup tomato sauce, rice, Pecorino Romano, onion, Italian seasoning, and black pepper. Spoon into bell peppers, dividing evenly.

2. Stand stuffed peppers in a 5- or 6-qt slow cooker. Pour remaining tomato sauce over peppers and sprinkle with parsley. Cover with tops of peppers. Into bottom of slow cooker, pour ¾ cup water. Cover and cook until bell peppers are tender but still hold their shape, about 4 hours on Low.

Per serving (1 stuffed pepper): 286 Cal, 6 g Total Fat, 3 g Sat Fat, 1,179 mg Sod, 47 g Total Carb, 7 g Sugar, 9 g Fib, 12 g Prot.

Prep ahead
Next time you're making rice, cook a double-batch so you'll have plenty on hand, ready to use in this recipe.

Vegetarian mains

Italian vegetable-bean stew

Prep 20 min   Cook 4 to 10 hr   Serves 6

Nearly every ingredient in this rich vegetarian stew (carrots, beans, mushrooms, and more) goes into the slow cooker at once. Then just start it and walk away!

¾	lb Yukon Gold potatoes, scrubbed and cut into 1-inch chunks
3	carrots, cut diagonally into ¾-inch slices
1	large onion, chopped
3	large garlic cloves, minced
1	tsp fennel seeds, lightly crushed
1	tsp dried oregano
¾	tsp salt
¼	tsp black pepper
1	(15½-oz) can red kidney beans, rinsed and drained
1	(14½-oz) can Italian-style stewed tomatoes
1	(10-oz) package cremini mushrooms, halved or quartered if large
1	large red bell pepper, cut into 1-inch pieces
¾	cup vegetable broth (or water)
1	(9-oz) box frozen Italian green beans, thawed
½	cup grated Pecorino Romano, plus more for sprinkling

Coarsely chopped flat-leaf parsley

1 In a 5- or 6-qt slow cooker, combine potatoes, carrots, and onion. Stir in garlic, fennel seeds, oregano, salt, and black pepper. Top with beans, tomatoes, mushrooms, and bell pepper. Add broth, stirring to combine. Cover and cook until vegetables are fork-tender, 4 to 5 hours on High or 8 to 10 hours on Low.

2 About 15 minutes before cooking time is up, stir in green beans. Divide stew evenly among 6 large shallow bowls; sprinkle with Pecorino Romano and parsley.

Per serving (1½ cups stew and generous 1 tbsp cheese): 242 Cal, 5 g Total Fat, 2 g Sat Fat, 1,051 mg Sod, 40 g Total Carb, 7 g Sugar, 9 g Fib, 10 g Prot.

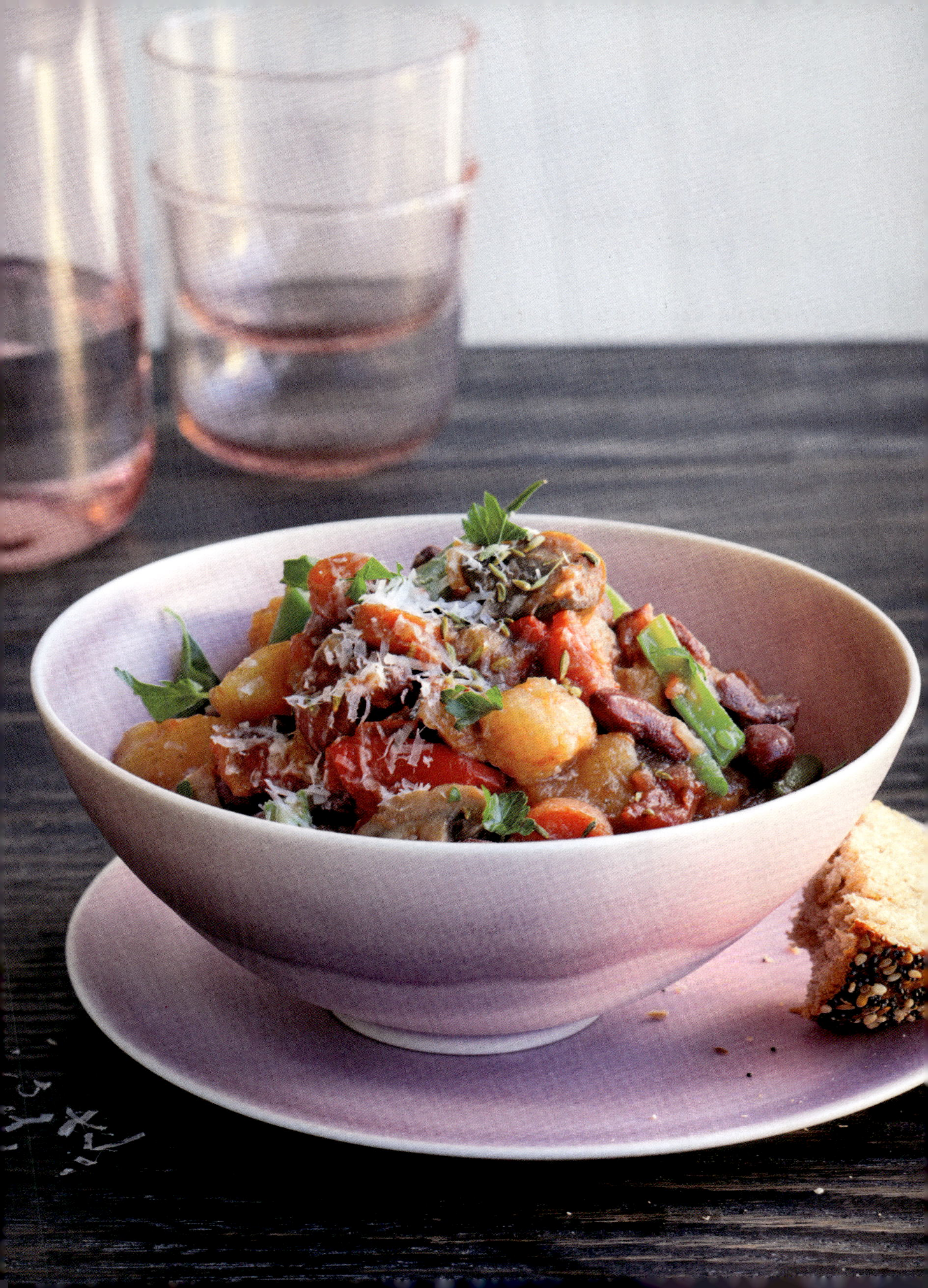

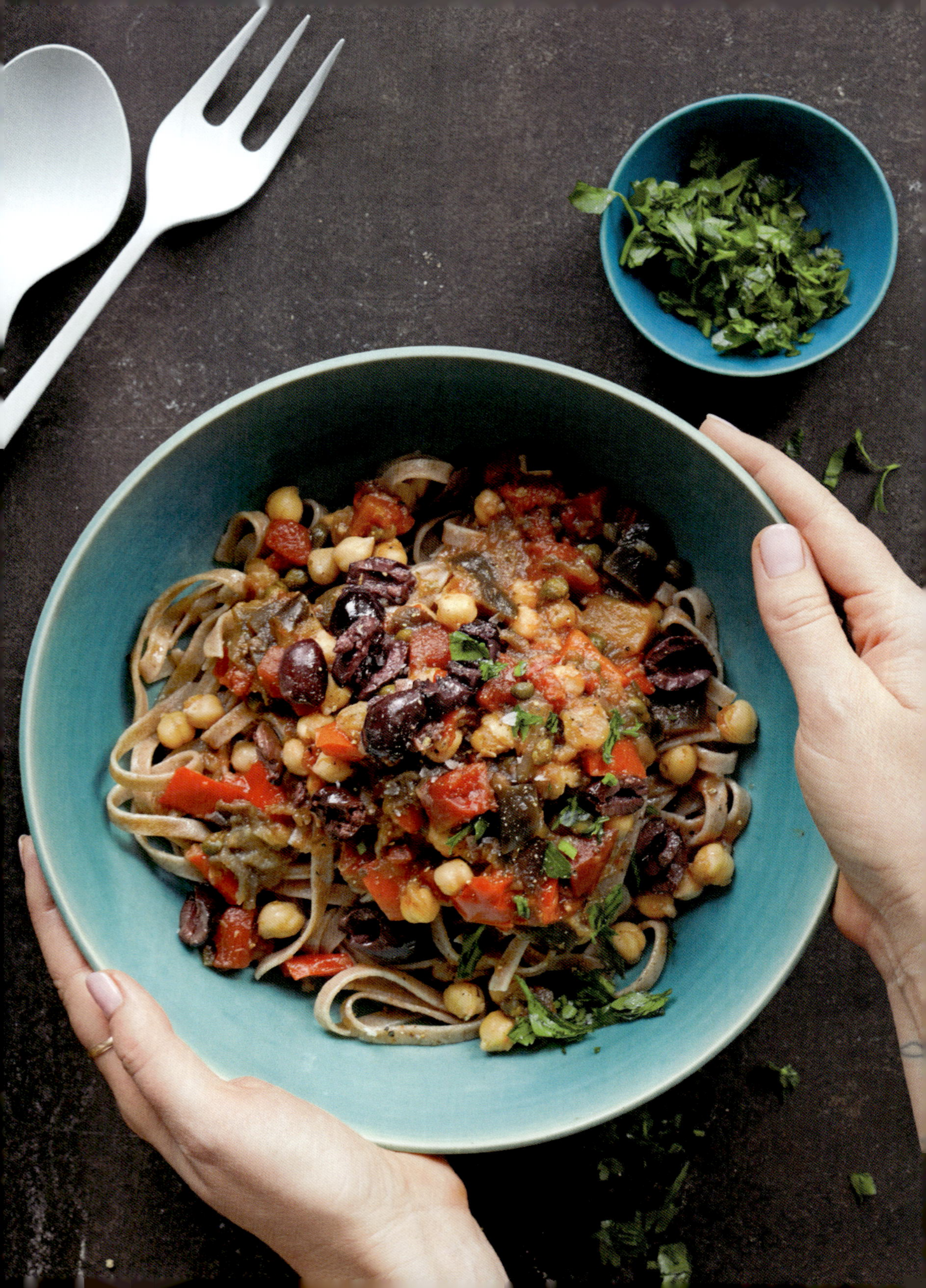

Tomato-eggplant puttanesca

Prep 10 min   Cook 2½ hr   Serves 6

This recipe is a testament to the usefulness of pantry and fridge staples! Capers, olives, canned tomatoes, pasta, and red pepper flakes (plus some eggplant, bell pepper, and parsley) are all you need to cook up an Italian classic.

1	(28-oz) can diced tomatoes
1	cup vegetable broth
1	small eggplant, unpeeled and cut into ½-inch dice
1	red bell pepper, cut into ½-inch dice
2	large garlic cloves, minced
2	tbsp nonpareil (tiny) capers
1	tsp dried oregano
½	tsp salt
½	tsp red pepper flakes
12	oz whole-wheat fettuccine
1	(15½-oz) can chickpeas, rinsed and drained
⅓	cup pitted Kalamata olives, halved
⅓	cup chopped flat-leaf parsley

1 In a 5- or 6-qt slow cooker, combine tomatoes, broth, eggplant, bell pepper, garlic, capers, oregano, salt, and red pepper flakes. Cover and cook until vegetables are softened, 2½ hours on Low, stirring after 1 hour of cooking time.

2 Meanwhile, cook fettuccine according to package directions. Drain and cover to keep warm.

3 Stir chickpeas and olives into tomato mixture. Toss together fettuccine and puttanesca sauce. Divide evenly among 6 large shallow bowls. Sprinkle with parsley.

Per serving (about 2 cups): 261 Cal, 2 g Total Fat, 0 g Sat Fat, 597 mg Sod, 53 g Total Carb, 6 g Sugar, 10 g Fib, 10 g Prot.

North African lentil-chickpea tagine

Prep 35 min   Cook 2½ to 4½ hr   Serves 6

Morroccan flavors do great things for lentils, butternut squash, and chickpeas. Make extra to freeze.

- 1 tbsp olive oil
- 1 large onion, chopped
- 4 large garlic cloves, minced
- 2 tbsp minced peeled ginger
- 2 tsp ground cumin
- ¾ tsp salt
- ½ tsp ground coriander
- ¼ tsp red pepper flakes
- 1 (1½-lb) butternut squash, peeled, seeded, and cut into 1-inch chunks
- 1½ cups brown or green lentils, picked over, rinsed and drained
- 3 cups vegetable broth
- 1 (15½-oz) can chickpeas, rinsed and drained
- 1 (14½-oz) can stewed tomatoes
- ⅓ cup chopped flat-leaf parsley, plus small sprigs for garnish
- ¾ cup plain fat-free Greek yogurt
- Smoked paprika
- 6 tbsp unsalted peanuts

1 In a medium skillet over medium heat, warm oil. Add onion and cook, stirring, until golden, about 8 minutes. Add garlic, ginger, cumin, salt, coriander, and red pepper flakes; cook, stirring, until fragrant, about 1 minute longer. Spoon into a 5- or 6-qt slow cooker.

2 Add squash, lentils, and broth to slow cooker, stirring well to combine. Cover and cook until lentils and squash are tender, about 2 hours on High or 4 hours on Low. Stir in chickpeas and tomatoes. Cover and cook 30 minutes on High. Stir in chopped parsley. Ladle evenly into 6 shallow bowls and dollop with yogurt; sprinkle with paprika and peanuts. Garnish with parsley sprigs.

Per serving (1½ cups tagine, 2 tbsp yogurt, and 1 tbsp peanuts): 398 Cal, 5 g Total Fat, 1 g Sat Fat, 920 mg Sod, 70 g Total Carb, 11 g Sugar, 14 g Fib, 22 g Prot.

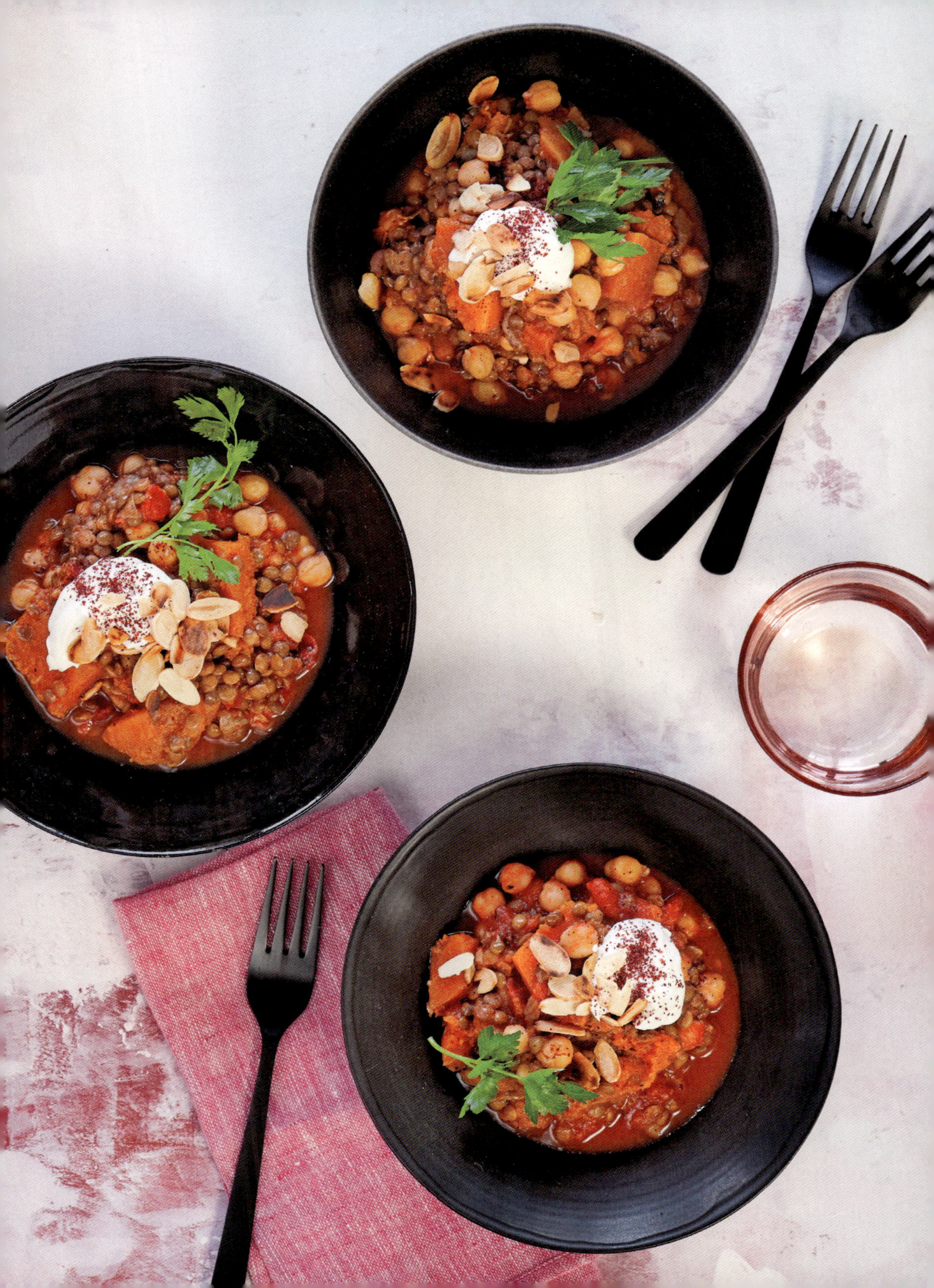

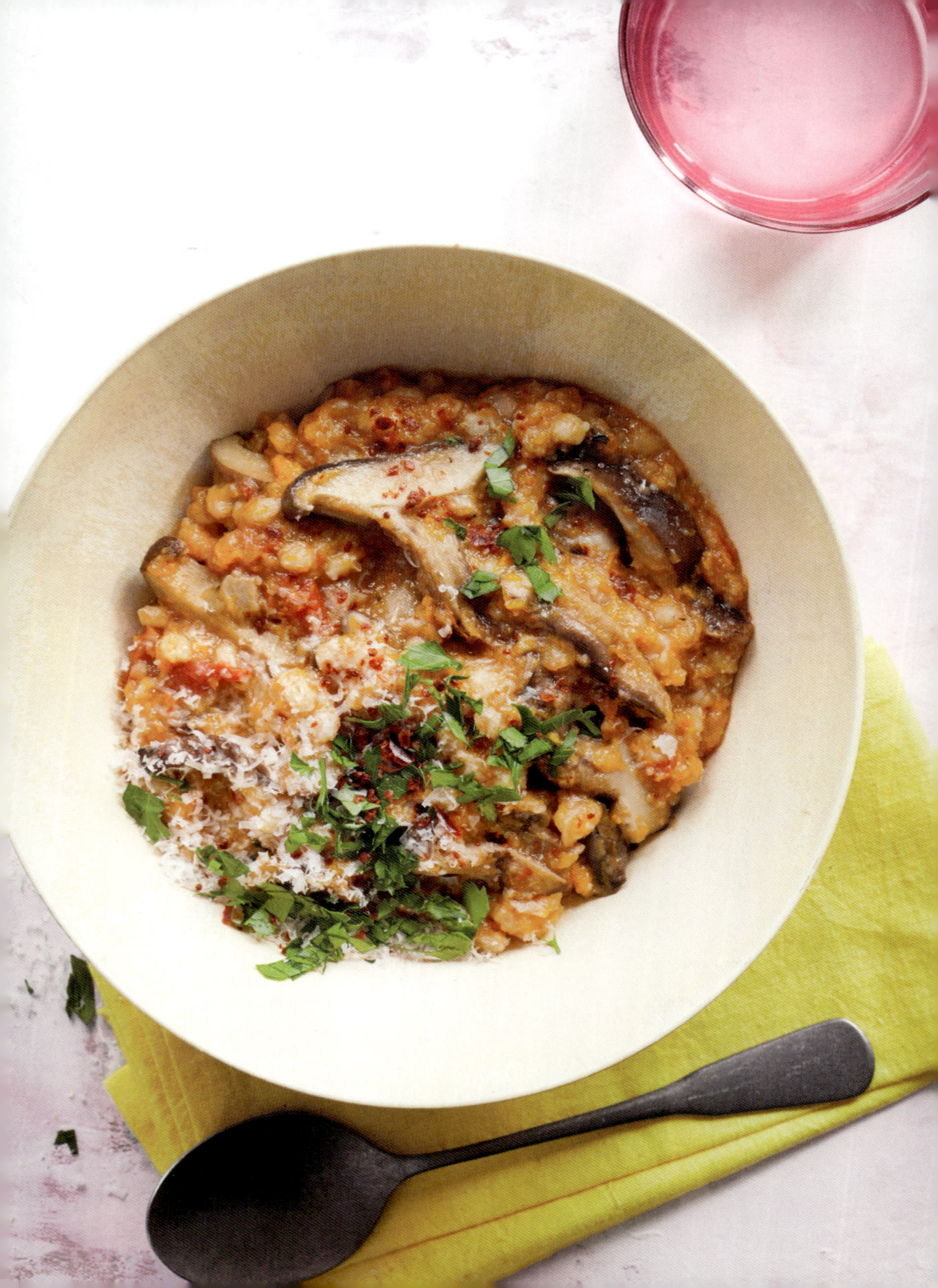

Farro and double-mushroom pot

Prep 32 min   Cook 3½ hr   Serves 8

Farro is a hearty grain with a texture somewhere between rice and barley. In this stew-like recipe it tastes fantastic with earthy mushrooms, diced canned tomatoes, butternut squash, and grated cheese sprinkled on top.

- ½ cup coarsely chopped flat-leaf parsley
- 4 large garlic cloves, minced
- Grated zest of ½ lemon
- ½ tsp plus pinch salt, divided
- ¼ tsp plus pinch black pepper, divided
- 1½ tbsp olive oil
- 1 (8-oz) package sliced white mushrooms
- 1 (3½-oz) package sliced shiitake mushrooms
- 1 large onion, chopped
- 1½ tbsp chopped thyme
- ¼ tsp red pepper flakes
- 1 (2-lb) butternut squash, peeled, seeded, and cut into ½-inch dice
- 1 (28-oz) can diced tomatoes
- 1 (32-oz) carton vegetable broth
- 1¼ cups farro, rinsed and drained
- ½ cup grated Grana Padano or Parmesan

1. In a cup, stir together parsley, one-third of garlic, lemon zest, a pinch salt, and a pinch black pepper. Refrigerate.

2. In a large nonstick skillet over medium heat, warm oil. Add mushrooms and onion; sprinkle with ¼ tsp salt and ⅛ tsp black pepper. Cook, stirring occasionally, until vegetables are softened and begin to brown, about 10 minutes. Add remaining garlic, thyme, and red pepper flakes and cook, stirring, until fragrant, about 30 seconds longer. Transfer vegetable mixture to a 5- or -6-qt slow cooker.

3. To slow cooker, add squash, tomatoes, broth, and farro; add remaining ¼ tsp salt and ⅛ tsp black pepper, stirring to mix. Cover and cook until farro and squash are tender, 3½ to 4 hours on High, stirring in additional broth or water to thin stew if needed. Divide stew evenly among 8 bowls. Sprinkle with reserved parsley mixture and cheese

Per serving (about 1½ cups stew and 1 tbsp cheese): 239 Cal, 5 g Total Fat, 1 g Sat Fat, 709 mg Sod, 43 g Total Carb, 9 g Sugar, 8 g Fib, 9 g Prot.

Vegetarian mains

Risotto-style barley and peas

Prep 10 min   Cook 4 hr   Serves 6

What do we mean by "risotto-style"? You'll know once you dig in. The creamy texture delivers the comfort-food satisfaction of a classic risotto—but using barley, a good-for-you whole grain. Baby peas and grated Parmesan add savory richness.

2¾ cups vegetable broth
½ cup dry white wine
1 cup pearl barley, rinsed
2 shallots, finely chopped
¼ tsp salt
¼ tsp black pepper
1½ cups frozen baby peas
⅓ cup grated Parmesan
Edible flowers (optional)

In a 4- or 5-qt slow cooker, combine broth, wine, barley, shallots, salt, and pepper. Cover and cook until barley is tender and liquid is almost absorbed, 4 to 5 hours on Low. Add peas and cook 5 minutes more. Stir in Parmesan. Garnish with edible flowers, if using.

Per serving (generous ¾ cup): 194 Cal, 2 g Total Fat, 1 g Sat Fat, 630 mg Sod, 34 g Total Carb, 3 g Sugar, 7 g Fib, 7 g Prot.

Cooking idea
Stir 1 or 2 diced carrots and celery stalks into the slow cooker along with the shallots for more flavor and color.

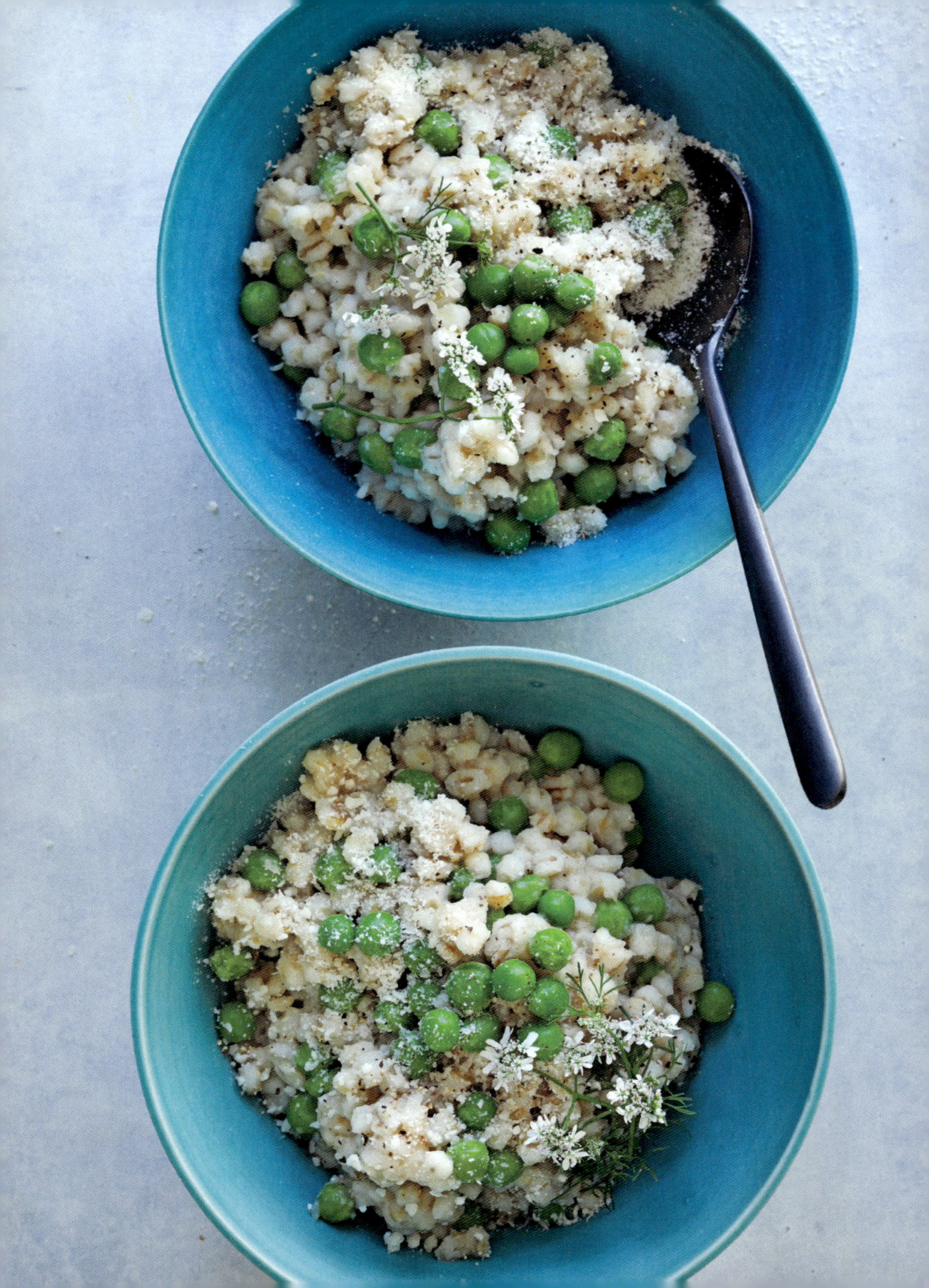

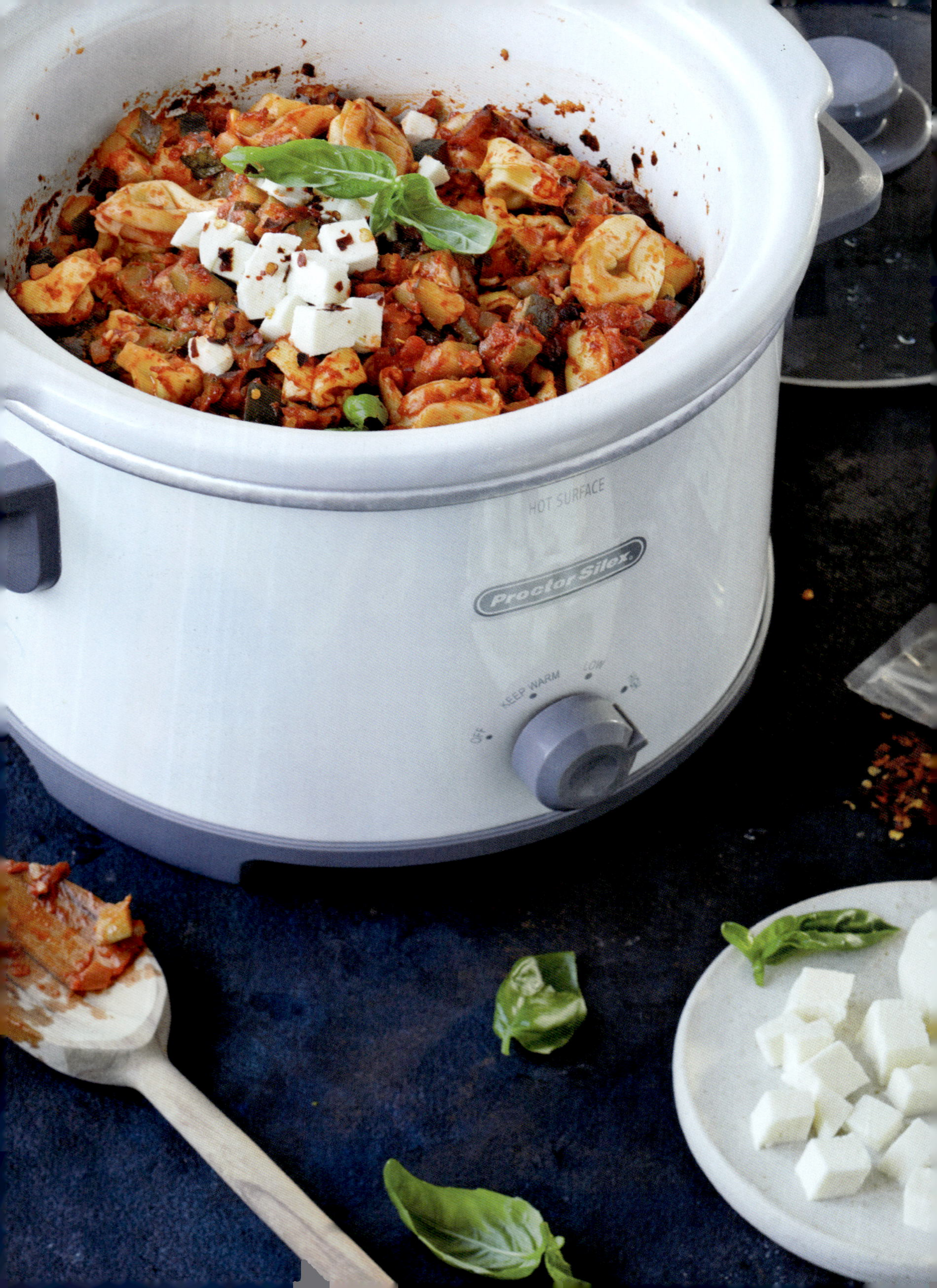
HOT SURFACE
Proctor Silex
KEEP WARM
LOW
OFF

Tortellini with garlicky tomato sauce

Prep 15 min   Cook 5 hr   Serves 8

Cooking frozen tortellini (or any frozen stuffed pasta) in your slow cooker is a revelation. Something magical happens with the pasta, cheese, and tomato sauce—and you get that from-scratch, baked pasta deliciousness with way less work.

2	tsp olive oil
6	small zucchini, trimmed and diced
1	onion, chopped
2	garlic cloves, minced
1½	cups marinara sauce
½	tsp kosher salt (or to taste)
½	tsp red pepper flakes
¼	tsp black pepper (or to taste)
8	cups tightly packed baby spinach (about 1 lb)
6	cups frozen cheese tortellini (about 18 oz)
½	cup diced part-skim mozzarella, divided

Basil leaves (optional)

1 In a large heavy nonstick skillet over medium-high heat, warm oil. Add zucchini and onion and cook, stirring frequently, until lightly browned, about 5 minutes. Add garlic and cook, stirring, until fragrant, about 30 seconds. Add marinara sauce, salt, red pepper flakes, and black pepper.

2 Add spinach in batches, adding more as each batch wilts. Reduce heat to medium and cook, covered, stirring once or twice, 3 minutes.

3 Spoon 2 cups marinara-spinach mixture into a 6-qt slow cooker. Place half of tortellini on top, forming even layer. Repeat with another 2 cups marinara-spinach mixture and remaining tortellini. Spoon remaining marinara-spinach mixture on top and sprinkle with ¼ cup mozzarella. Cover and cook until tortellini are tender, about 5 hours on Low. Sprinkle with remaining ¼ cup mozzarella. Garnish with basil leaves, if desired.

Per serving (1⅓ cups): 283 Cal, 9 g Total Fat, 4 g Sat Fat, 644 mg Sod, 44 g Total Carb, 6 g Sugar, 4 g Fib, 15 g Prot.

Serving idea
Grate some imported Parmigiano-Reggiano onto each serving. To be sure you're buying the real thing, look for "Parmigiano-Reggiano" stamped on the rind.

Ricotta-and-spinach stuffed cabbage

Prep 18 min   Cook 3 to 7 hr   Serves 4

Cabbage rolls stuffed with a creamy mixture of spinach, ricotta, scallions, and a touch of nutmeg is a welcome change from the usual beef. We like delicate Savoy cabbage—find it in the produce aisle next to the regular green kind.

- 8 large Savoy cabbage leaves
- 1 (15-oz) container part-skim ricotta
- 1½ cups chopped baby spinach
- 4 scallions, thinly sliced
- 1 large egg
- 2 tbsp grated Parmesan
- ½ tsp salt
- ¼ tsp black pepper
- ⅛ tsp ground nutmeg
- 1 cup tomato sauce
- Chopped basil
- 1 oz Parmesan, shaved, plus more for sprinkling

1. Place cabbage leaves on a large microwavable plate; cover with a damp paper towel. Microwave on High until softened, 3 to 4 minutes. Transfer cabbage to a cutting board. When cool enough to handle, trim thick ribs at base of leaves.

2. Meanwhile, to make filling: In a large bowl, stir together ricotta, spinach, scallions, egg, Parmesan, salt, pepper, and nutmeg.

3. Place ⅓ cup of ricotta mixture in center of each cabbage leaf. Fold in opposite sides and roll up to enclose filling. Place cabbage rolls, seam-side down, in a 5- or 6-qt slow cooker. Top with tomato sauce. Cover and cook until cabbage is fork-tender, 3 to 4 hours on High or 6 to 7 hours on Low.

4. Sprinkle cabbage rolls with basil and shaved Parmesan. Put 2 cabbage rolls on each plate; top with tomato sauce.

Per serving (2 cabbage rolls and 2 tbsp tomato sauce): 238 Cal, 12 g Total Fat, 7 g Sat Fat, 866 mg Sod, 14 g Total Carb, 4 g Sugar, 3 g Fib, 19 g Prot.

Serving idea
Stuffed cabbage goes great with a side of brown rice and a sprinkle of chopped herbs like parsley.

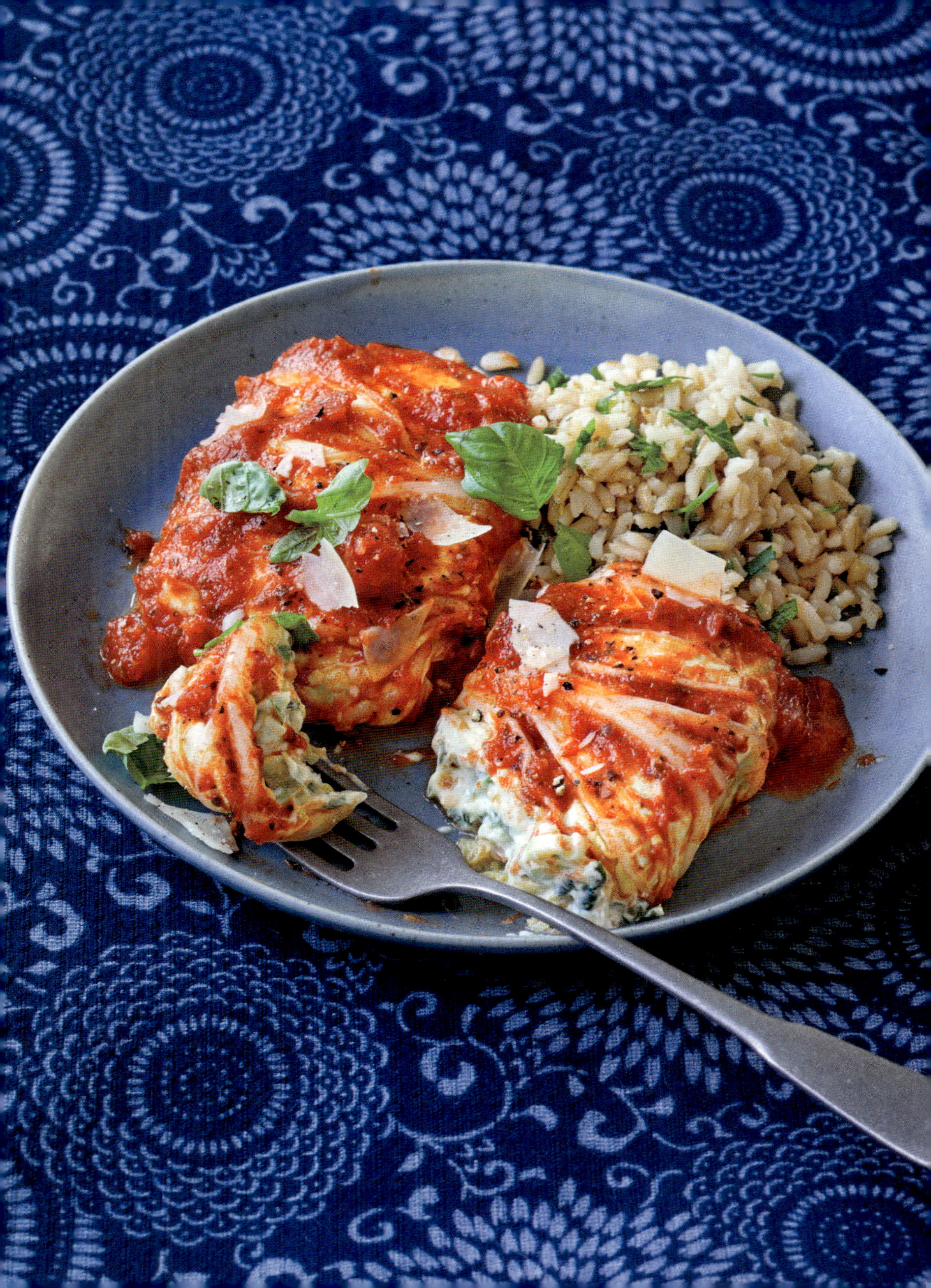

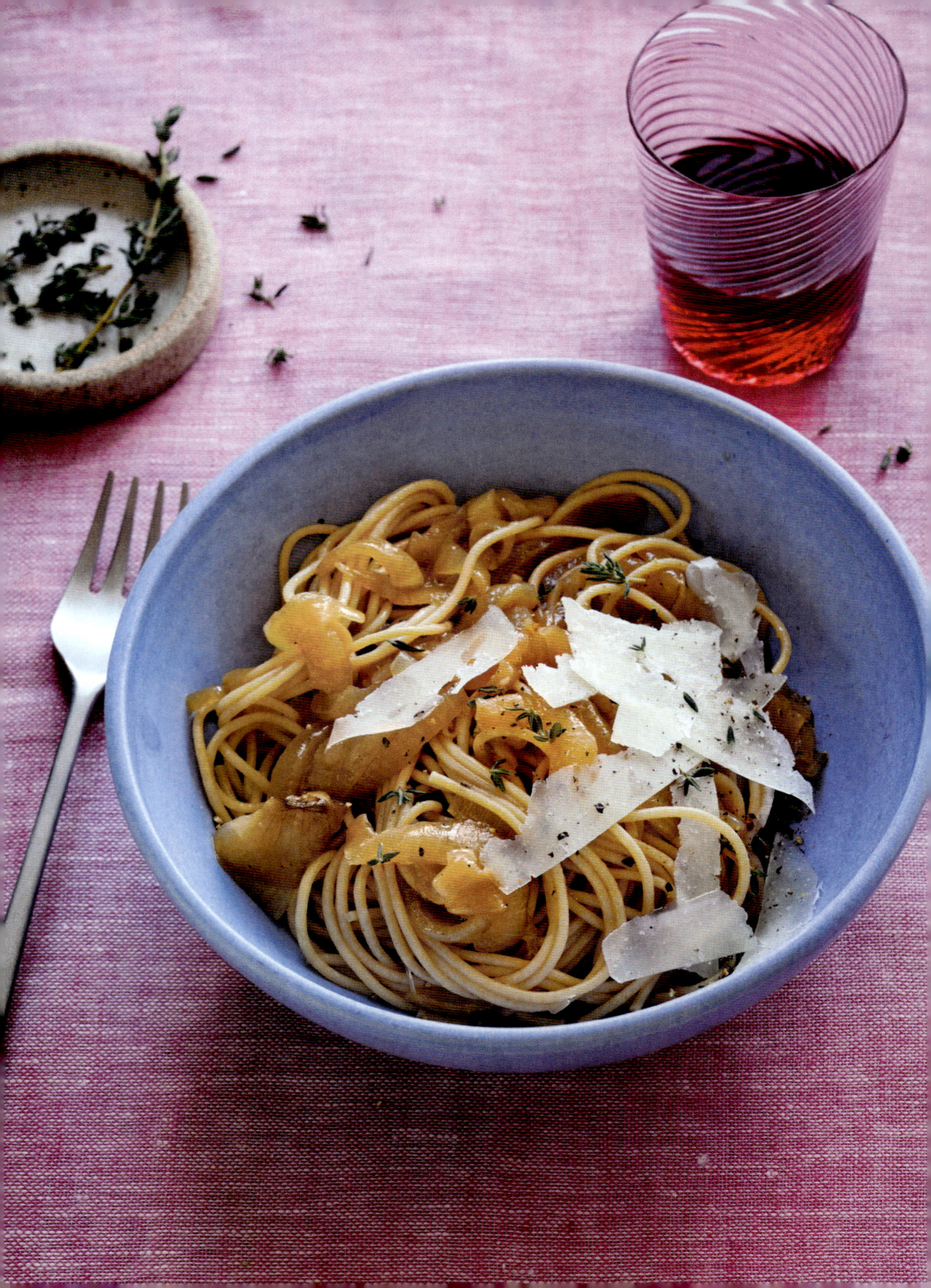

Spaghetti with caramelized onions

Prep 10 min   Cook 10 hr   Serves 6

Sweet, rich golden caramelized onions turn simple dishes into something special. We've used them here as a topping for pasta, but they also pair well with any grilled protein.

- 5 large sweet onions such as Texas Sweet or Vidalia (about 4½ lb), sliced
- 2 tbsp extra-virgin olive oil
- 1¼ tsp kosher salt, divided
- 1 large bay leaf
- 12 oz spaghetti
- ¼ tsp black pepper (or to taste)
- ¾ cup grated or shaved Parmesan
- Thyme leaves (optional)

1 In a 5- or 6-qt slow cooker, mix together onions, oil, and ½ tsp salt. Tuck in bay leaf. Cover and cook until onions are golden and softened, about 6 hours on Low.

2 Stir onions. Partially cover and cook, stirring once or twice, until onions are golden brown and most of liquid is evaporated, 4 to 5 hours on High. Stir in remaining ¾ tsp salt. Remove and discard bay leaf.

3 Meanwhile, cook spaghetti according to package directions. Drain and cover to keep warm.

4 Divide pasta evenly among 6 large shallow bowls and top with onion mixture. Sprinkle with pepper, Parmesan, and thyme, if using.

Per serving (about ½ cup onion, 1 cup pasta, and 2 tbsp cheese): 354 Cal, 9 g Total Fat, 3 g Sat Fat, 635 mg Sod, 56 g Total Carb, 7 g Sugar, 4 g Fib, 12 g Prot.

Prep ahead
Make an extra batch of these delicious caramelized onions to enjoy on top of burgers, tucked into omelets, or layered on your favorite sandwich.

Summer tomato sauce with pasta

Prep 20 min   Cook 5 to 9 hr   Serves 6

At the peak of summer, when farmers' markets are laden with juicy, ripe tomatoes at tempting prices, it's time to cook up a batch or two of this sauce. Make extra to freeze so you can thaw and cook with it all winter long.

1	tbsp olive oil
1	large onion, chopped
3	large garlic cloves, thinly sliced
2	tbsp tomato paste
1½	tsp kosher salt, divided
5	lb plum tomatoes, quartered lengthwise and seeded
2	cups firmly packed basil sprigs, plus ½ cup small leaves
½	tsp black pepper
12	oz penne

1. In a large skillet over medium heat, warm oil. Add onion and garlic and cook, covered, stirring occasionally, until onion is golden, about 8 minutes.

2. Transfer onion mixture to a 6- or 7-qt slow cooker. Stir in tomato paste and 1 tsp salt until mixed well; top with tomatoes. Place basil sprigs in center of 12-inch piece of cheesecloth; gather ends together and tie with kitchen twine to form a bundle.

3. Push basil bundle into tomatoes. Cover and cook until tomatoes have released their juices and are tender, 2½ to 3 hours on High or 5 to 6 hours on Low. Remove and discard basil bundle.

4. Puree tomato mixture with an immersion blender or let cool 5 minutes and puree in batches in a food processor. Cook, uncovered, until sauce is slightly thickened, 2 to 3 hours on High. Stir in ¼ cup basil leaves, remaining ½ tsp salt, and pepper.

5. Meanwhile, cook penne according to package directions. Drain and cover to keep warm. To serve, divide pasta evenly among 6 large shallow bowls; top each serving with ½ cup tomato sauce and remaining ¼ cup basil leaves. (Leftover tomato sauce can be refrigerated in an airtight container up to 5 days.)

Per serving (½ cup tomato sauce and 1 cup pasta): 257 Cal, 3 g Total Fat, 0 g Sat Fat, 237 mg Sod, 51 g Total Carb, 7 g Sugar, 3 g Fib, 9 g Prot.

Serving idea

Meatballs and tomato sauce are a perfect match. Try this sauce with our spicy turkey meatballs on page 73 or our Classic Italian version on page 85.

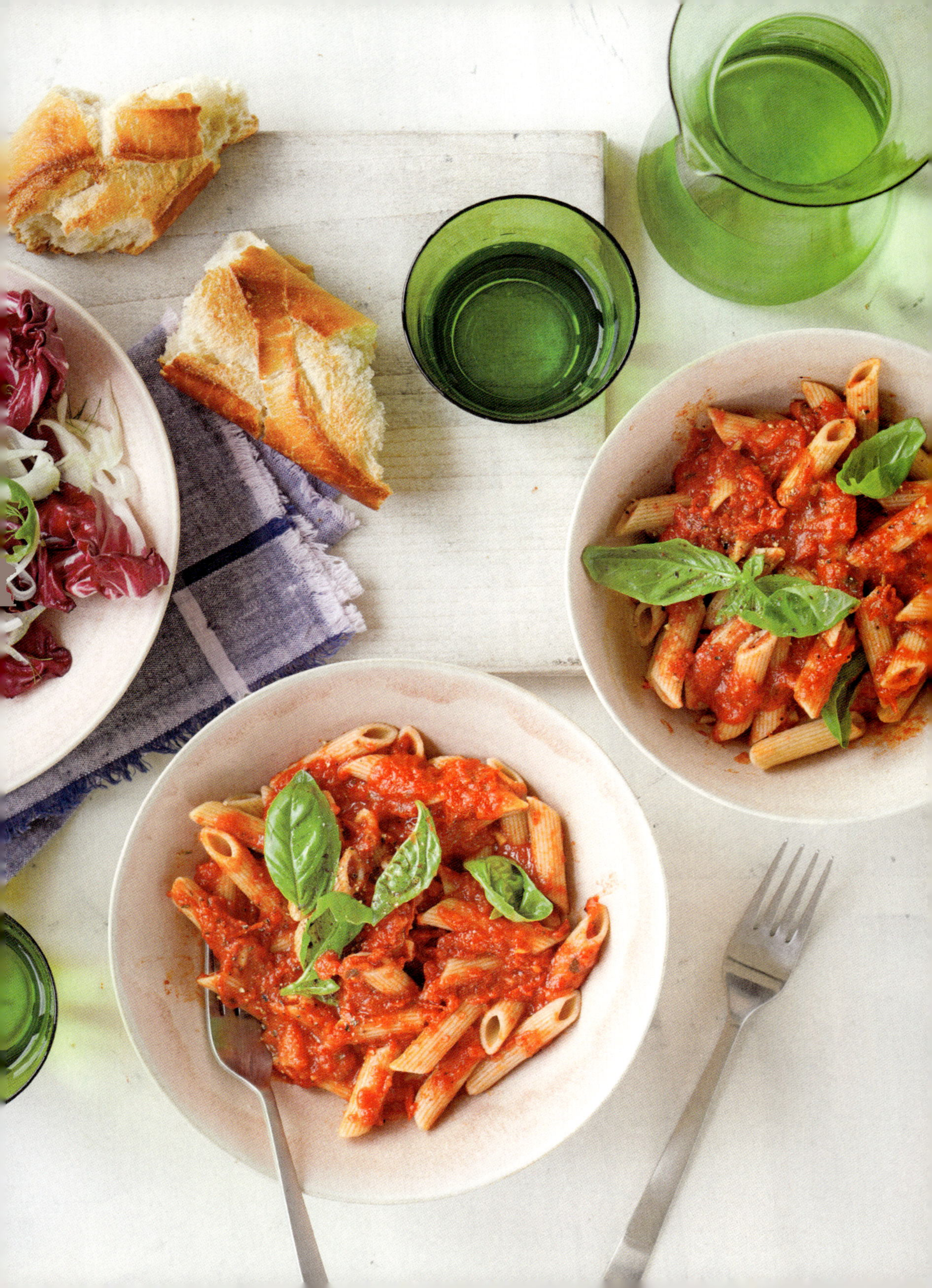

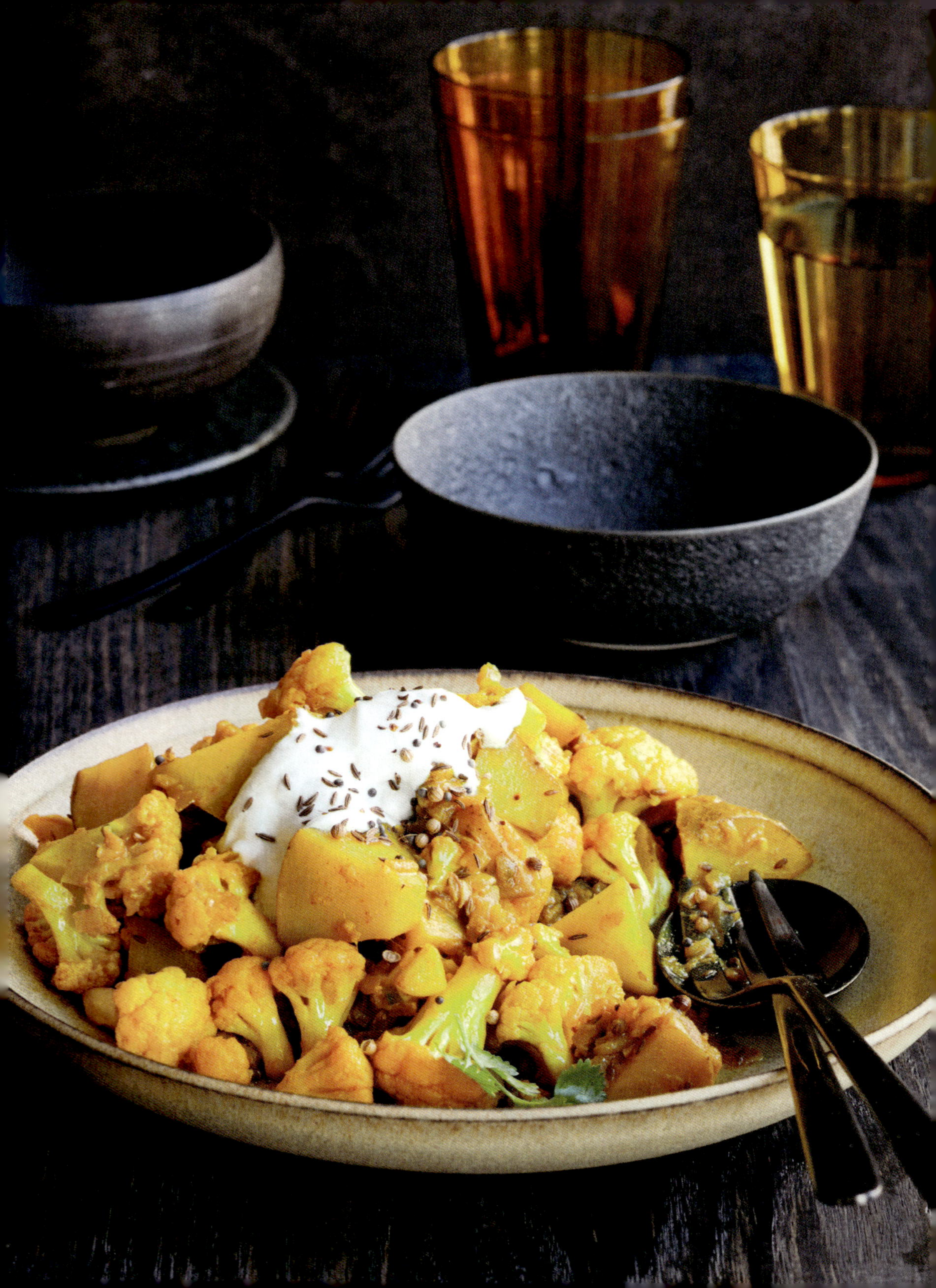

Indian-spiced potatoes with cauliflower

Prep 20 min   Cook 2 hr   Serves 4

What makes this potato and cauliflower dish so fabulously fragrant? The mix of Indian spices, including turmeric for taste and bright yellow color.

- 2½ tsp canola oil, divided
- 1 onion, cut into thin wedges
- 1 jalapeño pepper, cut into very thin rings
- 2 garlic cloves, minced
- 1 tbsp minced peeled ginger
- 2 tsp mustard seeds, preferably black, plus more for garnish
- 2 tsp cumin seeds, plus more for garnish
- 1½ tsp ground coriander
- ½ tsp ground turmeric
- ½ tsp salt
- 1 lb all-purpose potatoes, scrubbed and cut into 1-inch chunks
- ½ small head cauliflower, cut into 1-inch florets (about 3 cups)
- ½ cup plain fat-free yogurt

1 In a medium heavy nonstick skillet over medium-high heat, warm oil. Add onion and cook, stirring occasionally, until softened and lightly browned, about 5 minutes. Add remaining ½ tsp oil. Stir in jalapeño, garlic, ginger, mustard seeds, cumin seeds, coriander, and turmeric; cook, stirring constantly, until spices are toasted and fragrant, about 1 minute. Remove skillet from heat and stir in salt.

2 Combine potatoes and cauliflower in a 4- or 5-qt slow cooker. Add onion mixture and stir until well combined. Cover and cook until vegetables are fork-tender, about 2 hours on High, gently stirring after 1 hour to prevent vegetables from sticking to insert. Divide evenly among 4 bowls. Top each serving with yogurt, mustard seeds, and cumin seeds.

Per serving (1¼ cups potato mixture and 2 tbsp yogurt): 164 Cal, 4 g Total Fat, 0 g Sat Fat, 333 mg Sod, 29 g Total Carb, 6 g Sugar, 5 g Fib, 6 g Prot.

Cooking idea

For more satisfying protein, add a 15½-oz can of chickpeas, rinsed and drained, to the potato mixture about 10 minutes before the cooking time is up.

Artichoke and bell pepper paella

Prep 20 min   Cook 1½ to 3 hr   Serves 4

Paella—usually a major cooking project—becomes weeknight easy when you pair your slow cooker with convenience foods like yellow rice mix, store-bought broth, frozen artichoke hearts, and frozen mixed vegetables.

1	tbsp olive oil
2	bell peppers (in a variety of colors), diced
1	large onion, chopped
3	garlic cloves, minced
1	(7-oz) box yellow rice mix
2	cups vegetable broth (or water)
1	bay leaf
4	vegetarian sausage links, thinly sliced
1	(9-oz) box frozen artichoke hearts, thawed
1	(10-oz) box frozen mixed vegetables, thawed
	Cilantro leaves
½	lemon, cut into 4 wedges
	Hot pepper sauce

1 In a large skillet over medium heat, warm oil. Add bell peppers and onion and cook, stirring, until softened, about 5 minutes. Add garlic and cook, stirring constantly, until fragrant, about 30 seconds longer. Transfer to a 5- or 6-qt slow cooker.

2 Stir in rice mix, broth, and bay leaf. Cover and cook until rice is just tender and liquid is almost absorbed, about 1½ hours on High or 3 hours on Low.

3 About 20 minutes before cooking time is up, stir in sausages, artichoke hearts, and mixed vegetables. Remove and discard bay leaf. Sprinkle cilantro over paella. Serve with lemon wedges and hot sauce.

Per serving (2 cups): 293 Cal, 9 g Total Fat, 1 g Sat Fat, 823 mg Sod, 44 g Total Carb, 6 g Sugar, 9 g Fib, 12 g Prot.

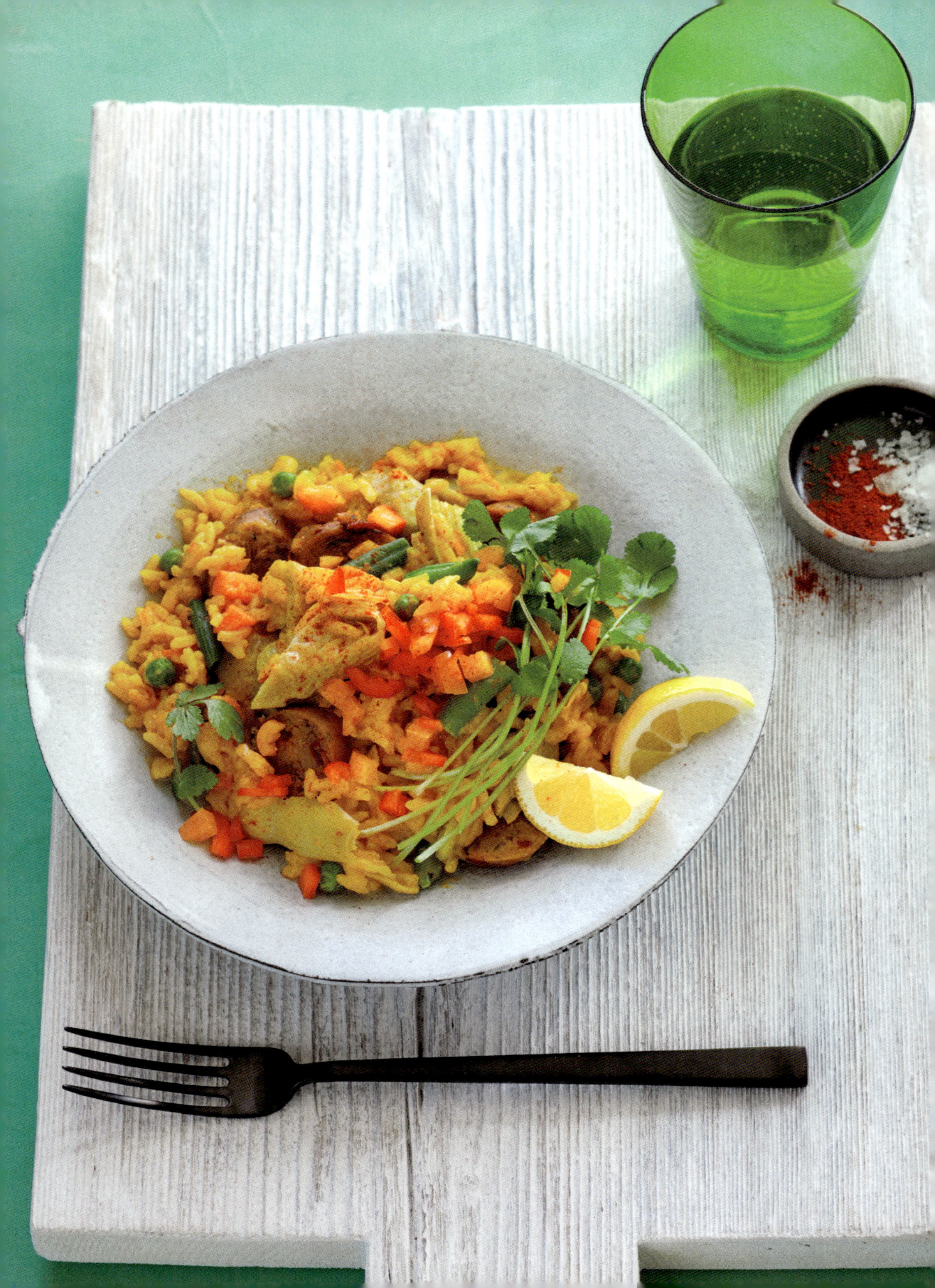

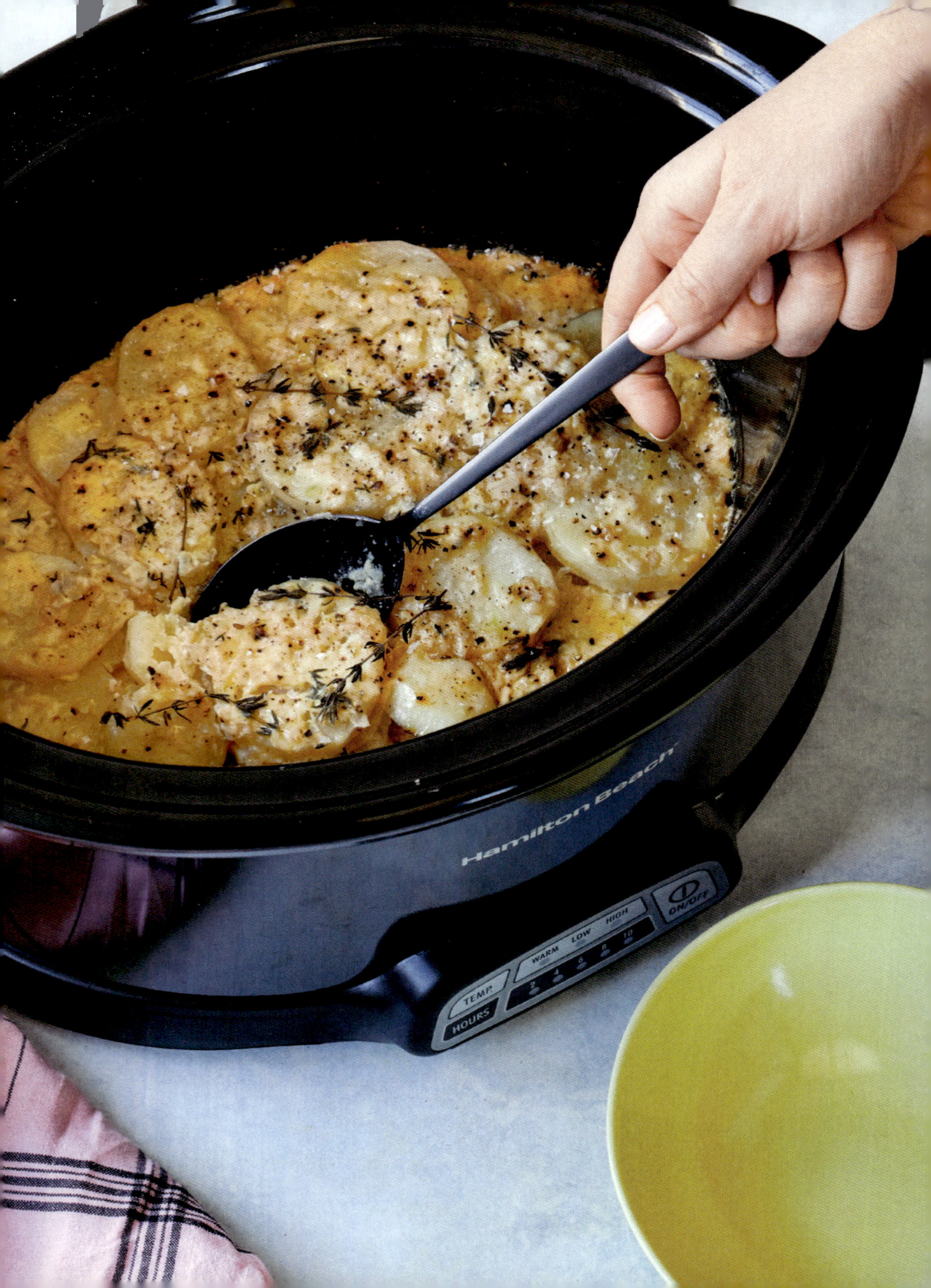
Hamilton Beach
TEMP
HOURS
WARM
LOW
HIGH
2
4
6
8
10
ON/OFF

Scalloped potatoes with thyme

Prep 28 min Cook 3 hr Serves 6

Serve these creamy, cheesy potatoes anytime, but especially when your oven is overloaded (Thanksgiving!).

Nonstick spray
- 1 tbsp olive oil
- 2 large shallots, finely chopped (about ⅓ cup)
- 1 large garlic clove, minced
- 1 tbsp all-purpose flour
- 1¼ cups reduced-fat (2%) milk
- 2 tsp chopped thyme, divided
- 1 tsp Dijon mustard
- ½ tsp kosher salt, divided
- ¼ tsp black pepper, divided, plus more for sprinkling
- ⅛ tsp ground nutmeg
- 1¾ lb all-purpose potatoes, peeled and cut into ⅛-inch slices
- 6 tbsp grated Parmesan

1 In a small saucepan over medium heat, warm oil. Add shallots and garlic and cook, stirring occasionally, until softened, about 3 minutes. Stir in flour and cook, stirring constantly, 2 minutes. Slowly pour in milk, stirring constantly with a wooden spoon until sauce bubbles; simmer, stirring, until sauce thickens, about 2 minutes longer. Stir in 1 tsp thyme, mustard, ¼ tsp salt, ⅛ tsp pepper, and nutmeg.

2 Spray the insert of a 4- or 5-qt slow cooker with nonstick spray. Arrange one-third of potatoes in bottom of slow cooker, overlapping as needed; sprinkle with ⅛ tsp salt, and a pinch pepper. Sprinkle with 2 tbsp Parmesan and one-third of sauce. Repeat layers with half of remaining potatoes, 2 tbsp Parmesan, half of remaining sauce, ⅛ tsp salt, and remaining pinch pepper. Decoratively arrange remaining potatoes on top and spoon remaining sauce over.

3 Cover and cook until potatoes are fork-tender, 2½ to 3 hours on High. Turn off slow cooker and sprinkle potatoes with remaining 2 tbsp Parmesan, 1 tsp thyme, and a sprinkle of pepper. Cover and let stand until cheese is melted, about 5 minutes.

Per serving (⅙ of potatoes): 187 Cal, 5 g Total Fat, 2 g Sat Fat, 566 mg Sod, 29 g Total Carb, 4 g Sugar, 3 g Fib, 6 g Prot.

Serving idea
Vegetarian sausage links can turn this classic side into a warming winter dinner.

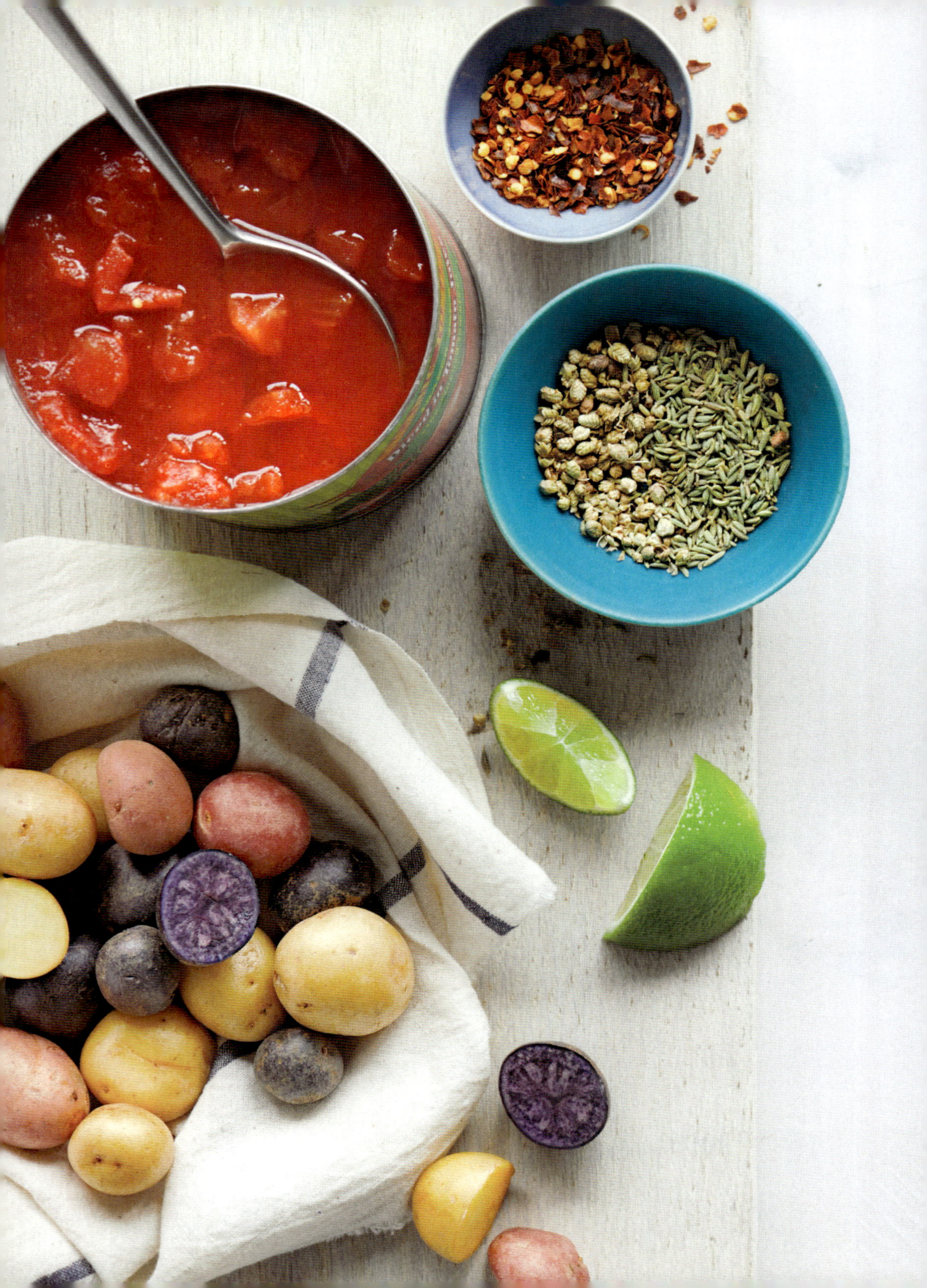

Chapter 3
Updated classics

Chicken with celery root and apple 58
Mushroom, tomato, and thyme chicken 61
Piled-high chicken nachos 62
Louisiana jambalaya 65
Old-fashioned chicken noodle soup 66
Chicken and white bean chili 69
Turkey–bell pepper meatloaf 70
Spicy turkey meatballs 73
Low-and-slow sloppy joes 74
Italian-style pot roast 77
Braciole with spicy tomato sauce 78
Hearty beef-barley stew 81
Beef 'n' bean chili 82
Classic Italian meatballs 85
Simply delicious lasagna 86
Rosemary-garlic pork roast 89
Pork chops with braised cabbage 90
Sicilian-style pork and fennel ragu 93
Double-mushroom and prosciutto soup 94
Parmesan-stuffed artichokes 97
Lamb-ricotta meatballs and sauce 98
San Francisco fisherman's stew 101
Garlicky shrimp with charred fennel 102
Creamy tomato soup with crab 105

Chicken with celery root and apple

Prep 40 min   Cook 3 to 6½ hr   Serves 4

We'll admit that celery root—gnarled and a bit hairy—doesn't look promising in the produce aisle. But once it's trimmed and peeled, this celery-scented veggie is a winner. Delicious cooked with chicken and apples, it's also great raw in slaws and salads.

4	(6-oz) bone-in chicken thighs, skin removed
¾	tsp salt, divided
¼	plus ⅛ tsp black pepper, divided
2	tsp olive oil
1	large onion, chopped
3	large garlic cloves, minced
1	cup chicken broth
1	(1½-lb) celery root, trimmed, peeled, and cut into 1-inch chunks
4	carrots, halved lengthwise and cut into 1-inch chunks
½	cup unsweetened apple juice or cider
2	tsp minced fresh thyme (or ½ tsp dried thyme)
1	apple, peeled, cored, and thinly sliced
1	tbsp Dijon mustard
¼	cup flat-leaf parsley leaves

1 Sprinkle chicken with ½ tsp salt and ¼ tsp pepper. In a large heavy nonstick skillet over medium-high heat, warm oil. Add chicken and cook until browned, about 4 minutes per side. Transfer to a plate.

2 Reduce heat to medium. Add onion to skillet and cook, stirring, until softened, about 5 minutes. Add garlic and cook, stirring constantly, until fragrant, about 30 seconds. Add broth and bring to a boil over high heat, scraping up browned bits from bottom of pan. Remove skillet from heat.

3 In a 5- or 6-qt slow cooker, combine celery root, carrots, apple juice, thyme, and remaining ¼ tsp salt and ⅛ tsp pepper. Stir in onion mixture and place chicken on top in single layer. Cover and cook until chicken and vegetables are fork-tender, 2½ to 3 hours on High or 5 to 6 hours on Low.

4 Transfer chicken to plate and cover to keep warm. Stir apple and mustard into slow cooker. Cover and cook until mixture simmers, about 30 minutes on High. Return chicken to slow cooker. Cover and cook until heated through, about 5 minutes more. Stir in parsley.

Per serving (1 chicken thigh with 1 cup vegetables and ⅓ cup sauce): 384 Cal, 10 g Total Fat, 2 g Sat Fat, 1,109 mg Sod, 36 g Total Carb, 15 g Sugar, 7 g Fib, 37 g Prot.

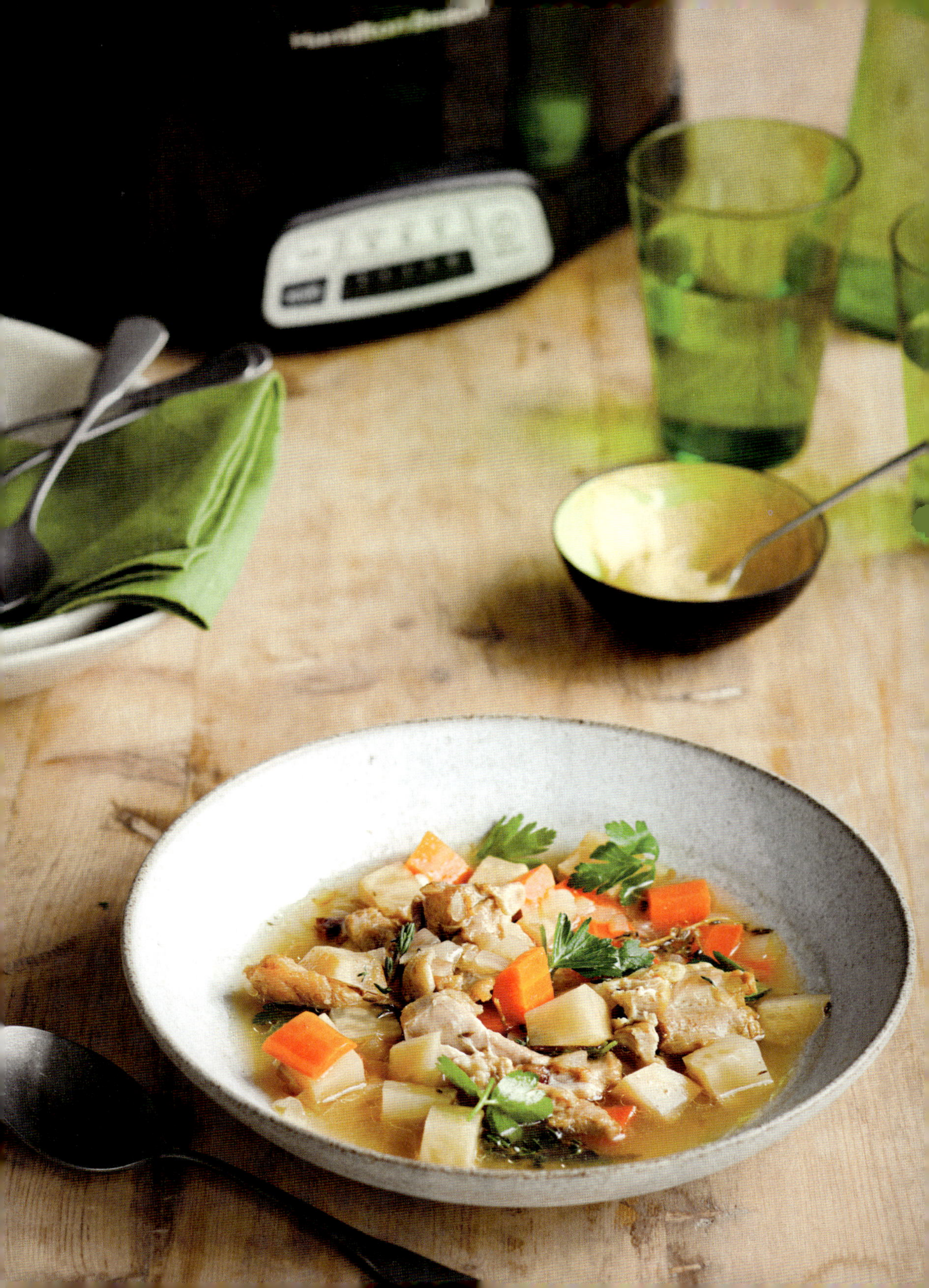

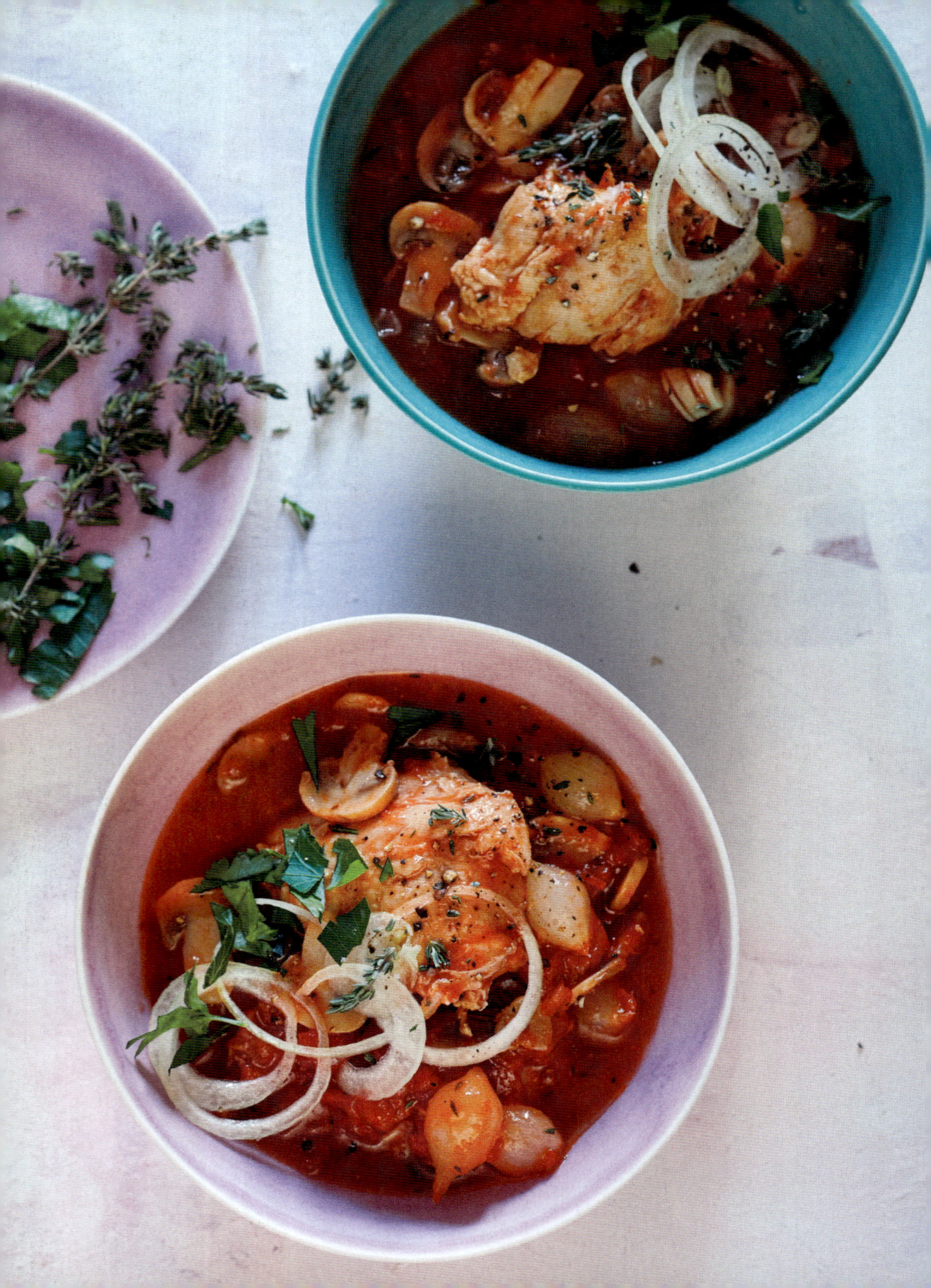

Mushroom, tomato, and thyme chicken

Prep 33 min   Cook 3 to 8 hr   Serves 6

Use frozen pearl onions—they're already peeled, trimmed, and par-boiled, which really cuts down on prep time.

- 6 (5-oz) bone-in chicken thighs, skin removed
- 1 tsp kosher salt, divided
- ½ tsp black pepper, divided
- 1 tbsp olive oil
- 1 cup frozen pearl onions, thawed
- 1 (8-oz) package sliced white or cremini mushrooms
- 2 garlic cloves, minced
- 1 (14½-oz) can petite diced tomatoes, drained
- 2 tbsp tomato paste
- 2 tsp dried thyme
- 1 tbsp balsamic vinegar
- Chopped flat-leaf parsley
- Thinly sliced sweet onion

1 Sprinkle chicken with ½ tsp salt and ¼ tsp pepper. In a large heavy nonstick skillet over medium-high heat, warm oil. Add chicken and cook until well browned, about 4 minutes per side. Transfer to a 5- or 6-qt slow cooker.

2 Pat pearl onions dry with a paper towel. Add to same skillet and cook, shaking pan occasionally, until lightly browned, about 3 minutes. Add mushrooms and cook, stirring frequently, until softened, about 3 minutes. Add garlic and cook, stirring constantly, until fragrant, about 30 seconds more. Add tomatoes, tomato paste, thyme, remaining ½ tsp salt, and remaining ¼ tsp pepper and bring to a boil, scraping up browned bits from bottom of pan.

3 Transfer onion mixture to slow cooker. Cover and cook until chicken is fork-tender, 3 to 4 hours on High or 6 to 8 hours on Low. Place chicken in 6 bowls. Stir vinegar into mushroom mixture; spoon over chicken. Top with parsley and sliced onion.

Per serving (1 chicken thigh and ¾ cup mushroom mixture): 194 Cal, 7 g Total Fat, 2 g Sat Fat, 598 mg Sod, 8 g Total Carb, 4 g Sugar, 2 g Fib, 24 g Prot.

Serving idea
Steamed or boiled baby potatoes would soak up some of the sauce in this recipe; use a potato masher to lightly crush them after cooking.

Piled-high chicken nachos

Prep 10 min   Cook 2½ to 5 hr   Serves 6

Double the chicken portion of this recipe to have leftovers that you can use to fill tacos, top a rice bowl, or add to a salad.

- 1 (15½-oz) jar fat-free salsa
- 1 cup chopped cilantro, divided, plus leaves for garnish
- 1 tbsp plus 1 tsp chili powder
- 2 tsp dried oregano
- ½ tsp salt, divided
- 1½ lb skinless boneless chicken breasts
- 36 tortilla chips
- ¾ cup shredded reduced-fat cheddar
- 1 cup diced plum tomatoes
- ¾ cup cooked corn kernels
- 1 lime, halved
- 1 Hass avocado, pitted, peeled, and thinly sliced
- Radishes, thinly sliced
- Red onion, thinly sliced

1 In a 5-qt slow cooker, stir together salsa, chopped cilantro, chili powder, oregano, and ¼ tsp salt. Add chicken, turning to coat evenly. Arrange chicken in single layer. Cover and cook until chicken is fork-tender, about 2½ hours on High or 5 hours on Low. Transfer chicken to a cutting board. With two forks, shred chicken; return to slow cooker.

2 Preheat broiler. Line a large rimmed baking sheet with foil.

3 On prepared baking sheet, make 6 piles of 6 slightly overlapping chips. Spoon chicken mixture over chips, dividing evenly; sprinkle with cheddar. Broil 4 inches from heat until cheese is melted, about 1 minute.

4 In a medium bowl, combine tomatoes, corn, remaining ½ cup cilantro, and remaining ¼ tsp salt; spoon on top of nachos. Squeeze lime juice over nachos. Top with cilantro leaves, avocado, radishes, and onion.

Per serving (6 garnished chips): 329 Cal, 12 Total Fat, 3 g Sat Fat, 1,029 mg Sod, 25 g Total Carb, 6 g Sugar, 6 g Fib, 33 g Prot.

Serving idea

Topping the nachos with quick-pickled red onion adds a surprise layer of flavor: Thinly slice red onion, put it into a bowl, and cover it with red-wine vinegar. Set aside for about 15 minutes. Drain.

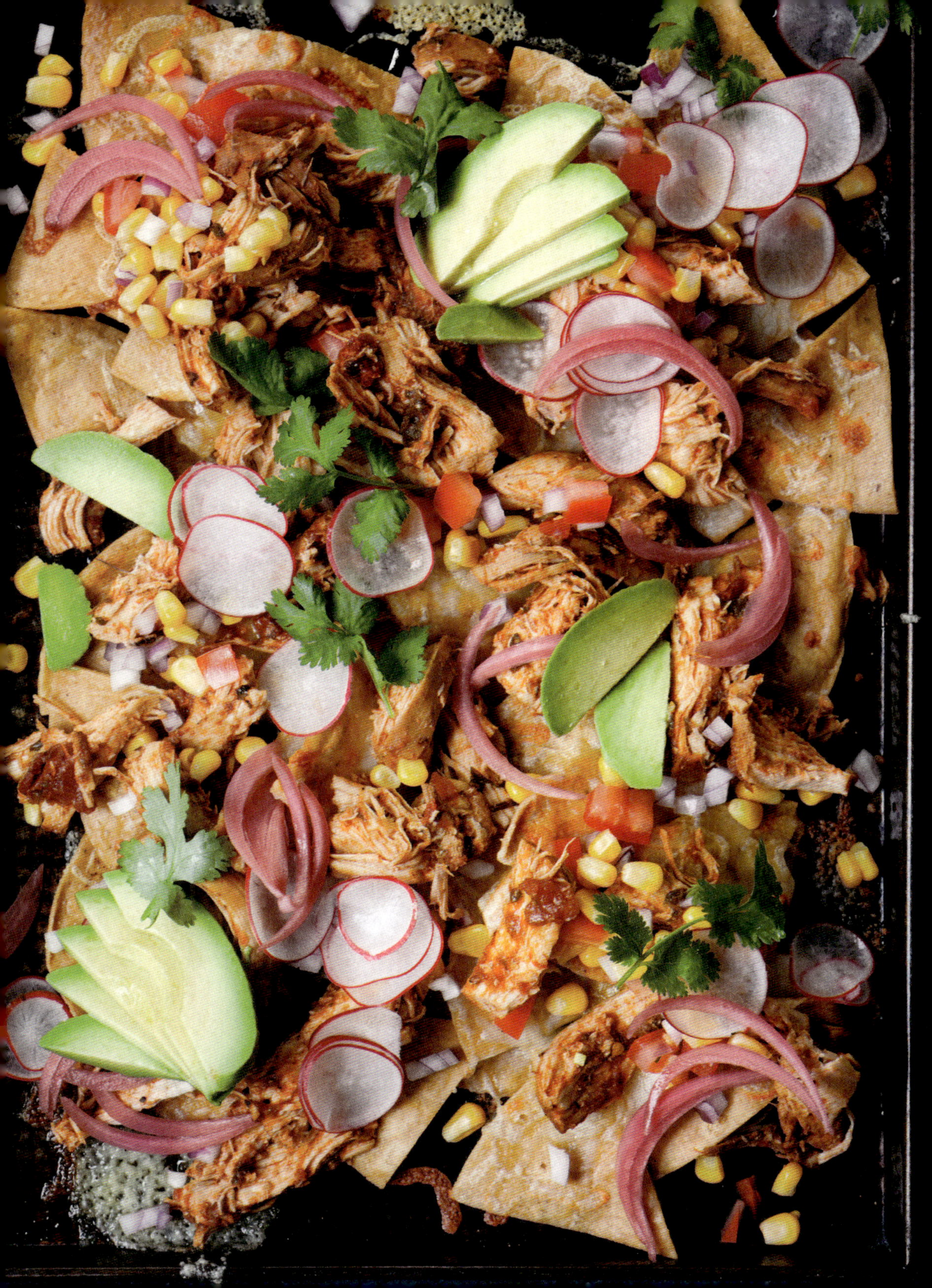

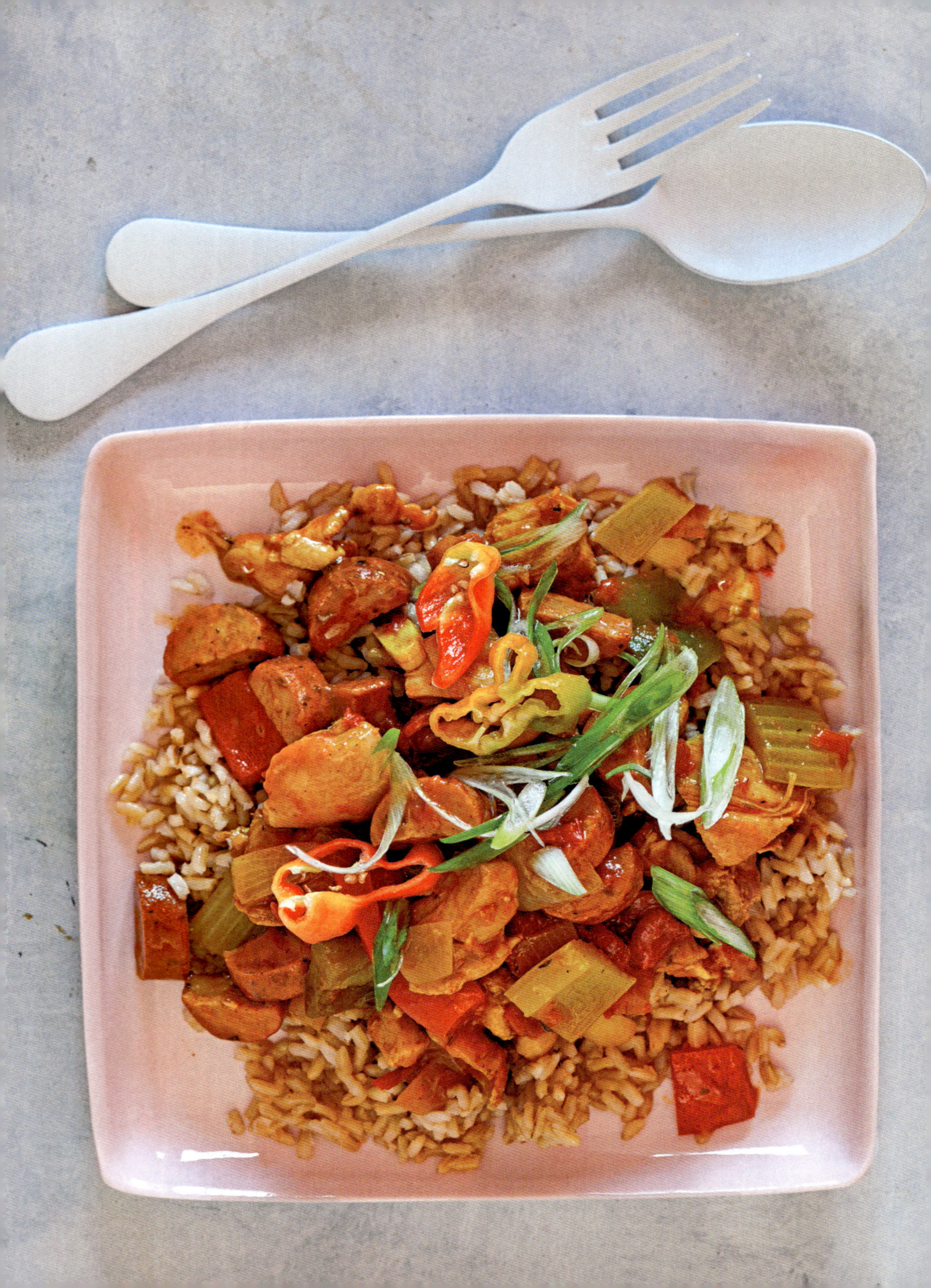

Louisiana jambalaya

Prep 36 min   Cook 2 to 6 hr   Serves 8

Jambalaya traditionally combines rice, sausage, and a protein such as shrimp, crawfish, chicken, or pork, but it's fine to play around with the ingredients. The only must-have element: the "holy trinity" of onion, bell pepper, and celery.

Canola-oil nonstick spray
- 1 tbsp Creole seasoning
- 2 lb skinless boneless chicken thighs, cut into 1½-inch chunks
- 3 (3-oz) cooked andouille turkey sausage links, halved lengthwise and sliced
- 2 red or green bell peppers, cut into 1½-inch pieces
- 1 large onion, chopped
- 2 celery stalks, chopped
- 3 garlic cloves, minced
- 1½ cups chicken broth
- 1 (14½-oz) can diced tomatoes
- 4 cups cooked long-grain white rice, warmed
- 3 scallions, sliced
- Sliced chile peppers (optional)

1 In a large bowl, sprinkle Creole seasoning over chicken, tossing until coated evenly. Spray a large skillet with nonstick spray and set over medium-high heat. Add chicken in batches and cook, turning occasionally, until browned, about 4 minutes per batch, transferring chicken to a 6- or 7-qt slow cooker as it is browned, coating skillet with nonstick spray between batches.

2 Spray same skillet with nonstick spray and reduce heat to medium. Add sausage, bell peppers, onion, celery, and garlic and cook, stirring, until vegetables are crisp-tender, about 5 minutes. Add broth and bring to a boil over high heat, scraping up browned bits from bottom of pan.

3 Transfer sausage-vegetable mixture to slow cooker. Stir in tomatoes. Cover and cook until chicken is cooked through and vegetables are tender, 2 to 3 hours on High or 4 to 6 hours on Low. Stir in rice. Spoon jambalaya evenly onto 8 plates or into 8 bowls. Sprinkle with scallions and chile peppers, if using.

Per serving (1½ cups): 331 Cal, 9 g Total Fat, 2 g Sat Fat, 839 mg Sod, 28 g Total Carb, 3 g Sugar, 2 g Fib, 33 g Prot.

Old-fashioned chicken noodle soup

Prep 25 min   Cook 4 to 10 hr   Serves 8

Who doesn't love a soul-soothing, belly-warming bowl of chicken soup? Our version is thick with egg noodles, and we've added leeks to the usual celery and carrots. If you happen to have homemade chicken broth stashed away, use it here.

- 1 (1-lb) bone-in chicken breast, skin removed
- 3 large celery stalks with leaves, cut diagonally into ½-inch slices
- 2 leeks (white and light green parts), sliced
- 2 large carrots, cut into ½-inch slices
- 1 small red bell pepper, diced
- 6 flat-leaf parsley sprigs plus ¼ cup chopped parsley
- 2 garlic cloves, lightly smashed with side of knife
- ½ tsp salt
- ¼ tsp black pepper
- 2 (32-oz) cartons chicken broth
- 1½ cups curly egg noodles

1. In a 5- or 6-qt slow cooker, combine chicken, celery, leeks, carrots, bell pepper, parsley sprigs, garlic, salt, and pepper; add broth. Cover and cook until chicken and vegetables are fork-tender, 4 to 5 hours on High or 8 to 10 hours on Low. Remove and discard garlic and parsley sprigs.

2. Transfer chicken to a cutting board. When cool enough to handle, remove and discard bones. Tear or cut chicken into bite-size pieces. Return chicken to slow cooker.

3. Meanwhile, cook noodles according to package directions; drain in colander. Stir into soup; cover and cook on High until chicken and noodles are heated through, about 10 minutes. Stir in chopped parsley. Ladle soup evenly into 8 bowls.

Per serving (1½ cups): 144 Cal, 2 g Total Fat, 0 g Sat Fat, 1,006 mg Sod, 15 g Total Carb, 4 g Sugar, 2 g Fib, 16 g Prot.

Serving idea
Make this a main dish by doubling the amount of chicken.

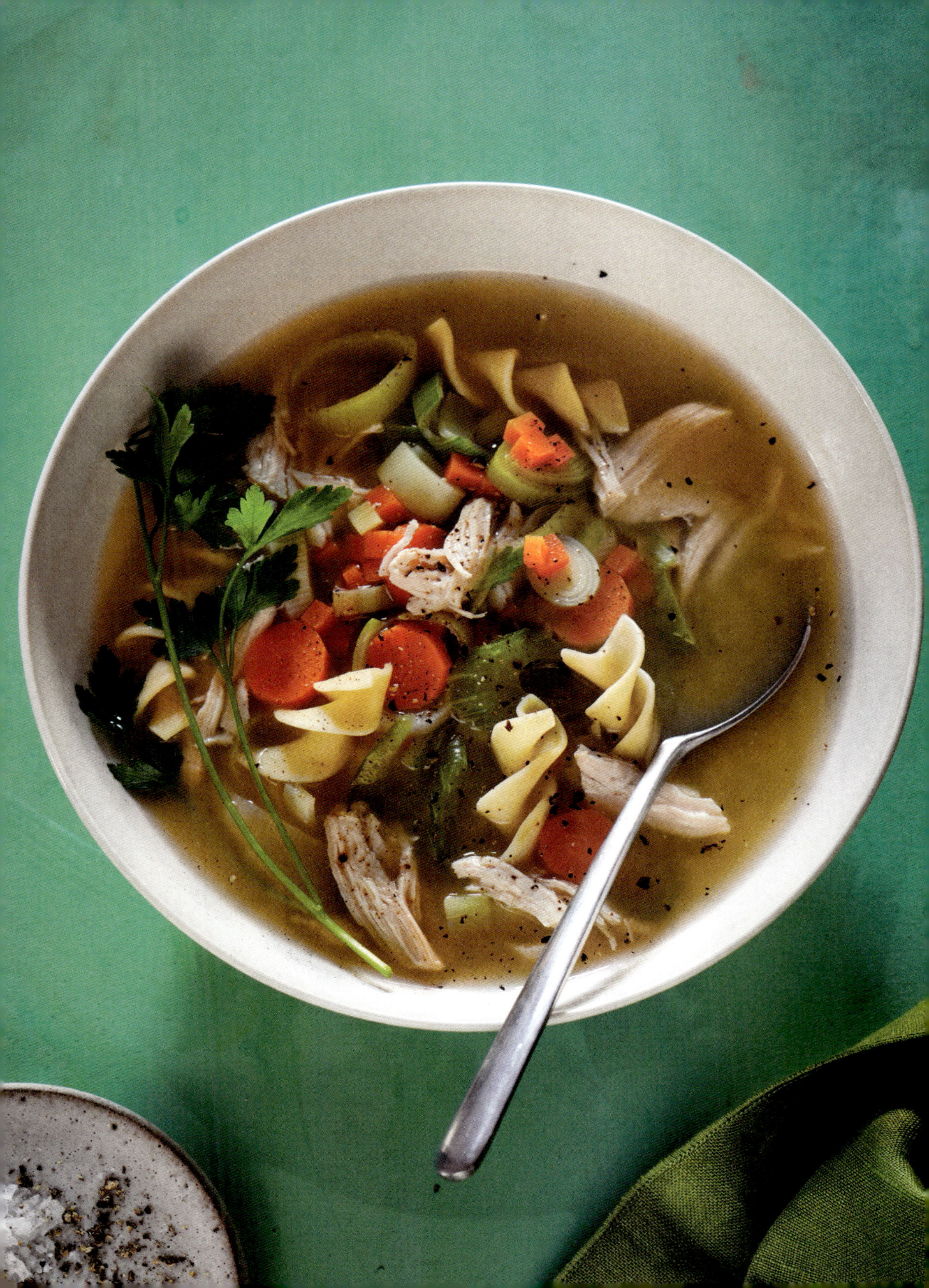

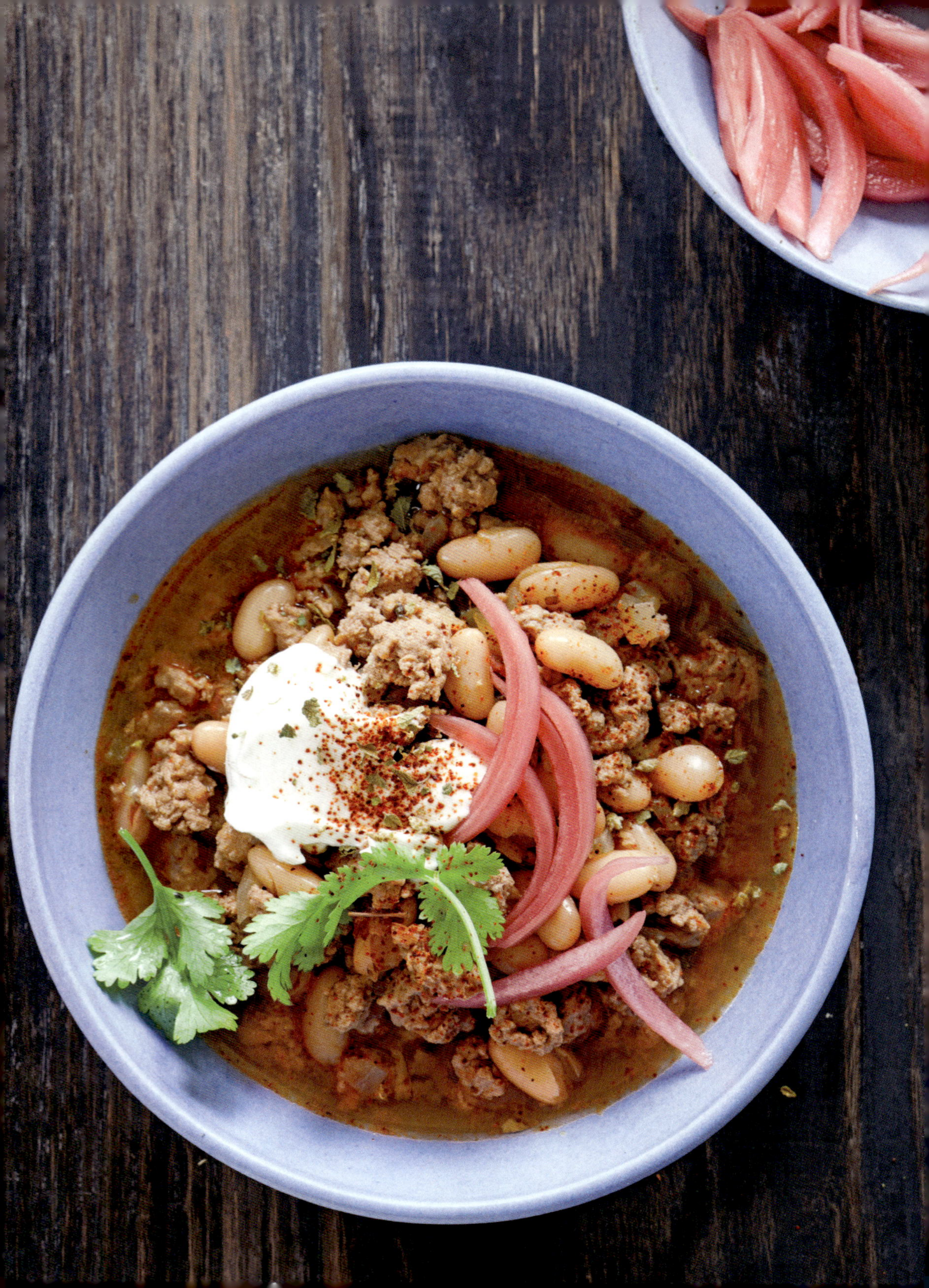

Chicken and white bean chili

Prep 25 min   Cook 4 hr   Serves 8

This chili leaves out the tomato so that the spices, garlic, and lime can shine, nicely complementing the white beans and chicken. We went light on the chili powder, but feel free to add more if you like extra heat.

4	tsp olive oil
2	lb ground chicken breast
1	large onion, chopped
2	garlic cloves, minced
1	(32-oz) carton reduced-sodium chicken broth
2	(15½-oz) cans cannellini (white kidney) beans, rinsed and drained
3	tbsp lime juice
1½	tsp ground cumin
1	tsp dried oregano
1	tsp chipotle chile powder
1	cup reduced-fat sour cream

Sliced red onion

Cilantro leaves

1 In a large heavy nonstick skillet over medium-high heat, warm oil. Add chicken, onion, and garlic and cook, breaking up chicken with wooden spoon, until lightly browned, about 10 minutes.

2 Transfer chicken mixture to a 3- or 4-qt slow cooker. Stir in broth, beans, lime juice, cumin, oregano, and chile powder. Cover and cook 4 hours on Low. Divide chili among 8 bowls. Top each serving with sour cream sprinkled with chile powder, red onion, and cilantro leaves.

Per serving (1 cup chili and 2 tbsp sour cream): 304 Cal, 8 g Total Fat, 3 g Sat Fat, 812 mg Sod, 21 g Total Carb, 1 g Sugar, 4 g Fib, 36 g Prot.

Cooking idea

While the chili cooks, throw together some additional toppings, like thinly sliced radishes, diced bell pepper, or paper-thin slices of jalapeño.

Turkey–bell pepper meatloaf

Prep 10 min   Cook 3 to 8 hr   Serves 6

Yes, slow cooker meatloaf is a thing! We tried it and loved the juicy results. Opt for 7% lean ground turkey (instead of ground turkey breast) for the best texture.

Nonstick spray
1½ lb lean (7% fat or less) ground turkey
1   green bell pepper, chopped
1   onion, chopped
1   large egg
¾   cup ketchup, divided
½   cup Italian-seasoned dried bread crumbs
1   tbsp yellow mustard
¼   tsp salt
¼   tsp black pepper
Oregano leaves
Parsley, chopped

1 With foil and nonstick spray, cover a wire rack small enough to fit into a 5- or 6-qt slow cooker.

2 In a large bowl, stir together turkey, bell pepper, onion, egg, ¼ cup ketchup, bread crumbs, mustard, salt, and black pepper until mixed well but not overmixed. Place turkey mixture on prepared rack. With damp hands, shape into 5 x 9-inch loaf.

3 Place meatloaf on rack in slow cooker. Spread remaining ½ cup ketchup over top of loaf. Cover and cook until an instant-read thermometer inserted into center of loaf registers 160°F, 3 to 4 hours on High or 6 to 8 hours on Low. Transfer meatloaf to cutting board and let stand 5 minutes. Sprinkle with oregano leaves and parsley. Cut into 6 thick slices.

Per serving (1 slice): 265 Cal, 11 g Total Fat, 3 g Sat Fat, 697 mg Sod, 18 g Total Carb, 8 g Sugar, 1 g Fib, 25 g Prot.

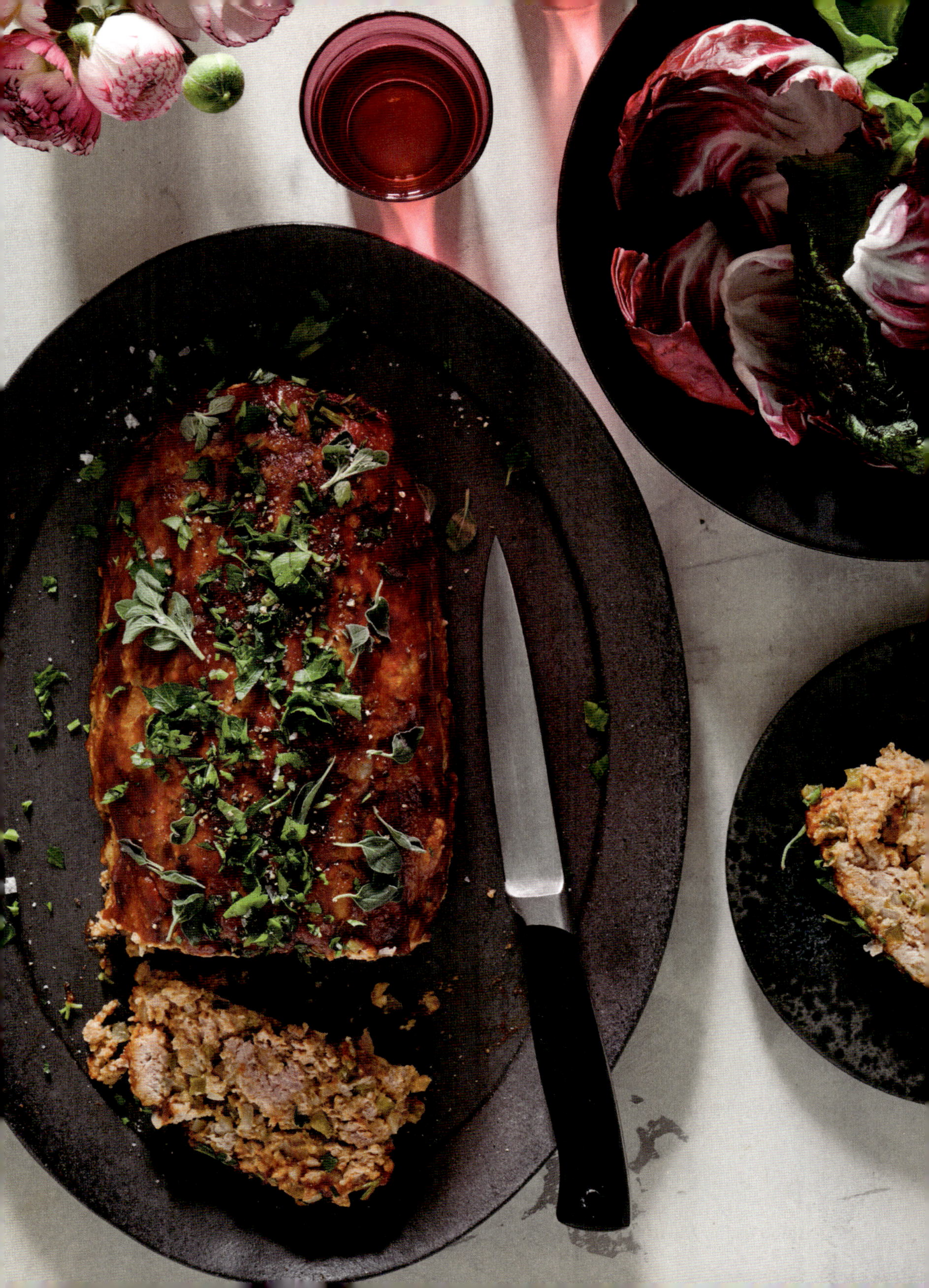

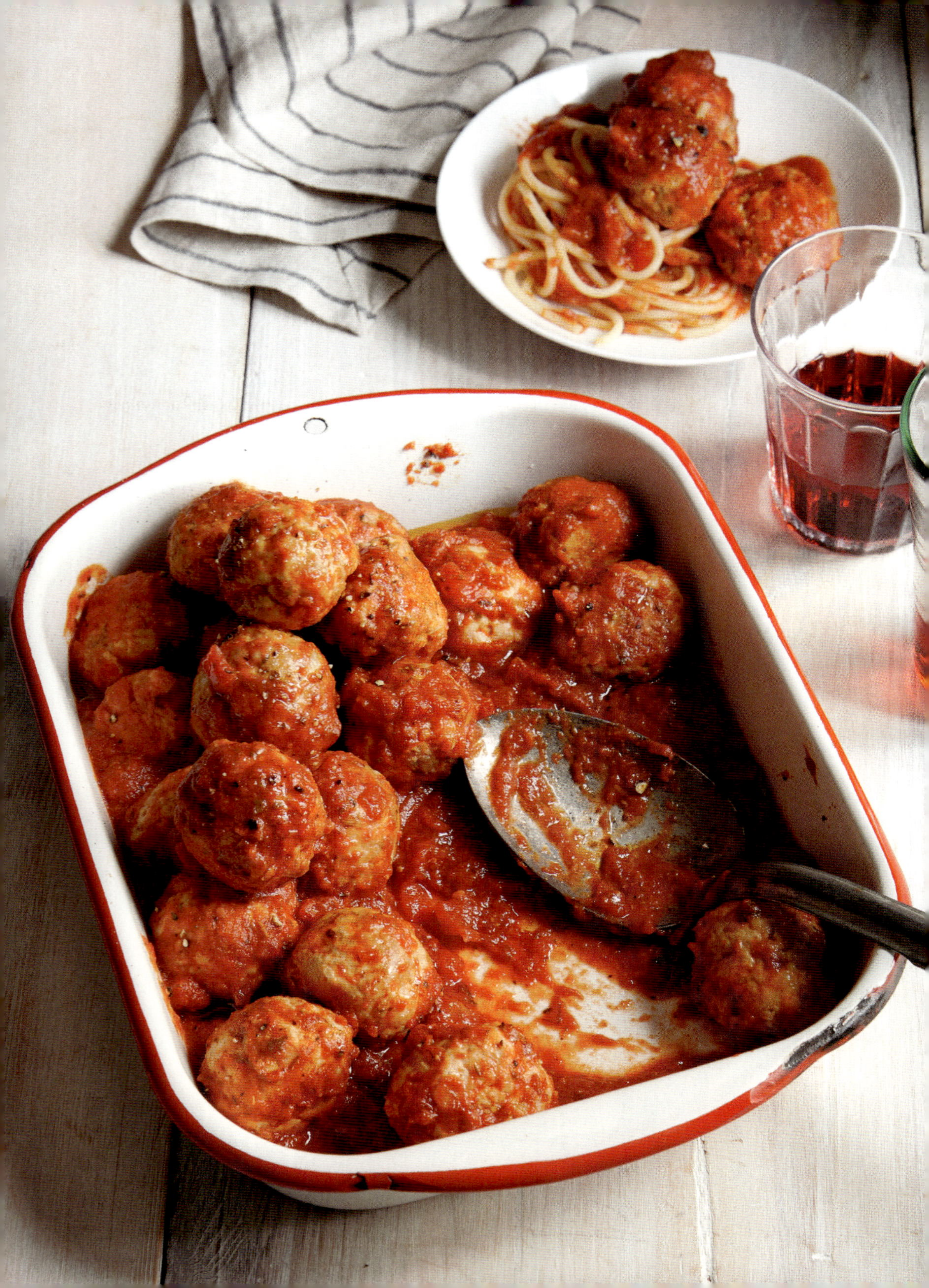

Spicy turkey meatballs

Prep 15 min   Cook 6 to 7 hr   Serves 8

Cooking this crowd-pleasing classic on Low ensures the turkey meatballs turn out juicy and tender.

1	(28-oz) can crushed tomatoes
⅓	cup tomato paste
2	tbsp balsamic vinegar
3	tsp dried oregano, divided
1	tsp salt, divided
¼	tsp red pepper flakes (or to taste)
2	lb lean (7% fat or less) ground turkey
½	cup whole-wheat panko bread crumbs
2	tbsp dried basil
1	tsp fennel seeds, crushed
½	tsp black pepper

1 In a 5- or 6-qt slow cooker, stir together tomatoes, tomato paste, vinegar, 2 tsp oregano, ½ tsp salt, and pepper flakes.

2 In a large bowl, mix together turkey, panko, basil, fennel seeds, remaining 1 tsp oregano, and remaining ½ tsp salt, and black pepper until combined well but not overmixed. With damp hands, shape turkey mixture into 24 meatballs. Add to slow cooker. Cover and cook until meatballs are cooked through and flavors are blended, 6 to 7 hours on Low.

Per serving (3 meatballs and ⅓ cup sauce): 231 Cal, 10 g Total Fat, 3 g Sat Fat, 536 mg Sod, 13 g Total Carb, 4 g Sugar, 3 g Fib, 24 g Prot.

Serving idea
Of course, you can serve these over pasta, but you can also try zucchini noodles if you want more veggies.

Updated classics

Low-and-slow sloppy joes

Prep 10 min Cook 3 to 8 hr Serves 6

We've made our version of kid-friendly sloppy joes mild enough to pass muster with even the pickiest eater, but don't worry—there's plenty of flavor here. Serve it with hot sauce for extra heat.

- 2 tsp olive oil
- 1 lb ground lean (7% fat or less) turkey
- 1 (14½-oz) can diced tomatoes
- 1 small onion, chopped
- 1 celery stalk, chopped
- 1½ tbsp dark brown sugar
- 2 tsp Worcestershire sauce
- 1½ tsp ground cumin
- 1 tsp vinegar
- 1 tsp chili powder
- ½ tsp kosher salt
- 6 whole-wheat hamburger buns, split and toasted

1. In a large skillet over medium-high heat, warm oil. Add turkey and cook, breaking apart with wooden spoon, until no longer pink, about 5 minutes.

2. Transfer turkey to a 5- or 6-qt slow cooker. Stir in all remaining ingredients except hamburger buns. Cover and cook until flavors blend and sauce is slightly thickened, 3 to 4 hours on High or 6 to 8 hours on Low.

3. Spoon about ½ cup turkey mixture into each hamburger bun.

Per serving (1 sandwich): 283 Cal, 10 g Total Fat, 2 g Sat Fat, 571 mg Sod, 30 g Total Carb, 9 g Sugar, 2 g Fib, 19 g Prot.

Serving idea

Dress up your sloppy joes with green leaf lettuce, thinly sliced tomato, thinly sliced sweet onion, and shredded carrot.

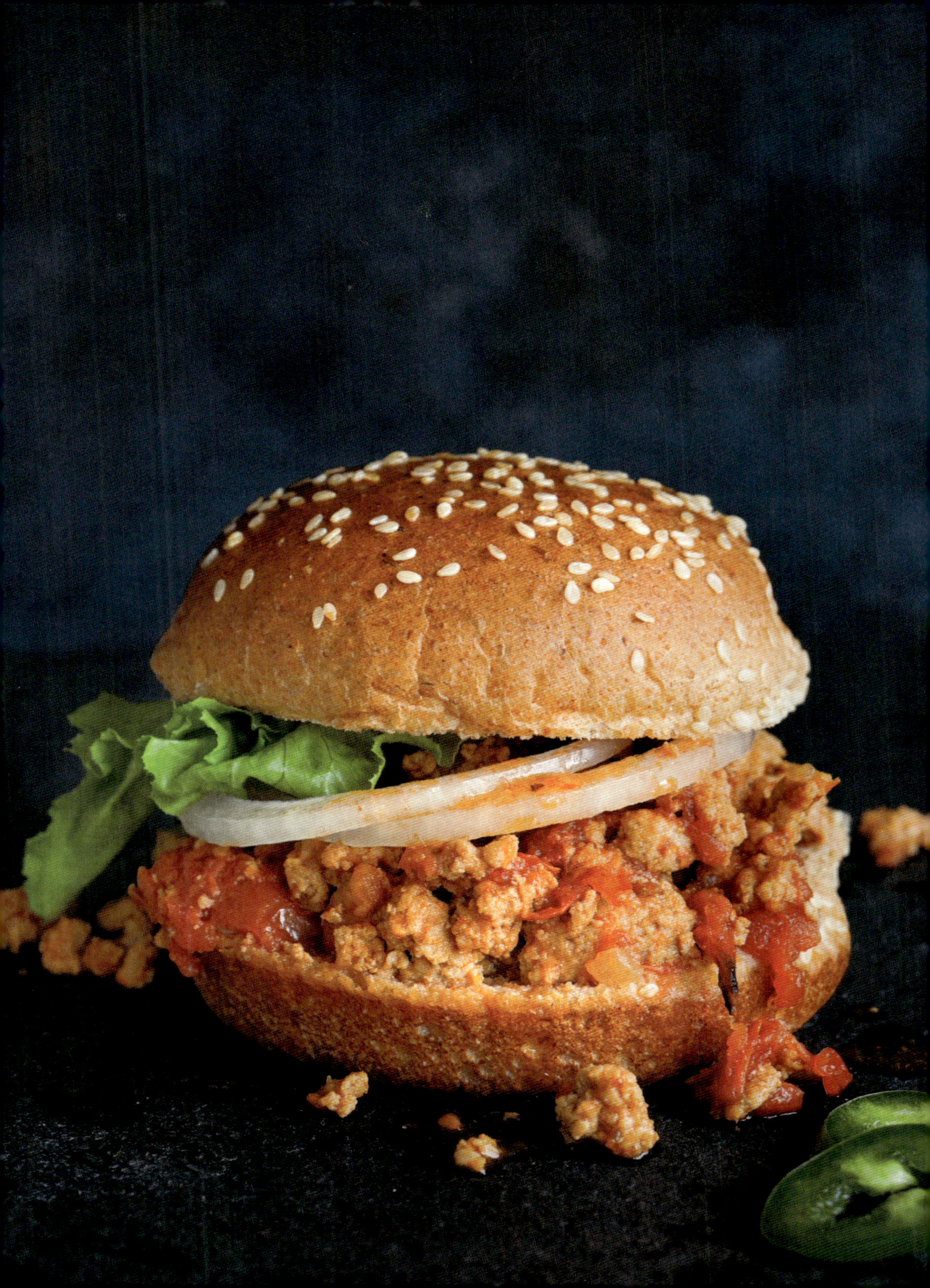

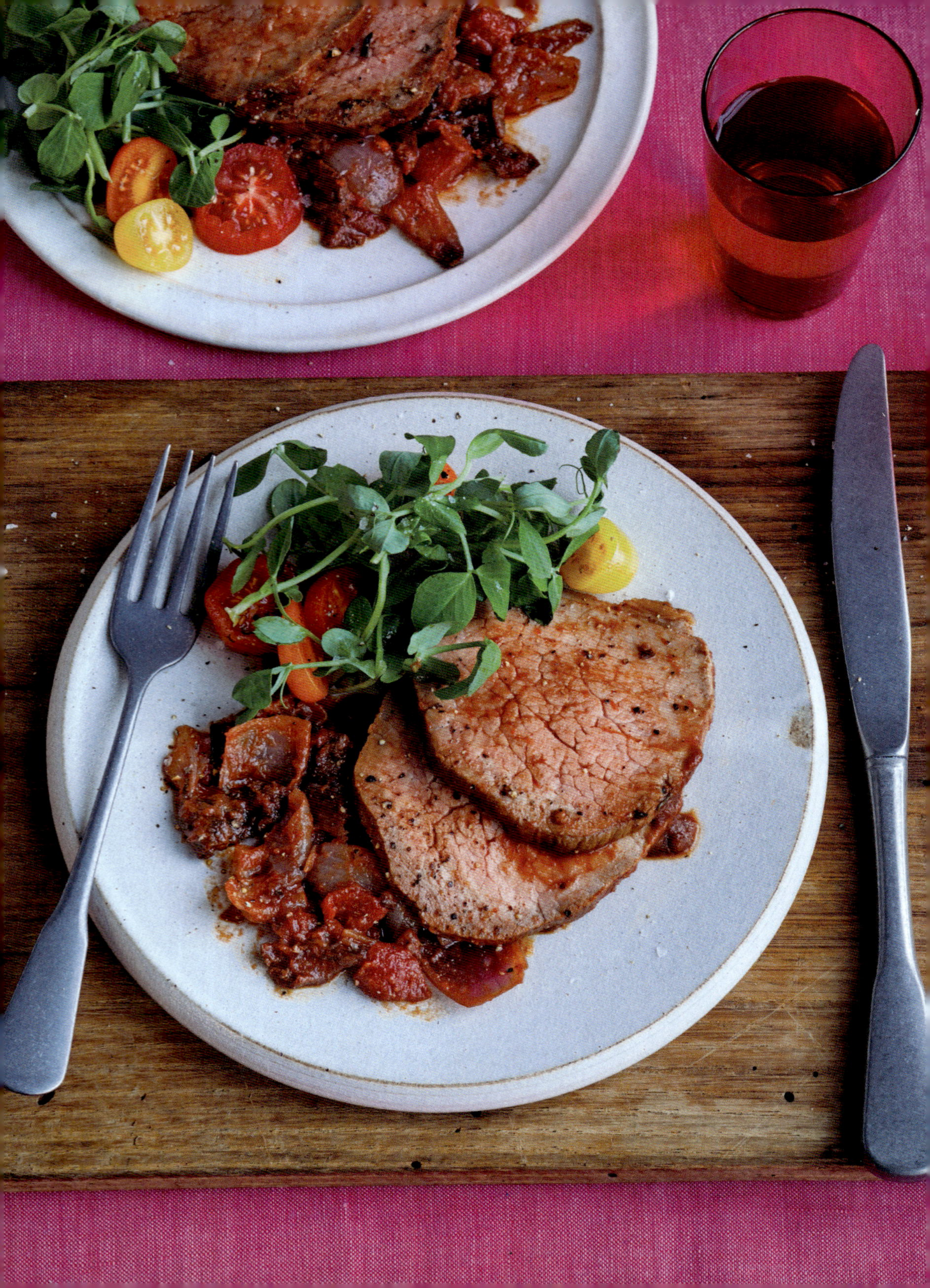

Italian-style pot roast

Prep 40 min   Cook 4 to 10 hr   Serves 8

Not sure what "fork-tender" means? With pot roast or poultry, as well as potatoes and other hard vegetables, it's when a fork can be inserted into food and then easily removed.

1	**(3-lb) lean bottom round beef roast, trimmed**
1½ tsp	**kosher salt, divided**
¼	**plus ⅛ tsp black pepper, divided**
2 tbsp	**all-purpose flour**
1 tbsp	**olive oil**
1	**large red onion, quartered and thinly sliced**
3	**large garlic cloves, minced**
1 tbsp	**finely chopped dried porcini mushrooms**
1 tbsp	**chopped fresh rosemary (or ¾ tsp dried)**
1	**(14½-oz) can diced tomatoes**
8	**flat-leaf parsley sprigs, tied together with kitchen twine**

1 Sprinkle roast with 1 tsp salt and ¼ tsp pepper. Place beef on a sheet of wax paper; sprinkle with flour, gently pressing so it adheres.

2 In a large skillet over medium-high heat, warm oil. Add beef and cook until browned on all sides, about 10 minutes. Transfer to a 5- or 6-qt slow cooker.

3 Reduce heat to medium. Add onion to skillet and cook, stirring, until softened, about 5 minutes. Add garlic, dried mushrooms, and rosemary and cook, stirring constantly, until fragrant, about 1 minute. Transfer onion mixture to slow cooker; stir in tomatoes, parsley sprigs, remaining ½ tsp salt, and remaining ⅛ tsp pepper. Cover and cook until beef is fork-tender, 4 to 6 hours on High or 8 to 10 hours on Low. Remove and discard parsley sprigs. Transfer beef to a cutting board; let stand loosely covered 10 minutes.

4 Meanwhile, pour pan liquid and vegetables into a medium saucepan and bring to a boil over high heat. Boil until reduced to about 2 cups.

5 Cut beef against grain into 16 slices. Serve with sauce and vegetables.

Per serving (2 slices beef and ¼ cup sauce with vegetables): 277 Cal, 10 g Total Fat, 4 g Sat Fat, 545 mg Sod, 7 g Total Carb, 2 g Sugar, 1 g Fib, 38 g Prot.

Serving idea

In Italy, slow-cooked pot roast is called *stracotto*, which means "overcooked." Serve it up the way Italians do with a side of soft-cooked polenta.

Updated classics

Braciole with spicy tomato sauce

Prep 20 min   Cook 4 to 9 hr   Serves 8

This Italian beef roll looks fancy but it's easy to make and uses simple ingredients like egg, garlic, and bread crumbs. It's great for a dinner party or big family meal.

- ¼ cup Italian-seasoned dried bread crumbs
- ¼ cup chopped flat-leaf parsley
- ¼ cup grated Pecorino Romano
- 1 large egg, hard-boiled, coarsely chopped
- 2 garlic cloves, minced
- 2 tsp olive oil, divided
- 8 (¼-inch) slices lean top round steak (3 oz each), trimmed
- ¼ tsp salt
- 1 (24-oz) jar arrabbiata sauce
- ½ cup dry red wine

1 To make filling: In a medium bowl, stir together bread crumbs, parsley, Pecorino Romano, egg, garlic, and ½ tsp oil.

2 Between two pieces of plastic wrap, place steaks in one layer. With a meat mallet or rolling pin, pound to ⅛-inch thickness. Remove top piece of plastic. Sprinkle about 2 tbsp filling onto each steak, leaving a ½-inch border, gently pressing so it adheres. From short end, roll steaks up to enclose filling. Tie each at 1-inch intervals with kitchen twine. Sprinkle with salt.

3 In a 5- or 6-qt slow cooker, combine arrabbiata sauce and wine.

4 In a large heavy skillet over medium-high heat, warm remaining 1½ tsp oil. Add beef rolls and cook, turning occasionally, until browned, about 4 minutes. Transfer rolls to slow cooker, spooning sauce over. Cover and cook until beef is fork-tender, 4 to 5 hours on High or 8 to 9 hours on Low. Remove twine from rolls. Serve with sauce.

Per serving (1 beef roll and scant ¼ cup sauce): 262 Cal, 14 g Total Fat, 4 g Sat Fat, 566 mg Sod, 9 g Total Carb, 4 g Sugar, 1 g Fib, 0 g Prot.

Serving idea
Steamed lacinato kale sprinkled with crispy garlic chips is a delicious accompaniment to this braciole.

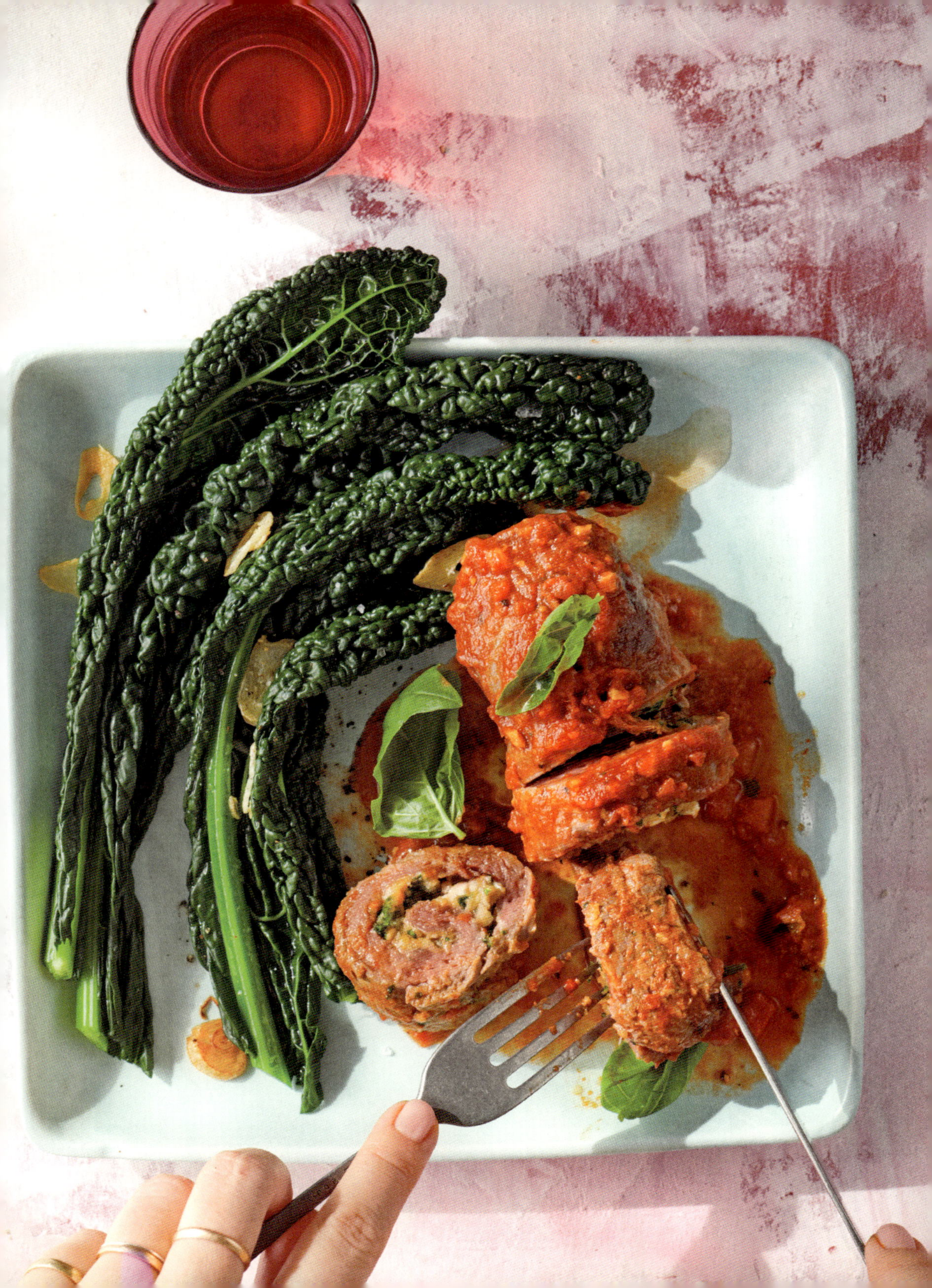

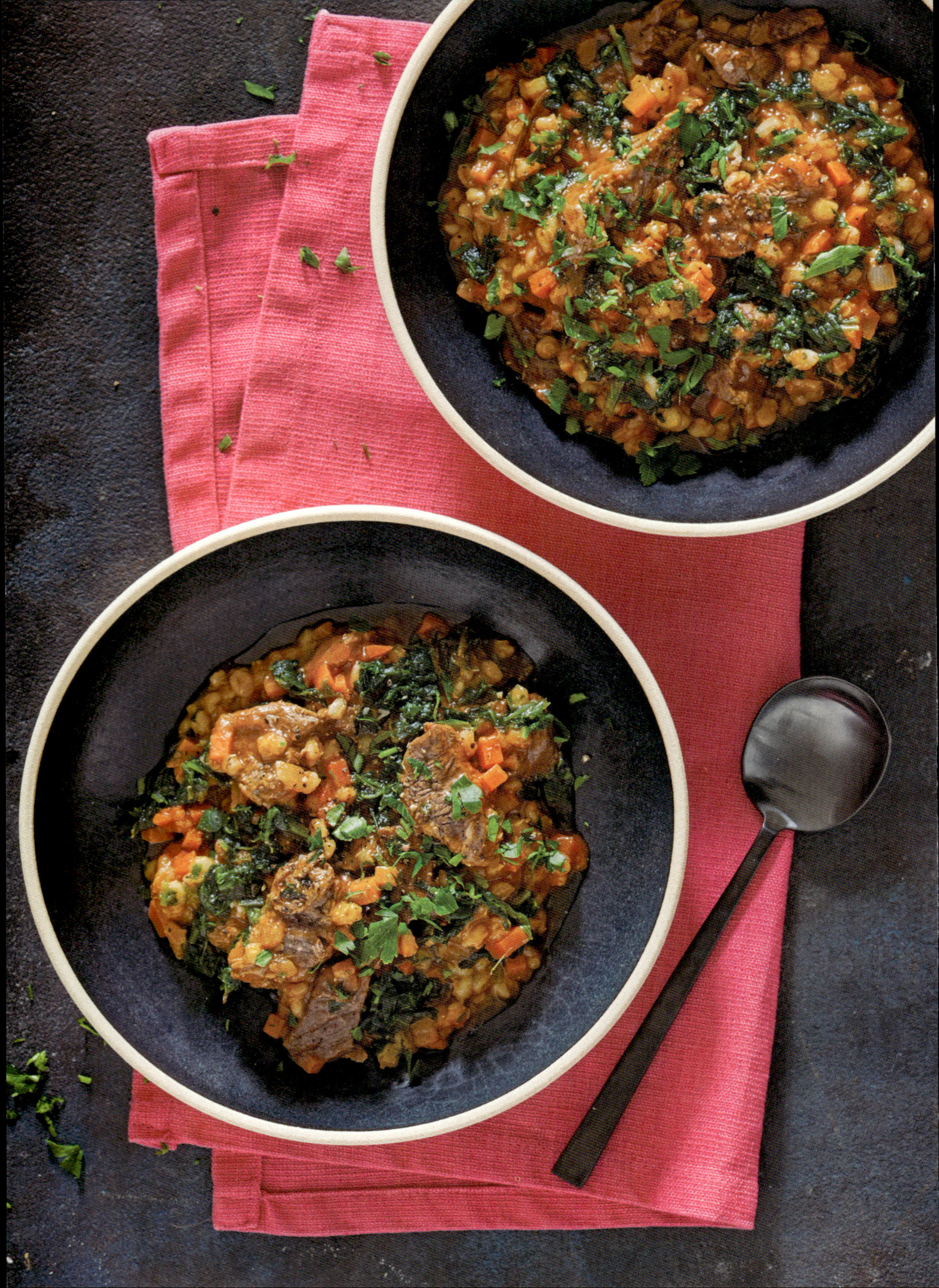

Hearty beef-barley stew

Prep 20 min Cook 4 to 10 hr Serves 8

Barley adds chewy, satisfying texture to this stew, and slow cooking turns the beef meltingly tender. A secret shortcut here? Tomato juice, to give the broth body and flavor.

¾	cup pearl barley
3	carrots, cut into ¼-inch dice
1	onion, chopped
3	garlic cloves, minced
1	tbsp chopped rosemary
1	(32-oz) carton beef broth
3	cups low-sodium tomato juice
2	tsp Worcestershire sauce
¾	tsp kosher salt
¼	tsp black pepper
1	(1-lb) lean beef bottom round roast, trimmed and cut into 1½- to 2-inch chunks
10	oz frozen chopped spinach, thawed

Flat-leaf parsley, chopped

1 In a 5- or 6-qt slow cooker, combine barley, carrots, onion, garlic, rosemary, broth, tomato juice, 2 cups water, Worcestershire sauce, salt, and pepper. Add beef. Cover and cook until barley is softened and beef is fork-tender, 4 to 5 hours on High or 8 to 10 hours on Low.

2 With tongs, transfer beef to cutting board. With two forks, break beef into chunks and return to slow cooker. Add spinach and cook until heated through, about 10 minutes. Serve sprinkled with parsley.

Per serving (1½ cups): 195 Cal, 3 g Total Fat, 1 g Sat Fat, 684 mg Sod, 24 g Total Carb, 5 g Sugar, 6 g Fib, 17 g Prot.

Beef 'n' bean chili

Prep 28 min   Cook 6 to 7 hr   Serves 6

Chili is a go-to party food. This beef and bean version is easy to make, and you can serve it straight from the slow cooker. Set out sour cream, shredded cheese, scallions, and a bottle of hot sauce, and let guests help themselves.

2	tsp olive oil
1	lb lean (7% fat or less) ground beef
1	large onion, chopped
2	large garlic cloves, minced
2	tbsp chili powder
2	tsp ground cumin
2	tsp smoked paprika
1	tsp dried oregano
¾	tsp kosher salt
⅛	tsp cayenne (or to taste)
1	(10-oz) can diced tomatoes with green chiles, drained, juice reserved
¼	cup tomato paste
¾	lb plum tomatoes, coarsely chopped
2	large red bell peppers, cut into ½-inch dice
1	(15½-oz) can red kidney beans, rinsed and drained
6	tbsp light sour cream
6	tbsp shredded reduced-fat cheddar

Scallions, thinly sliced

1 In a large nonstick skillet over medium heat, warm oil. Add beef and cook, breaking up with a wooden spoon, until no longer pink, about 5 minutes. With a slotted spoon, transfer to a plate. To skillet, add onion and garlic and cook, stirring, until onion is softened, about 5 minutes. Add chili powder, cumin, paprika, oregano, salt, and cayenne and cook, stirring, until fragrant, about 3 minutes longer. Spoon beef mixture into a 5- or 6-qt slow cooker.

2 Into a medium bowl, pour reserved tomato juice. Whisk in tomato paste until smooth. Add to slow cooker, along with tomatoes and bell peppers. Cover and cook 6 to 7 hours on Low, stirring halfway through cooking time. About 30 minutes before cooking time is up, stir in beans.

3 Ladle chili evenly into 6 bowls. Serve with sour cream, cheddar, and scallions.

Per serving (1⅓ cups chili, 1 tbsp sour cream, and 1 tbsp cheese): 288 Cal, 11 g Total Fat, 4 g Sat Fat, 880 mg Sod, 25 g Total Carb, 8 g Sugar, 7 g Fib, 24 g Prot.

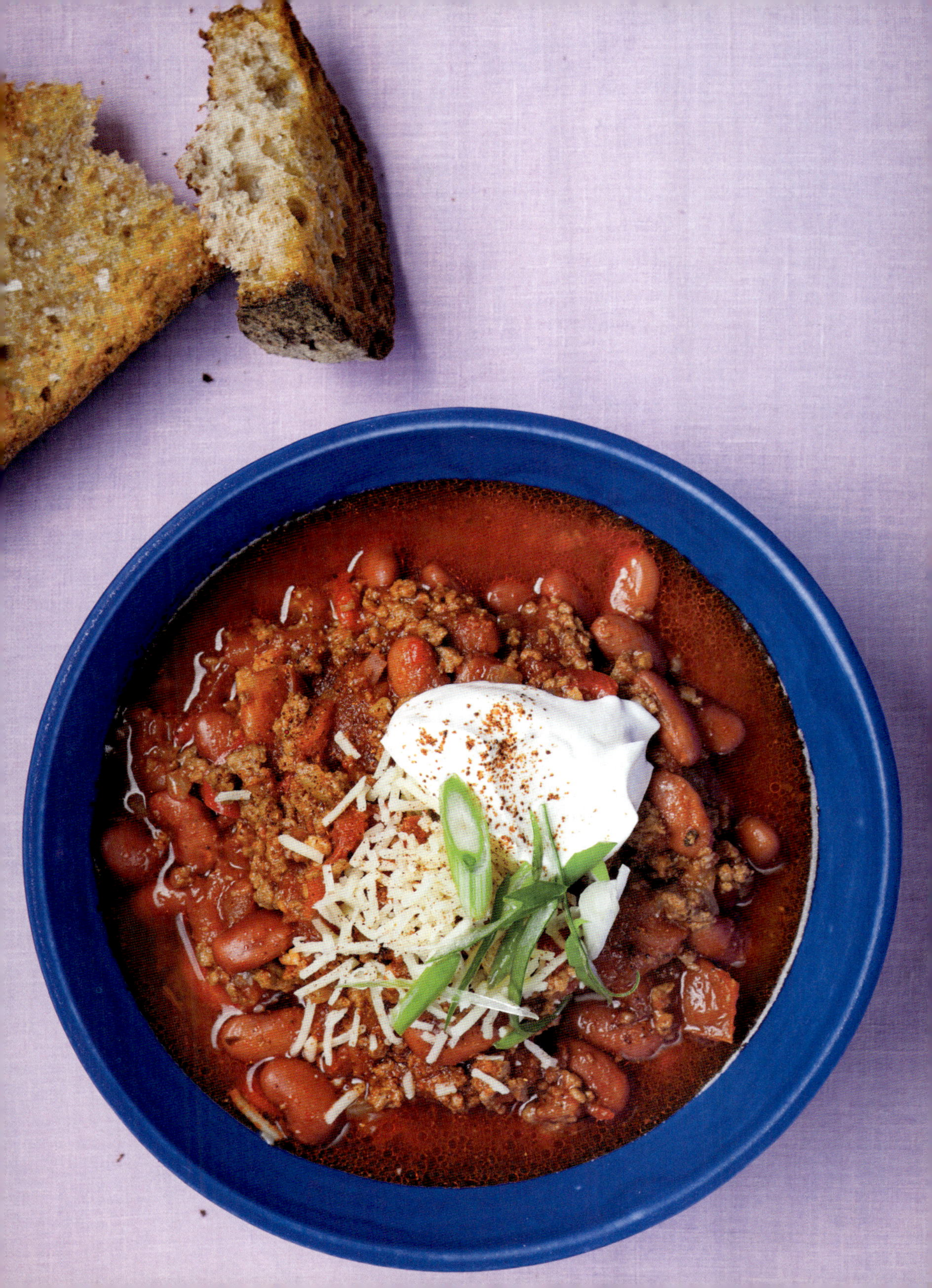

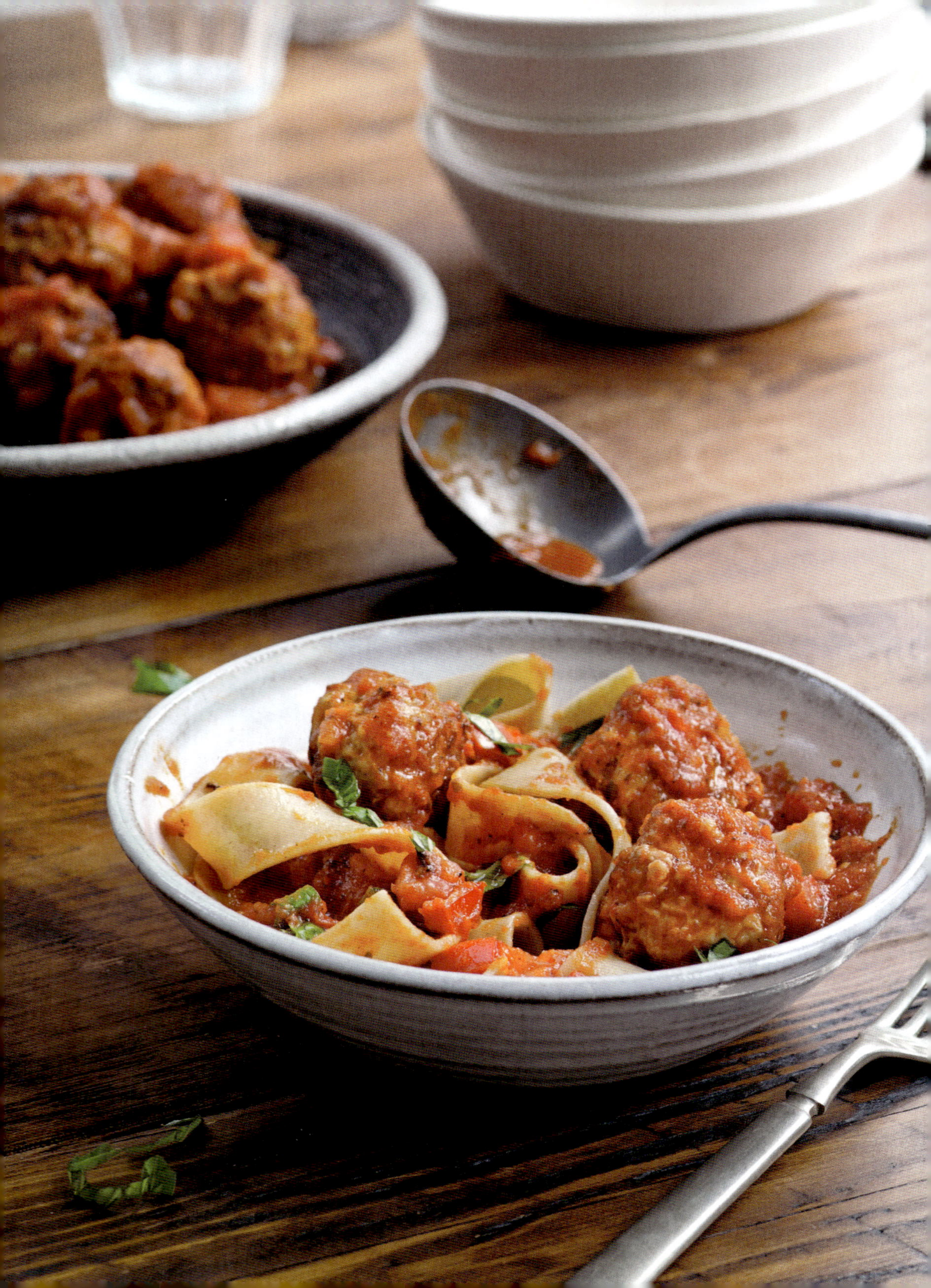

Classic Italian meatballs

Prep 35 min   Cook 3 hr   Serves 8

Fennel seeds give these meatballs an extra pop of Italian flavor. To ensure they come out nice and tender, handle the meat mixture as little as possible when mixing and shaping it.

1	lb lean (7% fat or less) ground beef
2	large eggs, lightly beaten
1	small onion, finely chopped
1	large garlic clove, crushed through a press or grated on a Microplane grater
¾	tsp fennel seeds, crushed
1	tsp kosher salt (or to taste)
¼	tsp black pepper (or to taste)
1	(26-oz) carton tomato sauce with basil
1	(14½-oz) can diced tomatoes with garlic and onion
⅓	cup all-purpose flour
1	tbsp olive oil
½	cup thinly sliced basil

1 In a medium bowl, stir together beef, eggs, onion, garlic, fennel seeds, salt, and pepper until combined well but not overmixed. With damp hands, shape into 24 meatballs.

2 In a 4- or 5-qt slow cooker, combine tomato sauce and diced tomatoes; set aside.

3 Spread flour on a sheet of wax paper; roll meatballs in flour until coated on all sides, shaking off excess.

4 In a large nonstick skillet over medium heat, warm oil. Cook meatballs in two batches, until browned on all sides, about 5 minutes per batch, transferring to slow cooker as they are browned. Spoon tomato sauce over meatballs. Cover and cook until meatballs are cooked through and sauce is slightly thickened, about 3 hours on Low; stir in basil. Divide meatballs and sauce evenly among 8 bowls.

Per serving (3 meatballs and about ½ cup sauce): 179 Cal, 7 g Total Fat, 2 g Sat Fat, 934 mg Sod, 13 g Total Carb, 5 g Sugar, 2 g Fib, 16 g Prot.

Serving idea

Saucy meatballs and pasta are a classic combination, especially when paired with regular or whole-wheat penne or spaghetti. Or try a spiral pasta, like gemelli, that the sauce can cling to.

Simply delicious lasagna

Prep 32 min   Cook 3 to 4 hr   Serves 8

The slow cooker makes an extra-creamy, gooey lasagna—the last word in comfort food.

Nonstick spray
- 1 lb white or cremini mushrooms, sliced
- 1 (9-oz) bag baby spinach
- ¾ tsp kosher salt, divided
- ¾ lb lean (7% fat or less) ground beef
- 1 small onion, chopped
- 2 large garlic cloves, minced
- 1 (28-oz) can crushed tomatoes
- 1 (15-oz) can tomato sauce
- 1 tsp dried oregano
- ¼ tsp red pepper flakes
- 1½ cups part-skim ricotta
- 1½ cups shredded part-skim mozzarella (about 6 oz), divided
- 5 tbsp grated Parmesan, divided
- ½ cup thinly sliced basil, divided
- 6 sheets lasagna noodles

1 Spray a large nonstick skillet with nonstick spray and set over medium heat. Add mushrooms and cook, stirring, until their liquid is released and almost evaporated, about 6 minutes. Add spinach in batches. Sprinkle with ¼ tsp salt. With a slotted spoon, transfer spinach mixture to a bowl. Discard liquid.

2 Spray same skillet with nonstick spray and set over medium heat. Add beef, onion, and garlic and cook, breaking up meat with a wooden spoon until no longer pink, about 5 minutes. Stir in crushed tomatoes, tomato sauce, oregano, red pepper flakes, and remaining ½ tsp salt. Simmer 5 minutes.

3 Meanwhile, in a medium bowl, stir together ricotta, ¾ cup mozzarella, 2 tbsp Parmesan, and ¼ cup basil.

4 In bottom of a 6-qt slow cooker, spread one-third of beef mixture. Break 3 lasagna noodles in half and arrange over beef, breaking to fit as needed. Scatter one-third of mushroom mixture over noodles and top with half of ricotta mixture. Spoon half of remaining beef on top; break remaining 3 noodles in half and arrange on top of beef. Top with remaining mushrooms, ricotta, beef, and mushrooms.

5 Cover and cook until noodles are tender when pierced with a knife, 3 to 4 hours on Low. Uncover and turn off slow cooker. Sprinkle remaining ¾ cup mozzarella and 3 tbsp Parmesan over lasagna. Cover and set aside until cheese is melted, about 10 minutes. Sprinkle with remaining ¼ cup basil. Cut into 8 portions.

Prep ahead

You can make the mushroom mixture and the tomato-beef mixture up to 1 day in advance. To keep the cooking time the same, be sure to take them out of the refrigerator about 1 hour before assembling the lasagna.

Per serving (1 portion): 314 Cal, 12 g Total Fat, 6 g Sat Fat, 848 mg Sod, 27 g Total Carb, 7 g Sugar, 4 g Fib, 27 g Prot.

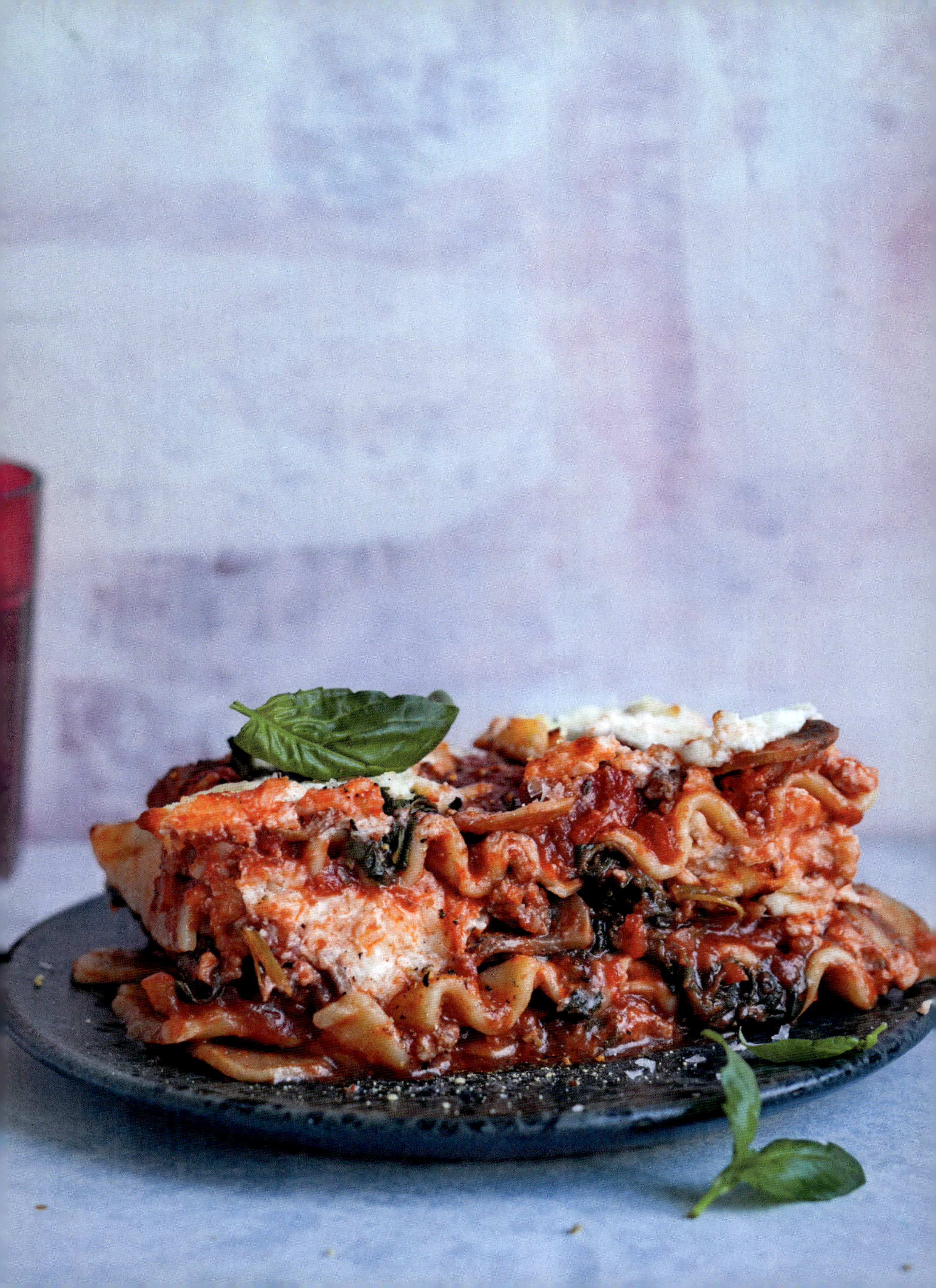

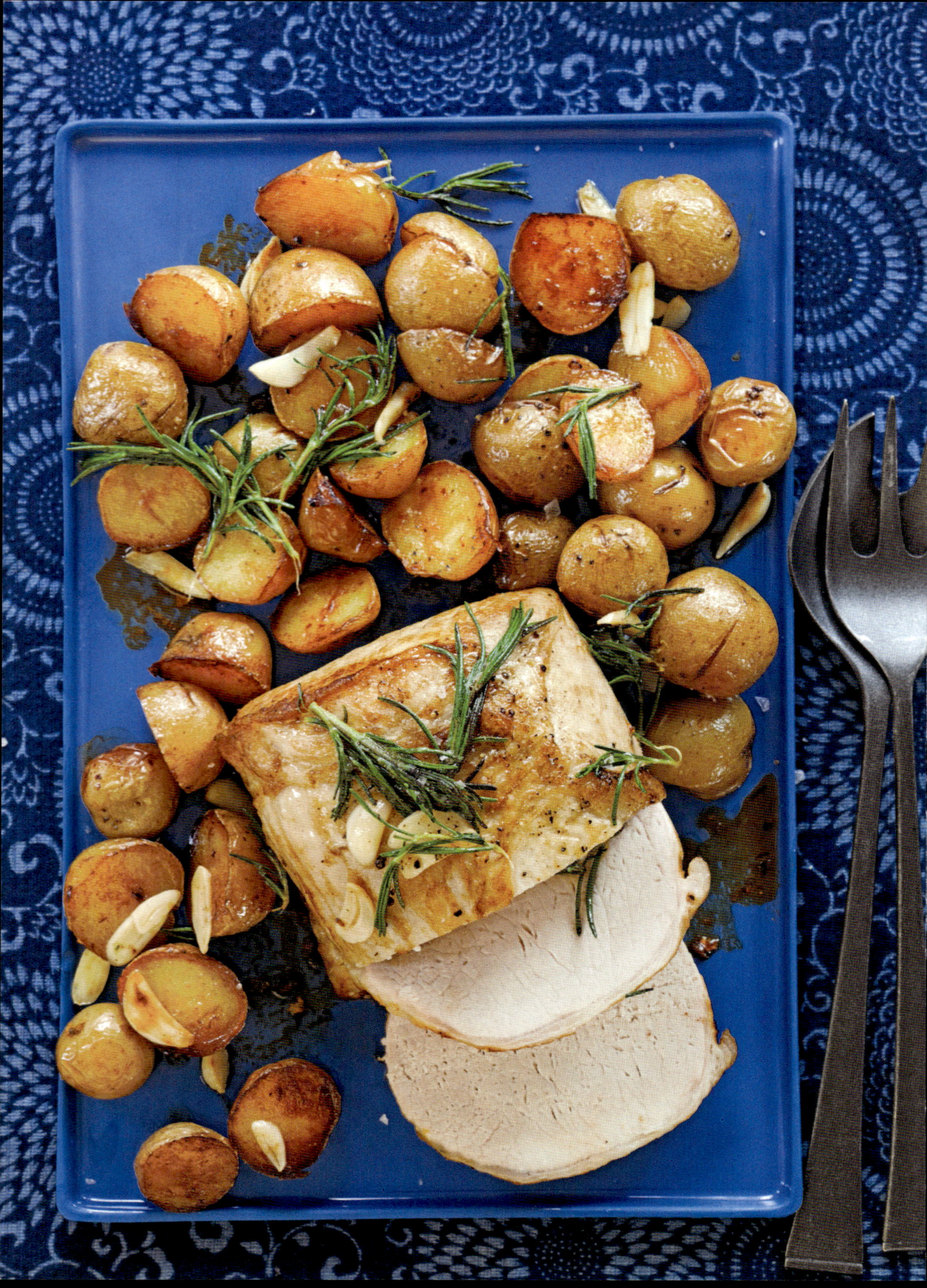

Rosemary-garlic pork roast

Prep 34 min   Cook 1½ hr   Serves 6

The trick to this super-moist pork? Rub it with minced garlic and fresh rosemary *after* browning, so those seasonings don't overcook. Also, use an instant-read thermometer to ensure the meat doesn't dry out.

- 1   (1½-lb) lean boneless center-cut pork loin roast, trimmed
- ¾   tsp kosher salt, divided
- ¾   tsp black pepper, divided
- 2   tsp olive oil
- 1½ lb Dutch yellow baby potatoes, scrubbed and halved
- ½   cup reduced-sodium chicken broth
- 1½ tbsp chopped rosemary
- 3   garlic cloves, minced

1 Sprinkle pork with ½ tsp salt and ½ tsp pepper. In a large skillet over medium-high heat, warm oil. Add pork and cook, turning occasionally, until well browned on all sides, about 6 minutes. Transfer pork to a cutting board; let cool slightly.

2 Meanwhile, add potatoes to skillet and cook, turning occasionally, until browned in spots (especially on cut side), about 7 minutes. Add broth and bring to a boil, scraping up browned bits from bottom of pan. Remove skillet from heat.

3 In a cup, mix together rosemary and garlic. Sprinkle all over pork, gently pressing so it adheres. Place pork in a 5- or 6-qt slow cooker. Spoon potatoes around pork and drizzle with broth mixture. Sprinkle potatoes with remaining ¼ tsp salt and ¼ tsp pepper. Cover and cook until an instant-read thermometer inserted into center of pork registers 145°F and potatoes are fork-tender, about 1½ hours on High.

4 Transfer pork to cleaned cutting board. Let stand 10 minutes, then cut into 6 thick slices (or 12 thin slices if you prefer) and arrange on a platter. With a slotted spoon, transfer potatoes to platter. Spoon pan juices over pork.

Per serving (1 thick slice pork with ¾ cup potatoes and 1½ tbsp juices): 259 Cal, 8 g Total Fat, 2 g Sat Fat, 365 mg Sod, 19 g Total Carb, 1 g Sugar, 3 g Fib, 27 g Prot.

Shopping tip

Any yellow-skinned potato can work in this recipe, but the extra-buttery Dutch baby will wow you. Prowl the produce aisle for them—they're worth it.

Pork chops with braised cabbage

Prep 25 min   Cook 4 hr   Serves 6

A little vinegar helps the red cabbage keep its brilliant color. Who knew?

- 4 tsp olive oil, divided
- 1 red onion, thinly sliced
- 1 tsp caraway seeds
- 2 Braeburn or Red Delicious apples
- ½ head red cabbage (about 1¼ lb), thinly sliced
- ¼ cup dried cranberries
- 3 tbsp unsweetened apple juice
- 2 tsp apple-cider vinegar
- 2 tsp kosher salt, divided
- ½ tsp black pepper, divided
- 6 (5-oz) lean boneless center-cut pork loin chops, trimmed

1. In a medium nonstick skillet over medium heat, warm 2 tsp oil. Add onion and caraway seeds and cook, stirring occasionally, until onion is softened, about 8 minutes.

2. Meanwhile, halve, core, and cut 1 apple into 1-inch chunks. Peel, halve, and core remaining apple and coarsely grate. Combine cabbage and both apples in a 5- or 6-qt slow cooker.

3. Stir in onion mixture, cranberries, apple juice, vinegar, 1 tsp salt, and ¼ tsp pepper. Cover and cook until cabbage is tender, about 4 hours on Low, stirring after 2 hours of cooking time.

4. Meanwhile, in a large skillet over medium-high heat, warm remaining 2 tsp oil. Sprinkle pork with remaining 1 tsp salt and ¼ tsp pepper. Add chops to skillet and cook, turning once, until an instant-read thermometer inserted into side of chop registers 145°F, about 4 minutes per side. Serve with cabbage.

Per serving (1 pork chop and 1 cup cabbage): 317 Cal, 11 g Total Fat, 3 g Sat Fat, 743 mg Sod, 24 g Total Carb, 16 g Sugar, 4 g Fib, 32 g Prot.

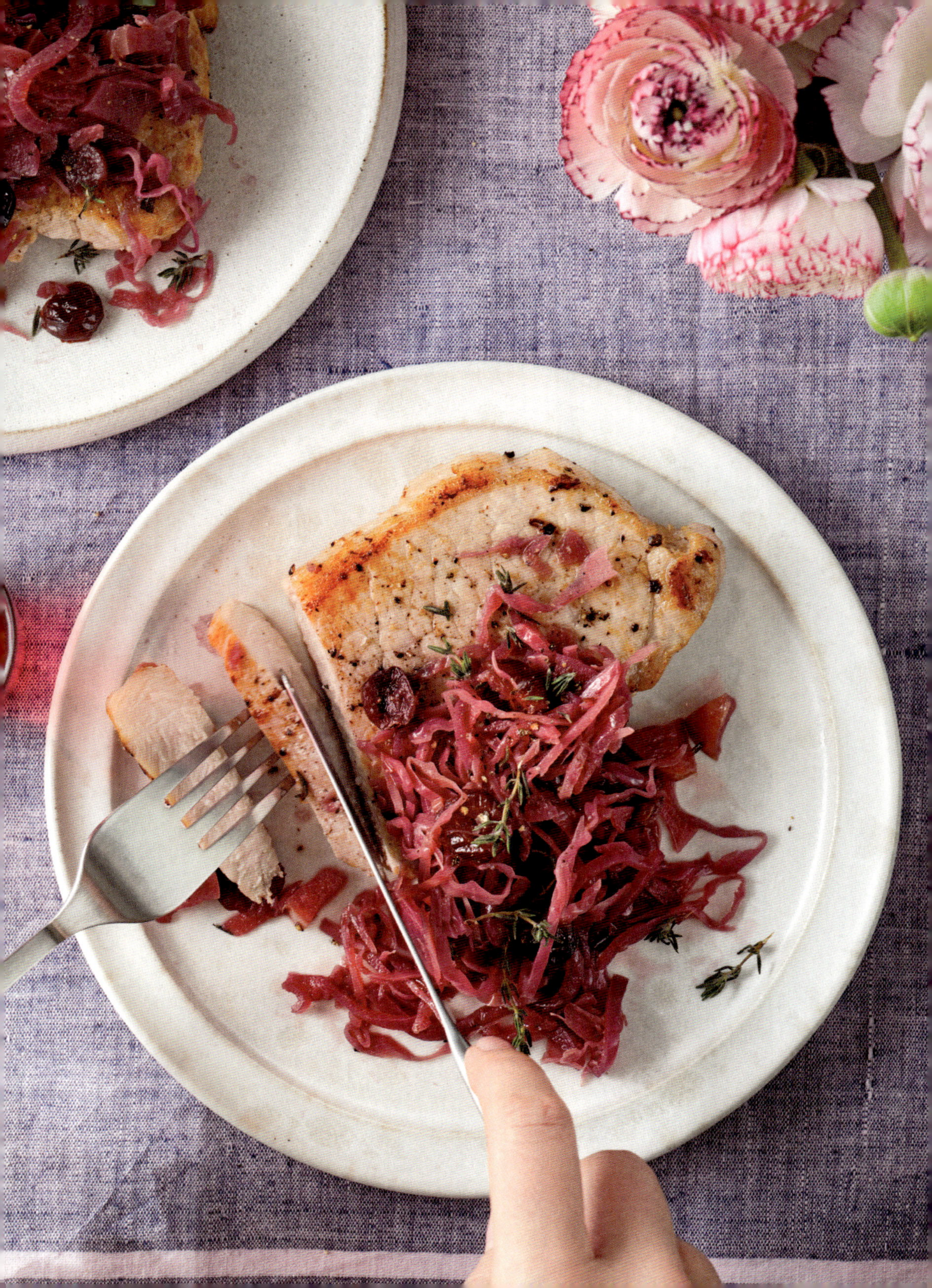

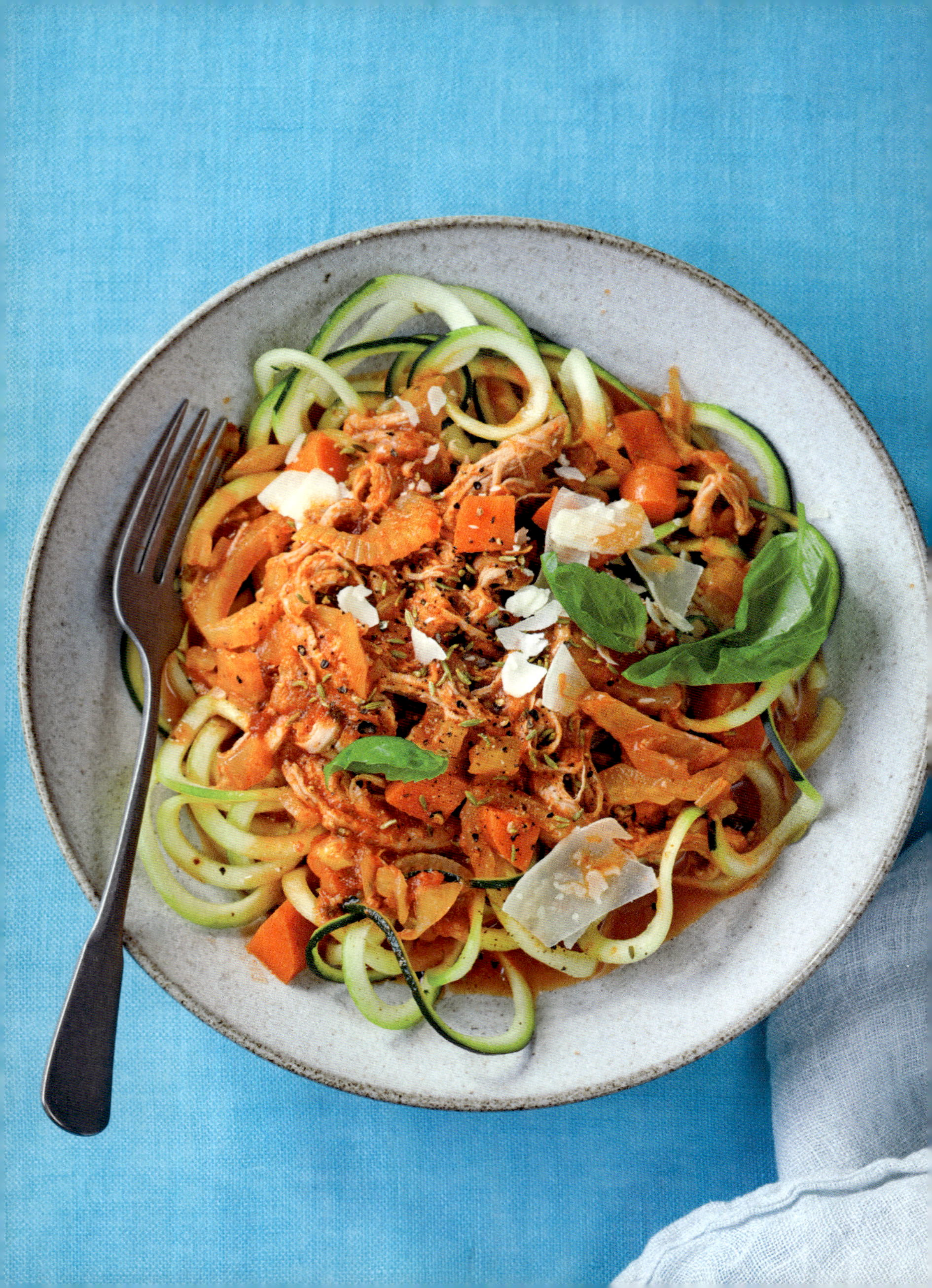

Sicilian-style pork and fennel ragu

Prep 30 min   Cook 3 to 8 hr   Serves 4

Sicilian cooks made the combo of pork, tomatoes, and fennel famous. The delicate licorice flavor of fresh fennel and the bolder taste of the seeds work especially well in this ragu.

1	(1-lb) lean pork tenderloin, trimmed
¼	tsp salt
⅛	tsp black pepper
2	tsp extra-virgin olive oil
1	cup thinly sliced fennel bulb
1	onion, chopped
1	large carrot, diced
1	large garlic clove, minced
1	tsp fennel seeds, crushed
⅓	cup dry white wine
1¾	cups reduced-fat marinara sauce
⅓	cup thinly sliced basil, plus small leaves for garnish
¼	cup grated or shaved Parmesan

1 Sprinkle pork with salt and pepper. In a large nonstick skillet over medium heat, warm oil. Add pork and cook until lightly browned on all sides, about 5 minutes. Transfer to a 5- or 6-qt slow cooker.

2 To skillet, add sliced fennel, onion, and carrot and cook, stirring, until vegetables are slightly softened, about 3 minutes. Stir in garlic and fennel seeds and cook, stirring, until fragrant, about 30 seconds. Add wine and bring to a boil, scraping up browned bits from bottom of pan. Transfer to slow cooker and stir in marinara sauce. Cover and cook until pork is fork-tender, 3 to 4 hours on High or 6 to 8 hours on Low. Transfer pork to a cutting board.

3 Cut pork crosswise into 3 or 4 pieces. With two forks, shred pork and return to slow cooker. Stir in sliced basil. Divide ragu evenly among 4 bowls; sprinkle with Parmesan and basil leaves.

Per serving (about 1¼ cups ragu and 1 tbsp cheese): 286 Cal, 8 g Total Fat, 2 g Sat Fat, 739 mg Sod, 17 g Total Carb, 8 g Sugar, 5 g Fib, 29 g Prot.

Serving idea
Toss the ragu over steamed or sautéed spiralized zucchini (aka "zoodles"). You can spiralize it yourself or buy it pre-cut in just about every major supermarket.

Updated classics

Double-mushroom and prosciutto soup

Prep 12 min, plus standing   Cook 3 to 6 hr   Serves 4

The amount of porcini mushrooms may look small, but this powerhouse ingredient packs a big flavor punch. Buy them in a specialty food store, and make sure they're imported from Italy.

1	(.35-oz) package dried porcini mushrooms
1	tbsp extra-virgin olive oil
1	small red onion, quartered and thinly sliced
1	carrot, halved lengthwise and sliced
1	celery stalk with leaves, thinly sliced
1	large garlic clove, minced
½	lb small cremini mushrooms, sliced
1	tsp kosher salt
¼	tsp black pepper
3	cups reduced-sodium beef broth
4	(½-oz) slices prosciutto
½	cup grated or shaved Parmesan
2	tbsp coarsely chopped flat-leaf parsley

1 In a 1-cup glass measure, combine porcini mushrooms and ½ cup boiling water. Let stand until mushrooms are softened, about 20 minutes. Transfer mushrooms with their liquid to a sieve set over a medium bowl. Reserve liquid. Rinse mushrooms to remove any grit, then pat dry and finely chop. Pour reserved mushroom liquid into a 3- or 4-qt slow cooker.

2 In a large nonstick skillet over medium heat, warm oil. Add onion and cook, stirring, until softened, about 5 minutes. Add carrot and celery and cook, stirring, until slightly softened, about 4 minutes. Add garlic and cook, stirring constantly, until fragrant, about 30 seconds longer.

3 In slow cooker, combine porcini mushrooms, cremini mushrooms, onion mixture, salt, pepper, and broth. Cover and cook 3 hours on High or 6 hours on Low.

4 Meanwhile, wipe skillet clean and set over medium heat. Arrange prosciutto in one layer and cook until crisp, about 5 minutes per side. Transfer to a paper towel–lined plate to drain. When cool, break into 1-inch pieces. Set aside.

5 Ladle soup evenly into 4 bowls. Top each serving with 2 tbsp Parmesan and one-fourth of prosciutto; sprinkle with parsley.

Per serving (about 1 cup soup and 2 tbsp cheese): 180 Cal, 11 g Total Fat, 4 g Sat Fat, 1,113 mg Sod, 10 g Total Carb, 3 g Sugar, 2 g Fib, 13 g Prot.

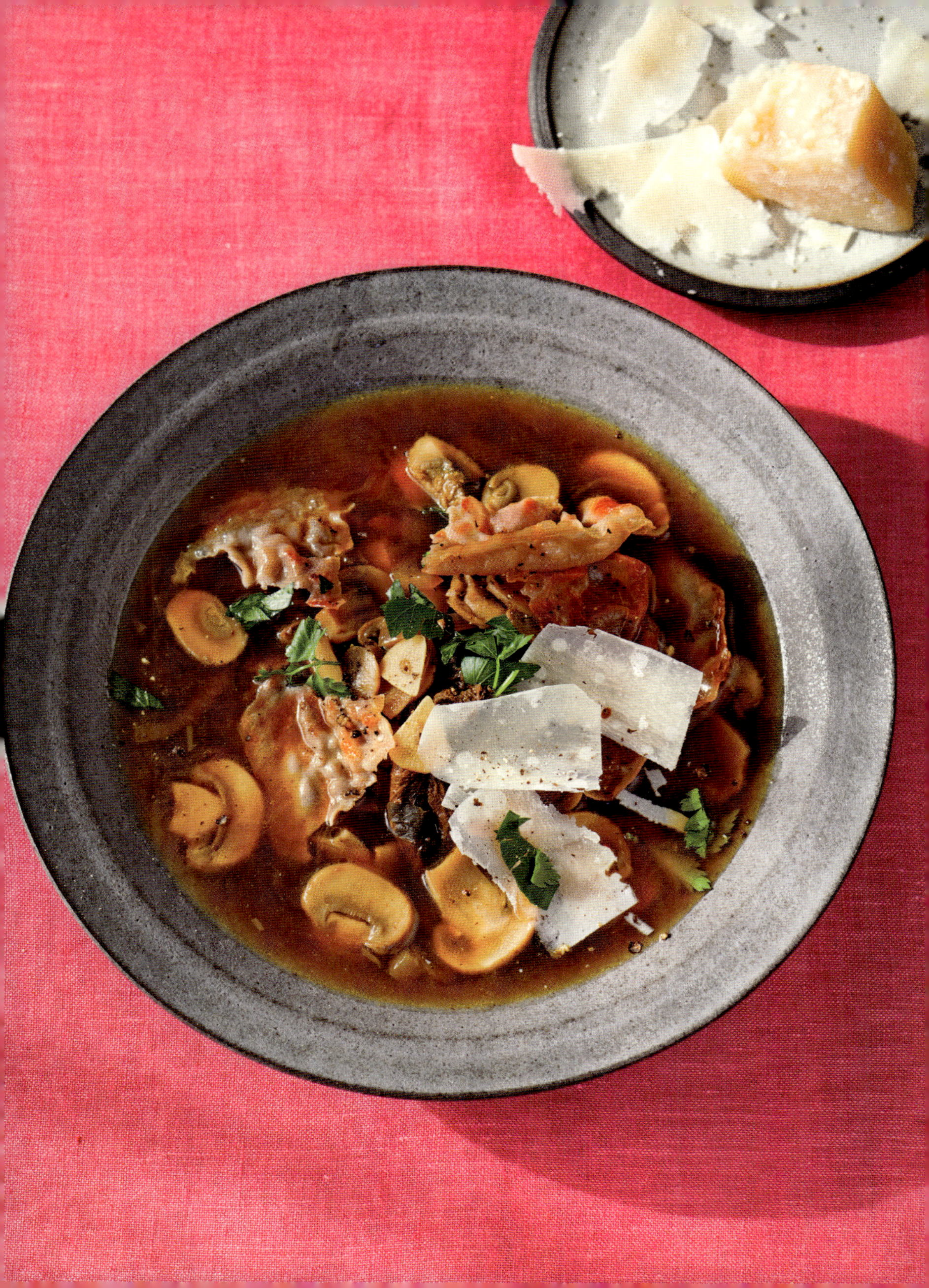

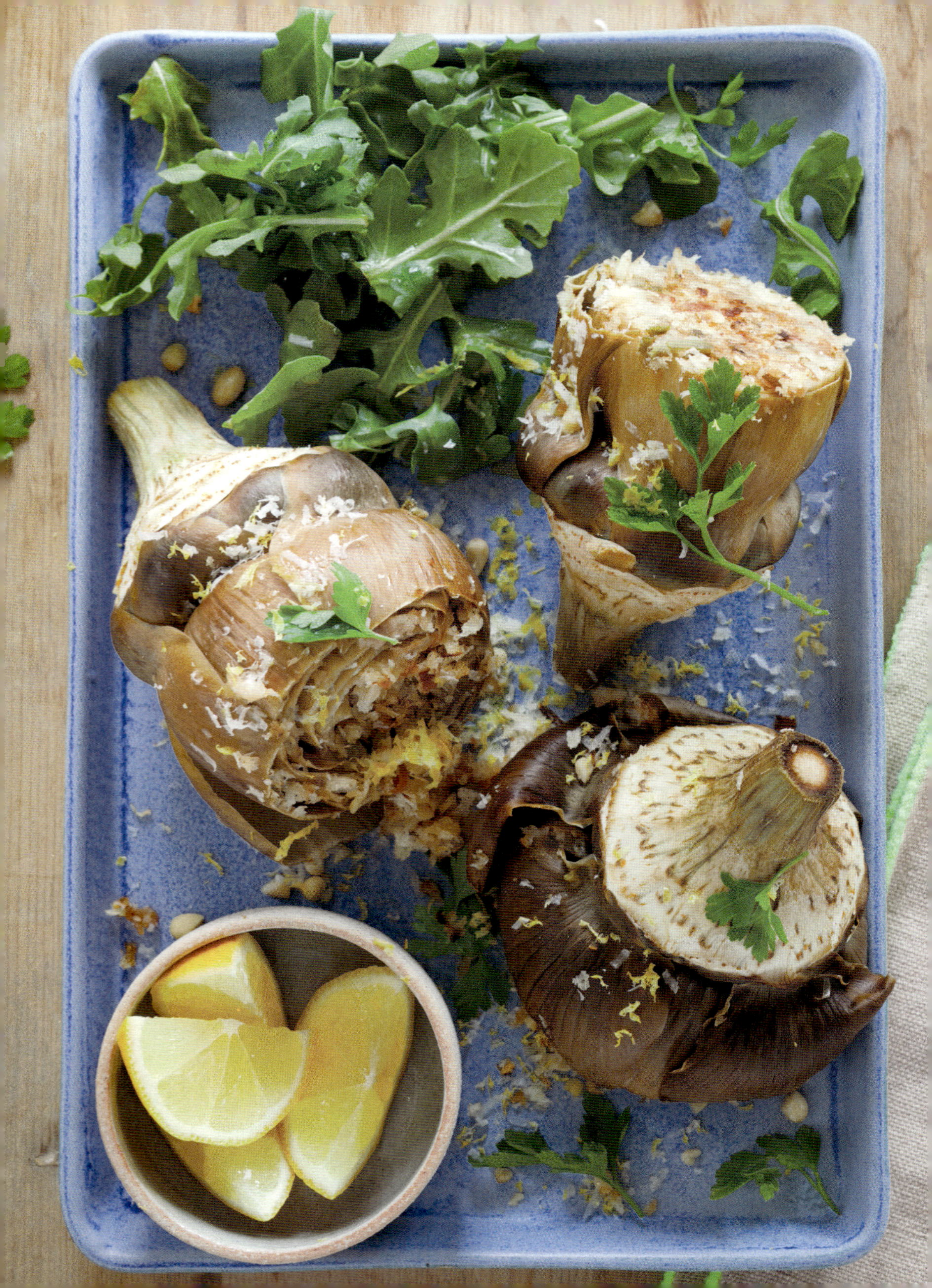

Parmesan-stuffed artichokes

Prep 38 min   Cook 3 hr   Serves 4

7 7 7

The most wonderful thing to do with artichokes? Slow-cook them stuffed with prosciutto, bread crumbs, and Parmesan.

1	lemon
4	(8-oz) artichokes
4	tsp extra-virgin olive oil
2	large shallots, finely chopped (about ⅓ cup)
2	garlic cloves, minced
2	(½-oz) slices prosciutto, trimmed and chopped
¾	cup panko bread crumbs
⅓	cup grated Parmesan
2	tbsp pine nuts, toasted and chopped
1	tsp dried oregano
¼	tsp kosher salt
⅛	tsp black pepper

Serving idea
These special-occasion artichokes are great with a salad of baby arugula dressed with balsamic or red-wine vinegar, extra-virgin olive oil, salt, and pepper.

1 Grate ½ tsp zest from lemon and set aside; squeeze lemon juice. To a bowl containing 1 cup water, add 1 tbsp lemon juice. Cut the stalk off each artichoke base and add to lemon water. Snap off tough green leaves from around base; discard. Slice 1 inch off tops of artichokes. Dip cut surfaces in lemon water. With kitchen scissors, trim thorny tops from leaves.

2 Spread open center leaves of artichoke. With the tip of a spoon, scoop out violet-tipped leaves and scrape out fuzzy choke. Place artichoke in lemon water. Repeat with remaining artichokes. Peel artichoke stems and chop.

3 In a medium nonstick skillet over medium heat, warm 2 tsp oil. Add stems, shallots, and garlic and cook, stirring, until softened, about 2 minutes. Add prosciutto and cook, stirring, until slightly crisp. Add panko and cook, stirring, until golden, 3 to 4 minutes. Remove skillet from heat and stir in Parmesan, reserved lemon zest, pine nuts, oregano, salt, and pepper. Stir in 2 tsp lemon juice and water to moisten stuffing.

4 Place artichokes, upside down, on paper towels to drain. Turn artichokes and lightly pack stuffing into cavities and between leaves. Pour 1 inch water into a 4-qt slow cooker; stand stuffed artichokes in slow cooker. Place a sheet of foil on top. Cover and cook until bottom of artichoke can be pierced easily with knife, about 3 hours on High.

5 Remove foil. Transfer artichokes to paper towels to drain. Arrange on a platter and drizzle with remaining 2 tsp oil.

Per serving (1 stuffed artichoke): 289 Cal, 13 g Total Fat, 3 g Sat Fat, 758 mg Sod, 35 g Total Carb, 5 g Sugar, 9 g Fib, 13 g Prot.

Lamb-ricotta meatballs and sauce

Prep 40 min   Cook 2½ to 5½ hr   Serves 10

The unexpected addition of ricotta makes these lamb meatballs tender and juicy. Be sure not to overmix the meat, and handle it gently for the best texture.

Olive-oil nonstick spray
- 1 large egg
- ⅔ cup part-skim ricotta
- ⅓ cup Italian-seasoned dried bread crumbs
- 2 tbsp chopped flat-leaf parsley
- 1 tbsp chopped oregano, plus small leaves for garnish
- 1 tsp salt, divided
- ¼ tsp red pepper flakes
- ¼ tsp black pepper
- 1½ lb lean ground lamb
- 1 onion, chopped
- 2 garlic cloves, minced
- 1 (28-oz) can crushed tomatoes, preferably San Marzano

1 Line a large rimmed baking sheet or broiler rack with foil and spray with nonstick spray. Preheat broiler.

2 In a large bowl, beat eggs. Stir in ricotta, bread crumbs, parsley, chopped oregano, ½ tsp salt, red pepper flakes, and black pepper. Add lamb and stir until mixed well but not overmixed. With damp hands, form 30 meatballs.

3 Arrange meatballs on prepared baking sheet. Broil 5 inches from heat, turning, until meatballs are firm, about 5 minutes. Transfer to a 5- or 6-qt slow cooker.

4 Spray a large nonstick skillet with nonstick spray and set over medium heat. Add onion and cook, stirring occasionally, until softened, about 5 minutes. Add garlic and cook, stirring constantly, until fragrant, about 30 seconds. Add tomatoes and remaining ½ tsp salt and bring to a boil. Transfer tomato mixture to slow cooker. Cover and cook until meatballs are tender, 2 to 3 hours on High or 4 to 5 hours on Low. Serve sprinkled with oregano leaves.

Per serving (3 meatballs and about ¼ cup sauce): 238 Cal, 16 g Total Fat, 8 g Sat Fat, 447 mg Sod, 8 g Total Carb, 3 g Sugar, 1 g Fib, 16 g Prot.

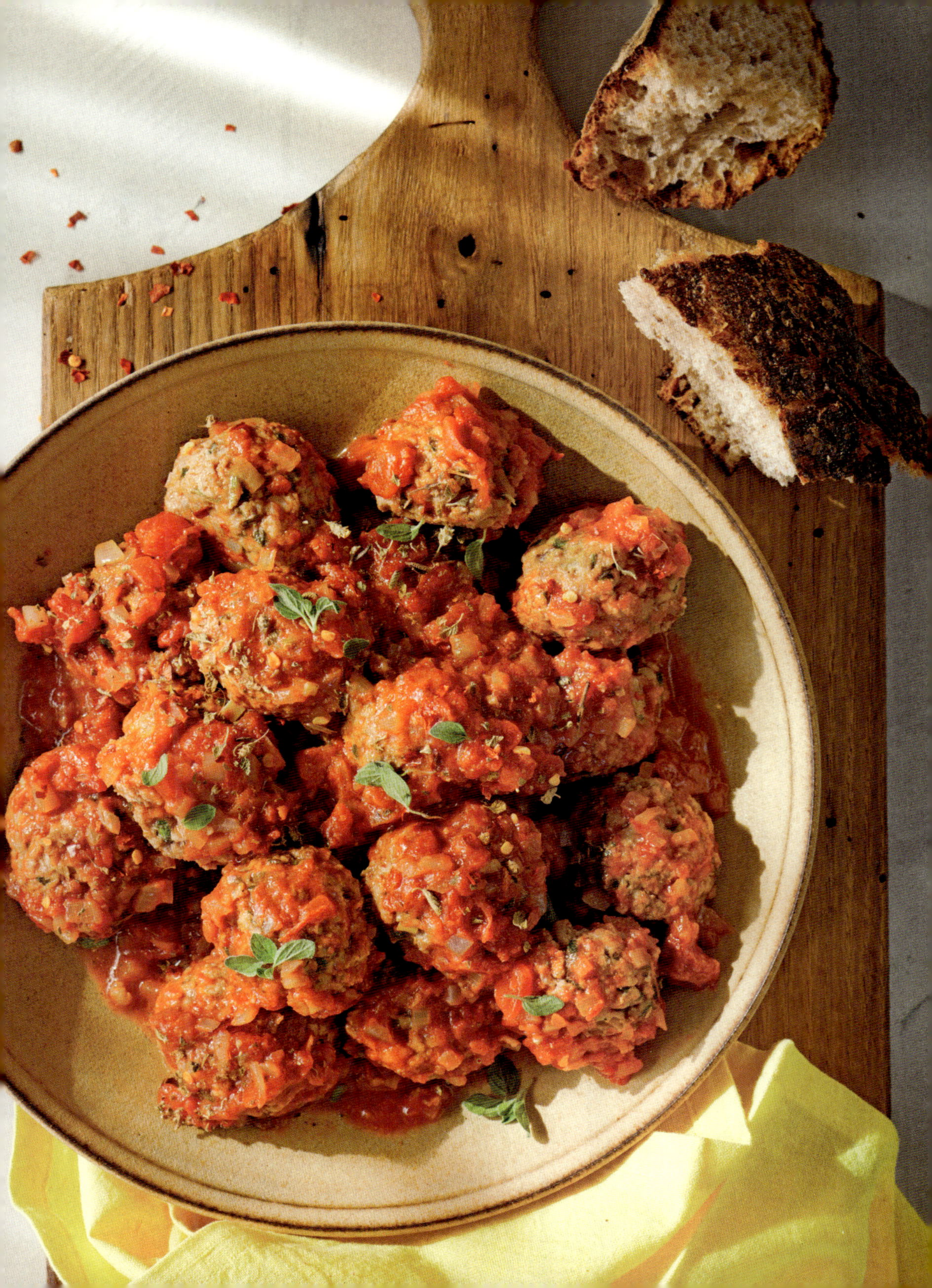

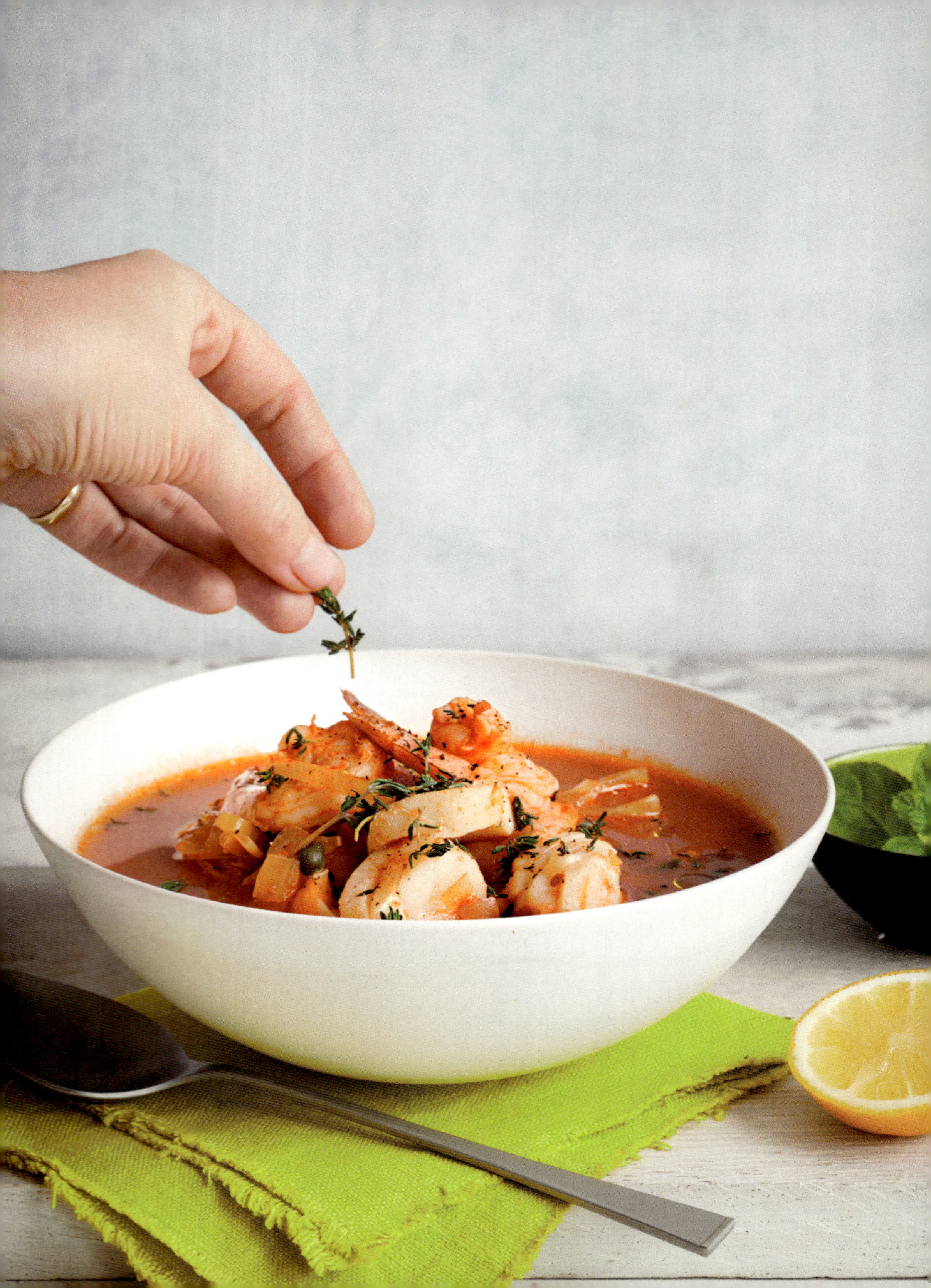

San Francisco fisherman's stew

Prep 25 min   Cook 3 to 6 hr   Serves 4

Also called *cioppino,* this tomato-based seafood stew usually contains Dungeness crab, but we've used shrimp to make your shopping easier.

- 1 (28-oz) can whole tomatoes in puree, tomatoes broken up, undrained
- 1 (14½-oz) can chicken broth
- 1 small fennel bulb, chopped
- 1 small onion, chopped
- 1 small carrot, cut into ¼-inch dice
- 1 large garlic clove, minced
- 1 tbsp nonpareil (tiny) capers, drained
- 2 tsp chopped thyme, plus whole leaves for garnish
- 1 tsp dried oregano
- ⅛ tsp red pepper flakes (or to taste)
- ¾ lb medium shrimp, peeled and deveined
- ¾ lb halibut, cod, and/or striped bass fillets, cut into 1-inch chunks
- 4 tsp fruity extra-virgin olive oil

1 In a 5- or 6-qt slow cooker, combine tomatoes with puree, broth, fennel, onion, carrot, garlic, capers, chopped thyme, oregano, and red pepper flakes. Cover and cook 3 hours on High or 6 hours on Low. (At this point, stew can be kept on warm setting up to 3 hours.)

2 Stir in shrimp and halibut. Cover and cook until shrimp are just opaque in center, about 10 minutes on Low. Ladle stew evenly into 4 large shallow bowls and drizzle each serving with 1 tsp oil. Sprinkle with thyme leaves.

Per serving (about 2 cups): 199 Cal, 6 g Total Fat, 1 g Sat Fat, 1,025 mg Sod, 14 g Total Carb, 7 g Sugar, 4 g Fib, 25 g Prot.

Garlicky shrimp with charred fennel

Prep 35 min   Cook 2 hr   Serves 4

Campari tomatoes are medium-size, grown hydroponically (without soil), and sold on the vine. Pesticide-free with great taste, they work beautifully in this recipe alongside fennel and shrimp.

Olive-oil nonstick spray
- 6 tsp olive oil, divided
- 2 (½-lb) fennel bulbs, cut lengthwise into ½-inch slices plus ¼ cup thinly sliced fennel ribs
- 1 orange bell pepper, cut into 8 pieces
- 5 garlic cloves, thinly sliced
- 1½ tsp chopped rosemary
- ¼ tsp kosher salt
- ¼ tsp black pepper
- ⅓ cup dry white wine
- 1 (10-oz) package Campari (cocktail) tomatoes
- 1 lb large shrimp, peeled and deveined
- 12 pitted Kalamata olives

Shopping tip
We used pitted Kalamata olives because they're simpler—and easier to find—but you could go authentically French and use Niçoise olives (sold with pits).

1 In a large heavy nonstick skillet over medium-high heat, warm 2 tsp oil. In skillet, arrange ½-inch sliced fennel, cut-side down, and cook, in batches if needed, until charred, about 3 minutes per side (spray fennel with nonstick spray as needed). Transfer to a 5-qt slow cooker. To skillet, add 2 tsp oil and bell pepper, skin-side down; cook until lightly charred, about 3 minutes. Add to slow cooker. Tuck one-third of garlic into vegetables and scatter rosemary on top. Sprinkle with salt and black pepper.

2 Into skillet, pour wine and boil until slightly reduced, about 1 minute. Add 2 tbsp water and cook 1 minute (you should have about 2 tbsp liquid). Pour over fennel mixture and place tomatoes with vines on top. Cover and cook until fennel and bell peppers are tender, about 2 hours on High.

3 About 5 minutes before cooking time is up, wipe skillet dry. Warm remaining 2 tsp oil over medium heat. Add remaining garlic and cook, stirring constantly, until light golden, about 1 minute; transfer to cup. Add shrimp to skillet and cook, turning once, until just opaque throughout, about 3 minutes. Remove skillet from heat.

4 With slotted spoon, transfer tomatoes to plate. Spoon fennel mixture onto platter. Remove tomatoes from vine, if desired, and place on top of fennel mixture; sprinkle with olives and fennel ribs and drizzle with juices. Add shrimp and scatter garlic on top.

Per serving (about 1 cup fennel mixture and about 8 shrimp): 232 Cal, 10 g Total Fat, 2 g Sat Fat, 1,026 mg Sod, 17 g Total Carb, 8 g Sugar, 5 g Fib, 18 g Prot.

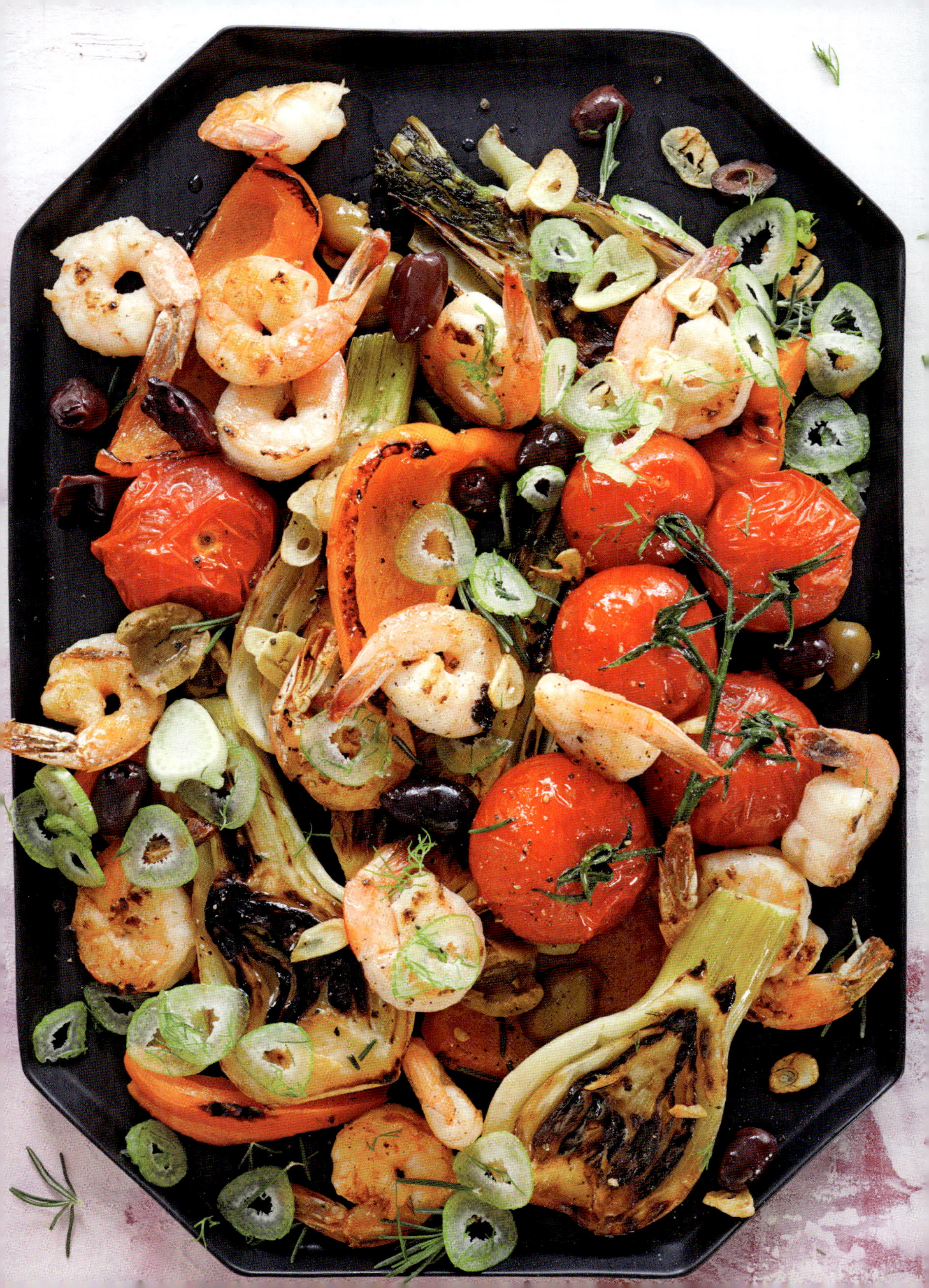

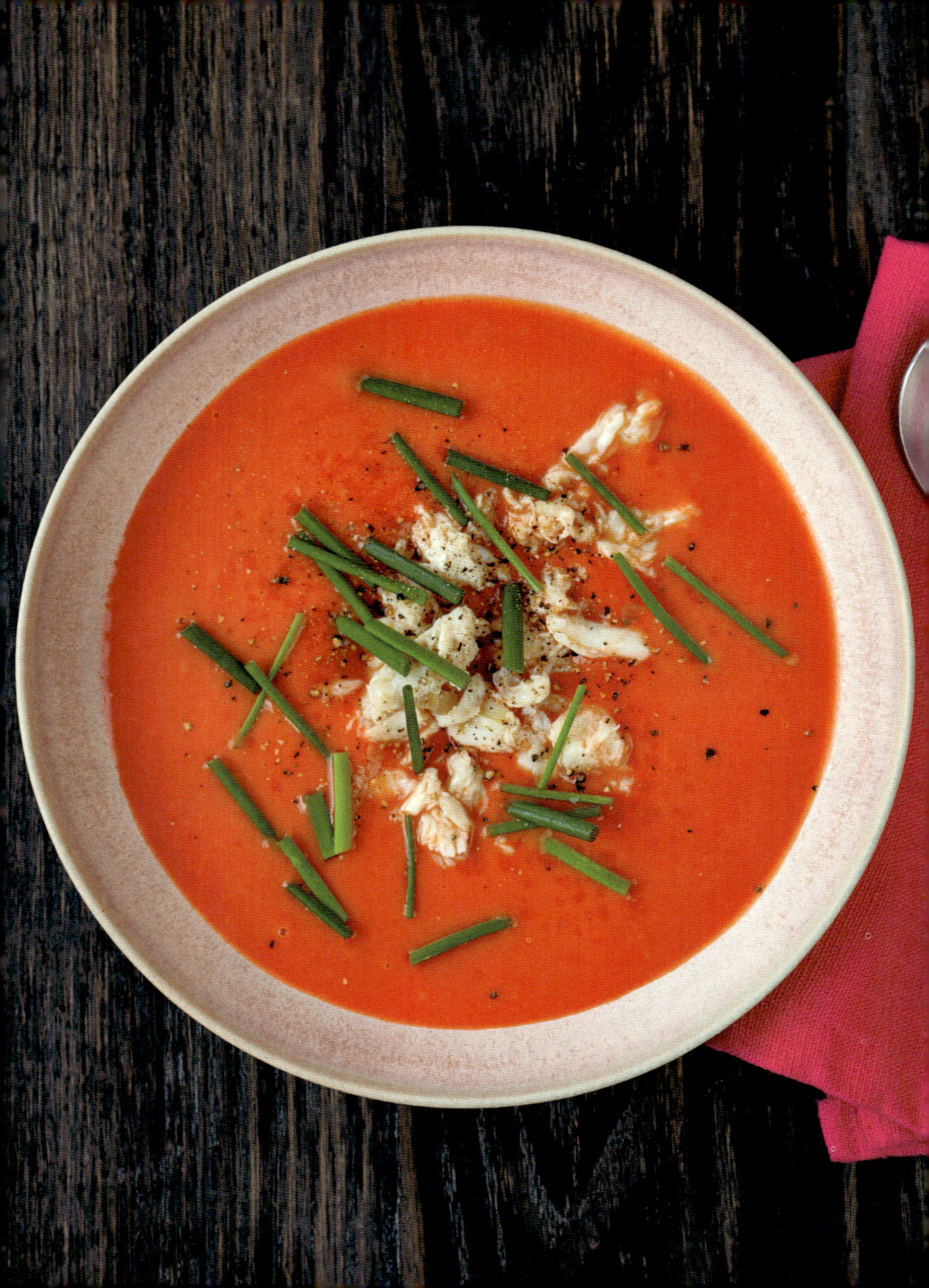

Creamy tomato soup with crab

Prep 16 min   Cook 4½ to 10½ hr   Serves 8

This soup delivers luscious texture without any cream or extra fat. The secret ingredient? One potato.

- 2 tsp olive oil
- 3 onions, sliced
- 3 large garlic cloves, minced
- ¾ tsp kosher salt
- ¼ tsp black pepper, plus more for sprinkling
- 2 (28-oz) cans whole peeled tomatoes, undrained, tomatoes broken up
- 1 (32-oz) carton vegetable broth (or water)
- 1 Yukon Gold or russet potato, peeled and cubed
- 1 cup half-and-half
- 1 lb lump crabmeat, picked over
- Chives, sliced

1 In a large nonstick skillet over medium heat, warm oil. Add onions and cook, stirring, until softened, about 5 minutes. Add garlic, salt, and black pepper and cook, stirring constantly, until fragrant, about 30 seconds.

2 Transfer onion mixture to a 5- or 6-qt slow cooker. Add tomatoes with their juice, broth, and potato, stirring well. Cover and cook until potato is tender and flavors are blended, 4 to 5 hours on High or 8 to 10 hours on Low.

3 Using an immersion blender, puree soup. (Or puree in batches in a blender or food processor.) Stir in half-and-half. Cover and cook until heated through, about 15 minutes on Low.

4 Ladle soup evenly into 8 bowls. Top evenly with crabmeat and sprinkle with chives and black pepper.

Per serving (1⅓ cups soup and about ¼ cup crabmeat): 151 Cal, 2 g Total Fat, 1 g Sat Fat, 925 mg Sod, 19 g Total Carb, 9 g Sugar, 3 g Fib, 14 g Prot.

Shopping tip
In place of lump crabmeat, feel free to opt for small shrimp or chunks of sweet lobster.

Updated classics

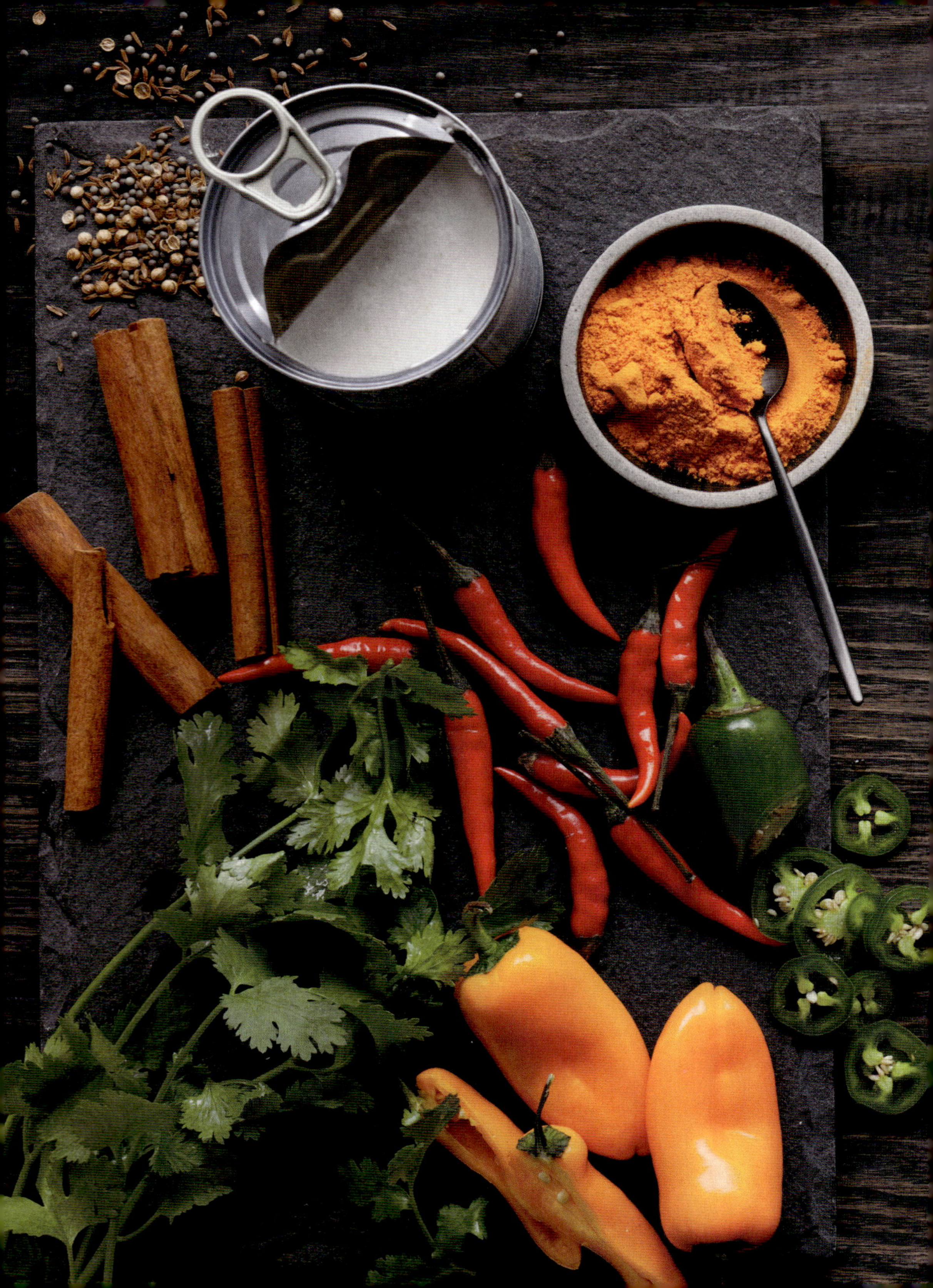

Chapter 4
Global favorites

Thai coconut-curry chicken 108
Chicken tacos with pineapple slaw 111
Moroccan chicken 112
Szechuan chicken and broccoli 115
Thai curry with noodles 116
Mexican chicken soup 119
Vietnamese lemongrass chicken soup 120
Jamaican jerk chicken 123
Meatballs in chipotle chile sauce 124
Mojo-style steak tacos 127
Beef carnitas tacos 128
Korean food truck tacos 131
Beef soup with lemongrass and coconut 132
Marrakesh-style pork 135
Teriyaki pork tenderloin 136
Five-spice pork stew 139
Sausage, chicken, and shrimp stew 140
Pork in green chile sauce 143
Indian fish curry 144
Hot-and-sour soup with shiitakes and tofu 147

Thai coconut-curry chicken

Prep 15 min   Cook 2½ to 6 hr   Serves 6

Coconut milk and red curry paste create the foundation for this Thai-inspired dish, but the key addition is peanut butter. Add a sprinkle of scallions, cilantro, crunchy peanuts, and lime juice to tie all the flavors together.

- 1 (13½-oz) can light (low-fat) coconut milk
- 7 tsp red curry paste, divided
- 1 tsp salt
- ½ head cauliflower, broken into small florets
- 1 lb all-purpose potatoes, scrubbed and cut into ¾-inch chunks
- 1 sweet potato, peeled and cut into ¾-inch chunks
- 1 red bell pepper, cut into ¾-inch pieces
- 2 carrots, cut into ½-inch slices
- 6 (5-oz) skinless boneless chicken breasts
- 2 tbsp creamy peanut butter
- ⅓ cup chopped cilantro
- 3 scallions, thinly sliced
- 2 tbsp chopped salted dry-roasted peanuts
- 1 lime, cut into 6 wedges

1 In a 4- to 6-qt slow cooker, whisk together coconut milk, 4 tsp curry paste, and salt until blended. Add cauliflower, both potatoes, bell pepper, and carrots; toss until mixed well.

2 Rub 2 tsp curry paste all over chicken and place on top of vegetable mixture. Cover and cook until chicken is cooked through and vegetables are tender, 2½ to 3 hours on High or 5 to 6 hours on Low.

3 Transfer chicken to a cutting board and cut into bite-size pieces or shred using two forks. Cover and keep warm.

4 In a cup, stir together peanut butter and remaining 1 tsp curry paste. Stir into slow cooker; add chicken, stirring until combined well. Spoon chicken-vegetable mixture evenly onto 6 plates or into bowls. Sprinkle with cilantro, scallions, and peanuts, and serve with lime wedges.

Per serving (1½ cups chicken curry and 1 tsp peanuts): 380 Cal, 12 g Total Fat, 4 g Sat Fat, 699 mg Sod, 32 g Total Carb, 6 g Sugar, 6 g Fib, 38 g Prot.

Serving idea

Cooked white rice, like jasmine, is a classic partner for this dish. But brown would also work well, adding an earthiness to the curry.

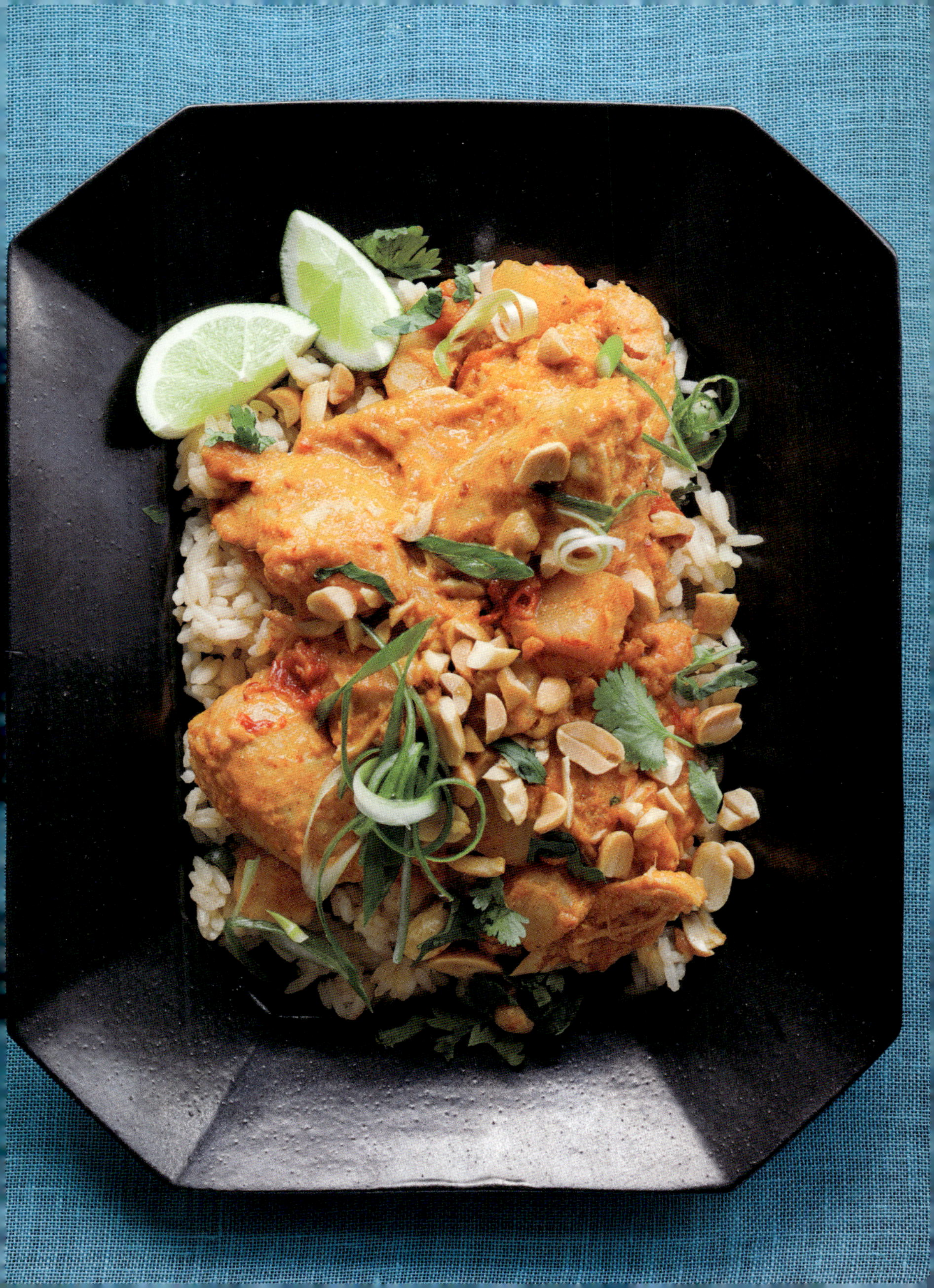

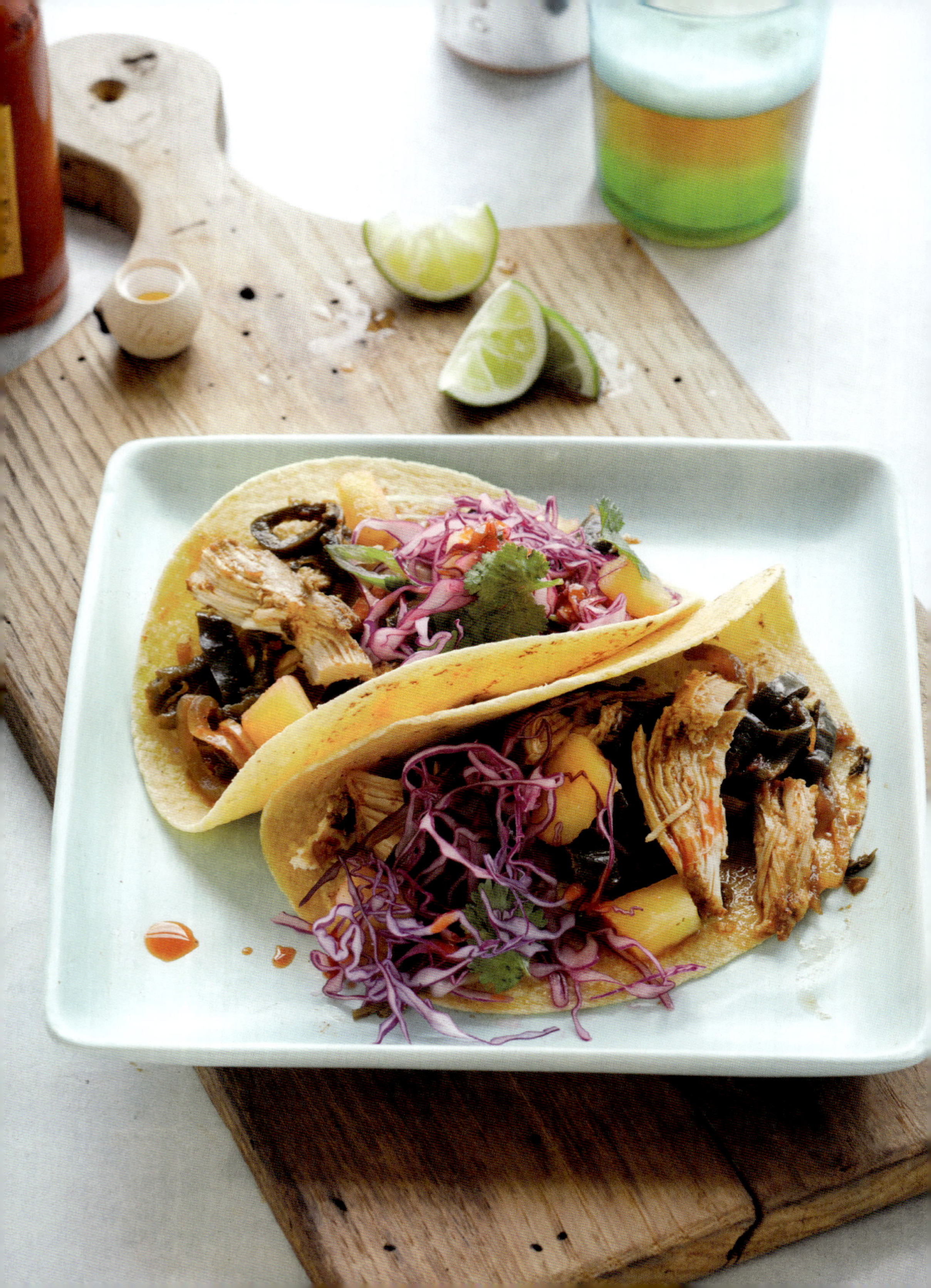

Chicken tacos with pineapple slaw

Prep 20 min   Cook 2½ hr   Serves 4

Take taco night to the next level: The chicken is seasoned with chili powder, adobo, cumin, and orange juice and simmered with poblanos, cilantro, and garlic. The bright pineapple slaw is a perfect pairing.

2	poblano peppers, seeded and sliced
½	large red onion, sliced
1	cup chopped cilantro, divided
3	garlic cloves, finely chopped
2	tsp chili powder
2	tsp adobo sauce (from chipotle chiles en adobo)
2	tsp orange or pineapple juice
1½	tsp ground cumin
1	tsp salt (or to taste), divided
1¼	lb skinless boneless chicken breasts
1½	cups thinly sliced red cabbage
1	cup diced or chopped pineapple
2	small scallions, thinly sliced
8	(6-inch) corn tortillas, warmed
½	lime, cut into 4 wedges

1. In a 5- or 6-qt slow cooker, stir together poblanos, onion, ½ cup cilantro, and garlic.

2. In a cup, mix together chili powder, adobo sauce, orange juice, cumin, and ½ tsp salt. Rub over chicken breasts. Place chicken on top of poblano mixture and spoon poblano mixture over chicken. Cover and cook until chicken is fork-tender, about 2½ hours on High.

3. Transfer chicken to a cutting board. With two forks, shred chicken, then return to slow cooker.

4. To make slaw: In a medium bowl, toss together cabbage, pineapple, remaining ½ cup cilantro, scallions, and remaining ½ tsp salt.

5. Lay tortillas on a work surface. Spoon about ½ cup chicken mixture on each tortilla and top with about ¼ cup slaw. Serve with lime wedges.

Per serving (2 tacos): 357 Cal, 6 g Total Fat, 1 g Sat Fat, 747 mg Sod, 42 g Total Carb, 10 g Sugar, 6 g Fib, 37 g Prot.

Global favorites

Moroccan chicken

Prep 20 min   Cook 2 to 6 hr   Serves 4

Your slow cooker acts like a traditional tagine in this perfectly spiced recipe.

- 1¾ tsp ground cumin, divided
- ¾ tsp salt, divided
- ¼ plus ⅛ tsp cinnamon, divided
- ¼ plus ⅛ tsp black pepper, divided
- ⅛ tsp cayenne (or to taste)
- 4 (5-oz) bone-in chicken thighs, skin removed
- 1 tsp olive oil
- 1 onion, chopped
- 2 garlic cloves, minced
- 1 tsp minced peeled ginger
- 1 (14½-oz) can diced tomatoes
- 1 (1-lb) container butternut squash chunks
- 1 (15½-oz) can chickpeas, rinsed and drained
- Cilantro leaves
- 2 tbsp sliced almonds, toasted
- 1 small lime, cut into 4 wedges

1 In a cup, mix together 1½ tsp cumin, ½ tsp salt, ¼ tsp cinnamon, ¼ tsp black pepper, and cayenne; sprinkle all over chicken. Transfer to a 5- or 6-qt slow cooker.

2 In a large nonstick skillet over medium heat, warm oil. Add onion and cook, stirring, until beginning to soften, about 3 minutes. Stir in garlic, ginger, and remaining ¼ tsp cumin, ¼ tsp salt, ⅛ tsp cinnamon, and ⅛ tsp black pepper; cook, stirring constantly, until fragrant, about 30 seconds.

3 Stir in tomatoes and bring to a boil. Add to slow cooker, along with squash and chickpeas, stirring to combine. Cover and cook until chicken and squash are fork-tender, 2 to 3 hours on High or 4 to 6 hours on Low. Spoon evenly into 4 large shallow bowls; sprinkle with cilantro and almonds, and serve with lime wedges.

Per serving (1 chicken thigh and 1½ cups vegetable mixture with sauce): 401 Cal, 11 g Total Fat, 2 g Sat Fat, 962 mg Sod, 48 g Total Carb, 11 g Sugar, 12 g Fib, 33 g Prot.

Serving idea
A steaming bowl of Israeli couscous would make a great side—or go gluten-free with brown rice.

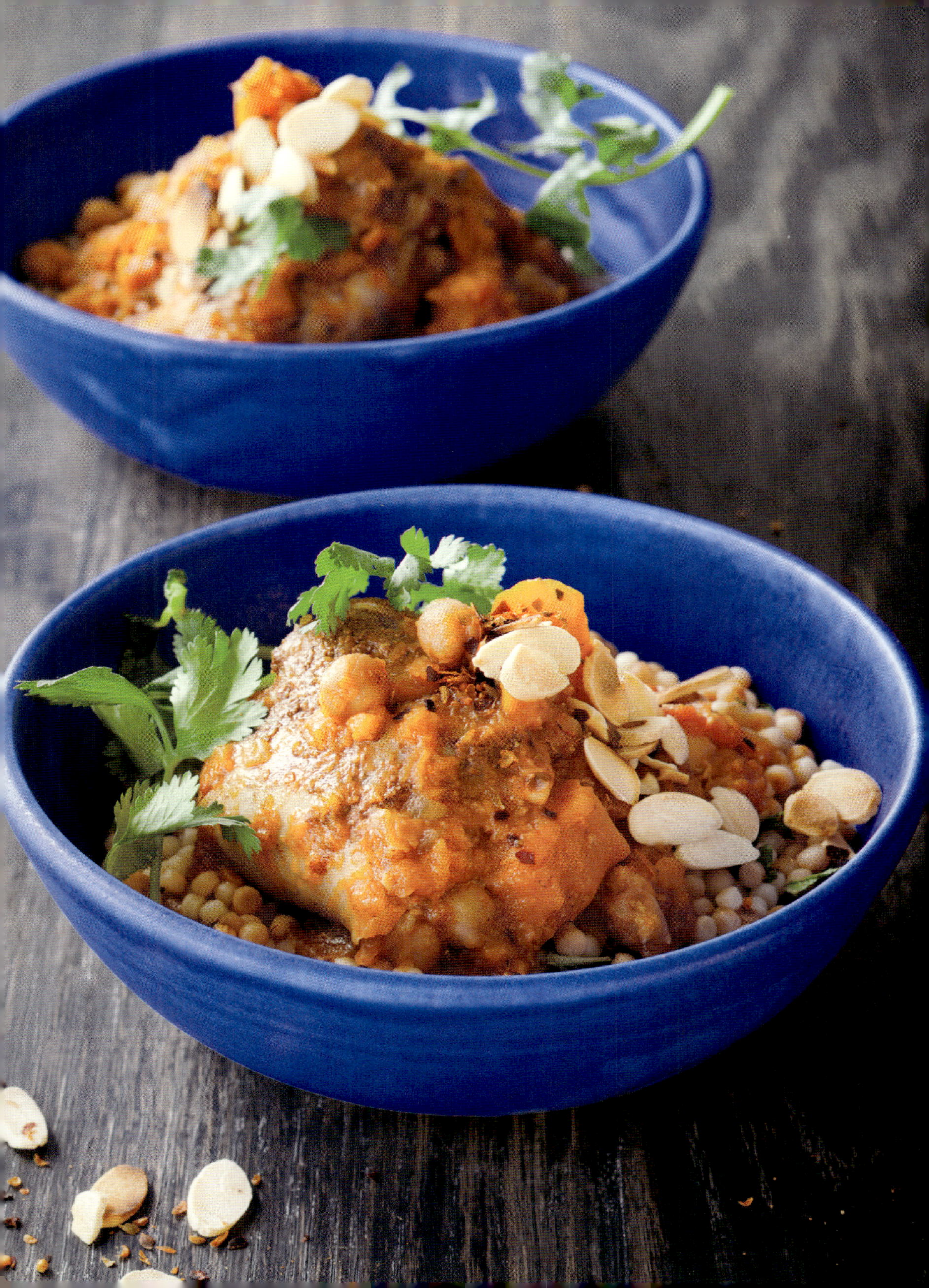

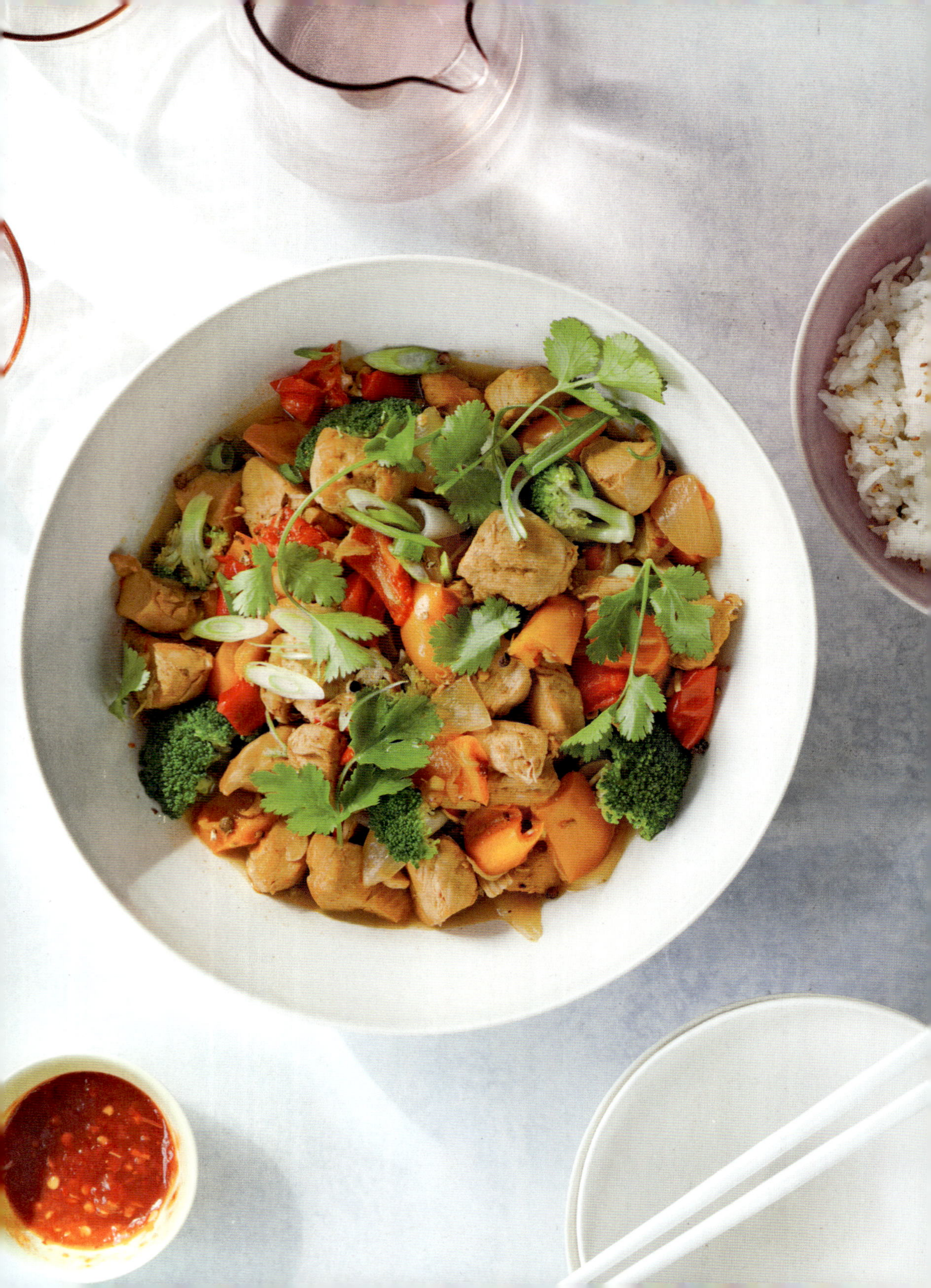

Szechuan chicken and broccoli

Prep 40 min   Cook 2 to 6 hr   Serves 4

Szechuan peppercorns have a pungent lemony aroma and a generous amount of heat that goes well with ginger, garlic, and onion. Crushed whole black peppercorns can be substituted if you can't find the Szechuan kind.

1½ lb	skinless boneless chicken breasts, cut into 1-inch chunks
1½ tsp	Szechuan peppercorns, crushed
1 tbsp	cornstarch
4 tsp	peanut or canola oil, divided
1	onion, thickly sliced
3	large garlic cloves, minced
2 tsp	minced peeled ginger
1 cup	chicken broth
⅓ cup	reduced-sodium soy sauce
¼ cup	rice wine or dry sherry
2 tsp	chili-garlic sauce (or to taste)
2	red or orange bell peppers, diced
3 cups	small broccoli florets
3	scallions, thinly sliced
	Cilantro leaves or small sprigs

1 Sprinkle chicken with peppercorns; dust with cornstarch. In a large skillet over medium-high heat, warm 2 tsp oil. Add chicken and cook until golden, 3 to 4 minutes per side. Transfer to a 5- or 6-qt slow cooker.

2 In same skillet, warm remaining 2 tsp oil. Add onion, garlic, and ginger and cook, stirring, until onion is lightly browned, about 6 minutes. Add broth and bring to boil, scraping up browned bits from bottom of pan. Transfer broth mixture to slow cooker. Stir in soy sauce, rice wine, and chili sauce. Cover and cook 1 hour on High or 2 hours on Low. Stir in bell peppers; cover and cook until chicken and vegetables are tender, 1 to 2 hours on High or 2 to 4 hours on Low.

3 Put broccoli in a steamer basket and set over 1 inch boiling water in medium saucepan. Cover and cook until crisp-tender, about 3 minutes. Add broccoli to chicken mixture. Spoon chicken-vegetable mixture evenly into 4 large shallow bowls; sprinkle with scallions and cilantro leaves.

Per serving (1½ cups): 342 Cal, 9 g Total Fat, 2 g Sat Fat, 968 mg Sod, 17 g Total Carb, 6 g Sugar, 4 g Fib, 43 g Prot.

Thai curry with noodles

Prep 30 min   Cook 2 to 6 hr   Serves 6

Wide rice noodles are sometimes labeled as pad thai noodles. Find them in the Asian-food section of supermarkets and try them with this chicken curry.

Nonstick spray
- 1 (13½-oz) can light (low-fat) coconut milk
- ¼ cup Thai red curry paste
- 2 tbsp powdered peanut butter
- 2 tbsp soy sauce
- 1 serrano pepper, seeded and minced
- 2 red bell peppers, cut into 1½-inch pieces
- 1 onion, diced
- 1½ lb skinless boneless chicken thighs, cut into 1½-inch chunks
- 2 large garlic cloves, minced
- 1 tbsp minced peeled ginger
- ¼ tsp kosher salt (or to taste)
- ½ lb green beans, trimmed and cut into 1½-inch pieces
- ⅓ cup chopped cilantro
- 1 tsp grated lime zest, plus thin strips for garnish
- 2 tbsp lime juice
- 6 oz wide rice noodles, cooked according to package directions, rinsed, drained, and kept warm

Small basil leaves

Chile peppers, whole or sliced (optional)

1 In a 5- or 6-qt slow cooker, whisk together coconut milk, curry paste, powdered peanut butter, soy sauce, and serrano pepper until blended. Stir in bell peppers and onion.

2 Spray a large heavy deep skillet or wok with nonstick spray and set over high heat. Add chicken in a single layer; sprinkle with garlic, ginger, and salt; cook, without stirring, until chicken is browned, about 1 minute. Stir-fry until chicken is no longer pink, 2 to 3 minutes longer.

3 Transfer chicken to slow cooker. Cover and cook until chicken and vegetables are tender, 2 to 3 hours on High or 4 to 6 hours on Low. Stir in green beans. Cover and cook until crisp-tender, about 10 minutes on High. Stir cilantro and lime zest and juice into chicken mixture. Divide noodles evenly among 6 bowls. Spoon curry on top and sprinkle with lime strips, basil leaves, and chile peppers, if using.

Per serving (generous 1 cup curry and ½ cup noodles): 355 Cal, 11 g Total Fat, 4 g Sat Fat, 1,125 mg Sod, 37 g Total Carb, 4 g Sugar, 5 g Fib, 26 g Prot.

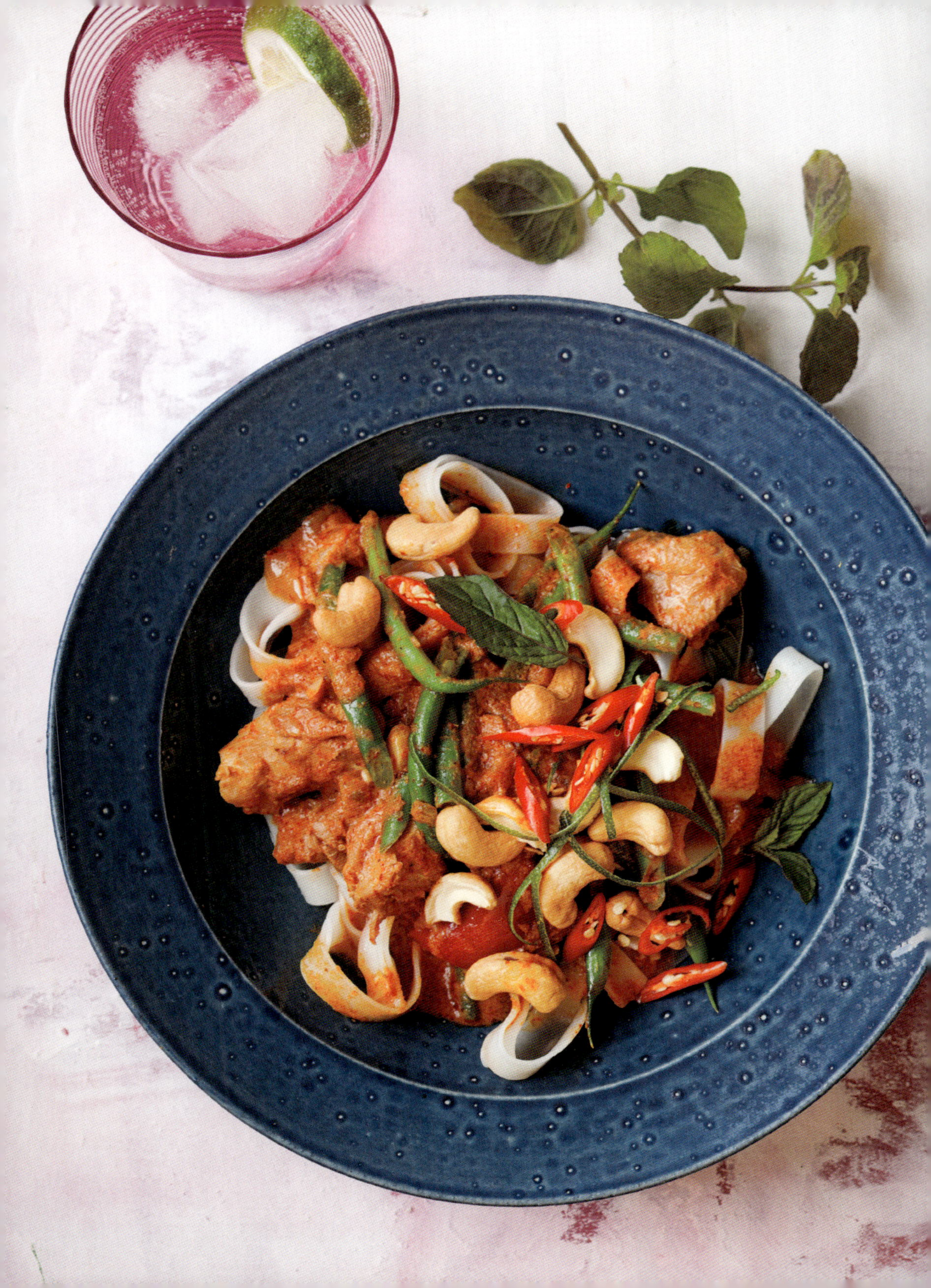

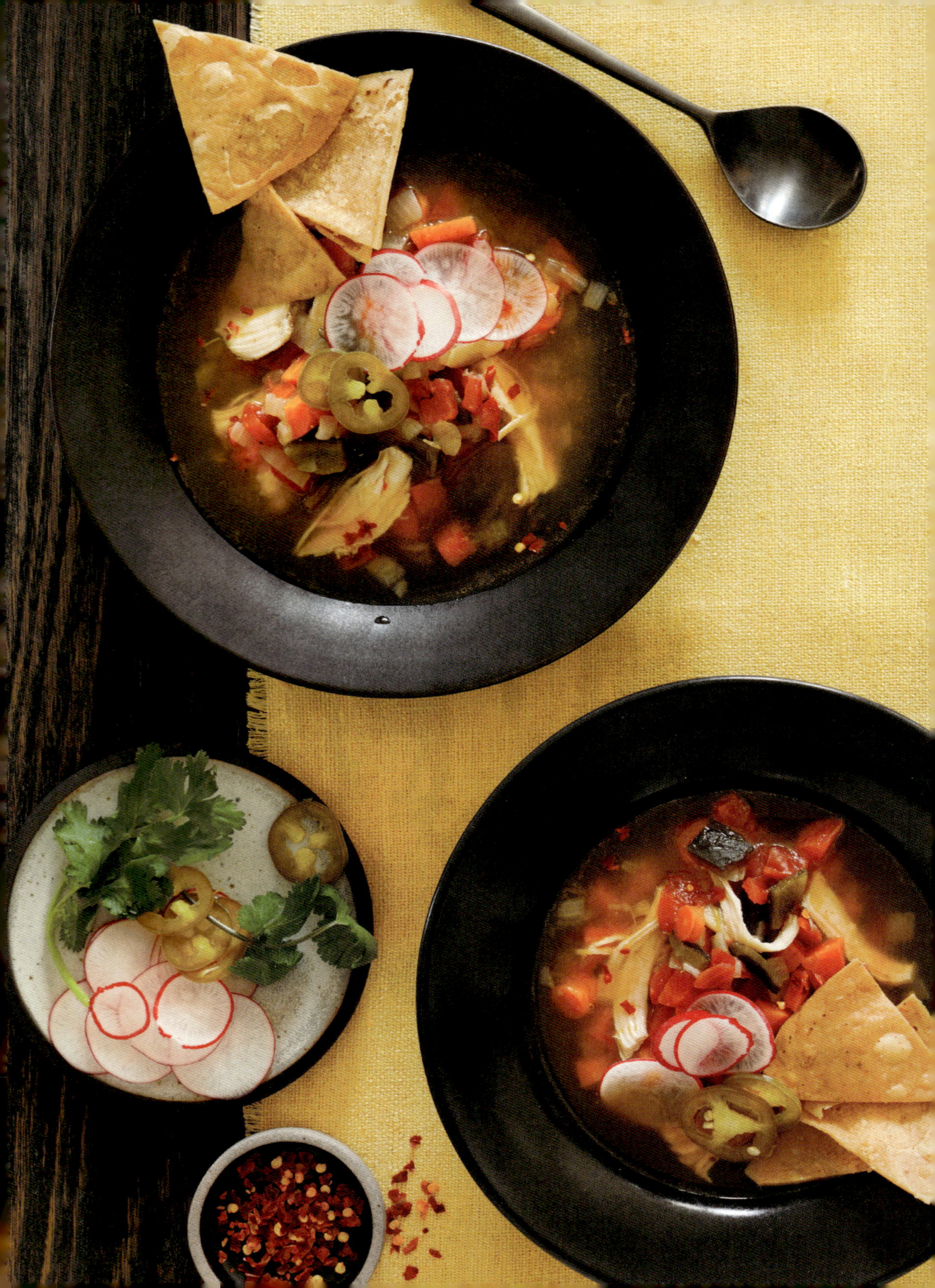

Mexican chicken soup

Prep 25 min   Cook 4½ to 10½ hr   Serves 6

What gives this chicken soup a Mexican twist? Poblano peppers, which are easy to find in your grocery store and rated mild for a family-friendly spice level.

1	tbsp olive oil
2	onions, chopped
2	large garlic cloves, sliced
1	(1-lb) bone-in chicken breast, skin removed
3	small carrots, sliced or diced
½	tsp salt
Pinch cayenne	
2	(32-oz) cartons reduced-sodium chicken broth
2	poblano peppers
1	(14½-oz) can diced fire-roasted tomatoes, drained
Cilantro leaves	
Radishes	
Picked sliced jalapeño peppers	

1. In a medium skillet over medium heat, warm oil. Add onions and cook, stirring, until softened, about 5 minutes. Add garlic and cook, stirring constantly, until fragrant, about 30 seconds longer. Transfer to a 5- or 6-qt slow cooker.

2. To slow cooker, add chicken, carrots, salt, and cayenne; pour in broth. Cover and cook until chicken and vegetables are fork-tender, 4 to 5 hours on High or 8 to 10 hours on Low.

3. Meanwhile, preheat broiler. Line broiler rack with foil.

4. Place poblano peppers on prepared rack and broil 5 inches from heat, turning, until skins are blistered and charred, 10 to 15 minutes. Transfer peppers to zip-close plastic bag. Squeeze out air and seal bag; let peppers steam 10 minutes. Peel peppers and remove stems and seeds; dice peppers and reserve.

5. With a slotted spoon, transfer chicken to a plate. When chicken is cool enough to handle, remove and discard bone. Tear or cut chicken into bite-size pieces.

6. Return chicken to slow cooker, along with poblanos and tomatoes. Cover and cook until heated through, about 15 minutes on High. Ladle soup evenly into 6 bowls. Top with cilantro leaves, radishes, and pickled peppers.

Serving idea

Want even more flavor? Top the soup with baked tortilla chips, thinly sliced radishes, and ultra-thin rings of jalapeño pepper— fresh or pickled.

Per serving (2 cups): 184 Cal, 5 g Total Fat, 1 g Sat Fat, 1,089 mg Sod, 15 g Total Carb, 7 g Sugar, 3 g Fib, 22 g Prot.

Vietnamese lemongrass chicken soup

Prep 25 min   Cook 4 to 10 hr   Serves 6

Known as *pho*, this soup is a staple in Vietnam and often eaten as the first meal of the day. Our version, with lemongrass and chicken, is satisfying but also light.

- 2   (½-lb) bone-in chicken breasts, skin removed
- 2   (32-oz) cartons reduced-sodium chicken broth
- 6   cilantro sprigs, plus torn leaves for garnish
- 3   scallions, white parts kept whole and green parts thinly sliced, divided
- 1   lemongrass stalk, trimmed and finely chopped (or 2 tsp refrigerated lemongrass paste)
- 2   garlic cloves, crushed with side of large knife
- 1   (3-inch) cinnamon stick
- ⅛   tsp black pepper
- Mint leaves
- ½   small red onion, very thinly sliced
- 1   lime, cut into wedges

1 In a 5- or 6-qt slow cooker, combine chicken, broth, cilantro sprigs, white part of scallions, lemongrass, garlic, cinnamon stick, and black pepper. Cover and cook until chicken is fork-tender, 4 to 5 hours on High or 8 to 10 hours on Low.

2 With a slotted spoon, transfer chicken to a plate. When cool enough to handle, remove and discard bones from chicken; cut or tear chicken into bite-size pieces.

3 Pour broth through a sieve set over a large bowl. Discard vegetables and spices. Return broth and chicken to slow cooker. Cover and cook until chicken is heated through, about 10 minutes on High.

4 Ladle soup evenly into 6 bowls; sprinkle with mint and onion. Serve with lime wedges.

Per serving (1⅔ cups): 117 Cal, 2 g Total Fat, 0 g Sat Fat, 779 mg Sod, 4 g Total Carb, 1 g Sugar, 1 g Fib, 20 g Prot.

Serving idea

Add even more zing and crunch by topping each bowl with mung bean sprouts, sliced scallion, and very thin slices of jalapeño.

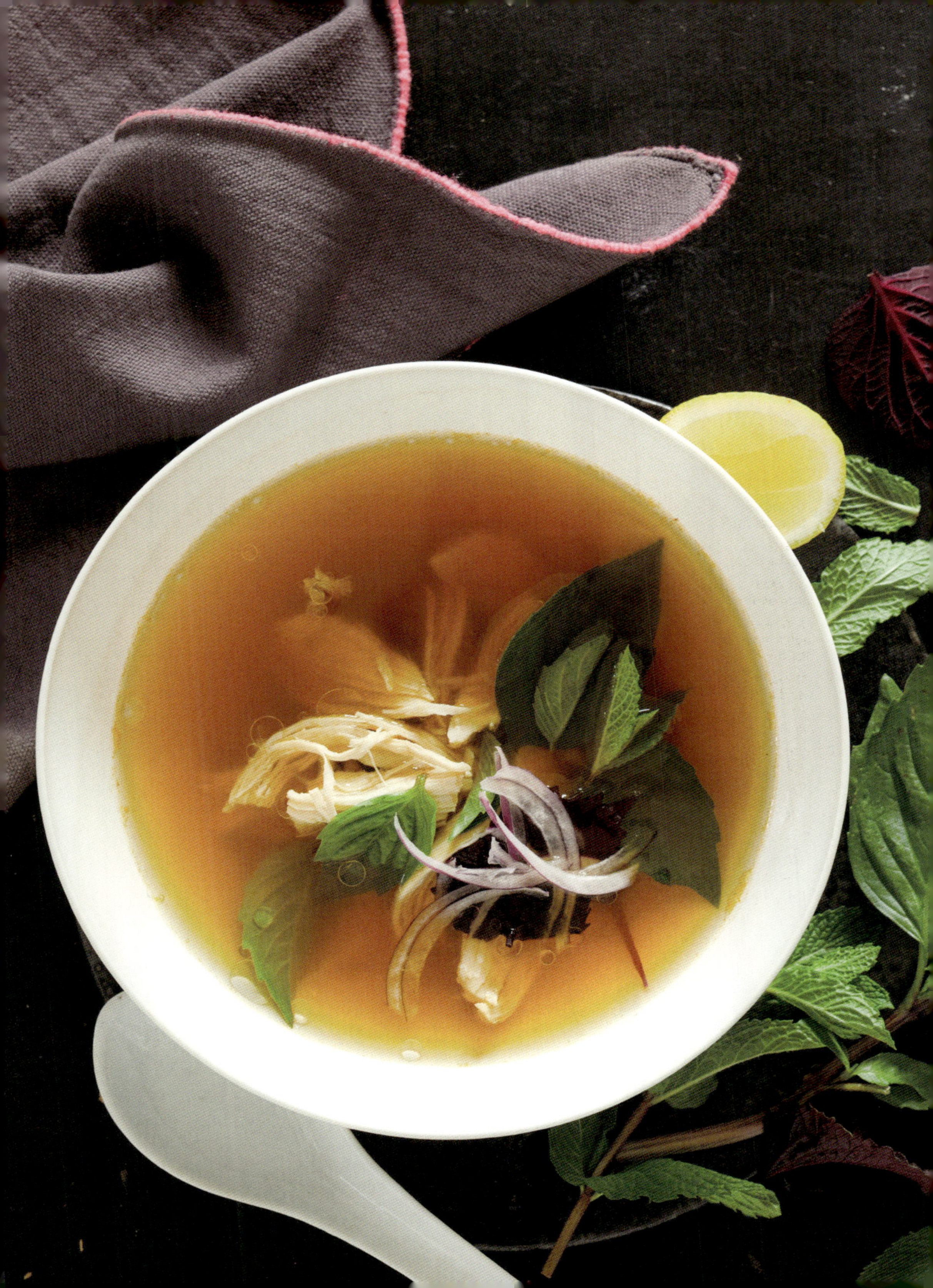

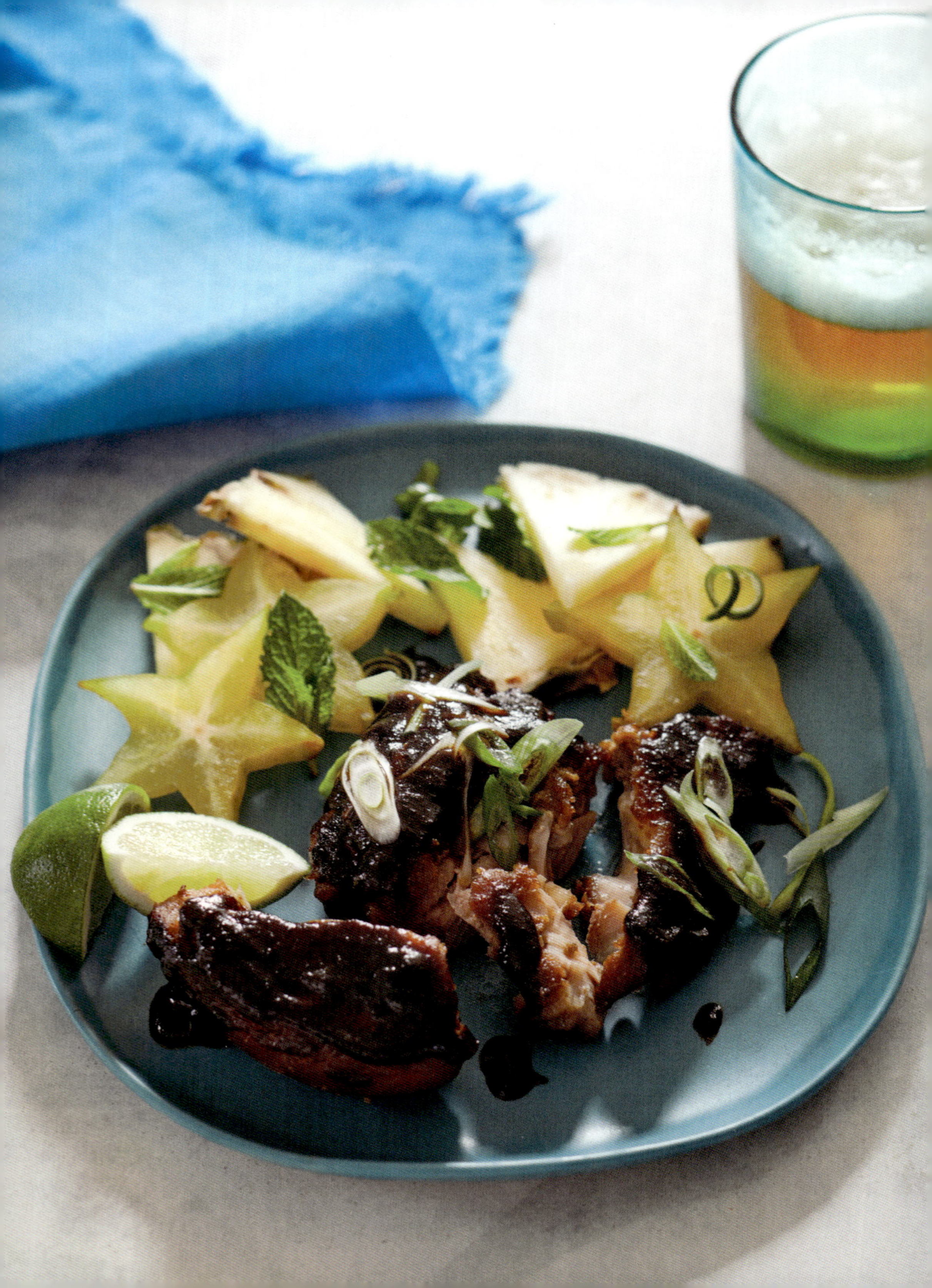

Jamaican jerk chicken

Prep 18 min   Marinate 8 hr   Cook 4 to 5 hr   Serves 6

In Jamaica, *jerk* means "barbecue," and jerk chicken is often grilled. However you cook it, you should always balance a mix of sweet, hot, herbal, and spicy flavors.

Nonstick spray
- 1   small onion, cut into chunks
- 6   scallions, cut into 1-inch lengths plus 1 scallion, thinly sliced diagonally
- 1   habanero pepper, halved and seeded
- 3   large garlic cloves
- 2   tbsp chopped peeled ginger
- Juice of 1 lime
- 1½ tbsp canola oil
- 1½ tbsp soy sauce
- 1½ tbsp molasses
- 1½ tbsp Jamaican jerk seasoning (or to taste)
- ⅛   tsp ground allspice
- 6   (5-oz) bone-in chicken thighs, skin removed
- 1   lime, cut into wedges

1 In a blender, combine onion, scallion lengths, habanero, garlic, ginger, lime juice, oil, soy sauce, molasses, jerk seasoning, and allspice; process until mixture forms a paste. Transfer ¼ cup of paste to a cup; cover and refrigerate.

2 In a large zip-close plastic bag, combine chicken and remaining seasoning paste. Squeeze out air and seal bag; massage paste onto chicken. Refrigerate 8 hours or up to overnight.

3 Transfer chicken and seasoning paste to a 5- or 6-qt slow cooker. Cover; cook until chicken is tender, 4 to 5 hours on Low.

4 Preheat broiler. Line a rimmed baking sheet with foil and spray with nonstick spray.

5 With tongs, transfer chicken to prepared baking sheet. Brush top of chicken with reserved ¼ cup seasoning paste. Spray chicken with nonstick spray. Broil until golden in spots, about 3 minutes. Sprinkle with sliced scallion; serve with lime wedges.

Per serving (1 thigh): 253 Cal, 10 g Total Fat, 2 g Sat Fat, 404 mg Sod, 11 g Total Carb, 6 g Sugar, 2 g Fib, 31 g Prot.

Serving idea
Cool things off by pairing this chicken with big chunks of fresh pineapple, halved strawberries, and sliced star fruit.

Meatballs in chipotle chile sauce

Prep 15 min Cook 2½ to 6 hr Serves 4

Grated zucchini adds moisture to these zesty Mexican-inspired turkey meatballs that cook in a chipotle-tomato sauce. Use the large holes of a box grater for the zucchini, and it'll be ready in a flash.

1	large egg
1½	tsp Mexican-style hot chili powder
1	tsp ground cumin
1	tsp salt
1	lb ground skinless turkey (7% fat or less)
1	small zucchini, coarsely grated
3	tbsp plain dried bread crumbs
2	(14½-oz) cans crushed fire-roasted tomatoes
½	cup chicken broth
¼	cup finely chopped red onion
3	garlic cloves, minced
2	chipotles en adobo, finely chopped
1	tsp dried oregano

Small oregano leaves (optional)

1 In a large bowl, whisk together egg, chili powder, cumin, and salt. Add turkey, zucchini, and bread crumbs; mix until well blended but not overmixed. With damp hands, shape into 12 meatballs. Set aside.

2 In a 5- or 6-qt slow cooker, combine tomatoes and broth. Stir in onion, garlic, chipotles en adobo, and oregano; add meatballs. Cover and cook until meatballs are tender, 2½ to 3 hours on High or 5 to 6 hours on Low. Divide meatballs and sauce evenly among 4 plates or large shallow bowls. Sprinkle with oregano, if using.

Per serving (3 meatballs and 1 cup sauce): 265 Cal, 12 g Total Fat, 3 g Sat Fat, 1,194 mg Sod, 16 g Total Carb, 7 g Sugar, 4 g Fib, 27 g Prot.

Serving idea
Spoon the meatballs over steamed zucchini noodles that can soak up all the tasty sauce.

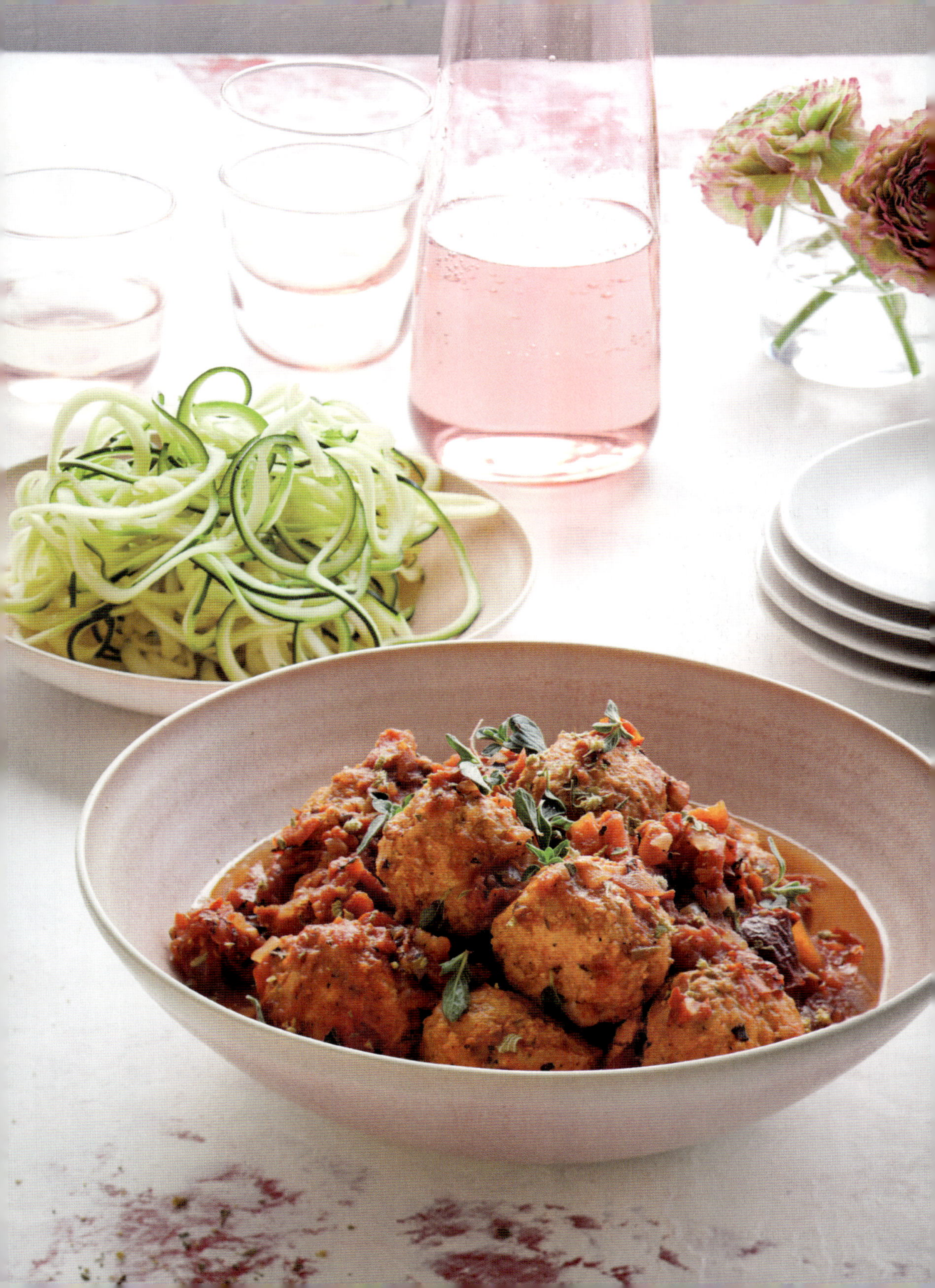

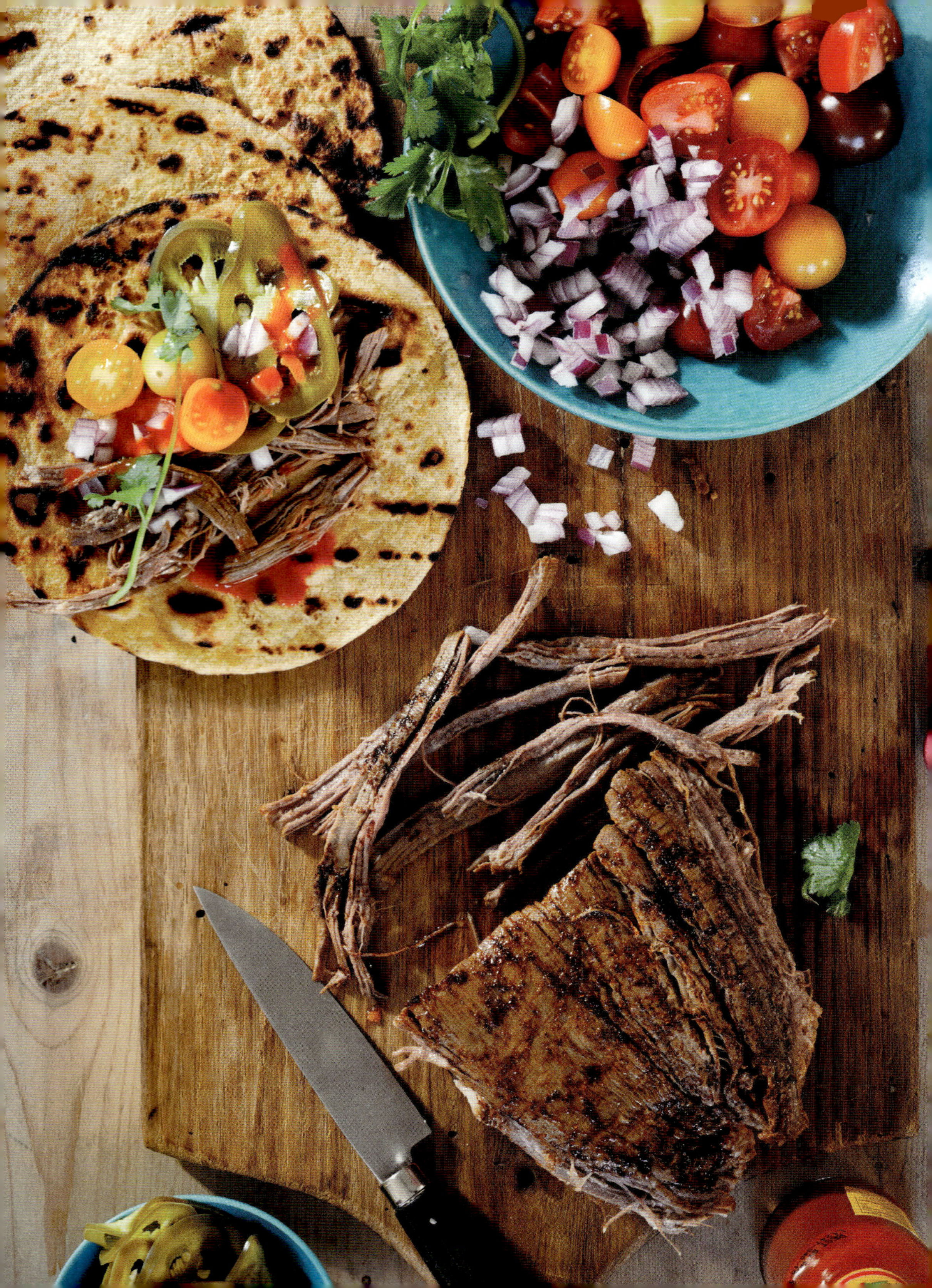

Mojo-style steak tacos

Prep 10 min   Cook 4 to 9 hr   Serves 4

Mojo is a sauce that originated in the Canary Islands. Ours has the traditional citrus juice, spices, and garlic, plus beer to flavor and tenderize the flank steak.

1	cup beer
½	cup orange juice
1	tbsp chili powder
1½	tsp ground cumin
1	tsp dried oregano
1	tsp salt
⅛	tsp cayenne, or to taste
1	(1-lb) lean flank steak, trimmed
8	(6-inch) corn tortillas, warmed
1	cup cherry tomatoes, halved
¼	cup diced red onion
¼	cup chopped cilantro
Hot pepper sauce	

1 In a 5- or 6-qt slow cooker, stir together beer, orange juice, chili powder, cumin, oregano, salt, and cayenne. Add steak, turning to coat well. Cover; cook until steak is very tender, 4 to 5 hours on High or 8 to 9 hours on Low.

2 Transfer steak to a cutting board; cut crosswise into 4 pieces. With two forks, shred steak.

3 Lay tortillas on a work surface. Divide steak evenly among tortillas; top with tomatoes, onion, and cilantro. Serve with hot sauce.

Per serving (2 tacos): 334 Cal, 8 Total Fat, 3 g Sat Fat, 734 mg Sod, 33 g Total Carb, 5 g Sugar, 4 g Fib, 29 g Prot.

Serving idea
Sprinkle each taco with 2 tbsp shredded reduced-fat Pepper Jack cheese.

Beef carnitas tacos

Prep 10 min   Cook 4 to 10 hr   Serves 8

Throughout central Mexico, carnitas is a favorite street food that's piled onto warm corn tortillas, topped with *pico de gallo* (fresh tomato and onion salsa), and wrapped in foil for easy eating.

1	(1-lb) lean flank steak, trimmed
1	cup beer
¼	cup orange juice
¼	cup lemon juice
2	tsp chili powder
1	tsp smoked paprika
1	tsp ground cumin
½	tsp salt
¼	tsp black pepper
8	(6-inch) corn tortillas, warmed
½	cup fat-free chunky salsa or pico de gallo
	Cilantro leaves
1	avocado, pitted, peeled, and diced
1	large lime, cut into 8 wedges

1. In a 5- or 6-qt slow cooker, combine flank steak, beer, orange juice, lemon juice, chili powder, paprika, cumin, salt, and black pepper. Cover and cook until beef is fork-tender, 4 to 5 hours on High or 8 to 10 hours on Low.

2. Transfer beef to a cutting board. Discard all but ½ cup cooking liquid. With two forks, shred beef into 1½- to 2-inch lengths. In a medium bowl, combine shredded beef with 2 tbsp cooking liquid, adding more cooking liquid if beef seems dry. Cover to keep warm.

3. To serve, lay tortillas on a work surface and top evenly with beef, salsa, cilantro, and avocado. Fold up tortillas to enclose filling. Serve with lime wedges.

Per serving (1 taco): 208 Cal, 8 g Total Fat, 2 g Sat Fat, 284 mg Sod, 19 g Total Carb, 2 g Sugar, 4 g Fib, 15 g Prot.

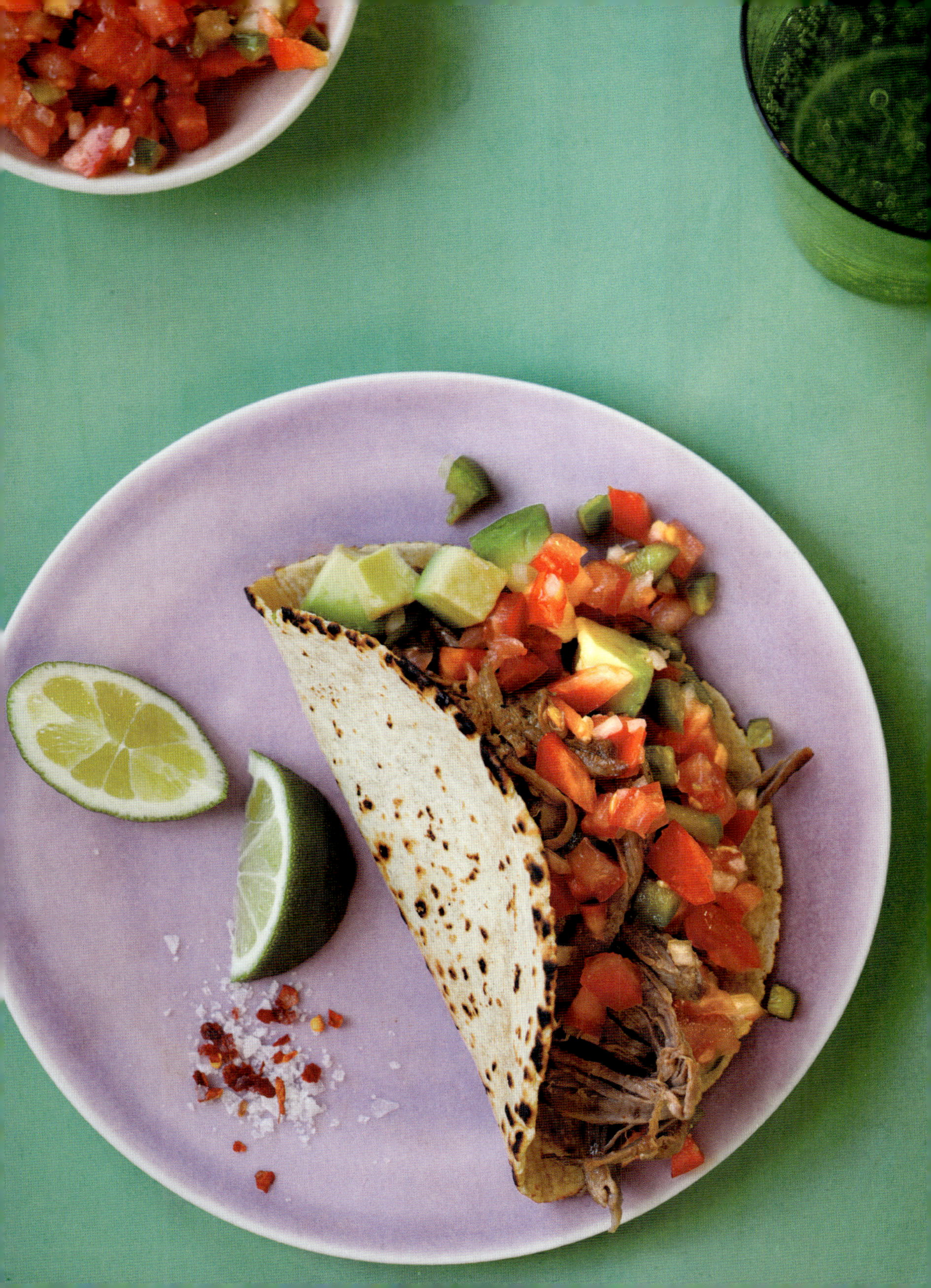

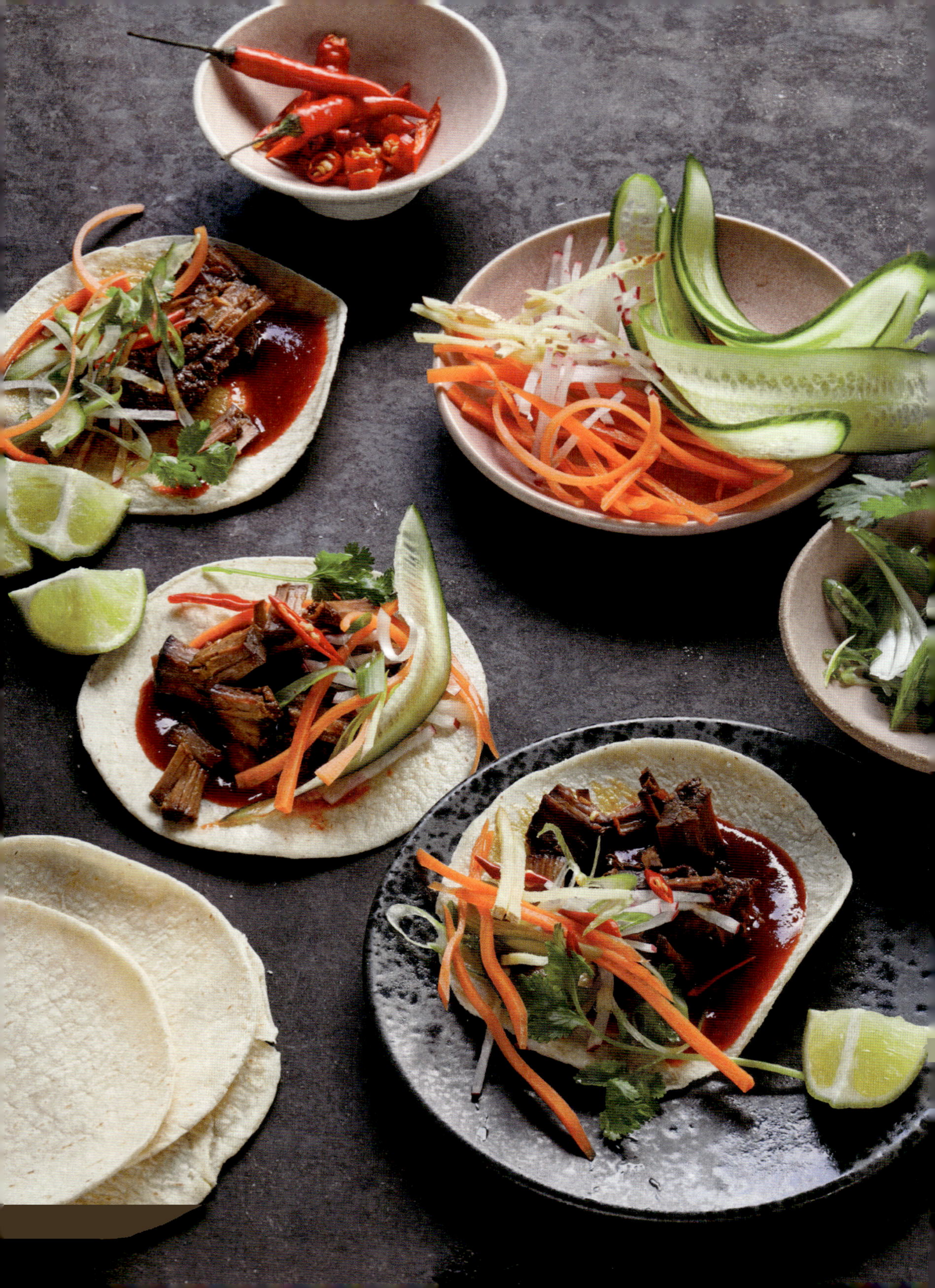

Korean food truck tacos

Prep 15 min   Marinate 6 to 8 hr   Cook 6 to 7 hr   Serves 8

Serve these steak tacos with Korean hot sauce (gochujang) for just the right amount of heat.

¼	cup reduced-sodium soy sauce
3	garlic cloves, minced
1	tbsp minced peeled ginger
1	tbsp honey
2	tsp dark sesame oil
1	(1½-lb) lean top round steak, trimmed
1	cup packaged matchstick-cut carrots
3	large radishes, cut into thin matchsticks
2	scallions, thinly sliced on diagonal
3	tbsp rice vinegar
½	tsp salt
16	(6-inch) flour tortillas, warmed
8	tsp gochujang or sriracha (or to taste)
2	large Kirby or medium regular cucumbers, cut lengthwise into very thin slices
	Cilantro leaves
1	large lime, cut into 8 wedges

1 In a large zip-close plastic bag, combine soy sauce, 2 tbsp water, garlic, ginger, honey, and sesame oil. Add beef and turn to coat. Squeeze out air and seal bag. Refrigerate 6 to 8 hours, turning bag over once or twice.

2 Transfer beef with marinade to a 5- or 6-qt slow cooker. Cover and cook until beef is fork-tender, 6 to 7 hours on Low.

3 Meanwhile, to make slaw: In a medium bowl, toss together carrots, radishes, scallions, vinegar, and salt.

4 With two forks, shred beef in slow cooker; stir until coated with cooking juices.

5 Lay tortillas on a work surface. Spread ½ tsp gochujang along center of each tortilla. Spoon ¼ cup shredded beef over gochujang. Drizzle with pan juices; top each taco with 3 tbsp slaw, a few slices cucumber, and a few cilantro leaves. Serve with lime wedges or squeeze juice over top.

Per serving (2 tacos): 362 Cal, 10 g Total Fat, 3 g Sat Fat, 837 mg Sod, 42 g Total Carb, 5 g Sugar, 3 g Fib, 25 g Prot.

Global favorites

Beef soup with lemongrass and coconut

Prep 15 min   Cook 4 to 9 hr   Serves 8

To prep lemongrass, cut off the green top and woody stem and discard. Peel away a tough outer layer or two to reveal the pale green inner stalk.

1	lemongrass stalk, trimmed and thinly sliced
8	garlic cloves, peeled
2	tbsp chopped peeled ginger
1 to 2	tbsp ground turmeric
2	tsp grated lime zest
1	tsp kosher salt (or to taste)
3	cups light (low-fat) coconut milk
2	lb lean beef chuck roast, trimmed and cut into 1-inch chunks
1	sweet onion, such as Vidalia, thinly sliced
½	lb small red potatoes, scrubbed and halved
½	lb baby carrots, peeled

Thinly sliced scallions

Cilantro leaves

1 In a food processor, combine lemongrass, garlic, ginger, turmeric, lime zest, and salt; pulse until a thick paste forms. Transfer to a 4- or 5-qt slow cooker. Add coconut milk; stir until combined. Add beef, onion, potatoes, and carrots, stirring well.

2 Cover and cook until beef and vegetables are fork-tender, 4 to 5 hours on High or 8 to 9 hours on Low. Ladle stew evenly into 8 bowls; sprinkle with scallions and cilantro.

Per serving (about 1 cup): 268 Cal, 13 g Total Fat, 8 g Sat Fat, 365 mg Sod, 13 g Total Carb, 2 g Sugar, 2 g Fib, 25 g Prot.

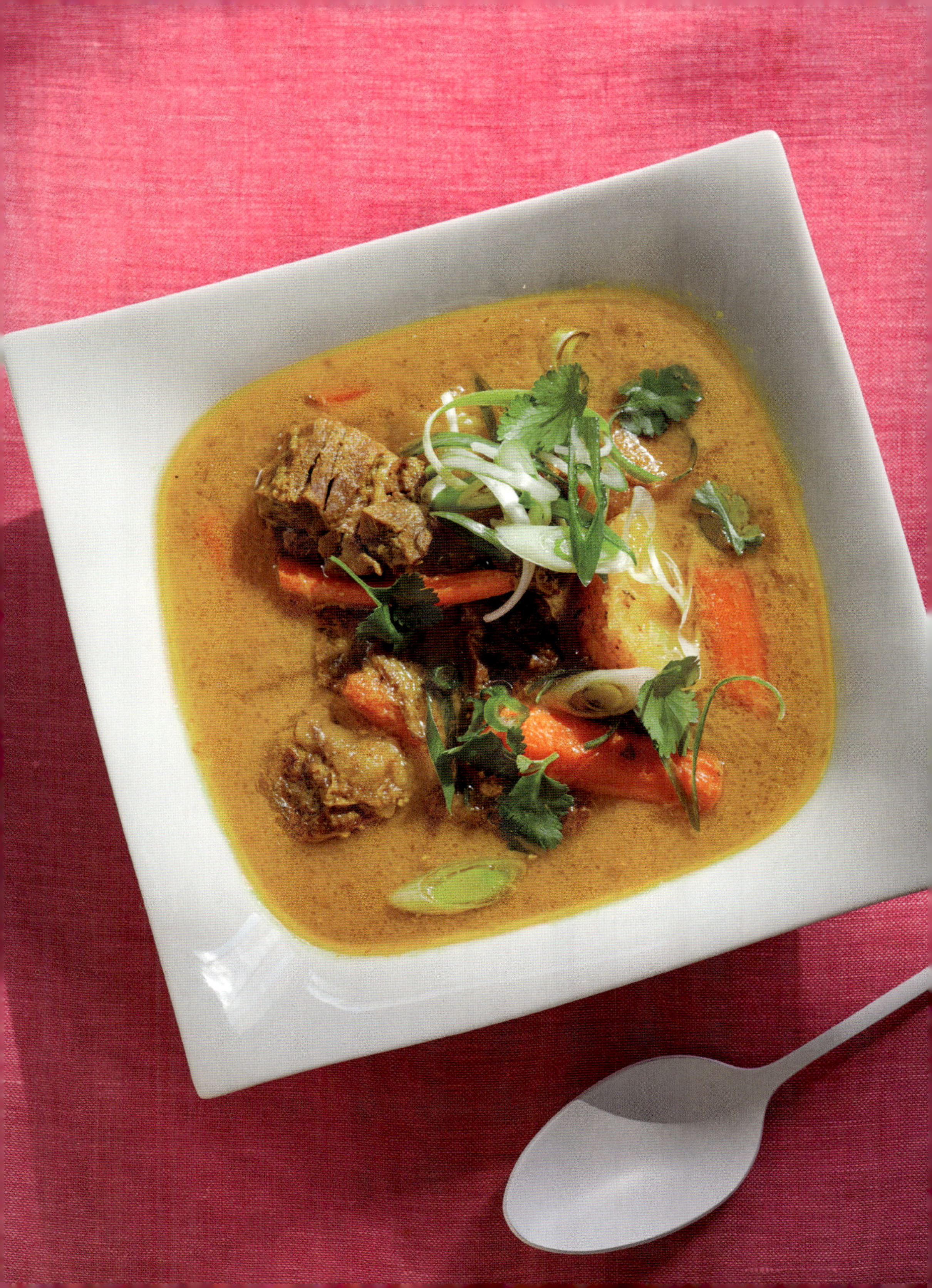

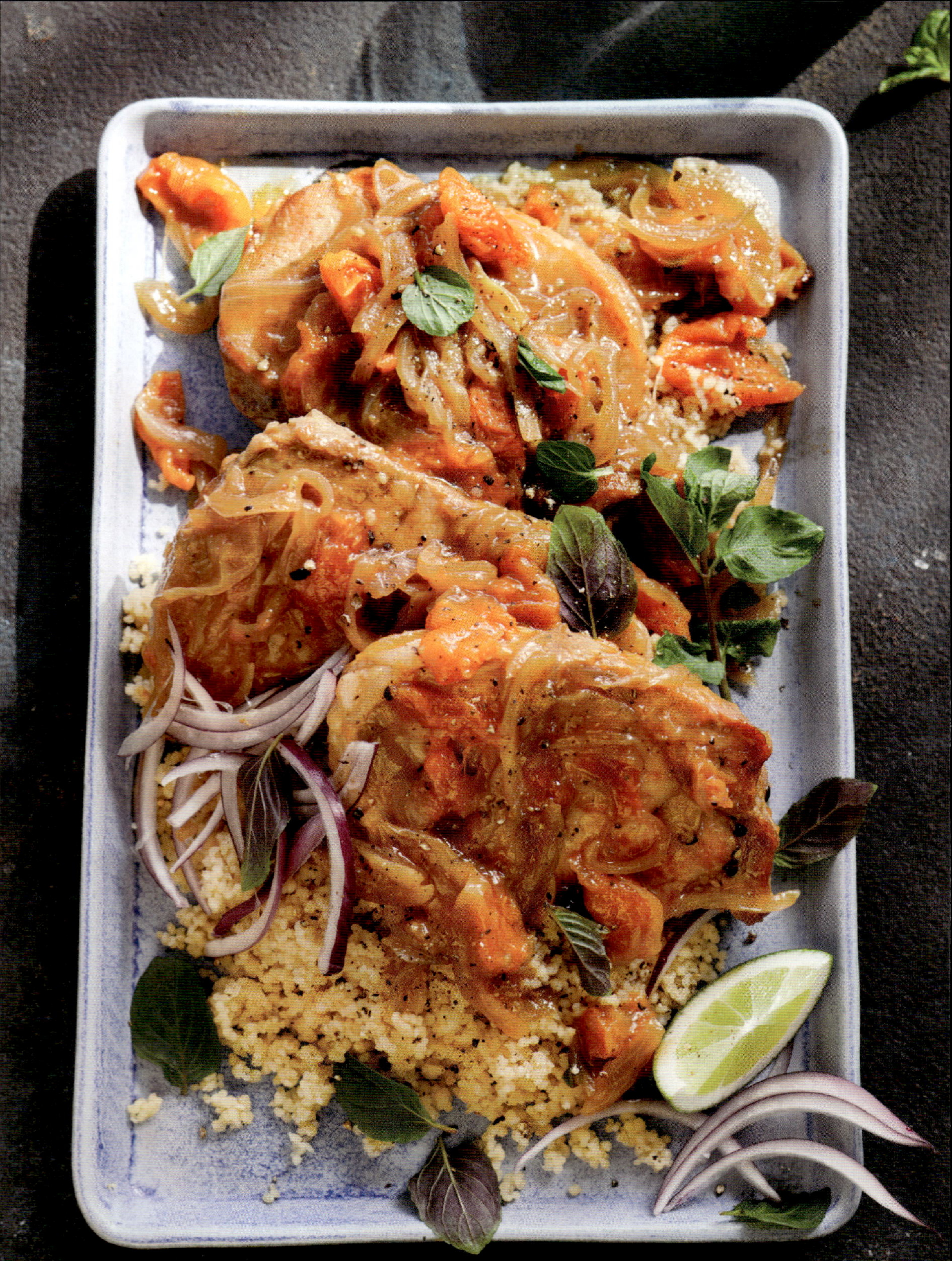

Marrakesh-style pork

Prep 18 min   Cook 3 to 8 hr   Serves 4

Slow-cooked pork chops get a sweet-tart smothering of onion with apricots and ginger in this North African–inspired dish.

2	tsp olive oil
4	(¼-lb) lean boneless pork chops, trimmed
1	tsp kosher salt, divided
¼	tsp black pepper
1	large red onion, quartered and thinly sliced
12	dried apricots, cut into ¼-inch strips
¾	cup unsweetened apple juice
2	tsp minced peeled ginger
1½	tsp chopped fresh thyme (or ½ tsp dried)
1	(3-inch) cinnamon stick
¼	cup cilantro or mint leaves
	Thinly sliced red onion

1. In a large heavy nonstick skillet over medium-high heat, warm oil. Sprinkle pork chops with ½ tsp salt and black pepper. To skillet, add pork and cook until browned, about 2 minutes per side. Transfer to a plate.

2. Reduce heat to medium. To skillet, add onion and sprinkle with remaining ½ tsp salt. Cook, stirring, until onion is golden, about 8 minutes. In a 5- or 6-qt slow cooker, combine half of onion and half of apricots. Top with pork chops and pour apple juice over. Mix together remaining onion, apricots, ginger, and thyme in a medium bowl. Spoon over pork and tuck in cinnamon stick.

3. Cover and cook until pork is fork-tender, 3 to 4 hours on High or 6 to 8 hours on Low. Remove and discard cinnamon. Serve sprinkled with cilantro and onion.

Per serving (1 pork chop and ⅓ cup onion mixture): 247 Cal, 9 g Total Fat, 3 g Sat Fat, 546 mg Sod, 16 g Total Carb, 12 g Sugar, 2 g Fib, 25 g Prot.

Serving idea
Make this dish more authentic by serving it atop whole-wheat couscous, with unsweetened mint tea on the side.

Teriyaki pork tenderloin

Prep 24 min   Cook 2½ to 3 hr   Serves 4

This 5-ingredient teriyaki sauce is so much better than anything you'll find in the supermarket, and it only takes a few minutes to prep. Make a double-batch to use on chicken or fish; it will keep in your fridge for up to 2 months.

- 1 tbsp canola oil
- 1 (1-lb) lean pork tenderloin, trimmed
- ½ cup reduced-sodium chicken broth
- ¼ cup soy sauce
- 1 tbsp seasoned rice vinegar
- 1 tbsp brown sugar
- 1 tbsp minced peeled ginger
- 2 garlic cloves, minced
- 2 tsp toasted sesame seeds
- Purple basil leaves (optional)

1. In a large heavy nonstick skillet over medium-high heat, warm oil. Add pork and cook until browned on all sides, about 6 minutes. Transfer to a 5- or 6-qt slow cooker. To skillet, add broth and bring to a boil, scraping up browned bits from bottom of pan. Add to slow cooker.

2. In a small bowl, stir together soy sauce, vinegar, brown sugar, ginger, and garlic and pour over pork. Cover and cook until an instant-read thermometer inserted into thickest part of pork registers 145°F, 2½ to 3 hours on Low.

3. Transfer pork to a cutting board and let stand 5 minutes. Cut into 8 slices. Place 2 slices pork on each of 4 plates; sprinkle with sesame seeds and drizzle with juices in cooker. Garnish with basil leaves, if desired.

Per serving (2 slices pork and 3 tbsp sauce): 184 Cal, 7 g Total Fat, 1 g Sat Fat, 1,002 mg Sod, 4 g Total Carb, 2 g Sugar, 0 g Fib, 26 g Prot.

Serving idea

Jasmine rice sprinkled with thinly sliced scallion and 2 tsp toasted sesame seeds complements the pork nicely.

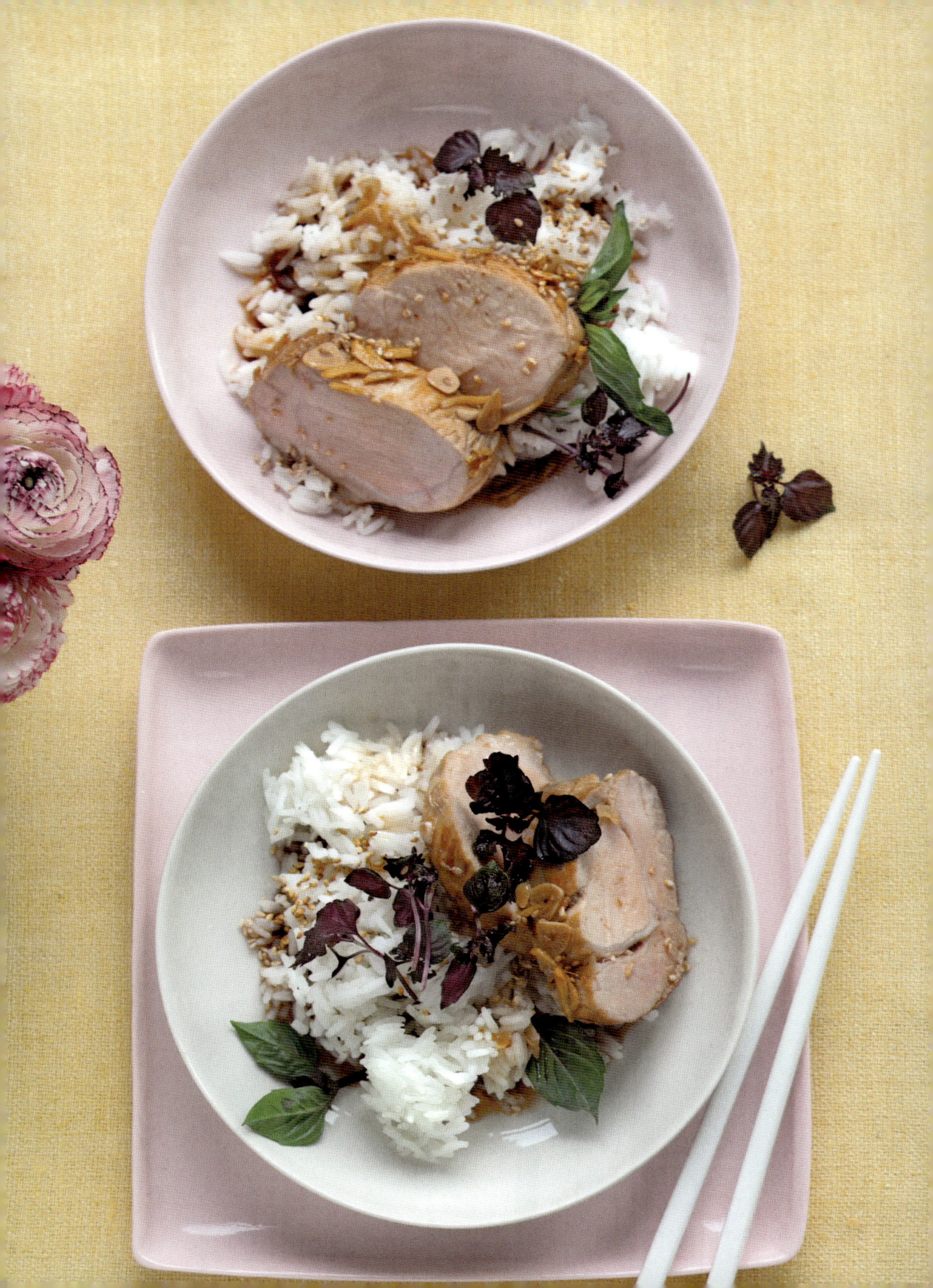

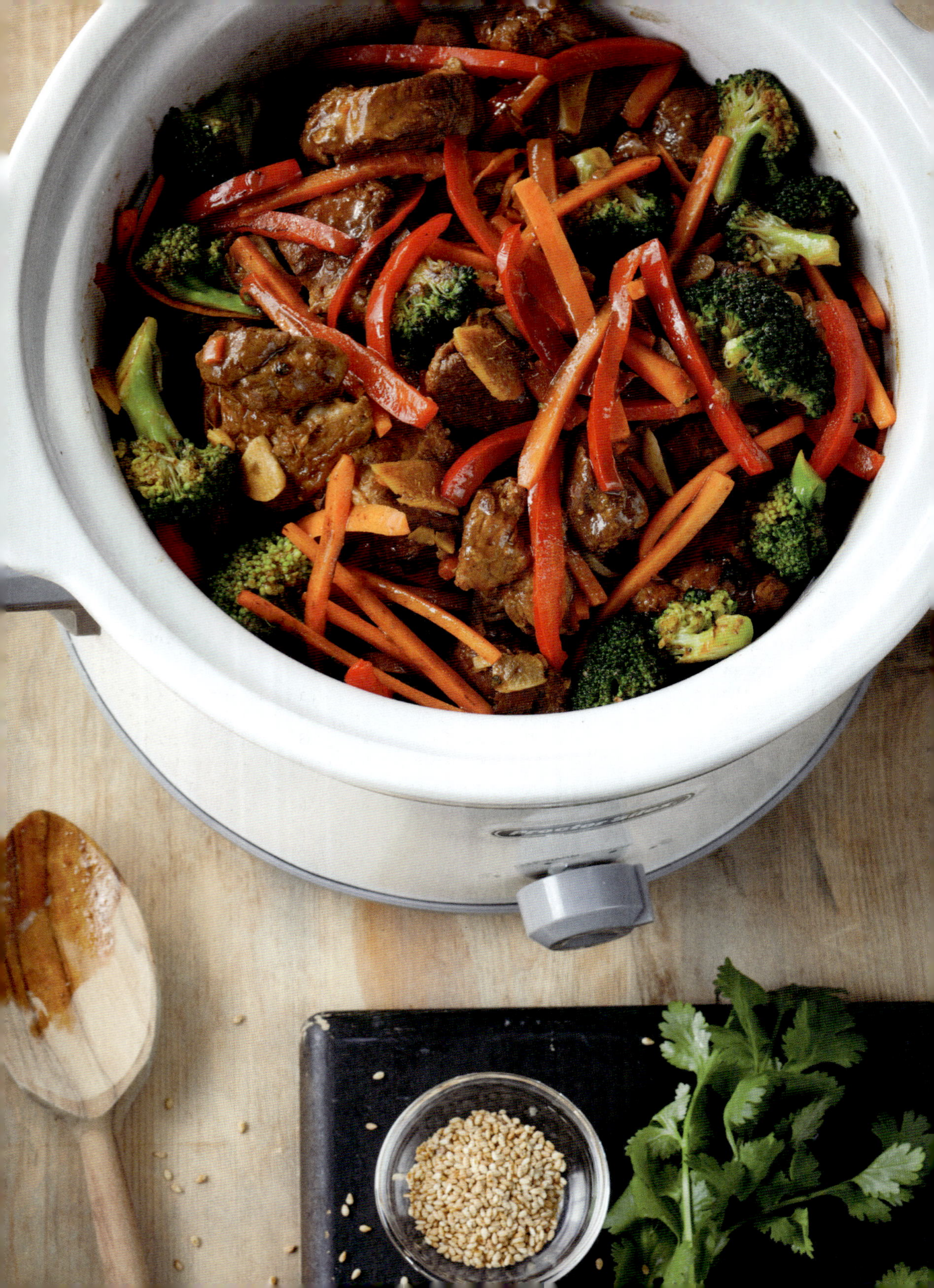

Five-spice pork stew

Prep 15 min   Cook 5 to 11 hr   Serves 6

Five-spice powder is a punchy combination of Szechuan peppercorns, star anise, whole cloves, cinnamon, and fennel seeds. To make things easy, use a store-bought mix.

1	(1½-lb) lean boneless pork loin roast, trimmed and cut into 1½-inch chunks
1	cup (¼-inch-thick) matchstick-cut carrots
1	(2-inch) piece ginger, peeled and minced
6	garlic cloves, minced
1	tsp five-spice powder
1½	cups chicken broth
¼	cup hoisin sauce
2	tbsp soy sauce
1	tbsp cornstarch
1	(16-oz) bag frozen broccoli stir-fry vegetables
2	tsp toasted sesame seeds

1 In a 5- or 6-qt slow cooker, combine pork, carrots, ginger, garlic, and five-spice powder. In a large glass measure, whisk together broth and hoisin sauce; pour over pork and vegetables. Cover and cook until pork is fork-tender, 4 to 5 hours on High or 8 to 10 hours on Low.

2 With a slotted spoon, transfer pork to a medium bowl; cover to keep warm.

3 In a small bowl, whisk together soy sauce and cornstarch until smooth. Whisk into slow cooker. Cover and cook until mixture simmers, about 10 minutes on High. Stir in stir-fry vegetables. Cover and cook until vegetables are tender, about 45 minutes. Return pork to slow cooker and cook until heated through, about 10 minutes more. Serve sprinkled with sesame seeds.

Per serving (about 1 cup): 255 Cal, 8 g Total Fat, 3 g Sat Fat, 768 mg Sod, 16 g Total Carb, 6 g Sugar, 3 g Fib, 29 g Prot.

Serving idea
Cooked brown or white long-grain rice makes a solid base for this stew.

Global favorites

Sausage, chicken, and shrimp stew

Prep 30 min   Cook 3⅓ to 4⅓ hr   Serves 6

This Cajun slow-cooker stew brings together sausage, chicken, and shrimp—there's even okra for variety!

1	tbsp olive oil
½	lb Italian-style turkey sausages, sliced
1	red bell pepper, diced
1	yellow bell pepper, diced
1	onion, chopped
1	celery stalk, diced
2	tbsp all-purpose flour
1	cup reduced-sodium chicken broth
1	lb skinless boneless chicken breasts, cut into 1½-inch chunks
1	(14½-oz) can diced tomatoes
2	tsp Cajun seasoning (or to taste)
½	lb large shrimp, peeled and deveined
1	(10-oz) box frozen cut okra, thawed
3	scallions, thinly sliced
	Hot pepper sauce

1 In a large heavy nonstick skillet over medium-high heat, warm oil. Add sausages and cook, turning, until browned, about 3 minutes. Transfer to a 5- or 6-qt slow cooker.

2 Reduce heat to medium. Add bell peppers, onion, and celery; cook, stirring, until softened, about 5 minutes. Sprinkle flour over vegetables and cook, stirring, 1 minute. Stir in broth and bring to a boil, scraping up browned bits from bottom of pan. Reduce heat and simmer 3 minutes. Transfer to slow cooker.

3 Add chicken, tomatoes, and Cajun seasoning to slow cooker, stirring to mix well. Cover and cook until chicken is cooked through and vegetables are tender, 3 to 4 hours on Low. Taste and season with additional Cajun seasoning, if desired.

4 Add shrimp and okra to slow cooker, stirring to mix well. Cover and cook until shrimp are just opaque in center, about 20 minutes longer. Sprinkle stew with scallions and serve with hot sauce.

Per serving (1⅓ cups): 184 Cal, 6 g Total Fat, 1 g Sat Fat, 996 mg Sod, 10 g Total Carb, 4 g Sugar, 2 g Fib, 23 g Prot.

Shopping tip
You could use fresh okra in this recipe, but we use the frozen version to make it simpler and cut back on prep time.

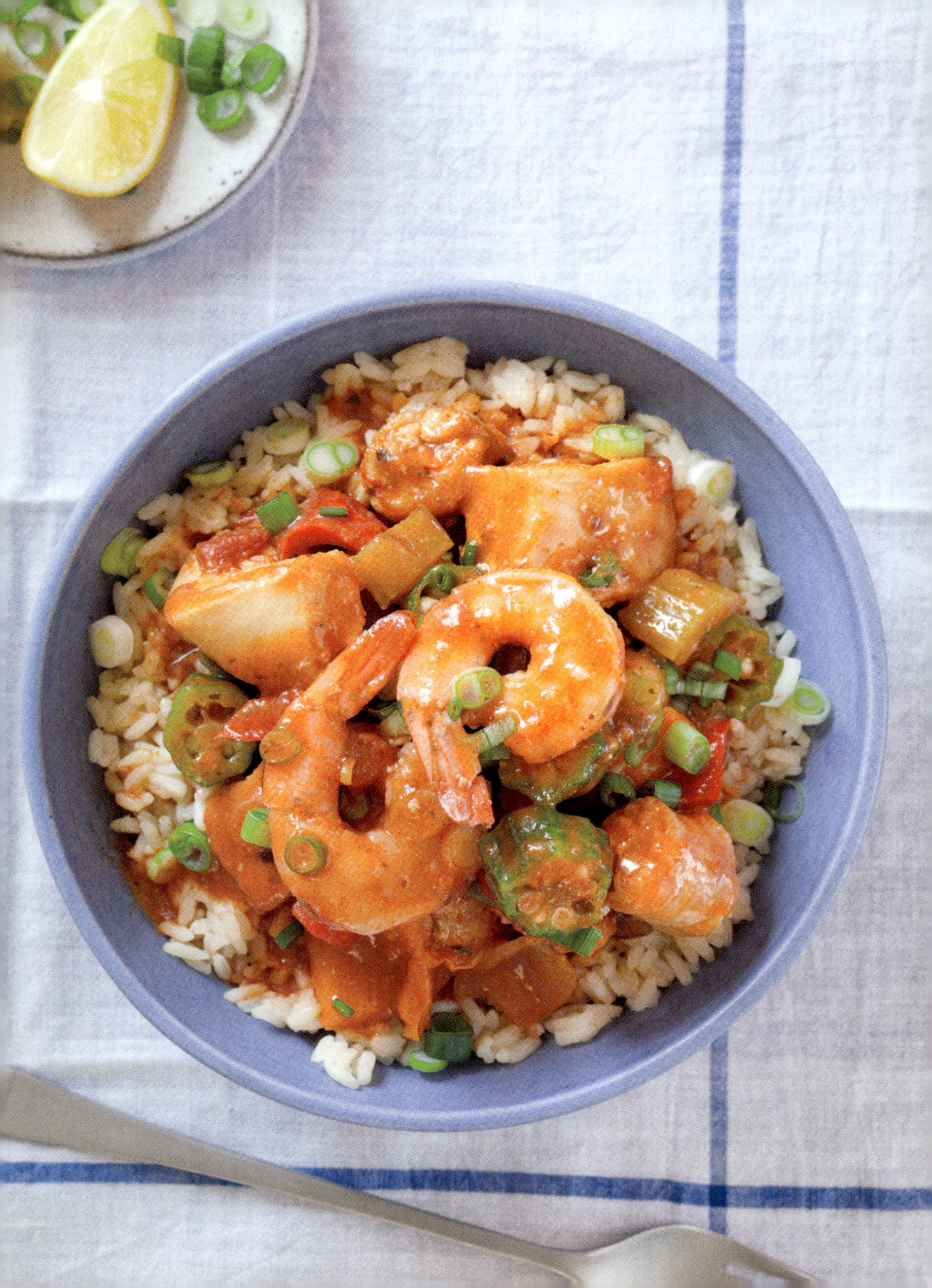

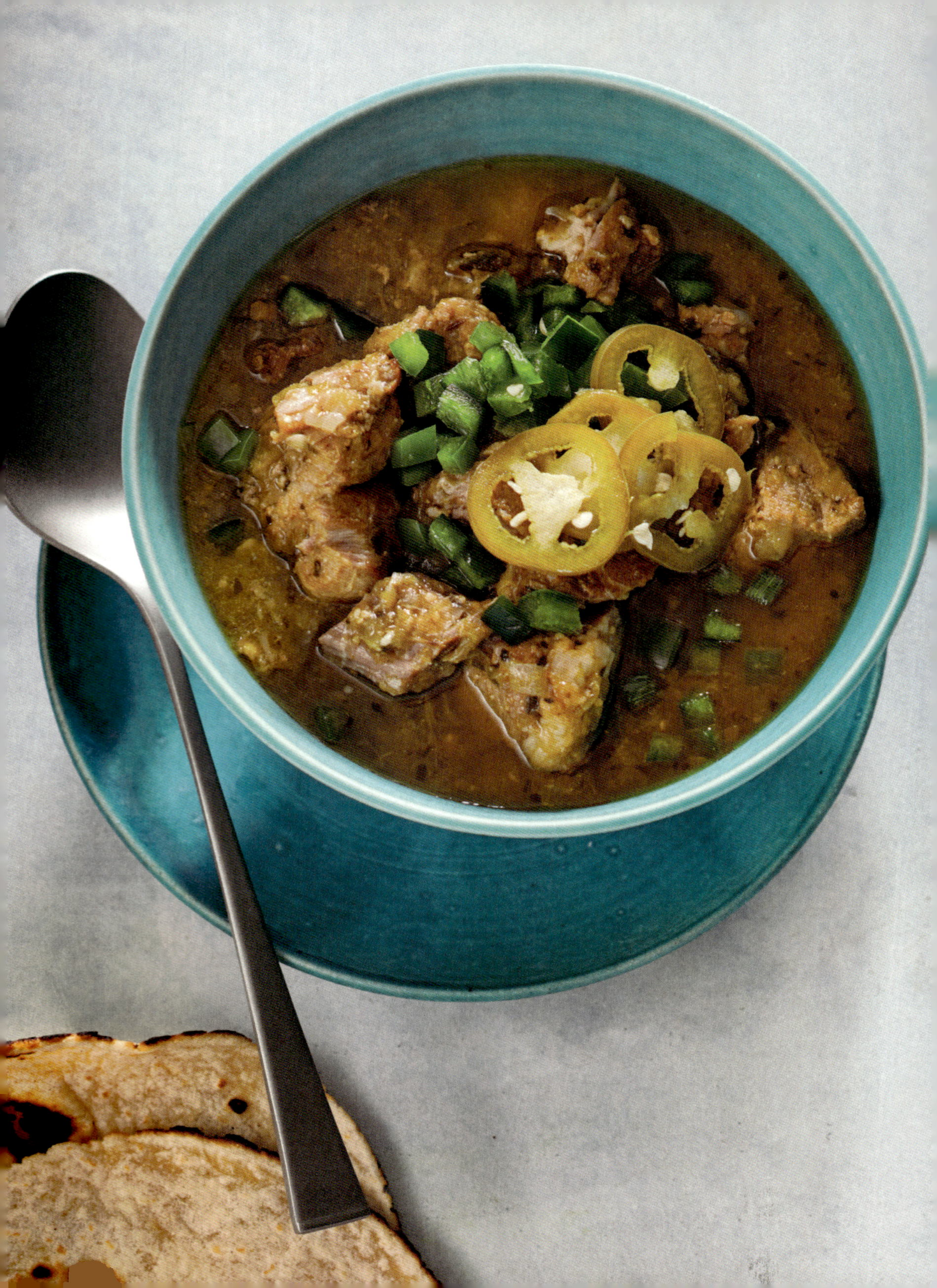

Pork in green chile sauce

Prep 35 min   Cook 2½ to 6 hr   Serves 4

Green chile sauce is excellent with pork and a nice change of pace from the usual tomato-based sauces. Tomatillos bring a bright acidity to our version.

Nonstick spray
1½ lb fresh tomatillos, papery skin removed, halved
1 large onion, cut into 1-inch pieces
2 poblano peppers, seeded and cut into 1-inch pieces
2 jalapeño peppers, halved lengthwise (seeds left in)
6 garlic cloves, peeled
2 tsp ground cumin
1½ tsp dried oregano
¾ tsp salt
¼ tsp black pepper
1½ lb lean boneless center-cut pork roast, trimmed and cut into 1½-inch chunks
½ cup chicken broth
⅔ cup chopped cilantro
½ cup chopped green bell pepper
⅓ cup sliced pickled jalapeño peppers (or to taste)

1 Preheat oven to 425°F. Line a large rimmed baking sheet with foil.

2 On prepared baking sheet, toss together tomatillos, onion, poblanos, jalapeños, and garlic. Spray vegetables with nonstick spray and toss until coated evenly; spread to form an even layer. Roast until vegetables are softened and browned, about 20 minutes. Transfer to a blender, in batches if necessary, and process until fairly smooth.

3 Meanwhile, in a cup, stir together cumin, oregano, salt, and black pepper. Sprinkle all over pork. Generously spray a large heavy nonstick skillet with nonstick spray and set over medium-high heat. Add half of pork and cook, turning occasionally, until browned on all sides, 4 to 5 minutes. Transfer to a 5- or 6-qt slow cooker. Repeat with remaining pork.

4 To skillet, add broth and bring to boil, scraping up browned bits from bottom of pan. Pour into slow cooker, along with tomatillo-chile sauce, stirring to coat pork. Cover and cook until pork is fork-tender, 2½ to 3 hours on High or 5 to 6 hours on Low. Stir in cilantro. Spoon pork and tomatillo-chile sauce evenly onto 4 plates or into bowls. Sprinkle with bell pepper and pickled peppers.

Serving idea
Corn tortillas that have been heated in a dry heavy skillet until lightly charred in spots are ideal with this dish.

Per serving (generous 1 cup): 350 Cal, 12 g Total Fat, 4 g Sat Fat, 766 mg Sod, 22 g Total Carb, 11 g Sugar, 6 g Fib, 40 g Prot.

Indian fish curry

Prep 25 min   Cook 3⅓–8⅓ hr   Serves 6

We've simplified the ingredient list (but kept all the Indian flavors) for this slow cooker curry, which works well with halibut or salmon.

4	tsp canola oil
1	onion, chopped
1	tbsp brown mustard seeds
3	large garlic cloves, minced
1	tbsp grated peeled ginger
4	small hot green chile peppers, such as Thai, seeded and minced, divided
2	tbsp Madras curry powder
1	tbsp tomato paste
2	cups chicken or vegetable broth
1	(14½-oz) can diced tomatoes
2	large carrots, diced
2	celery stalks, diced
1	tsp kosher salt, divided
2	lb halibut or salmon fillets, cut into 1½-inch chunks

Curry leaves (optional)

1 In a large skillet over medium heat, warm oil. Add onion and mustard seeds and cook, stirring occasionally, until onion is golden, about 8 minutes. Add garlic, ginger, and 3 chiles and cook, stirring frequently, until fragrant, about 1 minute. Add curry powder and tomato paste and cook, stirring frequently, until fragrant, about 1 minute longer. Add broth and bring to a boil, stirring to scrape up browned bits from bottom of pan.

2 Transfer broth mixture to a 5- or 6-qt slow cooker. Stir in tomatoes, carrots, celery, and ½ tsp salt. Cover; cook until vegetables are tender, 3 to 4 hours on High or 6 to 8 hours on Low.

3 Sprinkle halibut with remaining ½ tsp salt. Add to slow cooker, stirring gently to coat fish with liquid. Cover and cook until fish is just opaque in center, about 20 minutes on Low. Ladle evenly into 6 bowls. Garnish with curry leaves, if using.

Per serving (1⅓ cups): 221 Cal, 6 g Total Fat, 1 g Sat Fat, 875 mg Sod, 12 g Total Carb, 6 g Sugar, 3 g Fib, 31 g Prot.

Serving idea
Naan, a tasty flatbread available in supermarkets, is the perfect addition to this curry.

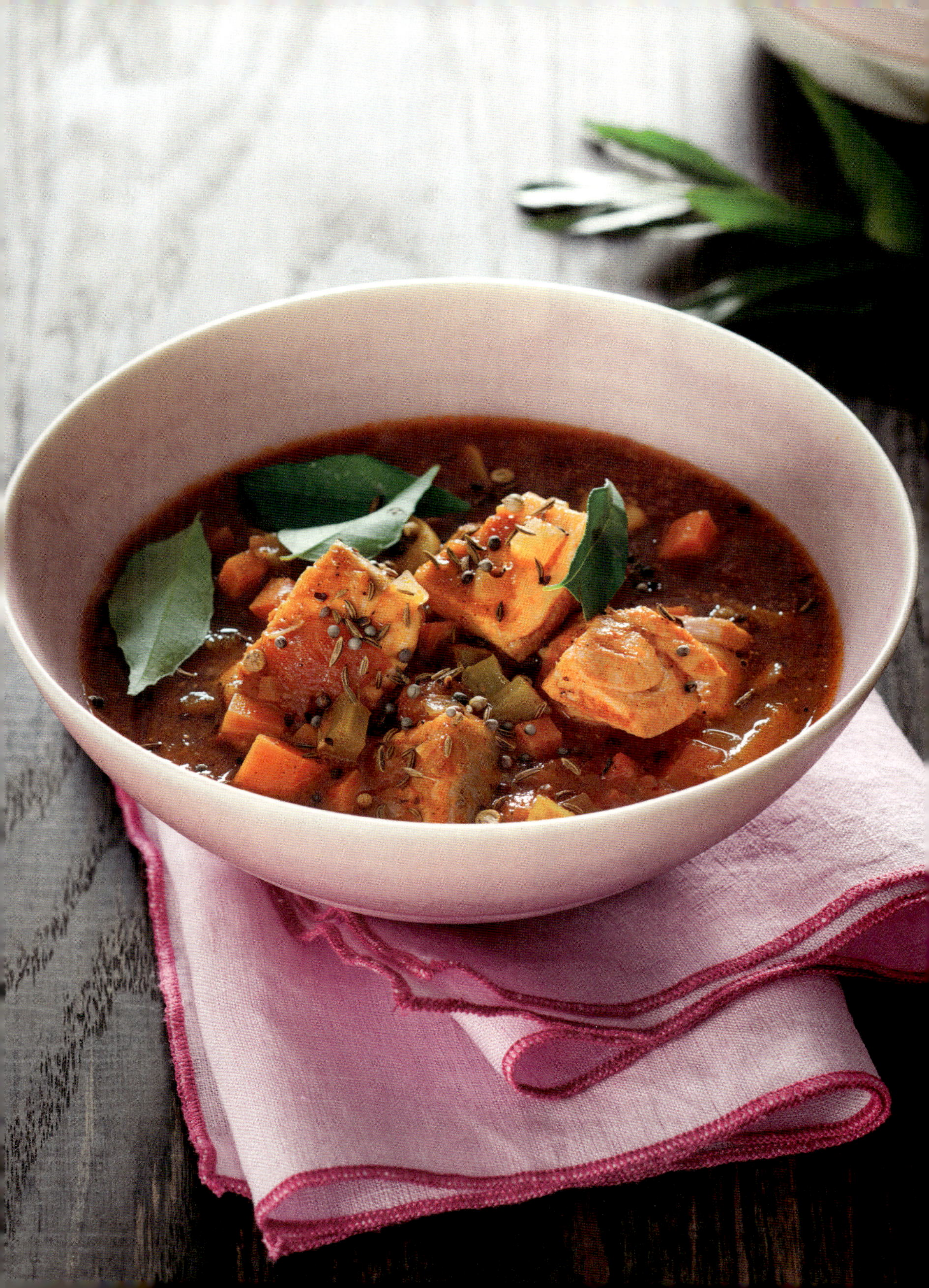

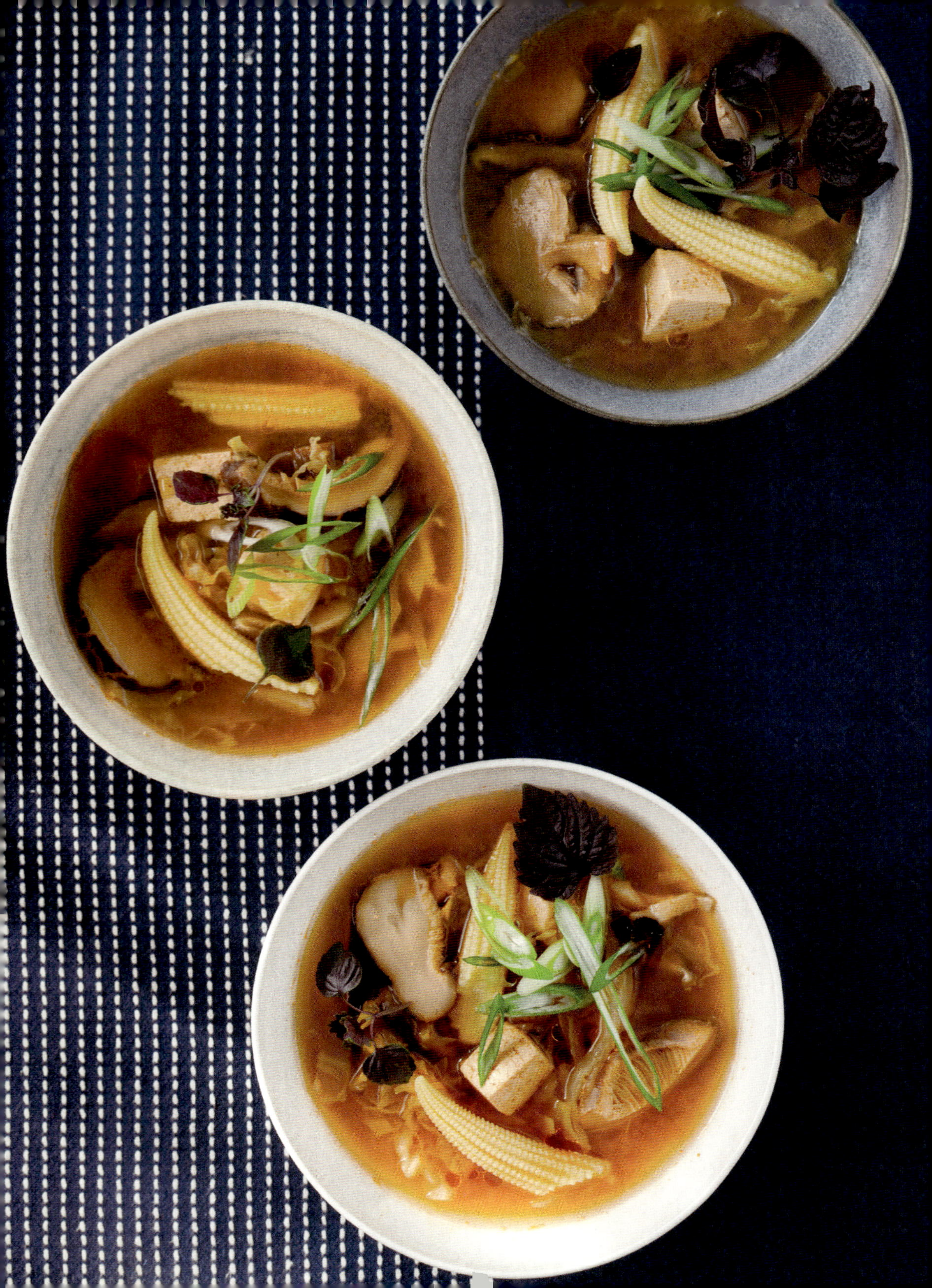

Hot-and-sour soup with shiitakes and tofu

Prep 20 min Standing time 20 min Cook 3 to 8 hr Serves 8

Shiitake mushrooms and tofu get a strong dose of heat from black pepper plus sriracha and a punch of sour from rice vinegar.

1	oz dried shiitake mushrooms
4	cups tightly packed thinly sliced green cabbage
6	oz fresh shiitake mushrooms, stems removed and caps sliced
2	tbsp soy sauce (or to taste)
¼	cup rice vinegar
4	tsp sriracha
1	tbsp minced peeled ginger
2	(32-oz) cartons vegetable broth
3	large eggs, lightly beaten
1	(15-oz) can baby corn, drained
1	(14-oz) package firm tofu, drained and diced
1	tbsp dark sesame oil
½	tsp black pepper
3	scallions, thinly sliced

Purple basil leaves (optional)

1 In a small bowl, combine dried mushrooms and 1 cup boiling water. Let stand until mushrooms are softened, about 20 minutes. Pour off water. Snip off mushroom stems and discard; slice mushroom caps.

2 In a 5- or 6-qt slow cooker, mix together cabbage, shiitakes, soy sauce, vinegar, sriracha, and ginger in a 5- or 6-qt slow cooker. Pour broth over. Cover and cook until vegetables are tender, 3 to 4 hours on High or 6 to 8 hours on Low.

3 To slow cooker, add eggs in a slow, steady stream, stirring constantly to form threads. Stir in corn, tofu, sesame oil, and black pepper. Cover and cook until corn is heated through, about 5 minutes on High. Ladle soup evenly into 8 bowls and sprinkle with scallions and basil leaves, if using.

Per serving (about 1¾ cups): 176 Cal, 8 g Total Fat, 1 g Sat Fat, 1,071 mg Sod, 16 g Total Carb, 4 g Sugar, 6 g Fib, 14 g Prot.

Cooking tip
Upgrade to a heartier main dish by stirring in 1 lb of cooked peeled and deveined medium shrimp along with the corn.

Global favorites

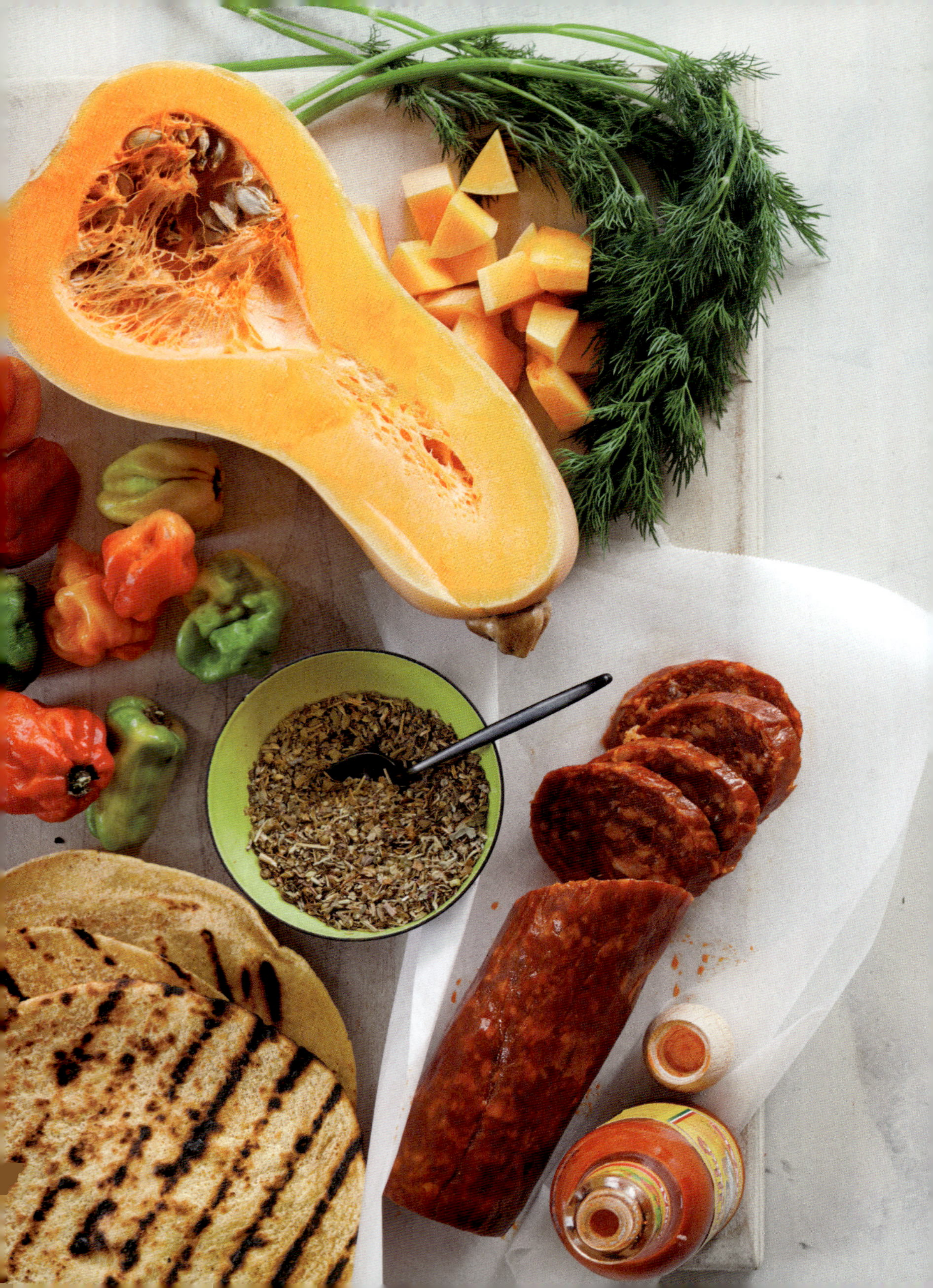

Chapter 5

Meals for 2

All these recipes are designed for a 2-qt slow cooker. If you only have a larger-size machine, double or triple the recipe because a slow cooker needs to be filled at least halfway for the best results.

Classic chicken cacciatore 150
Basque chicken with chorizo and peppers 153
Chicken tikka masala 154
Provençal-style beef stew 157
Carne guisada with charred tortillas 158
Lamb tagine with lemon and olives 161
Bouillabaisse 162
Vegetable bolognese 165
Cauliflower paprikash 166
Soft polenta with pecorino and mushrooms 169

Classic chicken cacciatore

Prep 10 min   Cook 2½ to 6 hr   Serves 2

The little bit of red wine in this dish makes a difference flavor-wise. But if you've got an open bottle of dry white hanging around, feel free to use that instead.

1	cup canned crushed tomatoes
¼	cup dry red wine
1	tbsp tomato paste
1	large garlic clove, minced
½	tsp dried oregano
½	tsp kosher salt (or to taste)
⅛	tsp black pepper
2	(5-oz) bone-in chicken thighs, skin removed
1	cup thickly sliced cremini mushrooms
1	small red or green bell pepper, thinly sliced
1	small onion, chopped
8	pitted green olives, quartered
1	tbsp coarsely chopped flat-leaf parsley

Grated zest of ½ lemon

In a 2-qt slow cooker, stir together tomatoes, wine, tomato paste, garlic, oregano, salt, and black pepper. Add chicken, mushrooms, bell pepper, and onion, stirring to combine. Cover and cook until chicken is fork-tender, 2½ to 3 hours on High or 5 to 6 hours on Low. Serve sprinkled with olives, parsley, and lemon zest.

Per serving (1 chicken thigh and about 1 cup vegetables with sauce): 286 Cal, 8 g Total Fat, 2 g Sat Fat, 1,077 mg Sod, 16 g Total Carb, 8 g Sugar, 4 g Fib, 33 g Prot.

Serving idea
Put some greens on your plate with a side of steamed broccoli rabe or Brussels sprouts.

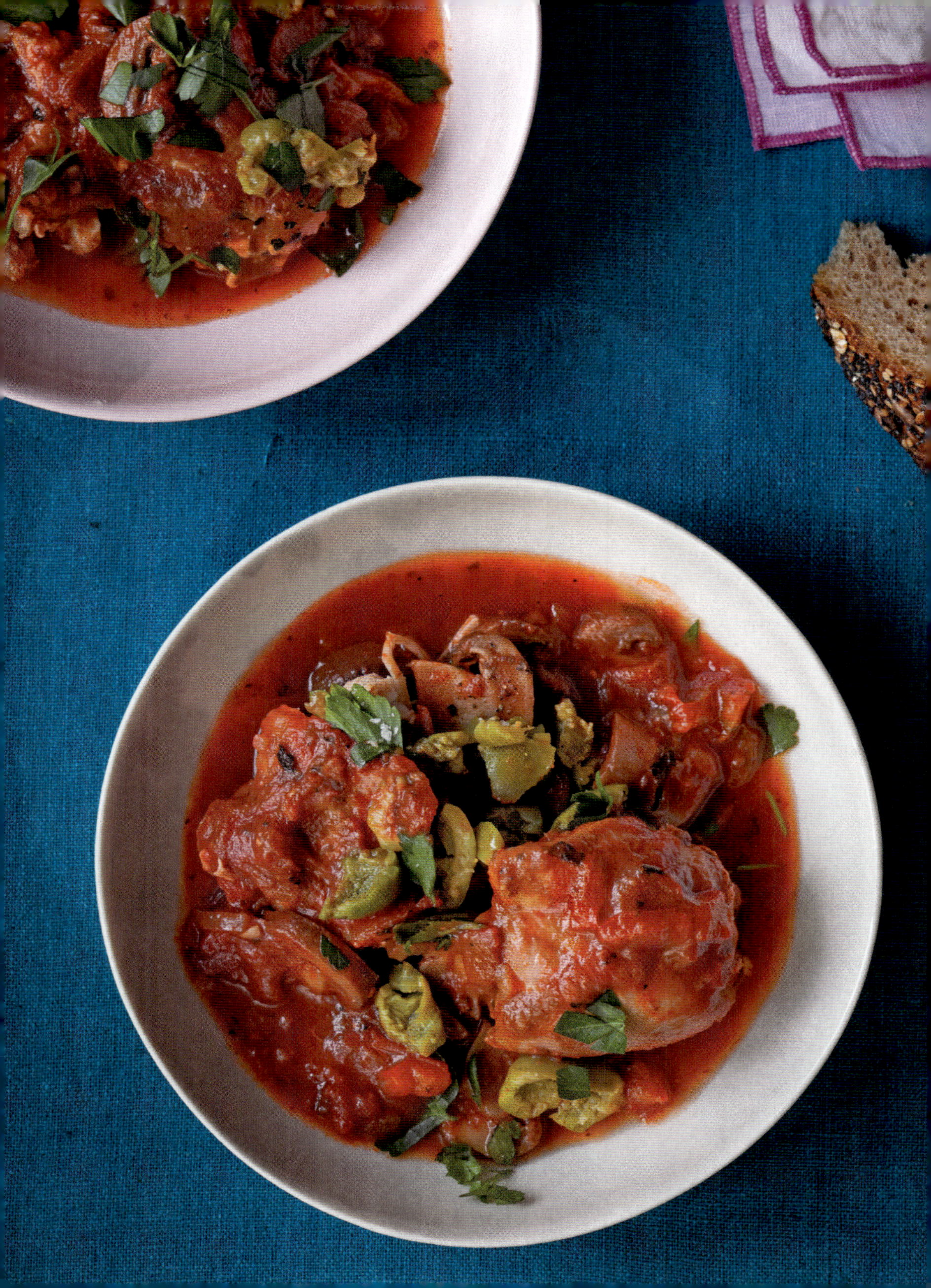

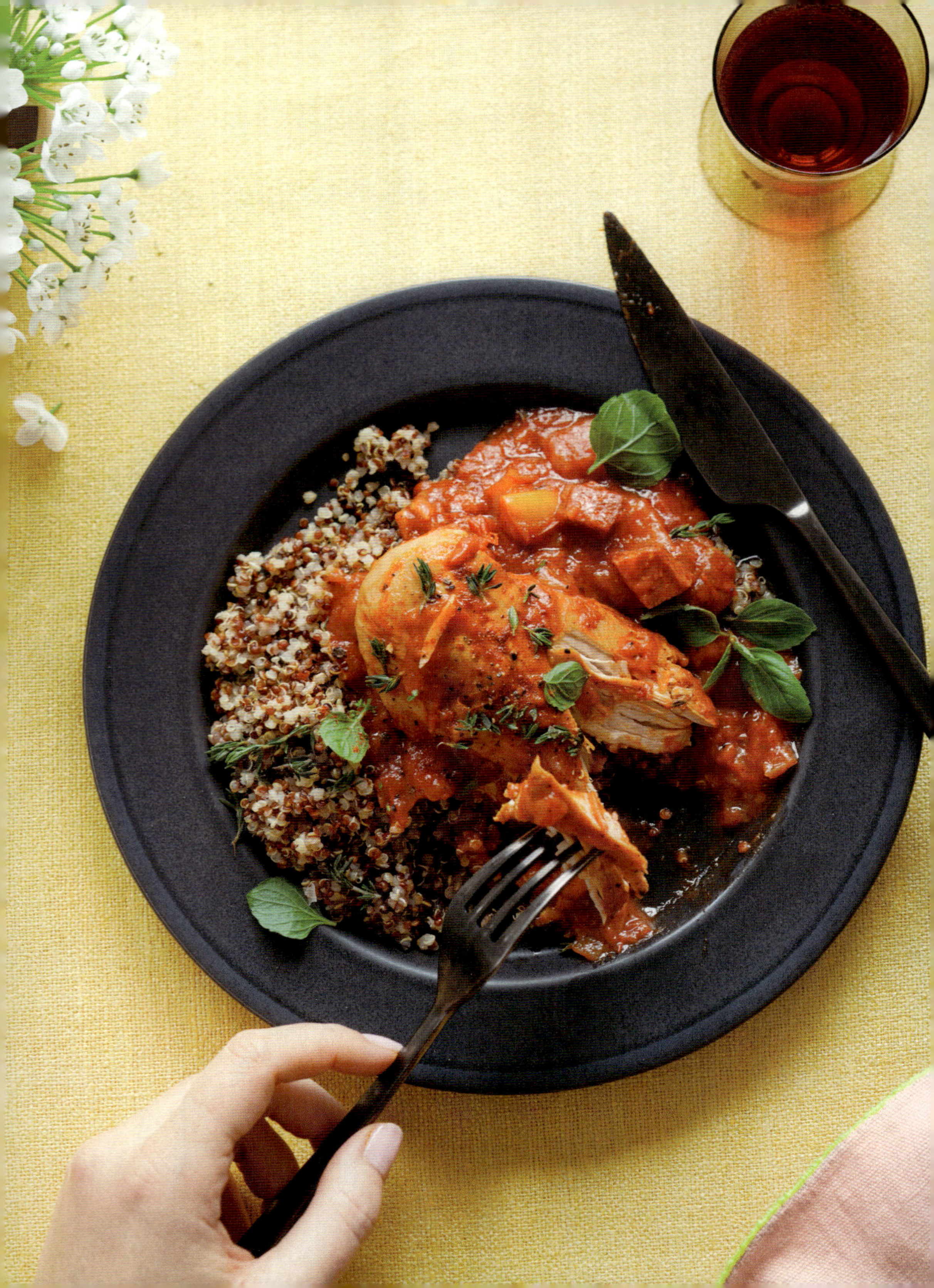

Basque chicken with chorizo and peppers

Prep 10 min   Cook 3 to 8 hr   Serves 2

The Basque region of northern Spain is home to almost 40 Michelin-starred restaurants. These people *know* good food. Our chicken dish highlights plenty of Basque ingredients, including chorizo, bell peppers, and smoked paprika.

1	cup canned diced fire-roasted tomatoes with juice
1	tbsp tomato paste
¾	tsp smoked paprika
½	tsp kosher salt
⅛	tsp black pepper
1	small onion, chopped
1	celery stalk, sliced
¼	cup chopped chorizo
2	(6-oz) skinless boneless chicken breasts
1	small yellow bell pepper, chopped
1½	tsp cornmeal

Thyme leaves

Basil leaves

1 In a 2-qt slow cooker, mix together tomatoes, 2 tbsp water, tomato paste, paprika, salt, and black pepper. Stir in onion, celery, and chorizo; top with chicken and bell pepper. Cover and cook until chicken and vegetables are fork-tender, 3 to 4 hours on High or 6 to 8 hours on Low.

2 About 20 minutes before cooking time is up, slowly stir cornmeal into slow cooker. Cover and cook until mixture thickens. Serve sprinkled with thyme and basil.

Per serving (1 chicken breast and 1¼ cups vegetables with sauce): 319 Cal, 9 g Total Fat, 3 g Sat Fat, 953 mg Sod, 15 g Total Carb, 7 g Sugar, 4 g Fib, 43 g Prot.

Serving idea
Quinoa, a good-for-you whole grain, is a heartier alternative to rice.

Chicken tikka masala

Prep 5 min   Cook 2 to 6 hr   Serves 2

Our slow cooker version of chicken tikka masala (aka butter chicken) uses Greek yogurt for creaminess, along with classic spices like garam masala, cumin, and coriander.

- ½ cup canned crushed tomatoes
- 1 small shallot, finely chopped
- 1 small garlic clove, minced
- 1 tsp grated peeled ginger
- 1¼ tsp garam masala
- ½ tsp dark brown sugar
- ½ tsp kosher salt
- ¼ tsp ground cumin
- ⅛ tsp ground coriander
- 2 (¼-lb) skinless boneless chicken thighs
- 2 tbsp plain low-fat Greek yogurt
- 2 tbsp chopped cilantro, plus sprigs for garnish
- Thinly sliced red onion

1. In a 2-qt slow cooker, stir together tomatoes, shallot, garlic, ginger, garam masala, brown sugar, salt, cumin, and coriander. Add chicken. Cover and cook 2 to 3 hours on High or 4 to 6 hours on Low. Stir in yogurt and chopped cilantro.

2. Divide evenly between 2 plates or shallow bowls. Garnish with cilantro sprigs and onion.

Per serving (1 chicken thigh and about ½ cup sauce): 172 Cal, 5 g Total Fat, 1 g Sat Fat, 684 mg Sod, 6 g Total Carb, 4 g Sugar, 1 g Fib, 25 g Prot.

Serving idea

Warm naan bread can swap in for traditional rice as a side for this classic Indian dish.

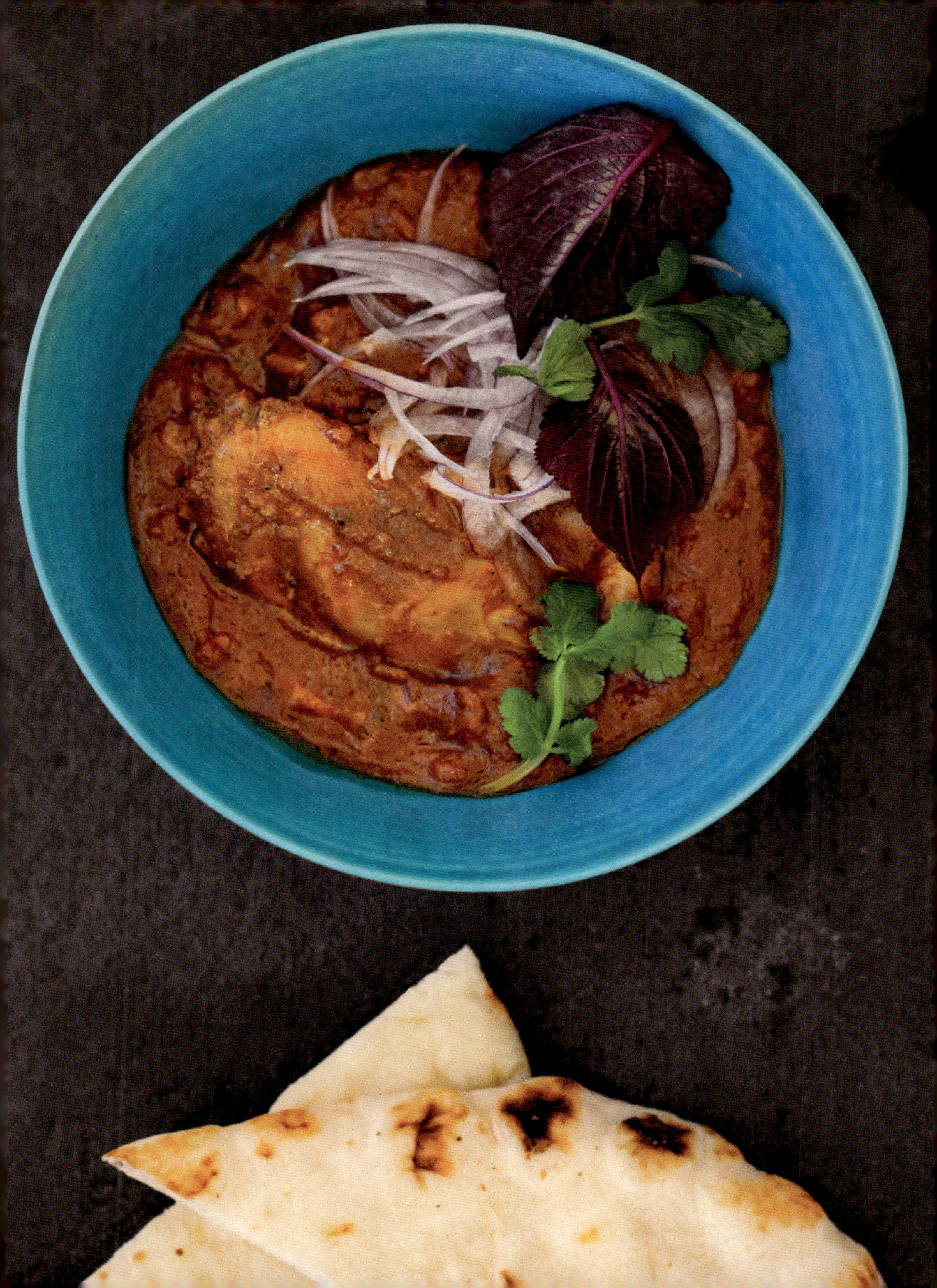

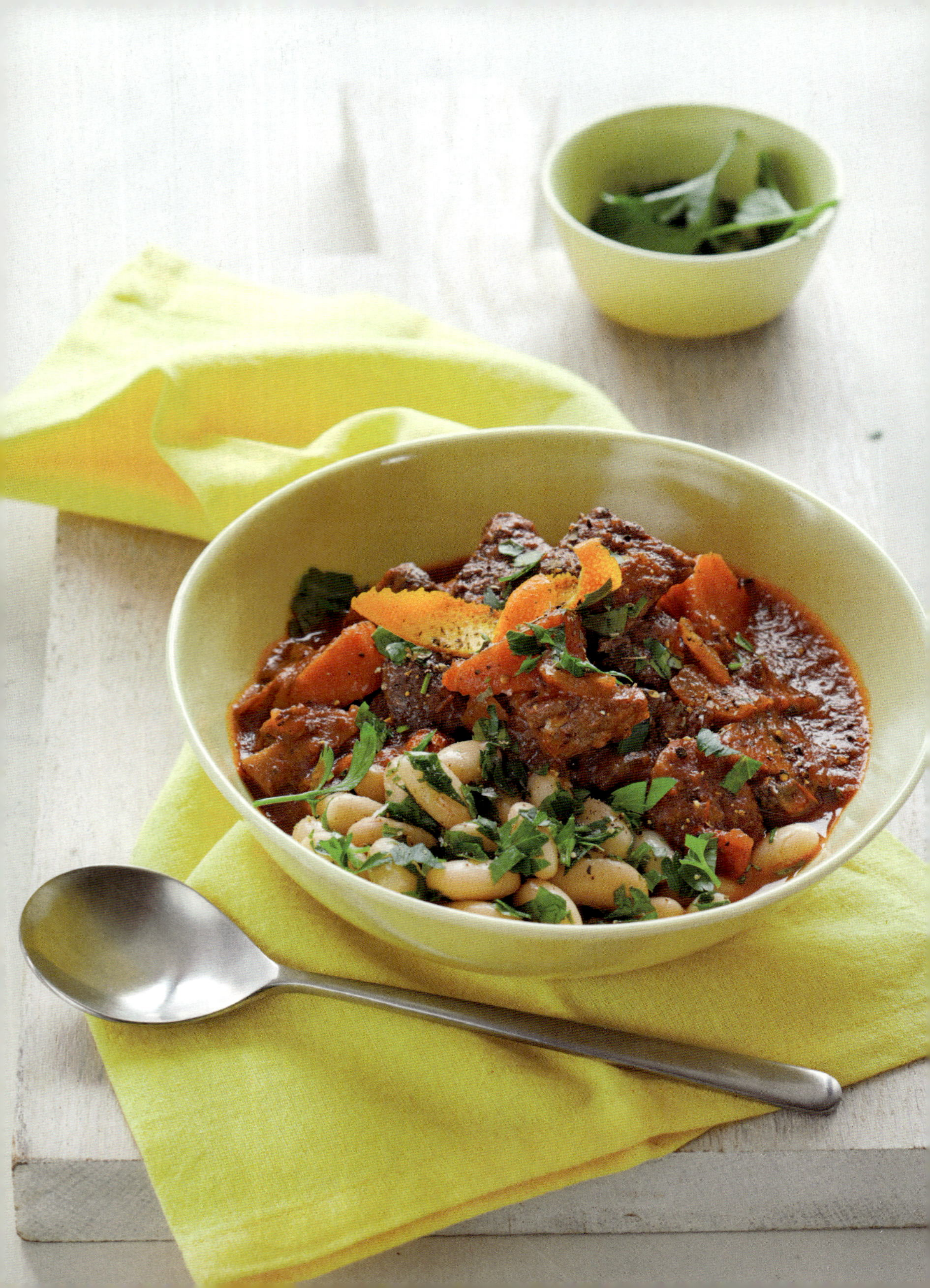

Provençal-style beef stew

Prep 30 min   Cook 3 to 8 hr   Serves 2

If you don't have herbes de Provence, you can substitute a mix of equal parts dried thyme, rosemary, and fennel seeds. The herbs, along with the wine, orange zest, and vegetables, give this beef stew the taste of southern France.

1½	tsp olive oil, divided
1	carrot, thickly sliced
1	small onion, coarsely chopped
1	large garlic clove, minced
⅓	cup dry red wine
½	lb lean boneless beef bottom round, trimmed and cut into 1-inch chunks
1	cup canned diced tomatoes with juice
2	(3-inch) strips orange zest
1	small bay leaf
½	tsp herbes de Provence
¼	tsp salt
⅛	tsp black pepper
1	(6-oz) package cremini mushrooms, halved or quartered if large

1 In a medium nonstick skillet over medium heat, warm 1 tsp oil. Add carrot and onion and cook, stirring, until onion is light golden, about 7 minutes. Stir in garlic and cook, stirring constantly, until fragrant, about 30 seconds longer. Transfer vegetable mixture to a 2-qt slow cooker.

2 Pour wine into same skillet and boil over high heat until reduced by half, about 2 minutes. Transfer to slow cooker, along with beef, tomatoes, orange zest strips, bay leaf, herbes de Provence, salt, and pepper. Cover and cook until beef is fork-tender, 3 to 4 hours on High or 6 to 8 hours on Low. Wipe skillet clean.

3 About 20 minutes before cooking time is up, heat remaining ½ tsp oil in same skillet over medium heat. Add mushrooms and cook, stirring often, until softened and liquid is evaporated, about 6 minutes. Stir mushrooms into stew. Cover and cook until flavors are blended, about 10 minutes more. Remove and discard bay leaf.

Per serving (about 1½ cups): 291 Cal, 10 g Total Fat, 3 g Sat Fat, 563 mg Sod, 16 g Total Carb, 8 g Sugar, 4 g Fib, 29 g Prot.

Serving idea

Instead of pairing this stew with rice, mix things up by serving it with white beans sprinkled with coarsely chopped flat-leaf parsley and black pepper.

Carne guisada with charred tortillas

Prep 30 min   Cook 2 to 6 hr   Serves 2

We kicked this Latin braised beef stew up a notch with poblanos, garlic, and fresh cilantro. Slow-cooking allows the flavors to meld.

Nonstick spray

½	lb boneless lean beef chuck, trimmed and cut into 1-inch chunks
½	tsp kosher salt, divided
1	garlic clove, minced
1	tsp chili powder
½	tsp cumin seeds
½	tsp dried oregano
1	tbsp all-purpose flour
1	cup canned diced tomatoes with juice
1	small yellow bell pepper, chopped
1	small poblano pepper, chopped
1	scallion, sliced
¼	cup chopped cilantro, plus small sprigs for garnish
4	(6-inch) corn tortillas
2	tbsp shredded reduced-fat cheddar

Radishes, thinly sliced
Jalapeño pepper, thinly sliced

2	lime wedges

1. Sprinkle beef with ¼ tsp salt. Spray a medium nonstick skillet with nonstick spray and set over medium heat. Add beef and cook until browned on all sides, about 6 minutes. Transfer to a 2-qt slow cooker.

2. To skillet, add garlic, chili powder, cumin, and oregano; reduce heat to low and cook, stirring constantly, until fragrant, about 30 seconds. Sprinkle with flour and stir until coated evenly. Stir in tomatoes and remaining ¼ tsp salt and bring to a boil, scraping up browned bits from bottom of pan. Reduce heat and simmer 1 minute.

3. To slow cooker, add tomato mixture; stir in bell pepper and poblano. Cover and cook until beef is fork-tender, 2 to 3 hours on High or 4 to 6 hours on Low. Stir in scallion and cilantro.

4. About 5 minutes before cooking time is up, in a dry medium skillet over medium-high heat, warm tortillas, one at a time, until lightly charred in spots (or hold over a gas flame with tongs).

5. Spoon stew evenly into 2 bowls. Sprinkle each serving with cheddar, radishes, jalapeño, and cilantro sprigs; serve with tortillas and lime wedges.

Per serving (1 cup stew, 1 tbsp cheese, and 2 corn tortillas): 359 Cal, 9 g Total Fat, 4 g Sat Fat, 878 mg Sod, 41 g Total Carb, 7 g Sugar, 7 g Fib, 32 g Prot.

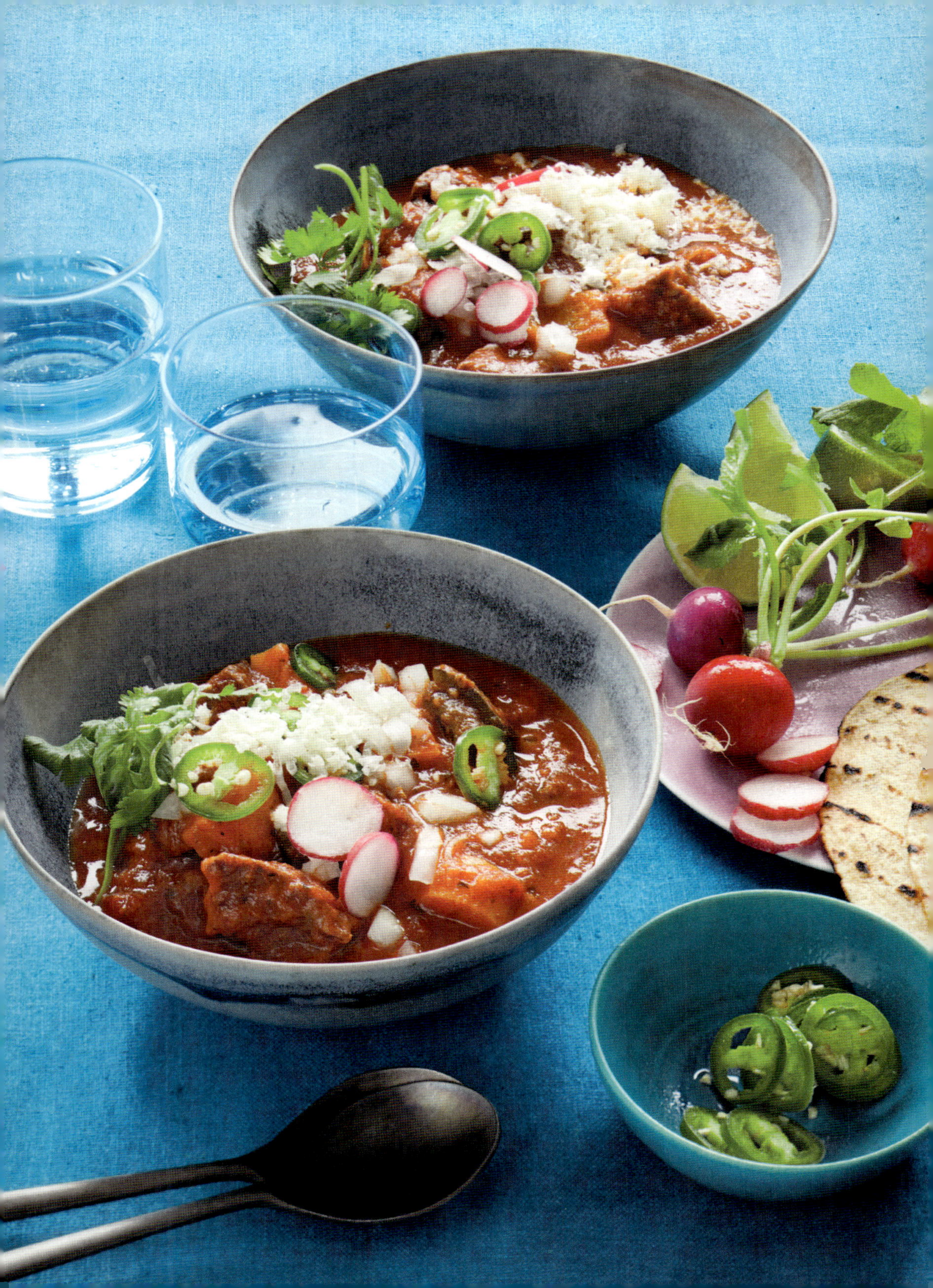

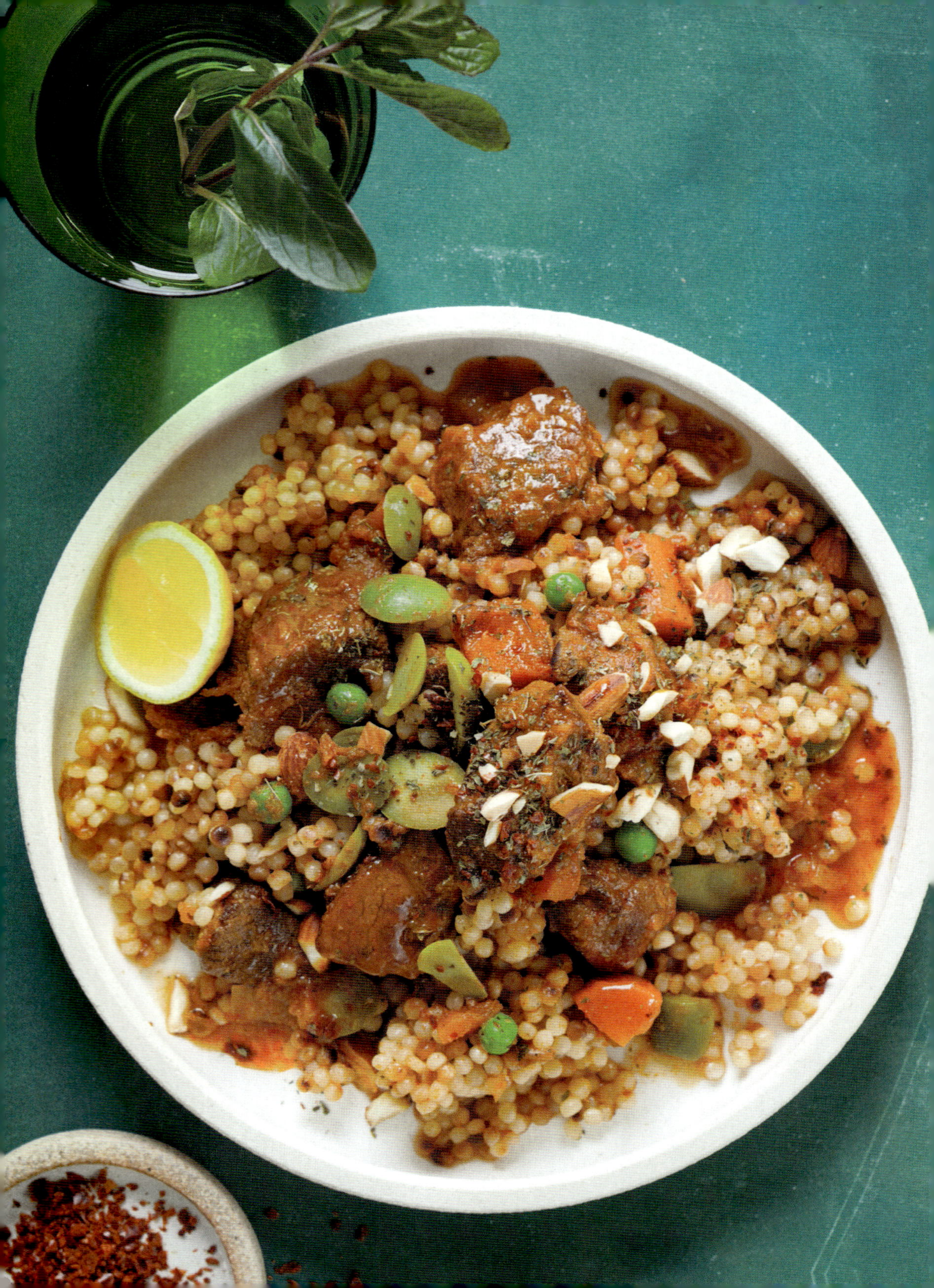

Lamb tagine with lemon and olives

Prep 32 min   Cook 3 to 8 hr   Serves 2

Spoon this tasty Moroccan stew over Israeli couscous. For extra flavor, toast the couscous in a skillet first, then cook it according to package directions.

½	lb lean boneless leg of lamb, trimmed and cut into 1½-inch chunks
¼	tsp kosher salt (or to taste), divided
¼	tsp black pepper, divided
1	tsp olive oil
1	small onion, chopped
1	large garlic clove, minced
1	tsp ground cumin
¾	tsp paprika
⅛	tsp cayenne
1	cup chicken broth
2	tsp tomato paste
1	carrot, cut into 1-inch chunks
½	lb peeled and seeded butternut squash chunks (about 2 cups)
1	small tomato, chopped
¼	cup frozen peas
2	tbsp sliced pitted Castelvetrano (large green) olives
1½	tsp lemon juice
2	tbsp chopped almonds
1	tsp dried mint

1 Sprinkle lamb with ⅛ tsp salt and ⅛ tsp black pepper. In a medium heavy nonstick skillet over medium-high heat, warm oil. Add lamb and cook until browned on all sides, about 5 minutes. Transfer to a plate.

2 Reduce heat to medium. Add onion and cook, stirring, until softened, about 5 minutes. Add garlic, cumin, paprika, and cayenne and cook, stirring constantly, until fragrant, about 30 seconds. Stir in ¼ cup broth and tomato paste until blended; cook, stirring, 1 minute.

3 In a 2-qt slow cooker, combine carrot and onion mixture. Top with lamb, squash, and chopped tomato. Sprinkle with remaining ⅛ tsp salt and ⅛ tsp black pepper. Pour in remaining ¾ cup broth. Cover and cook until lamb and vegetables are fork-tender, 3 to 4 hours on High or 6 to 8 hours on Low.

4 About 15 minutes before cooking time is up, stir in peas, olives, and lemon juice. Spoon stew evenly into 2 large shallow bowls. Sprinkle with almonds. With fingers, crush mint and sprinkle over stew.

Per serving (1½ cups stew and 1 tbsp almonds): 320 Cal, 10 g Total Fat, 2 g Sat Fat, 1,033 mg Sod, 28 g Total Carb, 9 g Sugar, 7 g Fib, 29 g Prot.

Bouillabaisse

Prep 30 min   Cook 4½ hr   Serves 2

If you're making a special dinner for two, try this famous Provençal fish stew, brimming with shrimp, red snapper, fennel, and leek.

Olive-oil nonstick spray
- ½ small fennel bulb, thinly sliced (about 1 cup)
- 1 small leek, thinly sliced (white and light green parts only)
- 1 small shallot, halved and thinly sliced
- 2 garlic cloves (1 finely chopped and 1 crushed through a press)
- 1 tsp tomato paste
- 3 tbsp dry white wine
- ½ cup canned diced tomatoes with juice
- 2 (3-inch) strips orange zest
- 1 tsp chopped thyme
- Pinch saffron threads
- 1¾ cups seafood stock or clam juice
- ⅛ tsp plus pinch black pepper, divided
- ½ lb red snapper or cod fillets, cut into 1½-inch chunks
- ¼ lb large shrimp, peeled and deveined
- 1 tsp olive oil
- 4 (½-oz) slices baguette
- Pinch coarse sea salt, such as Maldon's

1 Spray a large skillet with nonstick spray and set over medium heat. Add fennel, leek, and shallot and cook, stirring, until vegetables are softened, about 6 minutes. Stir in chopped garlic and tomato paste; cook, stirring, 1 minute. Pour in wine and cook until almost evaporated, about 2 minutes. Stir in tomatoes with juice, orange zest strips, thyme, saffron, and stock; bring to a boil.

2 Transfer vegetable-stock mixture from skillet to a 2-qt slow cooker. Wipe skillet clean and set aside. Cover slow cooker and cook 4 hours on Low. Stir in ⅛ tsp black pepper.

3 Add fish and shrimp to slow cooker. Cover; cook until fish and shrimp are just opaque in center, about 15 minutes on High.

4 In a cup, stir together oil and crushed garlic. Brush on both sides of slices of bread. Spray cleaned skillet with nonstick spray and set over medium-high heat. Add bread and cook, turning, until golden, about 2 minutes per side. Remove skillet from heat. Ladle bouillabaisse evenly into 2 large bowls and top with toasts; sprinkle with salt and pinch pepper.

Per serving (1½ cups bouillabaisse and 2 slices toast): 370 Cal, 7 g Total Fat, 1 g Sat Fat, 988 mg Sod, 30 g Total Carb, 9 g Sugar, 6 g Fib, 41 g Prot.

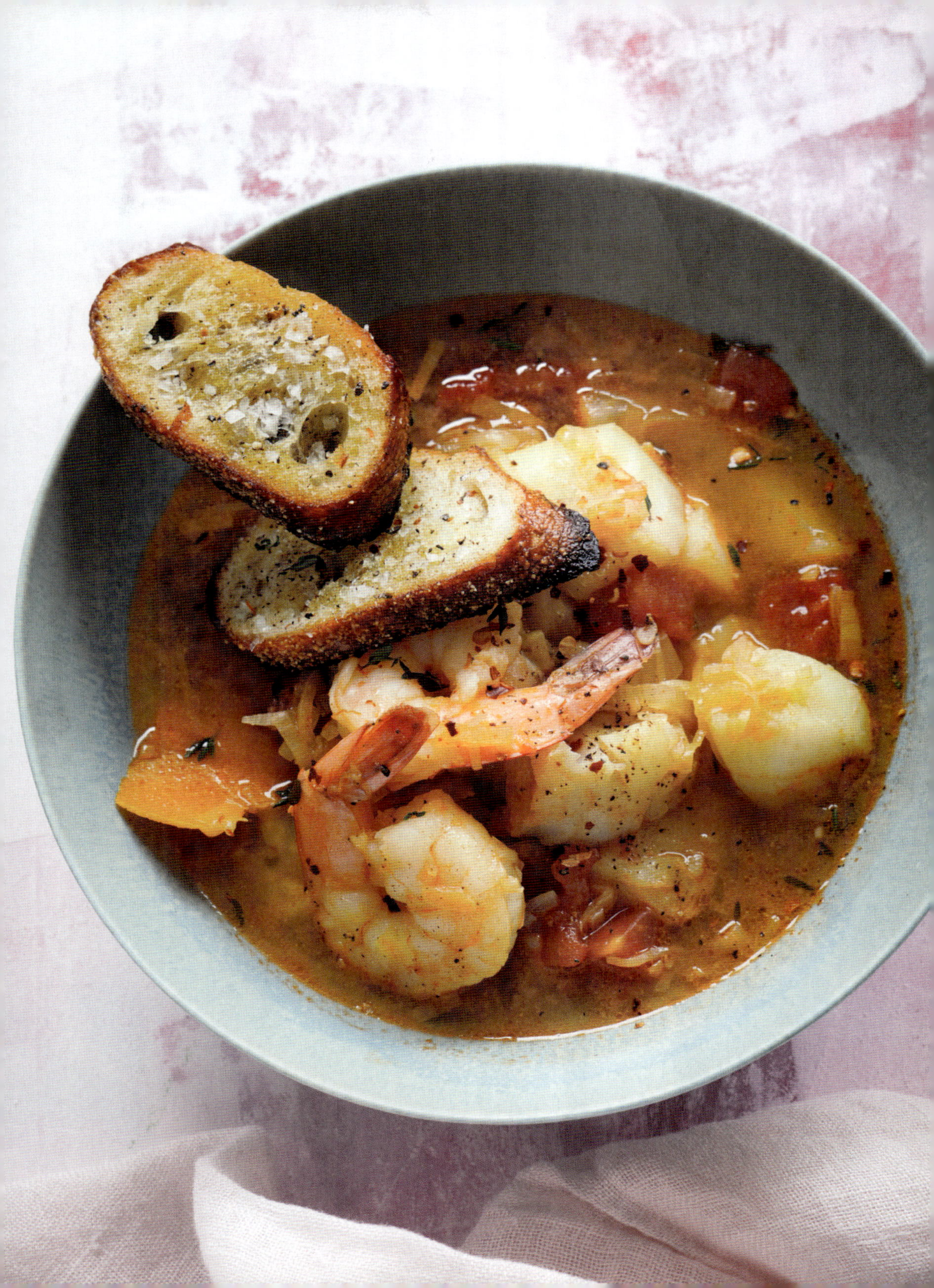

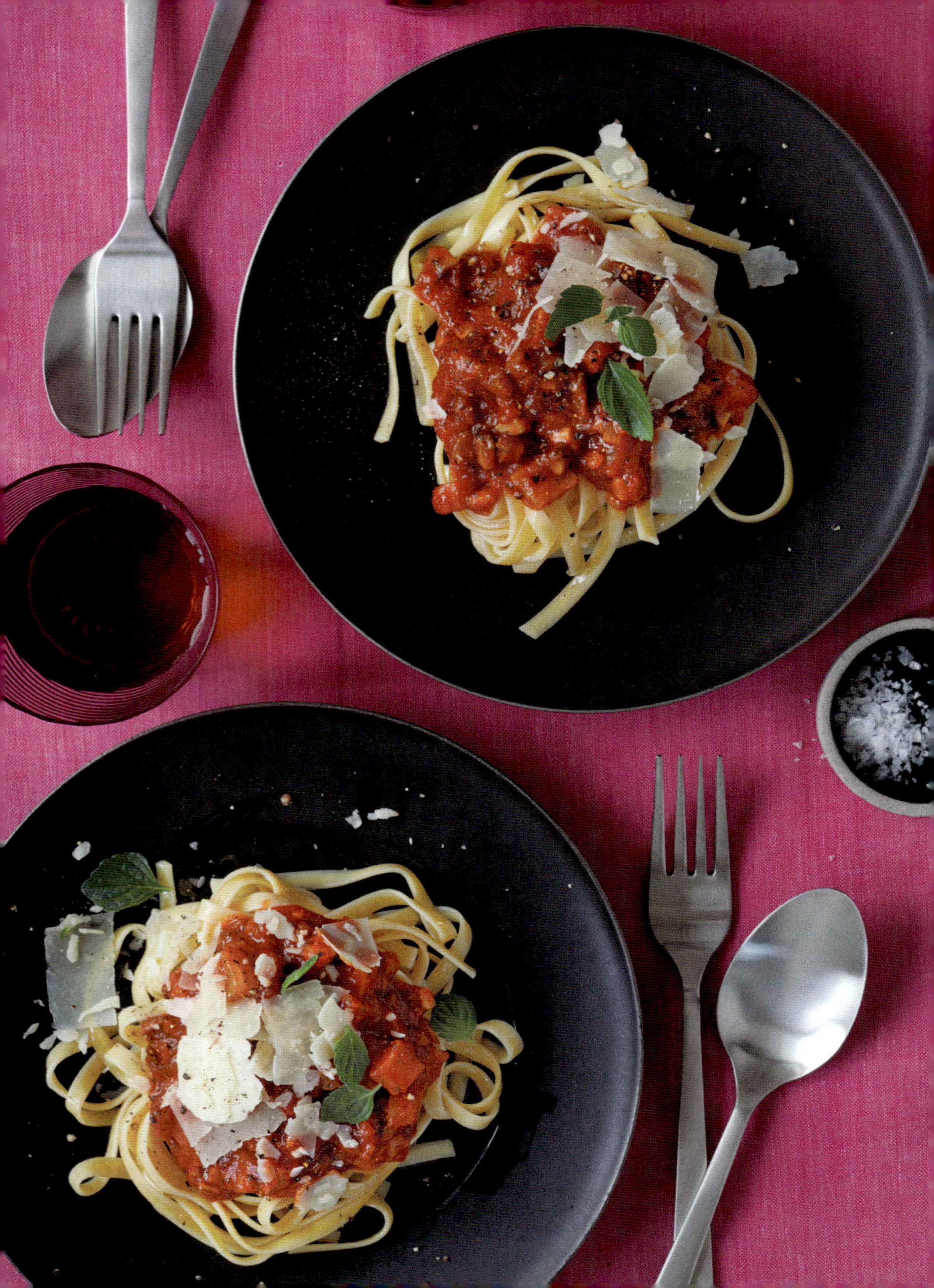

Vegetable bolognese

Prep 15 min   Cook 4 hr   Serves 2

Cremini mushrooms give this bolognese sauce a wonderful "meaty" texture. If your market carries interesting varieties—such as oyster, hen-of-the-woods, or chanterelles—sauté a mix of them for topping each serving.

- 1 tsp olive oil
- ¼ cup finely chopped fennel
- 3 tbsp finely chopped carrot
- 3 tbsp finely chopped celery
- 1 shallot, finely chopped
- 1 cup cremini mushrooms, finely chopped
- 1 small garlic clove, minced
- 1 cup canned petite diced tomatoes with juice
- ⅓ cup canned tomato sauce
- ¼ tsp kosher salt (or to taste)
- ⅛ tsp black pepper (or to taste)
- ¼ cup Parmesan shavings, divided
- 2 tbsp reduced-fat (2%) milk, at room temperature
- 4 oz linguine or spaghetti

1. In a medium nonstick skillet over medium heat, warm oil. Add fennel, carrot, celery, and shallot and cook, stirring, until shallot is softened, about 5 minutes. Add mushrooms and cook, stirring, 2 minutes. Add garlic and cook, stirring constantly, until fragrant, about 30 seconds more

2. Transfer vegetables to a 2-qt slow cooker. Stir in diced tomatoes, tomato sauce, salt, and pepper. Cover and cook until vegetables are softened and flavors are blended, about 3½ hours on Low. Stir 2 tbsp Parmesan and milk into vegetable mixture. Cover and cook 20 minutes on Low.

3. Meanwhile, cook pasta according to package directions. Drain and cover to keep warm. When ready to serve, divide pasta evenly between 2 shallow bowls; top evenly with bolognese and sprinkle with remaining 2 tbsp cheese.

Per serving (about 1½ cups sauce with pasta and 1 tbsp cheese): 336 Cal, 7 g Total Fat, 2 g Sat Fat, 836 mg Sod, 57 g Total Carb, 10 g Sugar, 5 g Fib, 14 g Prot.

Prep ahead
Shave a few minutes off your prep time by chopping the veggies in a food processor instead of by hand.

Cauliflower paprikash

Prep 20 min   Cook 1½ to 2 hr   Serves 2

Sun-dried tomato paste usually comes in a tube and should be stocked with other tomato products at your supermarket. Its richness takes this paprikash to the next level.

- 1½ tsp canola oil, divided
- 1 small onion, chopped
- 1 small red bell pepper, cut into ¾-inch pieces
- 1 large garlic clove, chopped
- 1¼ tsp smoked paprika
- ½ cup canned petite diced tomatoes with juice
- 2 tsp sun-dried tomato paste
- ½ tsp kosher salt
- ½ head cauliflower (about ¾ lb), trimmed and cut into ¾-inch florets
- ¼ lb cremini mushrooms, halved or quartered if large
- ¼ cup plain fat-free Greek yogurt
- 1½ cups cooked long-grain white rice
- 2 tsp chopped dill

1 In a large heavy skillet over medium-high heat, warm 1 tsp oil. Add onion and cook, stirring, until almost softened, about 4 minutes; add remaining ½ tsp oil. Stir in bell pepper, garlic, and paprika and cook, stirring, until onion starts to brown, about 2 minutes. Stir in tomatoes, 2 tbsp water, tomato paste, and salt.

2 In a 2-qt slow cooker, combine cauliflower and mushrooms; stir in tomato mixture. Cover and cook until cauliflower is tender, 1½ to 2 hours on High, stirring after 1 hour of cooking time. Stir in 2 tbsp yogurt, taking care not to break up cauliflower.

3 Divide rice evenly between 2 large shallow bowls; top with paprikash and remaining 2 tbsp yogurt. Sprinkle with dill.

Per serving (about 1½ cups paprikash, 1 tbsp yogurt, and ¾ cup rice): 312 Cal, 7 g Total Fat, 1 g Sat Fat, 666 mg Sod, 55 g Total Carb, 10 g Sugar, 8 g Fib, 13 g Prot.

Cooking tip

For a more veggie-heavy meal, add ½ cup frozen green peas to the paprikash about 30 minutes before the cooking time is up.

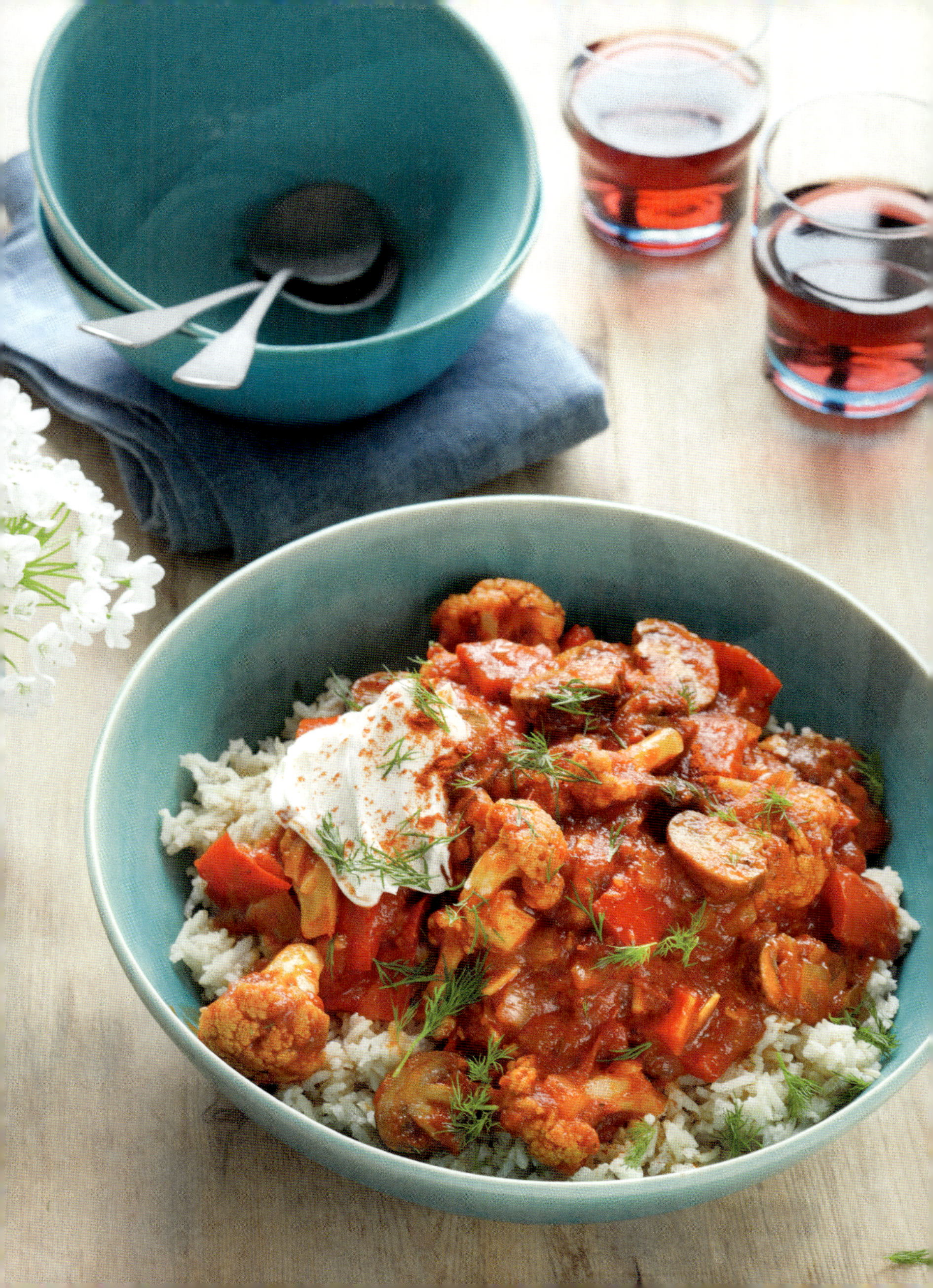

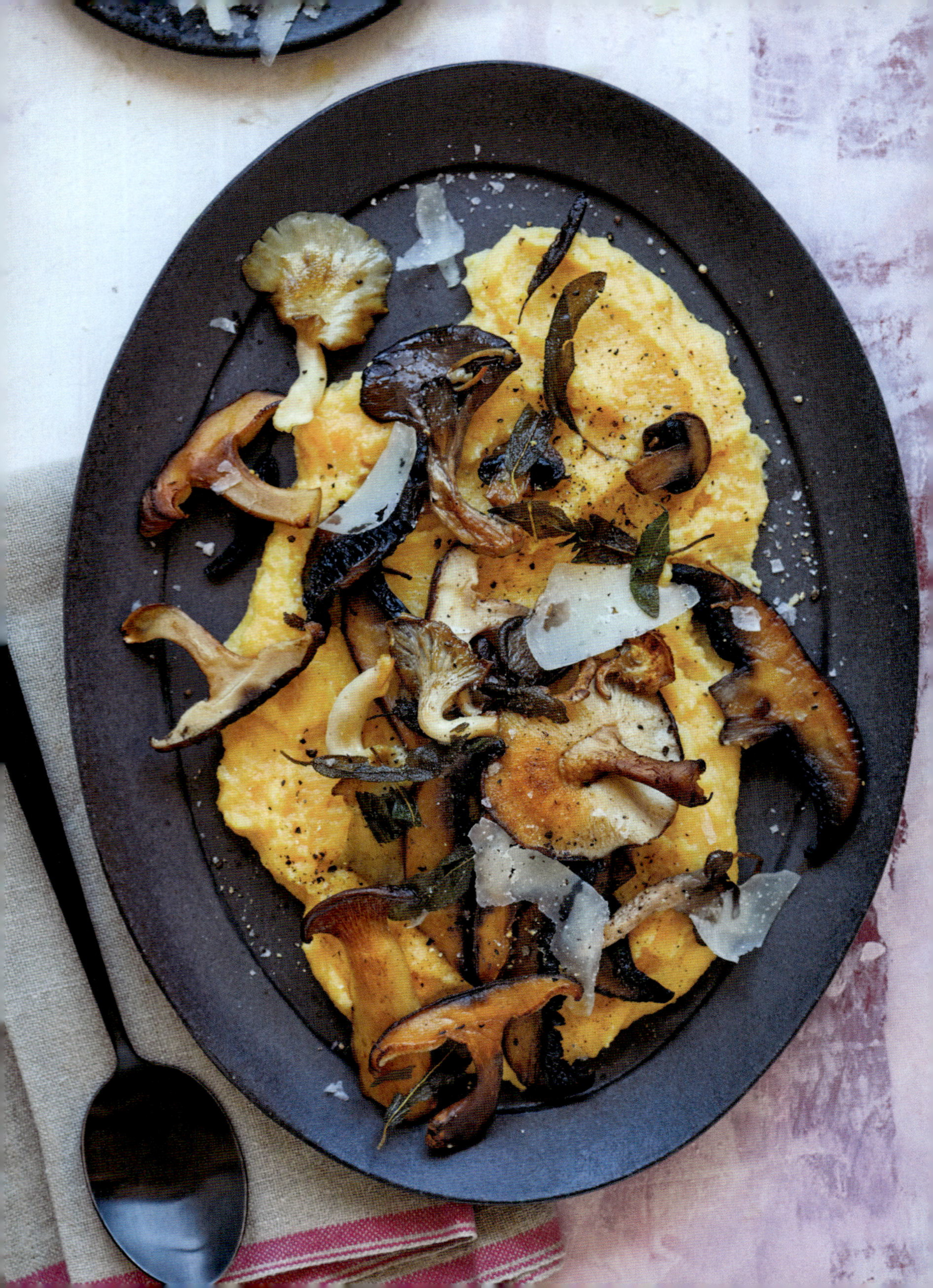

Soft polenta with pecorino and mushrooms

Prep 5 min   Cook 2 hr   Serves 2

Polenta firms up as it stands, so serve it as soon as it's ready. You can also loosen it by whisking in some warm broth or water until it's creamy and smooth again. Crispy sage leaves are the perfect garnish for this dish.

- 2 cups reduced-sodium vegetable broth
- ½ cup yellow cornmeal
- ¼ tsp kosher salt (or to taste), divided
- ¼ tsp black pepper, divided, plus more for garnish
- 2 tsp olive oil, divided
- 4 sage leaves, plus 1½ tsp finely chopped sage for garnish
- 1 (8-oz) container cremini or assorted mushrooms, cut into ½-inch slices
- 1 garlic clove, minced
- 3 tbsp grated or shaved Pecorino Romano

1 In a 2-qt slow cooker, stir together broth, cornmeal, ¼ tsp salt, and ⅛ tsp pepper. Cover and cook until polenta is thick and creamy, about 2 hours on Low, stirring about every 45 minutes to keep polenta lump free.

2 About 10 minutes before cooking time is up, warm 1 tsp oil in medium heavy nonstick skillet over medium-high heat. Add sage leaves and cook, turning, until crisp, 30 seconds to 1 minute. With tongs, transfer leaves to paper towel to drain; set aside.

3 To skillet, add remaining 1 tsp oil; add mushrooms and cook, stirring, until mushrooms are softened and golden, about 5 minutes. Stir in garlic and cook, stirring, 30 seconds longer. Remove skillet from heat and stir in chopped sage and remaining ¼ tsp salt and ⅛ tsp pepper. Remove skillet from heat. Cover to keep warm.

4 When polenta is done, stir in 2 tbsp Pecorino Romano. Spoon onto platter; top with mushrooms, fried sage leaves, remaining 1 tbsp cheese, and grinding of pepper.

Per serving (about 1 cup polenta with mushrooms): 219 Cal, 8 g Total Fat, 2 g Sat Fat, 960 mg Sod, 29 g Total Carb, 3 g Sugar, 4 g Fib, 9 g Prot.

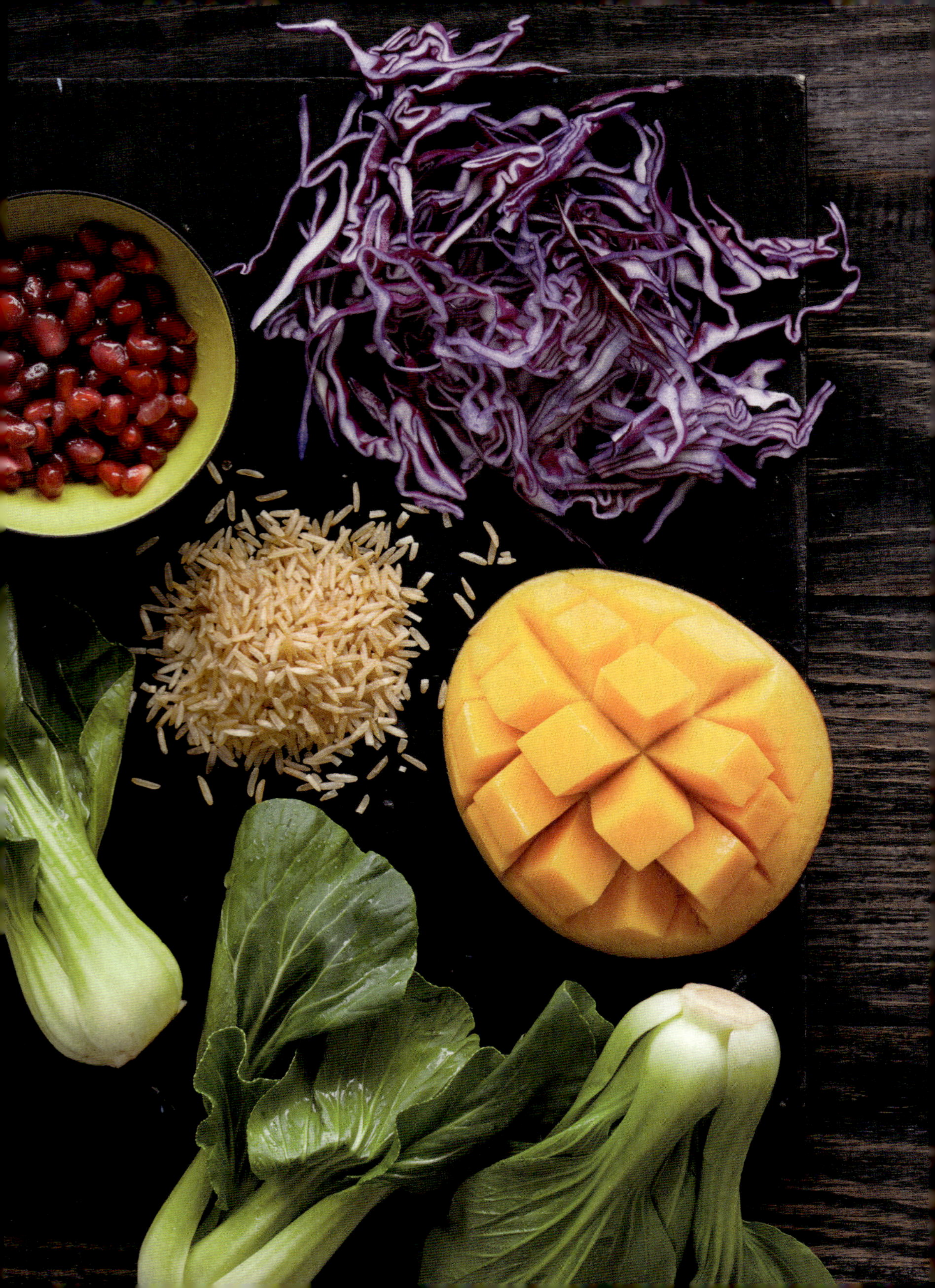

Bonus chapter

Instant Pot® & air fryer specials

INSTANT POT

White rice   172

Plain yogurt   172

Chicken stock   172

Soft-cooked and hard-cooked eggs   173

Hummus   173

Applesauce   173

Spiced-up rotisserie-style chicken   174

Cajun chicken-sausage jambalaya   177

Roman-style chicken cacciatore   178

Smoky beef brisket   181

Korean beef stew   182

Nonna's bolognese sauce   185

Tex-Mex red chile pork tacos   186

Lamb, apricot, and chickpea tagine   189

Cherry tomato and basil–topped spaghetti squash   190

Brown rice, kale, and sweet potato pilaf   193

Risotto with asparagus and chives   194

Cauliflower, potato, and bacon bisque   197

Beet borscht with beef and cabbage   198

AIR FRYER

Southern-style fried chicken   201

Super-simple chicken parmesan   202

Colombian beef and potato empanadas   205

Cornmeal-crusted fish fingers   206

Coconut shrimp with mango dipping sauce   209

Cheese-dusted potato fries   210

Crispy buttermilk onion rings   213

6 basic Instant Pot® recipes

The Instant Pot does some things better than any gadget we know: chicken stock to rival a restaurant, deeply flavored applesauce, perfectly hard-boiled eggs with shells that fall right off. Here are six essential recipes for your arsenal. You'll use them again and again.

White rice

Measure out 1 cup **long-grain white rice.** Put rice in a sieve and rinse under cool running water until water runs clear. Measure out 1 cup **water** (or up to 1¼ cups if you prefer softer rice); pour into a 4- to 6-qt Instant Pot. Add rice, stirring, so it settles into even layer. Lock lid, making sure vent is closed. Select Rice setting. When time is up, about 5 minutes, allow pressure to naturally release for 10 minutes. Press Cancel to turn off pot. Move steam release valve to Venting position to release remaining pressure. For brown rice, follow directions selecting Multigrain setting. Brown rice will take about 22 minutes.

Plain yogurt

Pour 4 cups reduced-fat (2%) or low-fat (1%) **milk** into 4- to 8-oz glass jars. Pour 1 cup **water** into a 6-qt Instant Pot and put metal rack in pot. Place jars on rack. Lock lid, making sure vent is closed. Press Steam and select High Pressure; set cooking time for 1 minute. When time is up, press Cancel to turn off pot. Allow pressure to naturally release. Remove lid and place jars on a work surface. Let milk cool to 115°F. Stir in 1 generous tsp **plain yogurt with live cultures** for each cup milk. Return jars to Instant Pot. Lock lid, making sure vent is closed. Press Yogurt and set cooking time for 3 hours for very mild yogurt or up to 8 hours for slightly tangy yogurt. When time is up, remove lid. Cover jars and refrigerate up to 2 weeks. Yogurt will continue to thicken upon standing.

Chicken stock

In a 6-qt Instant Pot, combine 3 lb **chicken wings** or other chicken parts; 2 **carrots**, halved; 2 or 3 **celery stalks**, cut up; 1 unpeeled **large onion**, halved; 4 or 5 **parsley sprigs;** 3 unpeeled large **garlic cloves;** 1 or 2 **bay leaves;** 10 whole **black peppercorns,** and 2 tsp **kosher salt.** Add enough **water** to cover, about 3 qt. (Water should not go above mark in pot.) Lock lid, making sure vent is closed. Press Pressure Cook and select High Pressure; set cooking time for 40 minutes. When time is up, press Cancel to turn off pot. Allow pressure to naturally release for 20 minutes. Move steam release valve to Venting position to release remaining pressure. Strain stock through a sieve set over a large bowl. Discard solids. Let stock cool; skim off fat from surface.

Soft-boiled and hard-boiled eggs

Into an Instant Pot, pour 1 cup **water.** Put a metal rack in pot and place **eggs** (as many as you like) on rack. Lock lid, making sure vent is closed. Press Pressure Cook and select High Pressure. For soft-boiled eggs (with firm white and runny yolk), set cooking time for 3 minutes. For hard-boiled eggs, set cooking time for 5 minutes. When time is up, press Cancel to turn off pot. Move steam release valve to Venting position to quickly release pressure. Cool eggs under cold running water.

Hummus

Put 1 cup **dried chickpeas** in a 6-qt Instant Pot; add enough **water** to cover by 1 inch (about 4 cups) and 1 tsp **kosher salt.** Lock lid, making sure vent is closed. Press Pressure Cook and select High Pressure; set cooking time for 45 minutes. When time is up, press Cancel to turn off pot. Allow pressure to naturally release for 15 minutes. Move steam release valve to Venting position to release remaining pressure. Remove lid. Beans should be soft and tender. If not, cook at High Pressure for another 5 minutes. Press Cancel to turn off pot. Move steam release valve to Venting position to quickly release pressure. Drain chickpeas, reserving about ½ cup liquid. Transfer chickpeas to food processor or blender. Add ¼ cup **bean liquid** along with ⅓ cup **tahini,** juice of ½ **lemon,** 1 or 2 **garlic cloves,** and **salt** to taste. Process until smooth adding more bean liquid if needed. Adjust seasoning.

Applesauce

Peel and core 3 lb **apples;** cut into chunks. Use one type or a mix of sweet and tart. Put into a 6-qt Instant Pot; add ¼ cup **water,** juice of ½ **lemon,** and ½ to 1 tsp **cinnamon** (optional). Toss until mixed well. Close lid, making sure vent is closed. Press Pressure Cook and select High Pressure; set cooking time for 5 minutes. When time is up, press Cancel to turn off pot. Allow pressure to naturally release. Mash apples with a potato masher or immersion blender. Transfer to airtight containers. Refrigerate up to 1 week or freeze up to 6 months.

Spiced-up rotisserie-style chicken

Prep 20 min   Cook 40 min   Serves 4

Your Instant Pot® hurries up this delectable roast chicken.

- 2 red Fresno or cherry peppers, cut into chunks (do not seed)
- 2 scallions, cut into 2-inch lengths
- 3 large garlic cloves, crushed with side of large knife
- 2 tbsp lime juice (reserve rind)
- 1 tbsp olive oil
- 2 tsp tomato paste
- 1¼ tsp dried thyme
- 1 tsp smoked paprika
- 1 tsp ground cumin
- ¾ tsp kosher salt
- ¾ cup chicken broth
- 1 (3¼-lb) whole chicken, skin and giblets removed (ask your butcher to skin the chicken, or do it yourself—there are easy-to-follow videos online)

1. In a blender, combine peppers, scallions, garlic, lime juice, oil, tomato paste, and seasonings; process until it forms a thick puree. In a cup, whisk together 3 tbsp puree and broth; reserve.

2. Place chicken, breast-side up, on a long sheet of foil. Tuck wings under; tie legs with kitchen twine. Insert 2 short bamboo skewers to secure thighs against body. Cut reserved lime rind into wedges and stuff into chicken. With a knife, poke holes in breast and leg. Brush remaining puree all over chicken.

3. Place a wire rack in a 6- to 8-qt Instant Pot. Pour in pepper-broth mixture. Lift chicken by foil and set on rack. Poke several holes in bottom of foil so juices can drain. Gather foil up to cover bottom half of chicken. Lock lid, making sure vent is closed. Press Pressure Cook and select High Pressure; set cooking time for 20 minutes for 6-qt Instant Pot and 16 minutes for 8-qt. When time is up, remove lid; instant-read thermometer inserted into thigh (not touching bone) should register 165°F. If needed, set for additional 5 minutes of cooking time.

4. When time is up, allow pressure to naturally release for 5 minutes. Press Cancel to turn off pot. Move steam release valve to Venting position to release remaining pressure. Remove lid. Lift chicken with rack and place on cutting board. Loosely cover with foil and let stand 15 minutes. Leave pan juices in pot. Remove skewers and cut chicken into 4 portions.

5. Press Sauté and set cooking time for 15 minutes. Let juices come to a boil; boil, uncovered, until slightly reduced, about 4 minutes. Press Cancel to turn off pot. Pour pan juices into a gravy boat and skim off fat from surface. Serve with chicken.

Per serving (¼ of chicken and ¼ cup pan juices): 279 Cal, 9 g Total Fat, 1 g Sat Fat, 692 mg Sod, 5 g Total Carb, 2 g Sugar, 1 g Fib, 42 g Prot.

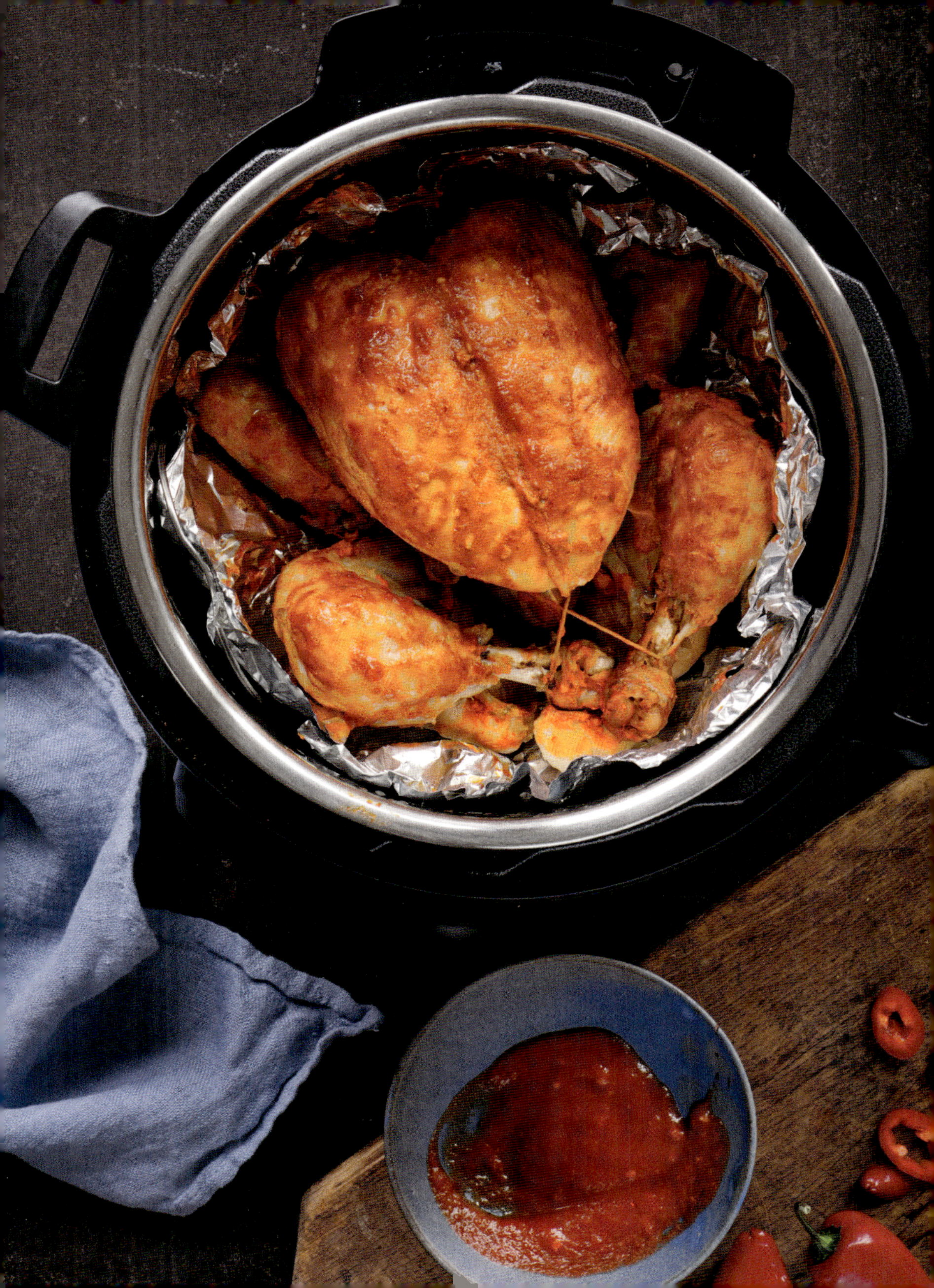

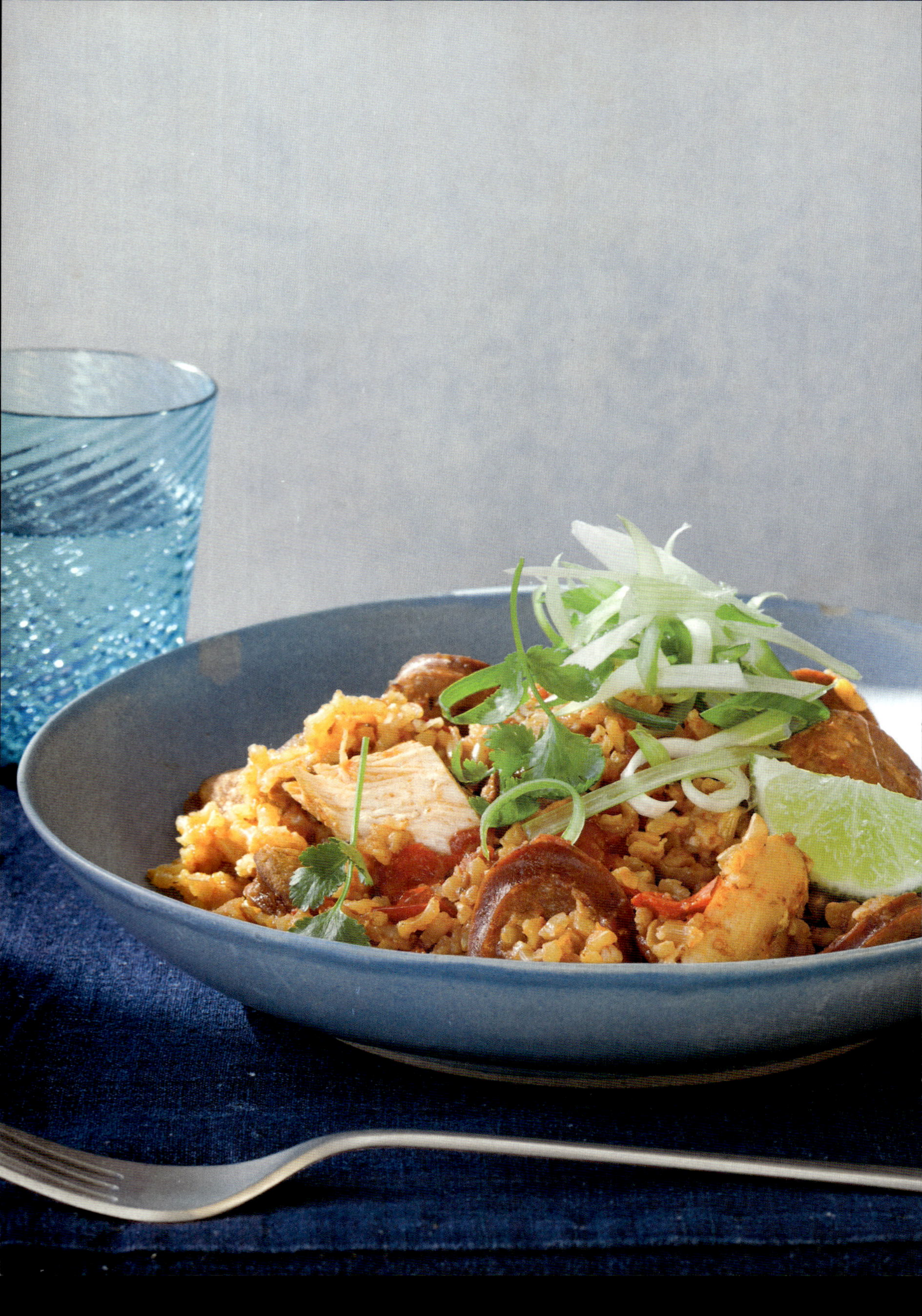

Cajun chicken-sausage jambalaya

Prep 10 min   Cook 23 min   Serves 4

Our homemade Cajun seasoning is fantastic on chicken and sausage. It's fresher and more intense than the pre-made kind and only takes a few minutes to prep.

Nonstick spray
- 6 oz turkey kielbasa, sliced
- 1 cup canned diced fire-roasted tomatoes, drained
- 1 cup chicken broth
- ¾ cup long-grain brown rice, rinsed well
- ¾ tsp salt, divided
- 1 onion, chopped
- 1 red bell pepper, cut into ½-inch dice
- 3 celery stalks, sliced
- 3 garlic cloves, finely chopped
- 3 tsp homemade Cajun seasoning, divided (see "Prep ahead," *below*)
- 2 (5-oz) skinless boneless chicken breasts, each cut crosswise into thirds
- 3 scallions, sliced
- Hot pepper sauce

1. Spray the bottom of a 6-qt Instant Pot with nonstick spray; press Sauté. When Hot is displayed, add kielbasa and cook, turning once, until browned, about 3 minutes. With a slotted spoon, transfer sausage to a plate. Press Cancel to turn off pot.

2. To pot, add tomatoes, broth, rice, and ¼ tsp salt, mixing well. Lock lid, making sure vent is closed. Press Rice setting and select Low Pressure; set cooking time for 15 minutes. When time is up, press Cancel to turn off pot. Move steam release valve to Venting position to quickly release pressure.

3. Remove lid. Stir in onion, bell pepper, celery, garlic, 2 tsp Cajun seasoning, and kielbasa. Place chicken on top and sprinkle with remaining 1 tsp Cajun seasoning and remaining ½ tsp salt. Lock lid, making sure vent is closed. Press Pressure Cook and select Low Pressure; set cooking time for 5 minutes. When time is up, press Cancel to turn off pot. Move steam release valve to Venting position to quickly release pressure. Remove lid.

4. Transfer chicken to a cutting board. Using two forks, pull chicken apart into bite-size pieces; stir back into rice mixture. Spoon jambalaya into serving bowl and sprinkle with scallions. Serve with hot sauce.

Per serving (1½ cups): 322 Cal, 7 g Total Fat, 2 g Sat Fat, 1,107 mg Sod, 37 g Total Carb, 4 g Sugar, 4 g Fib, 27 g Prot.

Prep ahead

To make Cajun seasoning, mix 4 tsp chili powder, 1 tbsp dried thyme, 2½ tsp smoked paprika, 2 tsp each garlic powder and onion powder, and 1 tsp each cayenne pepper and celery salt.

Roman-style chicken cacciatore

Prep 10 min   Cook 22 min   Serves 4

Unlike its tomato-heavy cousin, Roman-style cacciatore leans on fresh rosemary and mushrooms for a more sophisticated but still hearty dish.

Nonstick spray
- 4 (6-oz) bone-in chicken thighs
- 1 tsp kosher salt (or to taste), divided
- 4 carrots, cut into 2-inch lengths
- 1 large onion, sliced
- ½ lb small cremini mushrooms
- 1 (½-oz) package dried porcini mushrooms
- 1 tbsp chopped rosemary
- 4 garlic cloves, chopped
- ½ cup dry red wine
- ½ cup chicken broth
- 1 tbsp tomato paste
- 2 tsp cornstarch
- ½ cup grape tomatoes, halved
- ¼ tsp red pepper flakes

1 Spray chicken with nonstick spray and sprinkle with ½ tsp salt. Press Sauté on a 6-qt Instant Pot and set cooking time for 15 minutes. When Hot is displayed, add chicken, skin-side down, and cook until browned on both sides. Transfer to a plate.

2 To pot, add carrots, onion, mushrooms, rosemary, garlic, and remaining ½ tsp salt. Cook, stirring, until onion is slightly softened, about 2 minutes. In a small bowl, whisk together wine, broth, and tomato paste until blended; pour into pot. Place chicken, skin-side up, on top of vegetable mixture. Press Cancel to turn off pot. Lock lid, making sure vent is closed.

3 Press Pressure Cook and select Low Pressure; set cooking time for 7 minutes. When time is up, allow pressure to naturally release 5 minutes. Press Cancel to turn off pot. Move steam release valve to Venting position to release remaining pressure.

4 With a slotted spoon, transfer chicken and vegetables to a platter. Skim off fat from cooking juices. Press Sauté and set cooking time for 15 minutes. Bring juices to a boil.

5 Meanwhile, in a cup, whisk together 1 tbsp water and cornstarch. Stir into cooking juices and cook, uncovered, until sauce thickens, about 2 minutes. Stir in tomatoes. Press Cancel to turn off pot. Pour sauce over chicken and vegetables and sprinkle with pepper flakes. Remove chicken skin before eating.

Serving idea
Whole-wheat fettuccine is perfect with this chicken dish.

Per serving (1 chicken thigh and ½ cup vegetables with ¼ cup sauce): 322 Cal, 8 g Total Fat, 2 g Sat Fat, 829 mg Sod, 20 g Total Carb, 7 g Sugar, 4 g Fib, 37 g Prot.

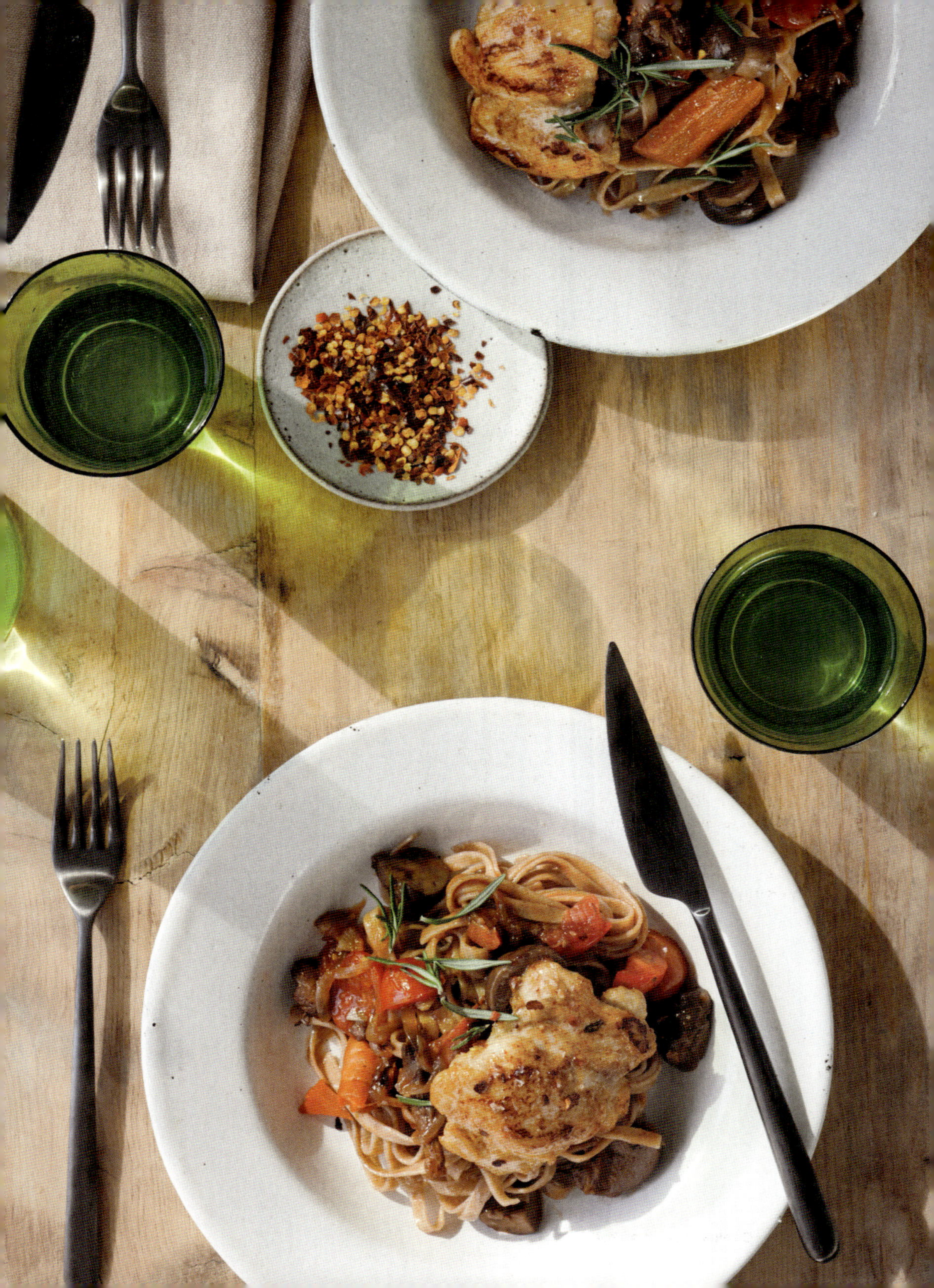

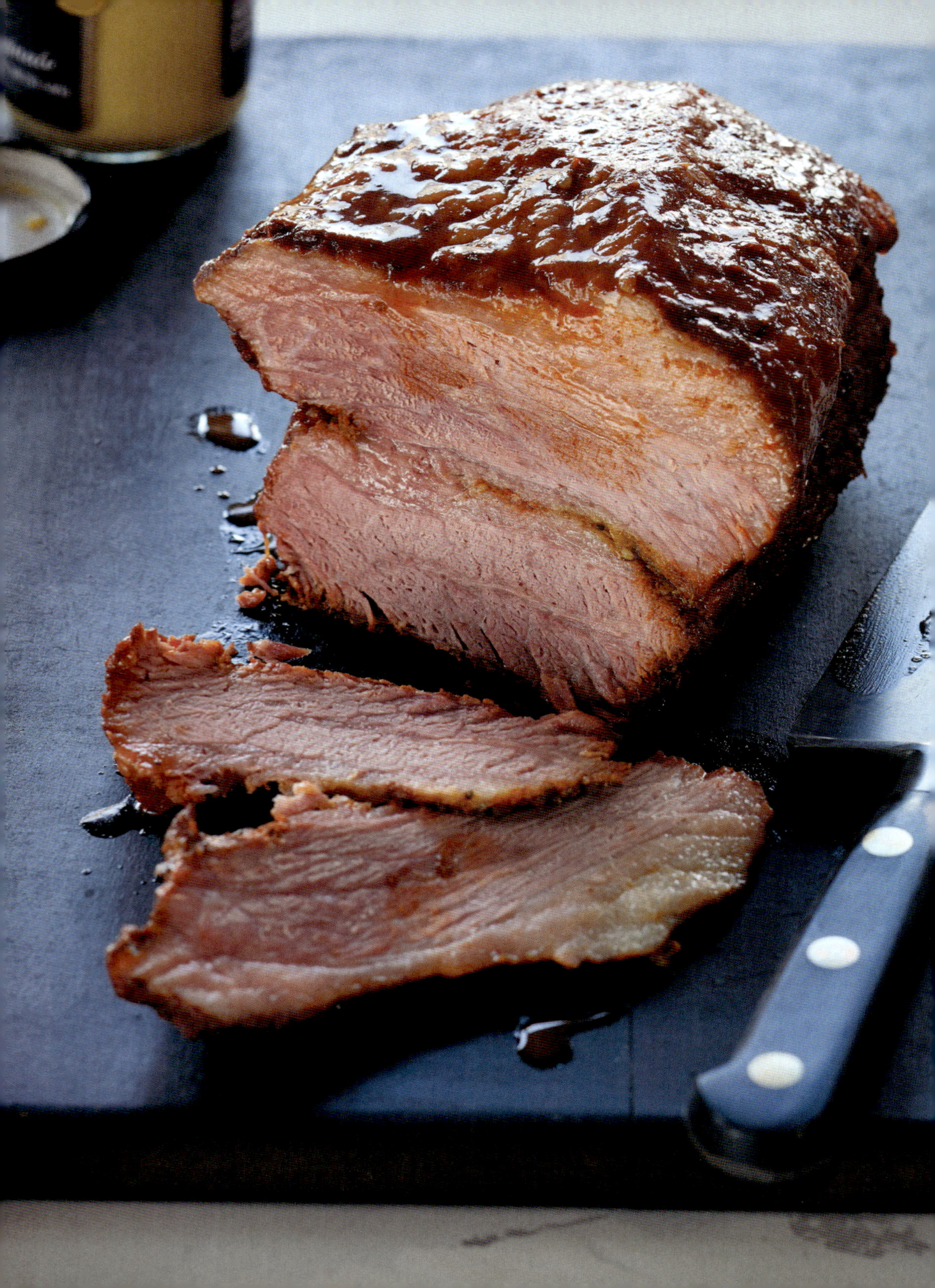

Smoky beef brisket

Prep 15 min   Marinate 6 to 8 hr   Cook 1 hr   Serves 8

Brisket is great for a big family meal (and people will fight over the leftovers). It's meant to be cooked low and slow or in a pressure cooker to break down the toughness for tender, juicy results.

- 2 tbsp garlic powder
- 1½ tbsp smoked paprika
- 1 tbsp brown sugar
- 1 tsp chipotle chile powder
- 1 tsp ground cumin
- 1 tsp dried oregano
- 1 tsp kosher salt
- 1 (3-lb) lean flat-cut brisket, trimmed
- ¾ cup regular or nonalcoholic beer
- ¼ cup barbecue sauce
- 2 tsp reduced-sodium Worcestershire sauce
- 1 tbsp apple-cider vinegar

1 In a cup, stir together garlic powder, paprika, brown sugar, chile powder, cumin, oregano, and salt. Rub all over brisket. Place brisket in a large zip-close plastic bag. Squeeze out air and seal bag; refrigerate at least 6 hours or up to 8 hours, turning once or twice.

2 Place brisket in a 6-qt Instant Pot (cut brisket crosswise in half and stack, if needed). In a glass measure, stir together beer, barbecue sauce, and Worcestershire sauce; pour over meat. Lock lid, making sure vent is closed.

3 Press Pressure Cook and select High Pressure; set cooking time for 50 minutes. When time is up, press Cancel to turn off pot. Allow pressure to naturally release 15 minutes. Move steam release valve to Venting position to release remaining pressure. Remove lid.

4 Transfer meat to a cutting board. Cover loosely with foil; let stand 15 minutes. Meanwhile, press Sauté and set cooking time for 15 minutes. Bring juices to a boil. Boil, uncovered, until reduced to 1½ cups, about 8 minutes. Press Cancel to turn off pot. Pour juices into a fat separator and pour off fat, or pour into glass measure and skim off and discard fat from surface; stir in vinegar. Thinly slice beef across grain into 24 slices; arrange on a platter. Spoon some pan juices over. Serve with remaining pan juices.

Per serving (3 slices brisket and 3 tbsp pan juices): 255 Cal, 7 g Total Fat, 3 g Sat Fat, 480 mg Sod, 7 g Total Carb, 4 g Sugar, 1 g Fib, 37 g Prot.

Korean beef stew

Prep 10 min Cook 50 min Serves 4

Gochugaru is Korea's answer to chili powder. Traditionally, it's made from sun-dried seeded red chile peppers that are coarsely ground. Can't find it in your grocery store? Aleppo pepper or ancho chile powder work in this recipe, too.

Nonstick spray
1 small Asian or Bosc pear, unpeeled and cut into chunks
1 shallot, halved
4 garlic cloves, peeled
1 (1½-inch) piece ginger, peeled and coarsely chopped
¼ cup rice vinegar
3 tbsp soy sauce
2 tsp gochugaru, divided
1 lb lean boneless beef chuck roast or boneless beef short ribs, trimmed and cut into 8 (2-inch chunks)
12 baby or baby-cut carrots (¾ lb)
4 (5-oz) baby bok choy, halved lengthwise
1½ tsp cornstarch
1 tsp toasted sesame seeds

1 In a blender, combine pear, shallot, garlic, ginger, vinegar, ¼ cup water, and soy sauce; puree. Stir in 1½ tsp gochugaru.

2 Press Sauté on a 6-qt Instant Pot; set cooking time for 15 minutes. When Hot is displayed, spray beef with nonstick spray; place in pot. Cook, turning, until browned. Add pear mixture. Press Cancel to turn off pot. Lock lid, making sure vent is closed.

3 Press Pressure Cook and select High Pressure; set cooking time for 35 minutes. When time is up, press Cancel to turn off pot. Move steam release valve to Venting position to quickly release pressure. Remove lid. Place carrots in pot. Top with bok choy, cut-side up. Lock lid, making sure vent is closed.

4 Press Pressure Cook and select High Pressure; set cooking time for 2 minutes. When time is up, press Cancel to turn off pot. Move steam release valve to Venting position to quickly release pressure. Remove lid. With tongs, transfer vegetables and beef to a platter. Cover to keep warm.

5 Skim off fat from liquid. In a cup, whisk 1 tbsp water and cornstarch; stir into pot. Press Sauté and set cooking time for 15 minutes. Bring to boil; cook, uncovered, about 1 minute. Press Cancel to turn off pot. Spoon sauce over beef and vegetables. Sprinkle with sesame seeds and remaining ½ tsp gochugaru.

Serving idea
You'll want rice—white or brown would both work—to soak up all the sauce in this dish.

Per serving (2 pieces beef, 2 pieces bok choy, 3 carrots, and ¼ cup sauce): 226 Cal, 8 g Total Fat, 3 g Sat Fat, 857 mg Sod, 13 g Total Carb, 5 g Sugar, 4 g Fib, 27 g Prot.

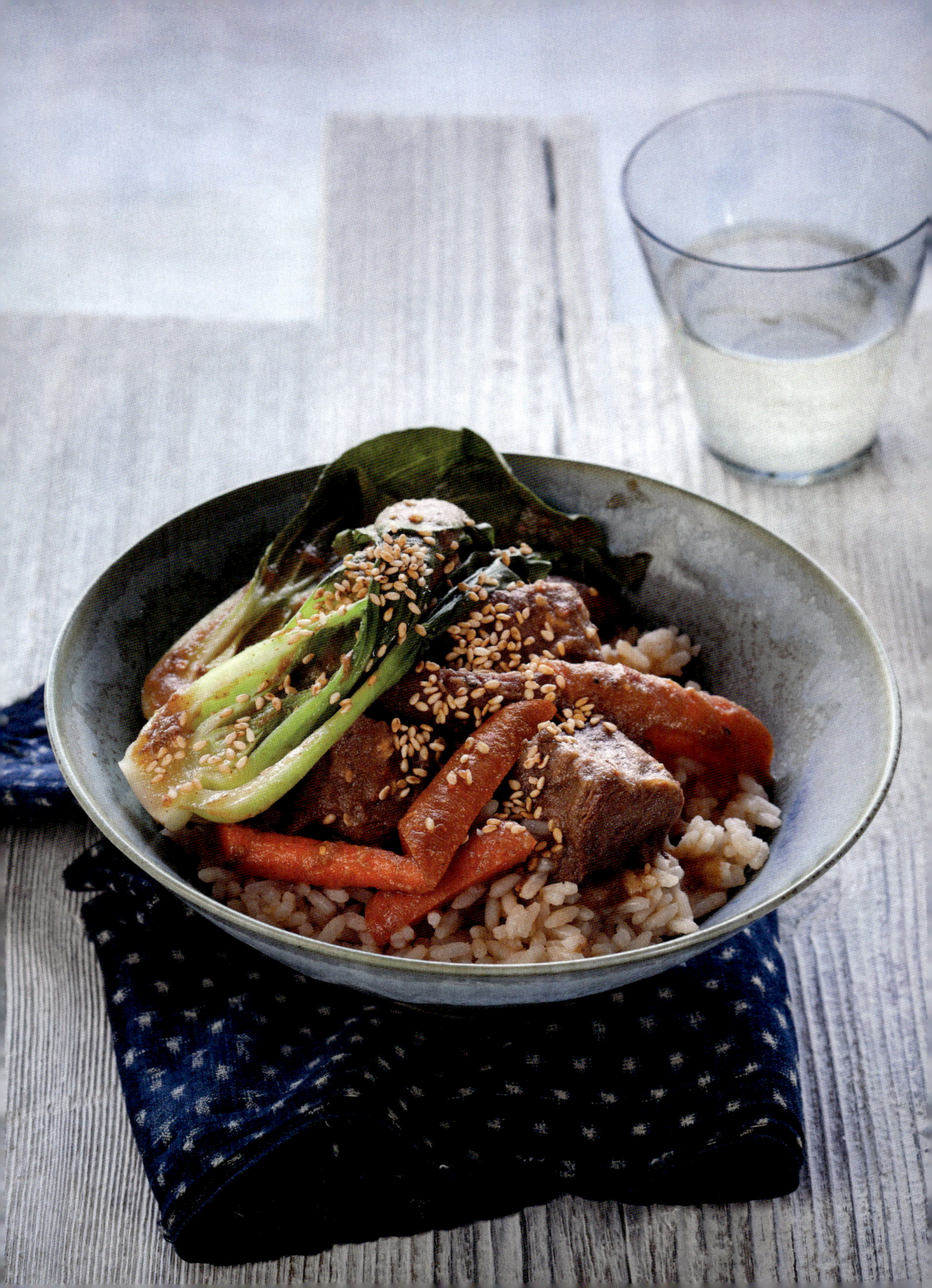

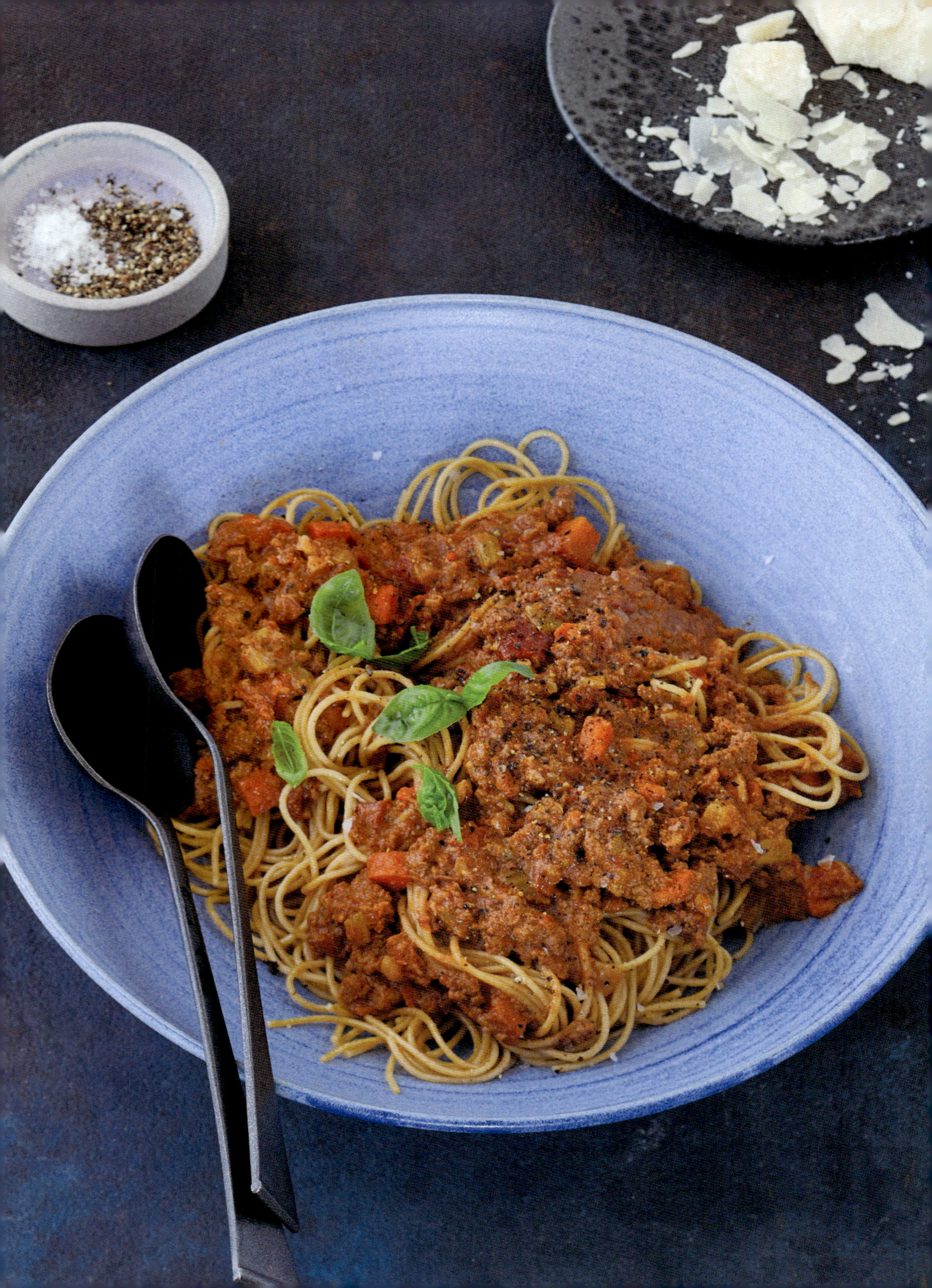

Nonna's bolognese sauce

Prep 15 min Cook 1 hr Serves 8

A little pancetta in your Instant Pot® lends this classic bolognese sauce rich flavor and texture.

3	basil sprigs
1	rosemary sprig
1	tsp olive oil
¼	cup diced pancetta
2	celery stalks, cut into ¼-inch dice
1	large carrot, cut into ¼-inch dice
1	small red onion, cut into ¼-inch dice
3	large garlic cloves, minced
3	tbsp tomato paste
1	lb lean (7% fat or less) ground beef
1	cup reduced-fat (2%) milk
1	(14½-oz) can petite diced tomatoes in puree
⅔	cup reduced-sodium beef broth
1½	tsp kosher salt (or to taste)
½	tsp black pepper
½	cup grated Parmesan

1 Tie basil and rosemary sprigs together with kitchen twine to form a bundle. Set aside.

2 Press Sauté on a 6-qt Instant Pot and set cooking time for 30 minutes. When Hot is displayed, add oil and pancetta to pot. Cook, stirring, until browned, about 2 minutes. Add celery, carrot, and onion and cook, stirring frequently, until vegetables are softened, about 3 minutes. Add garlic, and cook, stirring constantly, until fragrant, about 30 seconds. Stir in tomato paste until blended, about 1 minute longer.

3 Add beef to pot and cook, breaking into 1-inch clumps, until no longer pink, about 3 minutes. Add milk and bring to simmer. Cook, breaking meat up, until milk is almost evaporated, about 12 minutes. Stir in tomatoes, broth, salt, and pepper. Tuck in herb bundle. Press Cancel and lock lid, making sure vent is closed.

4 Press Pressure Cook and select High Pressure; set cooking time for 30 minutes. When time is up, press Cancel to turn off pot. Move steam release valve to Venting position to quickly release pressure. Remove lid. Remove and discard herb bundle. Skim off and discard any fat from surface. Stir in Parmesan.

Per serving (⅔ cup sauce): 186 Cal, 10 g Total Fat, 4 g Sat Fat, 745 mg Sod, 8 g Total Carb, 5 g Sugar, 1 g Fib, 17 g Prot.

Serving idea
Spoon the sauce over thin spaghetti for a more filling main meal.

Tex-Mex red chile pork tacos

Prep 15 min   Cook 45 min   Serves 12

The pineapple juice and vinegar in this recipe give the pork a nice sweet-sour taste and tenderize the meat at the same time.

Olive-oil nonstick spray
- 1 large red onion, thinly sliced
- ¼ cup apple-cider vinegar
- 1¼ tsp kosher salt
- 1 cup unsweetened pineapple juice
- 3 tbsp ancho chile powder
- 4 garlic cloves, crushed through a press or grated on Microplane grater
- 1 tsp ground cumin
- 1 tsp dried oregano
- 1 (2-lb) lean boneless pork shoulder roast, trimmed
- 12 taco shells, warmed
- 4 cups thinly sliced romaine or iceberg lettuce
- 6 large radishes, cut into thin matchsticks
- 2 small limes, each cut into 6 wedges

1 In a medium bowl, toss together onion, vinegar, and ¼ tsp salt; set aside, stirring occasionally. In a large glass measure, stir together pineapple juice, chile powder, garlic, cumin, oregano, and remaining 1 tsp salt; reserve.

2 Cut pork into 3 large pieces. Trim away visible fat and connective tissue; cut pork into 2-inch chunks.

3 Press Sauté on a 6-qt Instant Pot and set cooking time for 15 minutes. When Hot is displayed, spray pork with nonstick spray. Put pork into pot and cook, turning occasionally, until browned, about 10 minutes. Add pineapple juice mixture, stirring to scrape up browned bits from bottom of pot. Press Cancel to turn off pot. Lock lid, making sure vent is closed.

4 Press Pressure Cook and select High Pressure; set cooking time for 35 minutes. When time is up, press Cancel to turn off pot. Move steam release valve to Venting position to quickly release pressure; remove lid. With a slotted spoon, transfer pork to a large bowl. Let stand 5 minutes. Using two forks, shred pork. Cover to keep warm.

5 Transfer sauce from pot to a 2-cup glass measure; skim off and discard fat from surface. Add ¼ cup sauce to pork and stir until coated evenly. Transfer onion to a sieve to drain. Line taco shells with lettuce and top evenly with pork, onion, and radishes. Serve with remaining sauce and lime wedges.

Per serving (1 taco): 205 Cal, 9 g Total Fat, 3 g Sat Fat, 363 mg Sod, 15 g Total Carb, 3 g Sugar, 3 g Fib, 16 g Prot.

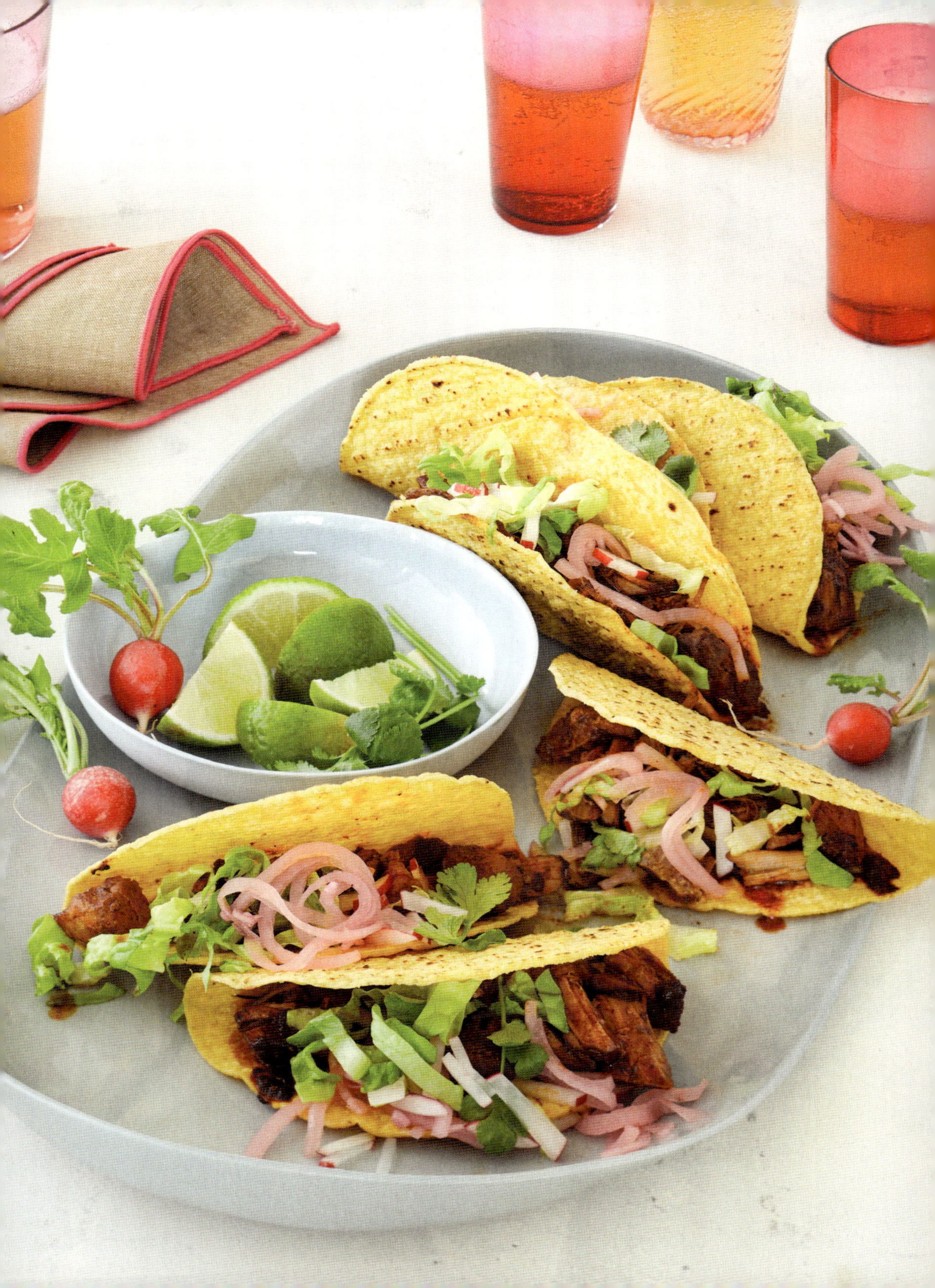

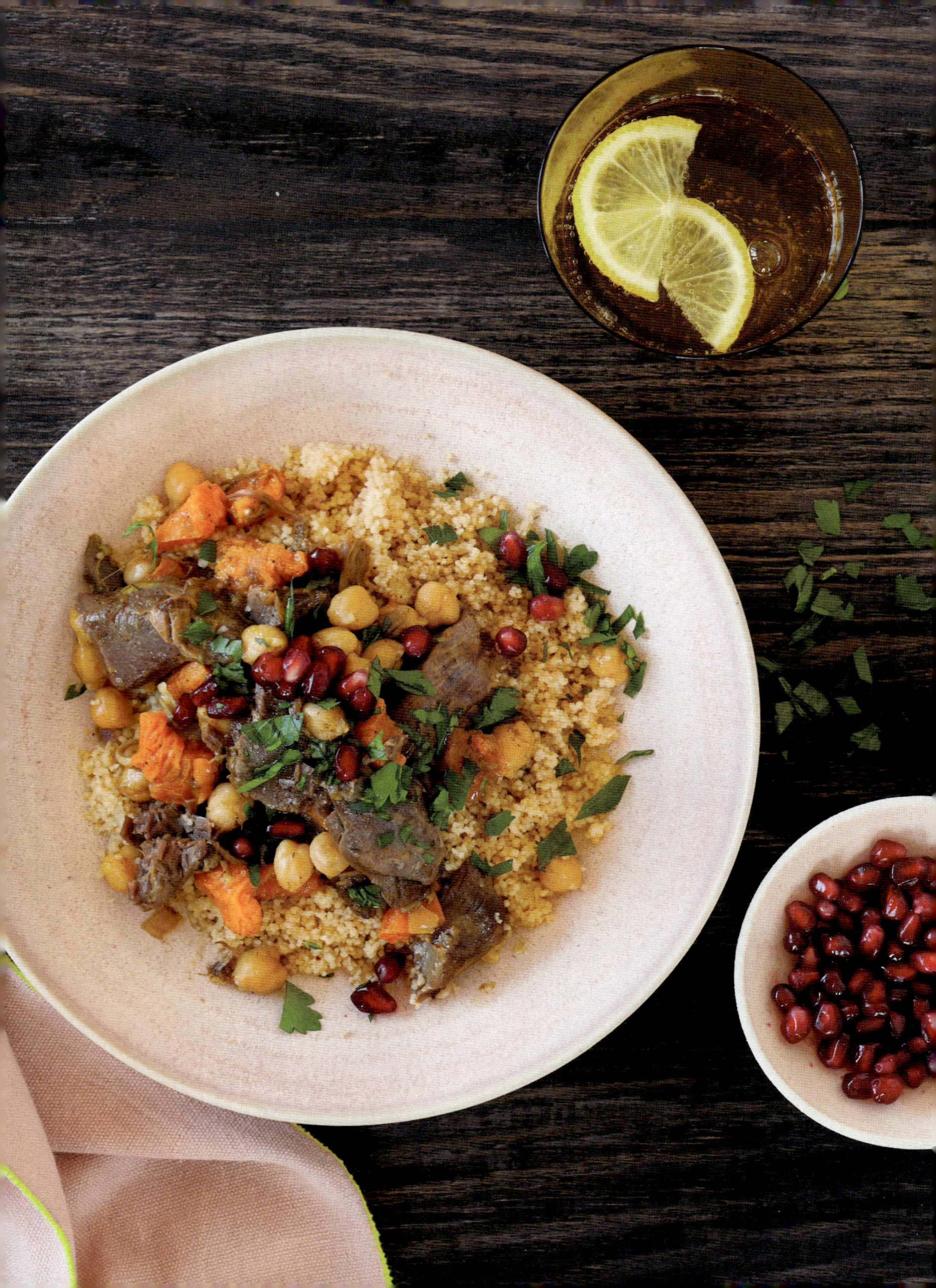

Lamb, apricot, and chickpea tagine

Prep 15 min   Cook 1 hr   Serves 4

Ras el hanout, the spice blend used in this North African stew, is sweet, savory, and spicy all at once. Find it in specialty-food stores, big-box stores, and online. If you can't find it, substitute garam masala.

1	tbsp plus 1½ tsp ras el hanout, divided
½	tsp kosher salt
3	(¾-lb) lean lamb shanks, trimmed
2	tsp olive oil
1	onion, chopped
3	garlic cloves, minced
1¾	cups beef broth
1	(15½-oz) can chickpeas, rinsed and drained
12	dried apricots, quartered
2	cups cooked whole-wheat couscous, kept warm
⅓	cup chopped cilantro
¼	cup pomegranate seeds (arils)

1 Sprinkle 1½ tsp ras el hanout and salt all over lamb. Set aside.

2 Press Sauté on a 6-qt Instant Pot. When Hot is displayed, add oil and onion; cook, stirring, until onion is softened, about 5 minutes. Add garlic and cook, stirring constantly, until fragrant, about 30 seconds. Stir in remaining 1 tbsp ras el hanout and cook, stirring, 1 minute; add broth. Arrange lamb shanks in pot. Press Cancel to turn off pot. Lock lid, making sure vent is closed.

3 Press Pressure Cook and select High Pressure; set cooking time for 55 minutes. When time is up, press Cancel to turn off pot. Move steam release valve to Venting position to quickly release pressure. Remove lid and stir in chickpeas and apricots. Lock lid, making sure vent is closed. Press Pressure Cook and select High Pressure; set cooking time for 2 minutes.

4 When time is up, press Cancel to turn off pot. Move steam release valve to Venting position to quickly release pressure. Remove lid and transfer lamb to cutting board. Cover pot. With a fork, pull large chunks of lamb from bones; discard bones. Stir meat back into pot.

5 Divide couscous evenly among 4 plates or shallow bowls. Spoon lamb mixture over. Sprinkle with cilantro and pomegranate seeds.

Per serving (1 cup stew, ½ cup couscous, and 1 tbsp pomegranate seeds): 482 Cal, 10 g Total Fat, 2 g Sat Fat, 1,023 mg Sod, 62 g Total Carb, 14 g Sugar, 14 g Fib, 38 g Prot.

Cherry tomato and basil–topped spaghetti squash

Prep 10 min   Cook 15 min   Serves 4

Spaghetti squash strands act a lot like pasta! And with your Instant Pot,® the large oval squash is ready in no time. When tomatoes are in season, this uncooked topping beats anything in a jar, hands down.

2	pints assorted color cherry or grape tomatoes, halved or quartered if large
12	large basil leaves, thinly sliced
3	scallions, finely chopped
1	tbsp plus 1 tsp olive oil
1	tbsp white balsamic vinegar
1	tsp kosher salt
¼	tsp black pepper (or to taste)
1	(3½-lb) spaghetti squash, halved crosswise, seeded
¼	cup grated or shaved Parmesan

1 In a serving bowl, mix together tomatoes, basil, scallions, oil, vinegar, salt, and pepper. Toss to mix well. Set aside.

2 Place a wire rack in bottom of a 6-qt Instant Pot; add 1 cup water. Press cut sides of squash halves together to re-form squash; place on rack. Press Pressure Cook and select High Pressure; set cooking time for 5 minutes. When time is up, press Cancel to turn off pot. Move steam release valve to Venting position to quickly release pressure. Remove lid. Let squash stand in pot 10 minutes. With tongs, transfer squash to a cutting board.

3 When squash is cool enough to handle, use a fork to scrape squash flesh into a large bowl, so that it forms spaghetti-like strands. Divide squash evenly among 4 plates. Spoon tomato-basil sauce over squash; top with Parmesan.

Per serving (2 cups squash, 1 cup sauce, and 1 tbsp cheese): 224 Cal, 9 g Total Fat, 2 g Sat Fat, 641 mg Sod, 35 g Total Carb, 7 g Sugar, 2 g Fib, 7 g Prot.

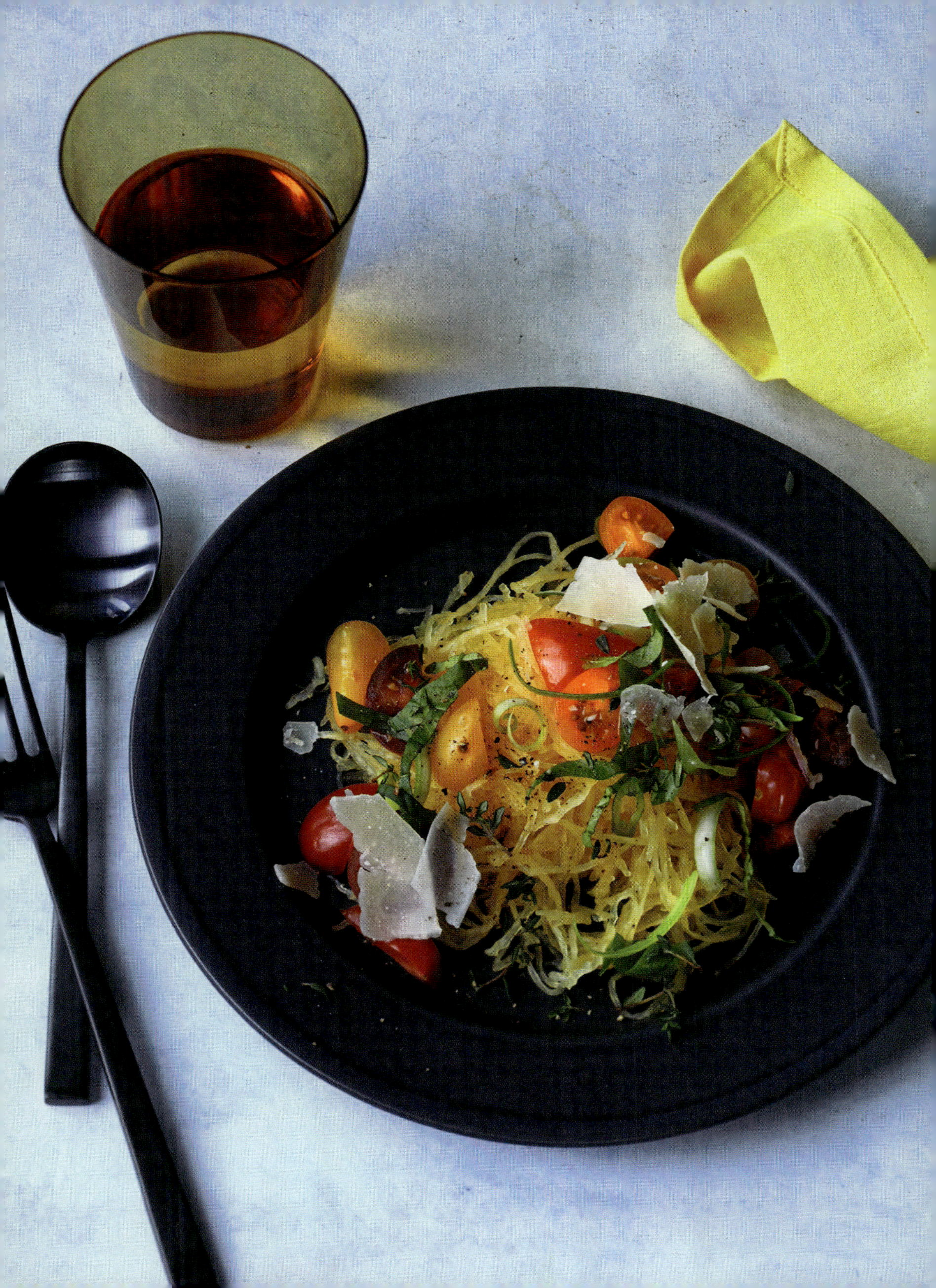

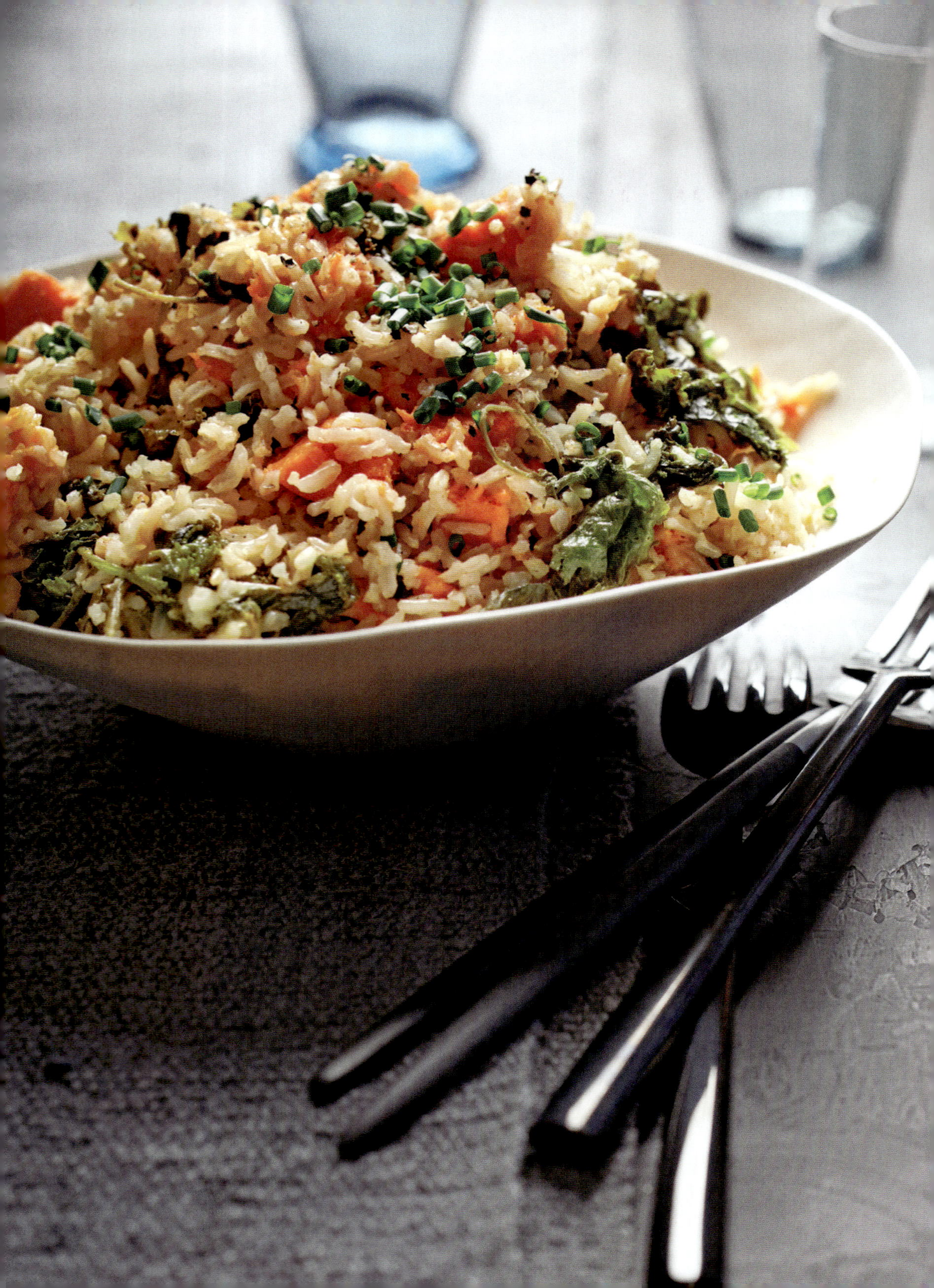

Brown rice, kale, and sweet potato pilaf

Prep 22 min   Cook 40 min   Serves 12

Warm spices round out the flavors in this satisfying vegetarian main dish. Basmati rice is extra-fragrant, but you could use long-grain white or brown rice.

Nonstick spray

1	small onion, chopped
2	tbsp minced peeled ginger, divided
2	cups brown basmati rice
1	large sweet potato, peeled and cut into ½-inch dice
1	tsp ground coriander
¾	tsp kosher salt
½	tsp ground nutmeg
½	tsp black pepper
1	(32-oz) carton reduced-sodium vegetable broth
4	cups tightly packed chopped kale
2	tbsp unsalted butter, cut into pieces
2	tbsp minced chives

1 Press Sauté on a 6-qt Instant Pot. When Hot is displayed, spray bottom of pot with nonstick spray. Add onion and 1½ tbsp ginger to pot. Cook, stirring, until onion is softened, about 4 minutes. Stir in rice and potato. Cook, stirring frequently, 1 minute. Stir in coriander, salt, nutmeg, and pepper and cook, stirring, until fragrant, about 20 seconds longer.

2 Add broth to rice mixture. Place kale on top, pressing to form a compact layer (do not stir). Lock lid, making sure vent is closed. Press Pressure Cook and select High Pressure; set cooking time for 33 minutes.

3 When time is up, press Cancel to turn off pot. Allow pressure to fall naturally for 10 minutes. Move steam release valve to Venting position to quickly release any remaining pressure. Remove lid. Stir in butter, chives, and remaining ½ tbsp ginger. Spoon pilaf into a serving bowl. (If you like, leave pilaf in pot; lock lid, leaving pressure valve open to keep warm up to 20 minutes.)

Per serving (⅔ cup): 164 Cal, 3 g Total Fat, 1 g Sat Fat, 276 mg Sod, 30 g Total Carb, 2 g Sugar, 2 g Fib, 4 g Prot.

Serving idea
If you're not going vegetarian, pair this good-for-you pilaf with a platter of broiled or grilled shrimp.

Bonus chapter 193

Risotto with asparagus and chives

Prep 20 min   Cook 25 min   Serves 4

Forget all that stirring. Risotto in your Instant Pot® is the hands-off way to go.

1	lb asparagus
2	tsp olive oil, divided
1	small leek (white and light green parts), finely chopped
1¼	cups medium-grain rice, such as Carnaroli or Arborio
½	cup dry white wine
1	tsp kosher salt
⅛	tsp saffron threads
½	cup grated Pecorino Romano
¼	tsp black pepper
4	tsp chopped chives
	Thinly sliced lemon zest

1 Cut off 2-inch lengths from asparagus tips and reserve. Cut off 3 inches from ends of asparagus stalks and set aside. Cut remaining asparagus into ½-inch slices and reserve.

2 To make stock: In a 6-qt Instant Pot, combine asparagus ends, ¾ cup reserved sliced asparagus, and 4 cups hot water; lock lid. Press Pressure Cook and select High Pressure; set cooking time for 10 minutes. When time is up, press Cancel to turn off pot. Move steam release valve to Venting position to quickly release pressure. Pour stock through a sieve set over a 4-cup glass measure, pressing on solids; discard. Set stock aside.

3 Press Sauté and set cooking time for 15 minutes. When Hot is displayed, add 1 tsp oil, reserved asparagus tips and remaining sliced asparagus. Cook, stirring, until crisp-tender, 4 to 5 minutes. With a slotted spoon, transfer asparagus to a bowl and cover with foil. Leave pot on sauté mode.

4 Add remaining 1 tsp oil and leek to pot; cook, stirring, until leek begins to soften, about 1 minute. Add rice and cook, stirring, until coated with oil, about 1 minute longer. Add wine and cook, stirring, until absorbed. Stir in reserved asparagus stock, salt, and saffron. Press Cancel to turn off pot.

5 Lock lid, making sure vent is closed. Press Pressure Cook and select Low Pressure; set cooking time for 5 minutes. When time is up, press Cancel to turn off pot. Move steam release valve to Venting position to quickly release pressure. Remove lid. Stir in reserved asparagus, ¼ cup Pecorino Romano, and pepper. Serve sprinkled with remaining ¼ cup cheese, chives, and lemon zest.

Per serving (1⅓ cups): 114 Cal, 2 g Total Fat, 1 g Sat Fat, 232 mg Sod, 19 g Total Carb, 1 g Sugar, 2 g Fib, 3 g Prot.

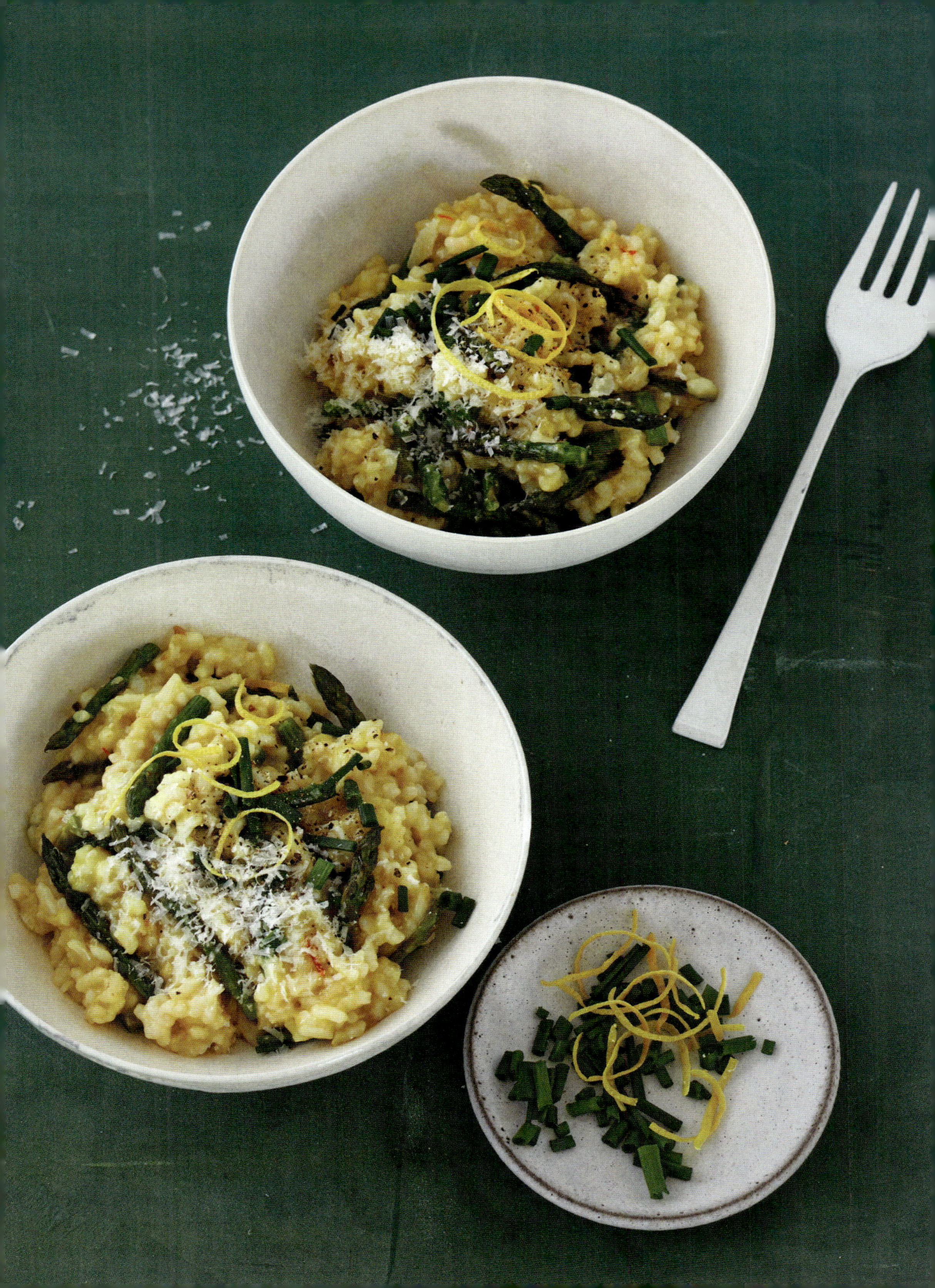

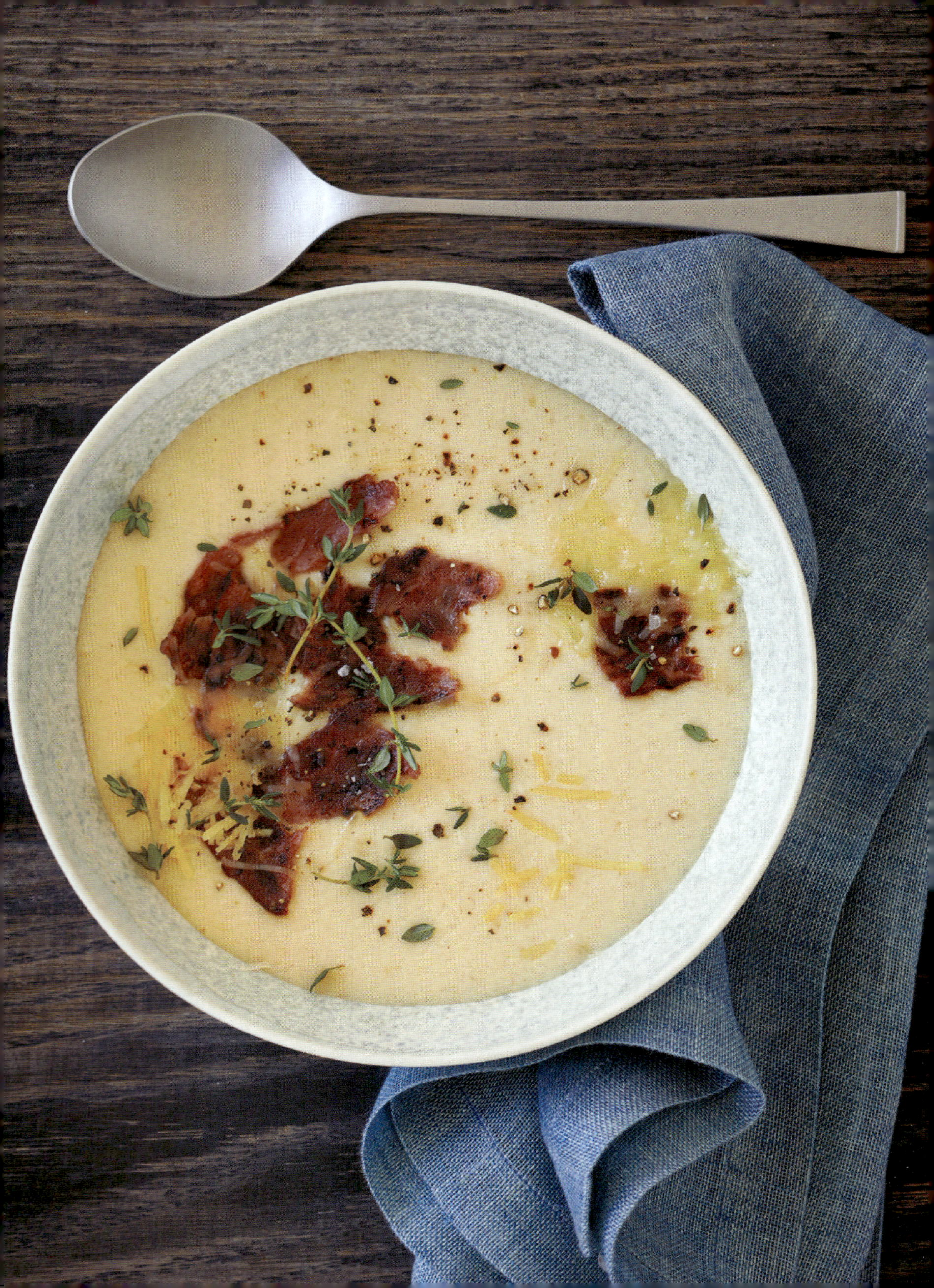

Cauliflower, potato, and bacon bisque

Prep 25 min   Cook 9 min   Serves 6

Get all the creaminess of a traditional bisque with no actual cream! Low-fat milk plus cauliflower and potato make this Instant Pot® soup velvety. If you don't have an immersion blender, just transfer the soup to a regular blender in batches and puree.

Nonstick spray
- 1 onion, chopped
- ½ small head cauliflower, cored and coarsely chopped (about 3 cups)
- 1 Yukon Gold or russet potato, peeled and diced (about 1 cup)
- 2 celery stalks, sliced
- 1 tbsp chopped thyme plus more for serving
- ¾ tsp kosher salt
- ¼ tsp black pepper (or to taste)
- 1½ cups reduced-sodium chicken broth
- 2 tbsp all-purpose flour
- 2 cups reduced-fat (2%) milk
- ¾ cup shredded reduced-fat cheddar
- 3 slices turkey bacon, crisp-cooked and broken into ½-inch pieces

1 Press Sauté on a 6-qt Instant Pot. When Hot is displayed, spray bottom of pot with nonstick spray. Add onion and cook, stirring, until softened, about 5 minutes. Stir in cauliflower, potato, celery, thyme, salt, and pepper.

2 In a small bowl, whisk together ½ cup broth and flour until smooth; add to pot along with remaining 1 cup broth and milk. Press Cancel to turn off pot. Lock lid, making sure vent is closed.

3 Press Pressure Cook and select Low Pressure; set cooking time for 4 minutes. When time is up, press Cancel to turn off pot. Move steam release valve to Venting position to quickly release pressure. Remove lid.

4 Stir ½ cup cheddar into soup. Using an immersion blender, puree soup. Ladle bisque evenly into 6 bowls; sprinkle with remaining ¼ cup cheddar and bacon. Sprinkle with additional thyme and pepper, if desired.

Per serving (1¼ cups soup, 2 tsp cheese, and ½ slice bacon): 135 Cal, 4 g Total Fat, 2 g Sat Fat, 653 mg Sod, 16 g Total Carb, 7 g Sugar, 3 g Fib, 10 g Prot.

Beet borscht with beef and cabbage

Prep 20 min Cook 35 min Serves 6

This wintery, Russian-style borscht is made with lean beef chuck roast; loads of beets, cabbage, and carrot; plus tomato paste and vinegar for a sweet-sour edge.

1	lb lean boneless beef chuck roast, trimmed and cut into ¾-inch pieces
1	(32-oz) carton reduced-sodium beef broth, heated
1½	lb beets, trimmed, scrubbed, and cut into ½-inch dice, plus thinly sliced beet and beet greens for garnish (optional)
1	(10-oz) bag thinly sliced red cabbage
1	large onion, sliced
2	cups shredded or matchstick-cut carrots (about 2 carrots)
2	tbsp tomato paste
1¼	tsp kosher salt
2	tbsp red-wine vinegar (or to taste)
⅓	cup chopped dill, plus small sprigs (optional)
¾	cup light sour cream
¼	tsp black pepper (or to taste)

1. Press Sauté on a 6-qt Instant Pot. When Hot is displayed, spray bottom of pot with nonstick spray. Add beef, in batches, and cook, stirring, until browned on all sides, about 6 minutes per batch. Return beef to pot along with broth. Press Cancel to turn off pot. Lock lid, making sure vent is closed.

2. Press Pressure Cook and select High Pressure; set cooking time for 16 minutes. When time is up, press Cancel to turn off pot. Move steam release valve to Venting position to quickly release pressure.

3. Remove lid and stir in beets, cabbage, onion, carrots, tomato paste, and salt. Lock lid, making sure vent is closed. Press Pressure Cook and select High Pressure; set cooking time for 7 minutes. When time is up, press Cancel. Move steam release valve to Venting position to quickly release pressure.

4. Remove lid and stir in vinegar and dill. Ladle soup evenly into 6 bowls. Top each serving with dollop of sour cream. Sprinkle with pepper. Garnish with sliced beet and beet greens, if desired.

Per serving (1½ cups borscht and 2 tbsp sour cream): 242 Cal, 8 g Total Fat, 4 g Sat Fat, 894 mg Sod, 24 g Total Carb, 14 g Sugar, 6 g Fib, 22 g Prot.

Serving idea
Stick with the Russian theme and slice up pumpernickel bread to serve on the side.

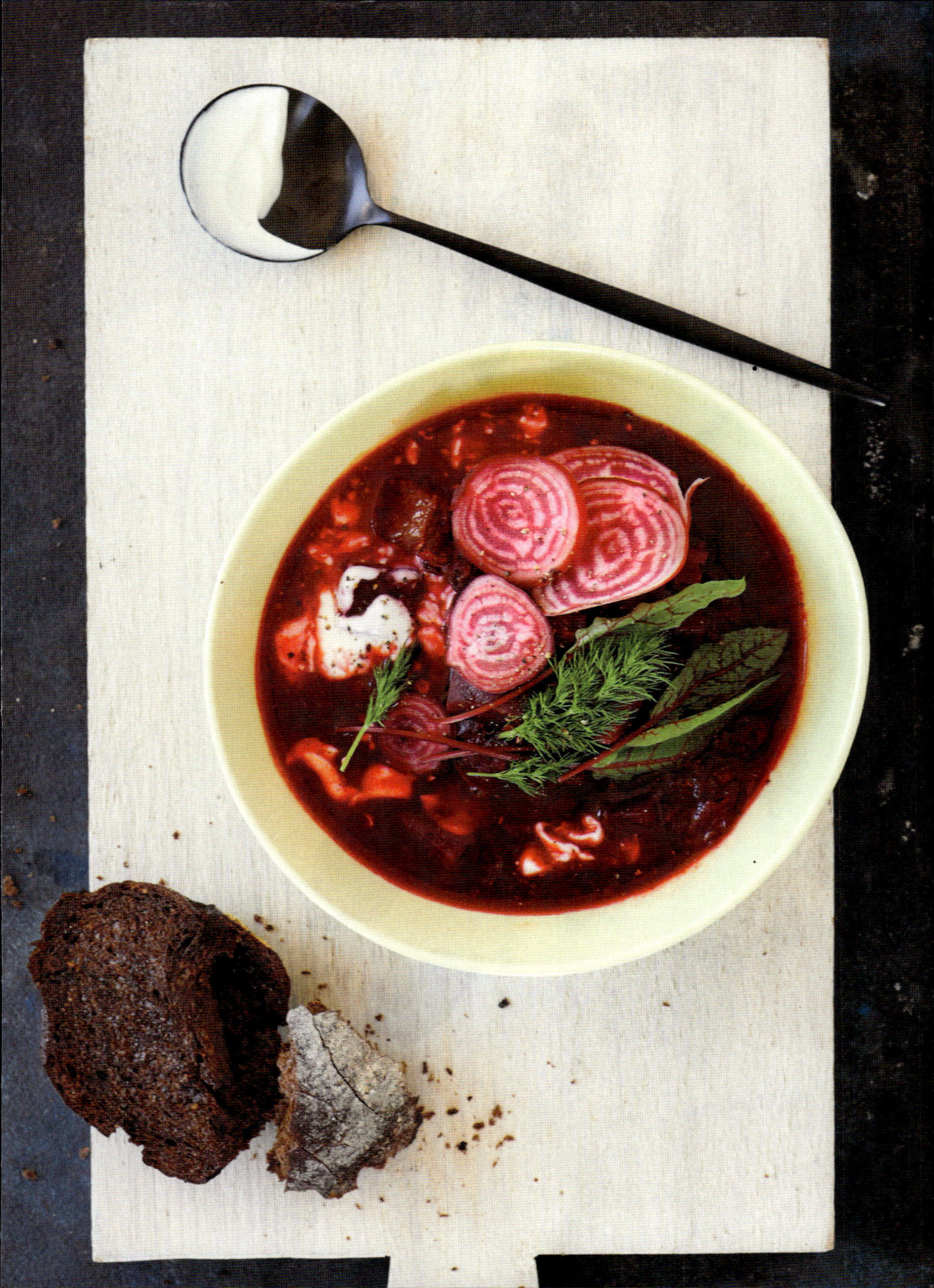

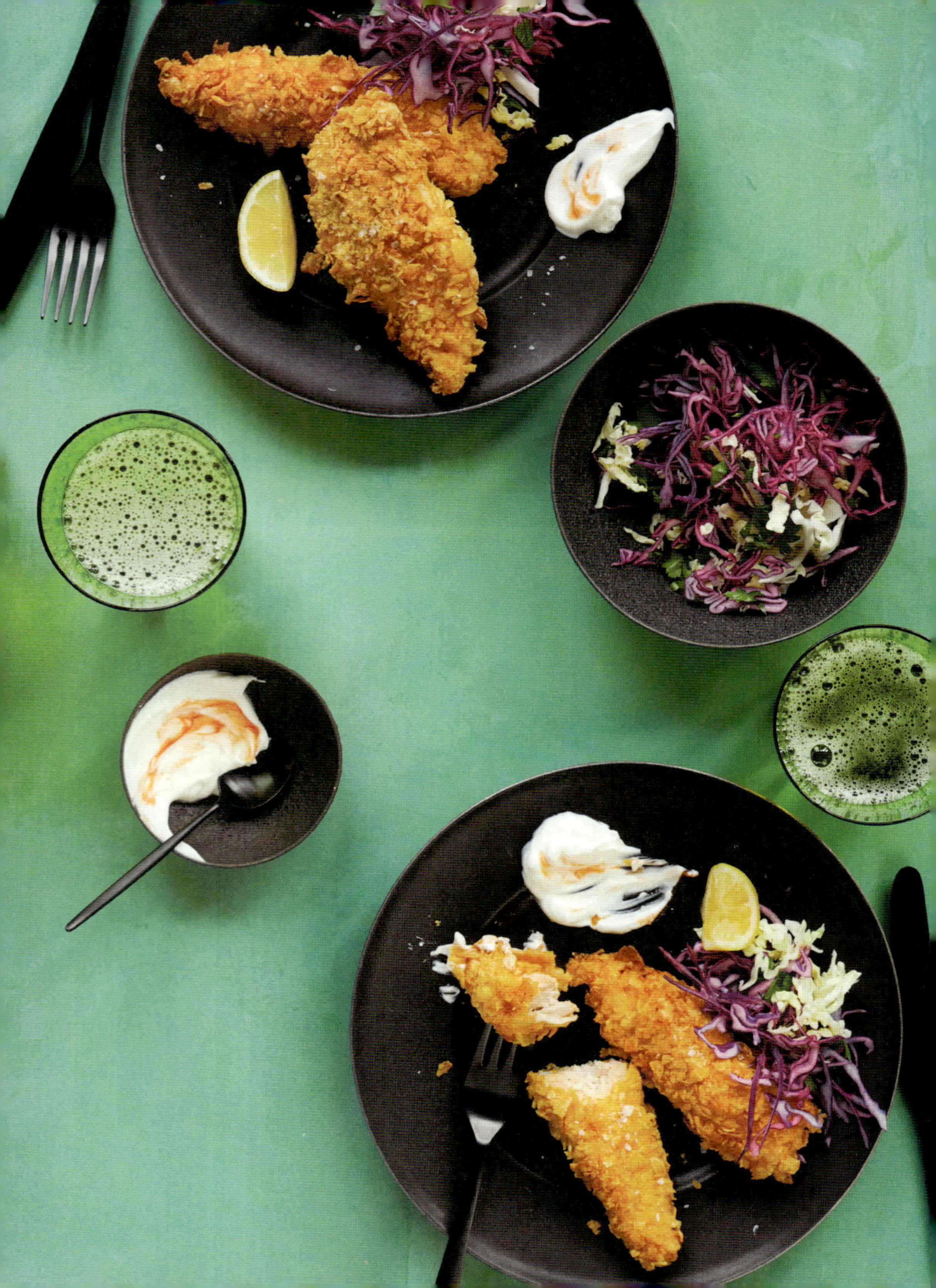

Southern-style fried chicken

Prep 20 min   Marinate 2 to 8 hr   Cook 10 min   Serves 4

7 · 4 · 4

Buttermilk makes this chicken tender, a just-right seasoning blend adds extra zing, and the air fryer brings the crispiness (without any oil).

Nonstick spray

- ¾ cup low-fat buttermilk
- 1 to 2 tbsp mild pepper sauce, such as Frank's plus more for serving
- 1 tsp garlic powder
- ¾ tsp poultry seasoning
- 4 (5-oz) skinless boneless chicken breasts, halved lengthwise
- ⅓ cup all-purpose flour
- 1 tsp paprika
- 1 tsp onion powder
- 1 tsp kosher salt, divided
- 1 large egg, beaten
- 1 cup crushed cornflake cereal or cornflake crumbs

1 In a 2-cup glass measure, stir together buttermilk, pepper sauce, garlic powder, and poultry seasoning until blended. Put chicken in a large zip-close plastic bag; add buttermilk mixture. Squeeze out air and seal bag; turn to coat chicken. Refrigerate at least 2 hours or up to overnight.

2 On a sheet of wax paper, mix together flour, paprika, onion powder, and ½ tsp salt. In a small shallow bowl, beat egg. Place crushed cornflakes on separate sheet of wax paper. Drain chicken in a colander, discarding buttermilk; sprinkle chicken with remaining ½ tsp salt. Dredge chicken in flour mixture, then dip in egg, allowing excess to drip off. Coat chicken with cornflakes, lightly pressing so they adhere. Spray nonstick spray all over chicken.

3 Depending on air fryer settings, preheat a 6- to 8-qt air fryer to 350°F or 360°F for 3 minutes. Spray bottom and side of basket with nonstick spray. Arrange chicken in basket, leaning pieces against side of basket as needed to fit. Air-fry 5 minutes. Turn breasts, being careful not to disturb coating. Air-fry until crust is golden and crispy and an instant-read thermometer inserted into chicken registers 165°F, 5 minutes longer. Serve with hot sauce.

Per serving (2 pieces chicken): 335 Cal, 6 g Total Fat, 2 g Sat Fat, 754 mg Sod, 30 g Total Carb, 5 g Sugar, 1 g Fib, 38 g Prot.

Serving idea

Fried chicken demands coleslaw! Use packaged coleslaw mix, a splash of vinegar, a sprinkling of chopped parsley, salt and pepper to taste, and a big dollop of plain fat-free yogurt for richness and tang.

Super-simple chicken parmesan

Prep 15 min   Cook 10 to 20 min   Serves 4

What's the difference between a skinless, boneless chicken breast and a chicken cutlet? Chicken cutlets are thin slices cut from the breast. Bonus with cutlets: they cook in minutes.

Olive-oil nonstick spray
- 1 large egg
- ½ cup Italian-seasoned dried bread crumbs
- 4 (¼-lb) chicken cutlets
- ½ cup low-fat pizza or marinara sauce
- 4 large basil leaves, thinly sliced
- 4 (½-oz) ultra-thin slices part-skim mozzarella
- 4 thick slices tomato
- ¼ cup grated Parmesan
- ¼ tsp black pepper

1 Whisk egg and 1 tbsp water in a large shallow bowl. Spread bread crumbs on sheet of wax paper. Dip chicken in egg, allowing excess to drip off; coat with crumbs, lightly pressing so they adhere. Spray nonstick spray all over cutlets.

2 Depending on air fryer settings, preheat a 6- to 8-qt air fryer to 360°F or 370°F for 3 minutes. Spray basket with nonstick spray and add 2 chicken cutlets. Air fry until golden and crisp, 4 to 5 minutes. Lift out basket. Turn chicken over; spread 2 tbsp pizza sauce on each cutlet and top with basil, slice of mozzarella, and slice of tomato. Sprinkle 1 tbsp Parmesan and pepper on each cutlet.

3 Air-fry until chicken is cooked through and crisp and mozzarella is melted, 2 to 3 minutes. Transfer to a plate and loosely cover with foil to keep warm. Air-fry remaining 2 cutlets.

Per serving (1 cutlet): 297 Cal, 10 g Total Fat, 4 g Sat Fat, 714 mg Sod, 15 g Total Carb, 3 g Sugar, 2 g Fib, 35 g Prot.

Serving idea
A side of steamed broccolini topped with sautéed slices of garlic and red pepper flakes takes just minutes to prepare.

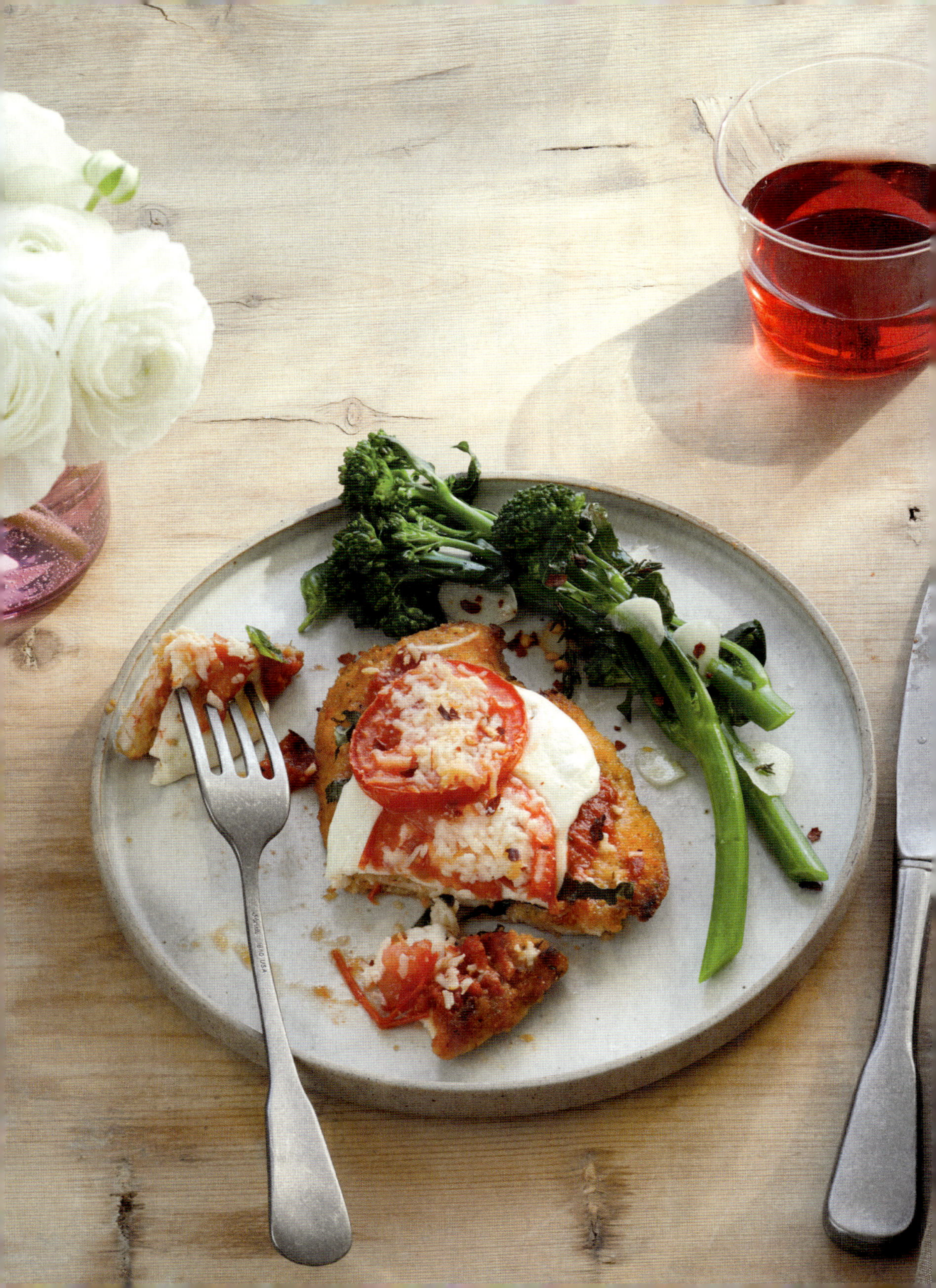

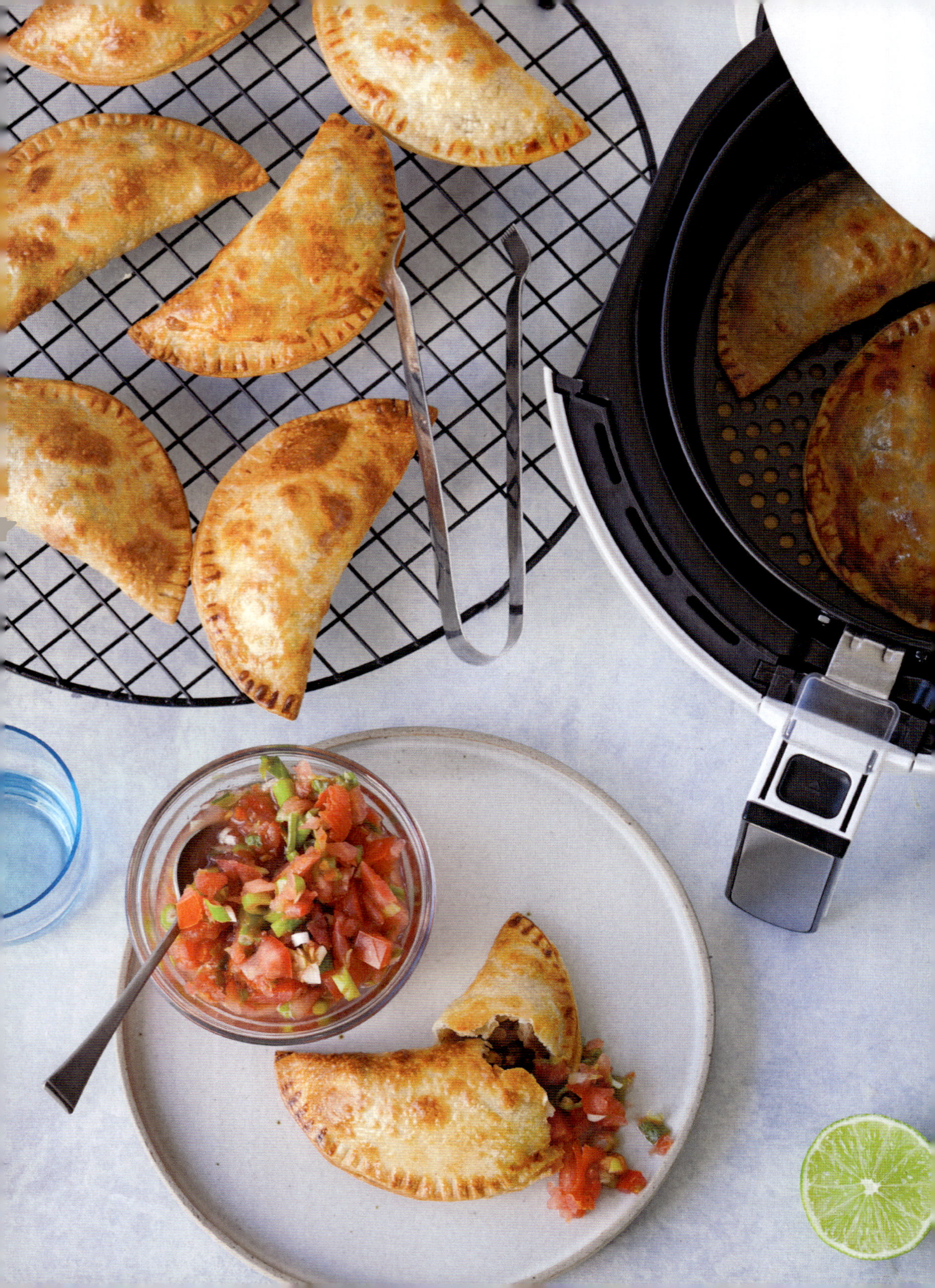

Colombian beef and potato empanadas

Prep 45 min   Chill 30 min   Cook 45 min   Serves 12

Colombian empanadas go heavy on the spices, which make them extra good. Using frozen dough is the key shortcut in this recipe.

1	tbsp olive oil
¾	lb beef stir-fry strips, cut into ¼-inch pieces
1	onion, cut into ¼-inch dice
1	Yukon Gold potato, peeled and cut into ¼-inch dice
1	large plum tomato, seeded and diced
3	garlic cloves, minced
2	tsp chili powder
2	tsp ground cumin
½	tsp kosher salt
⅓	cup chopped cilantro
12	frozen regular-size empanada dough disks for baking, thawed (like Goya)
1	large egg, lightly beaten

Aji picante (Colombian hot sauce; see "Prep ahead," *below*) or salsa

1. Preheat oven to 200°F. Line baking sheet with parchment paper.

2. To make empanada filling: In a large nonstick skillet over medium-high heat, warm oil. Add beef and onion and cook, stirring, until beef is browned and onion is softened, about 5 minutes. Add potato and reduce heat to medium. Cook, stirring, until potato is almost tender, about 10 minutes. Stir in tomato, garlic, chili powder, cumin, and salt. Reduce heat to medium-low; cook until potato is fork-tender, about 3 minutes longer. Transfer to a medium bowl and stir in cilantro. Let cool completely.

3. Mound 2 tbsp filling along middle of each empanada dough disk. Fold in half to form half-moon shape and press edges together to seal. Roll edge to form ½-inch rim; crimp with fork. Place on prepared baking sheet. Refrigerate until cold, about 30 minutes.

4. Line bottom of a 6- to 8-qt air fryer basket with parchment paper, slightly smaller than basket. Depending on air fryer settings, preheat to 360°F or 370°F for 3 minutes.

5. Place 4 empanadas in prepared basket. Brush tops with beaten egg. Air-fry 8 minutes. Turn empanadas over and brush with egg. Air-fry until golden brown and firm, about 6 minutes longer. Place on wire rack and keep warm in oven. Air-fry remaining empanadas. Serve warm with aji picante sauce.

Per serving (1 empanada and about 2½ tbsp sauce): 221 Cal, 7 g Total Fat, 2 g Sat Fat, 731 mg Sod, 31 g Total Carb, 4 g Sugar, 2 g Fib, 11 g Prot.

Prep ahead

Aji picante sauce is easy to make. Combine 1 cup cilantro leaves; 2 jalapeños, chopped; 3 scallions, chopped; 1 large tomato, chopped; 3 tbsp lime juice; 1 tbsp white vinegar; ½ tsp kosher salt; and ¼ tsp black pepper in food processor. Pulse until it forms a chunky puree. (Makes 2 cups.)

Cornmeal-crusted fish fingers

Prep 25 min   Cook 16 min   Serves 4

Forget frozen fish sticks because ours are a game changer. We like to use tilapia, a mild-flavored, firm-textured fish you can find anywhere.

Nonstick spray
- 1 lb thick tilapia or catfish fillets
- ¼ cup cornstarch or all-purpose flour
- 1 large egg
- ½ cup yellow cornmeal
- ¾ tsp kosher salt
- ¼ tsp cayenne

TARTAR SAUCE
- ¼ cup low-fat mayonnaise
- ¼ cup plain fat-free yogurt
- 3 tbsp sweet pickle relish, drained
- 2 tbsp chopped dill
- 1 tbsp minced shallot
- ¼ tsp grated lemon zest
- 1 tbsp lemon juice
- ¼ tsp black pepper

1 Preheat oven to 200°F. Line a small rimmed baking sheet with parchment paper.

2 Cut fish fillets lengthwise into ¾-inch-wide strips, then cut crosswise into 3-inch lengths (you should have about 20 fingers). Spread cornstarch on a sheet of wax paper. In a small bowl, beat egg. On a separate sheet of wax paper, mix together cornmeal, salt, and cayenne.

3 Dredge fish fingers in cornstarch, tapping off excess, then dip into egg, allowing excess to drip off. Coat fish with cornmeal mixture, pressing lightly so it adheres; arrange on prepared baking sheet. Lightly spray with nonstick spray.

4 Depending on air fryer settings, preheat a 6- to 8-qt air fryer to 390°F or 400°F for 3 minutes. Spray fryer basket with nonstick spray and add 10 fish fingers to basket. Air-fry 5 minutes. Turn fish over. Air-fry until golden brown and firm to touch, about 3 minutes longer. Transfer fish to wire rack and keep warm in oven. Air-fry remaining 10 fish fingers.

5 Meanwhile, to make tartar sauce: In a serving bowl, combine all tartar sauce ingredients until mixed well. Thin with water, if needed. (Makes about ¾ cup.) Serve with fish fingers.

Per serving (5 fish fingers and 3 tbsp tartar sauce): 270 Cal, 6 g Total Fat, 1 g Sat Fat, 648 mg Sod, 28 g Total Carb, 6 g Sugar, 1 g Fib, 25 g Prot.

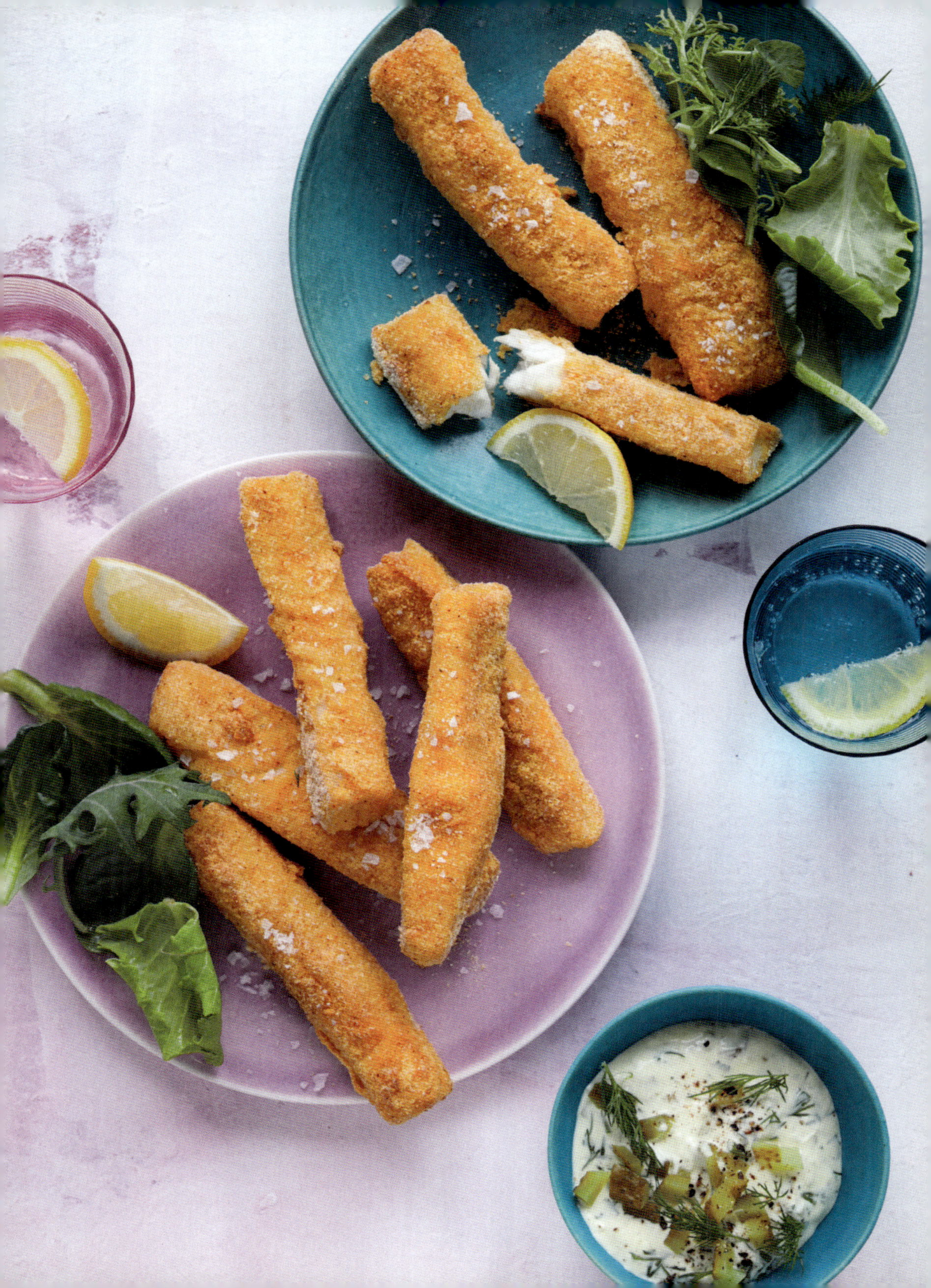

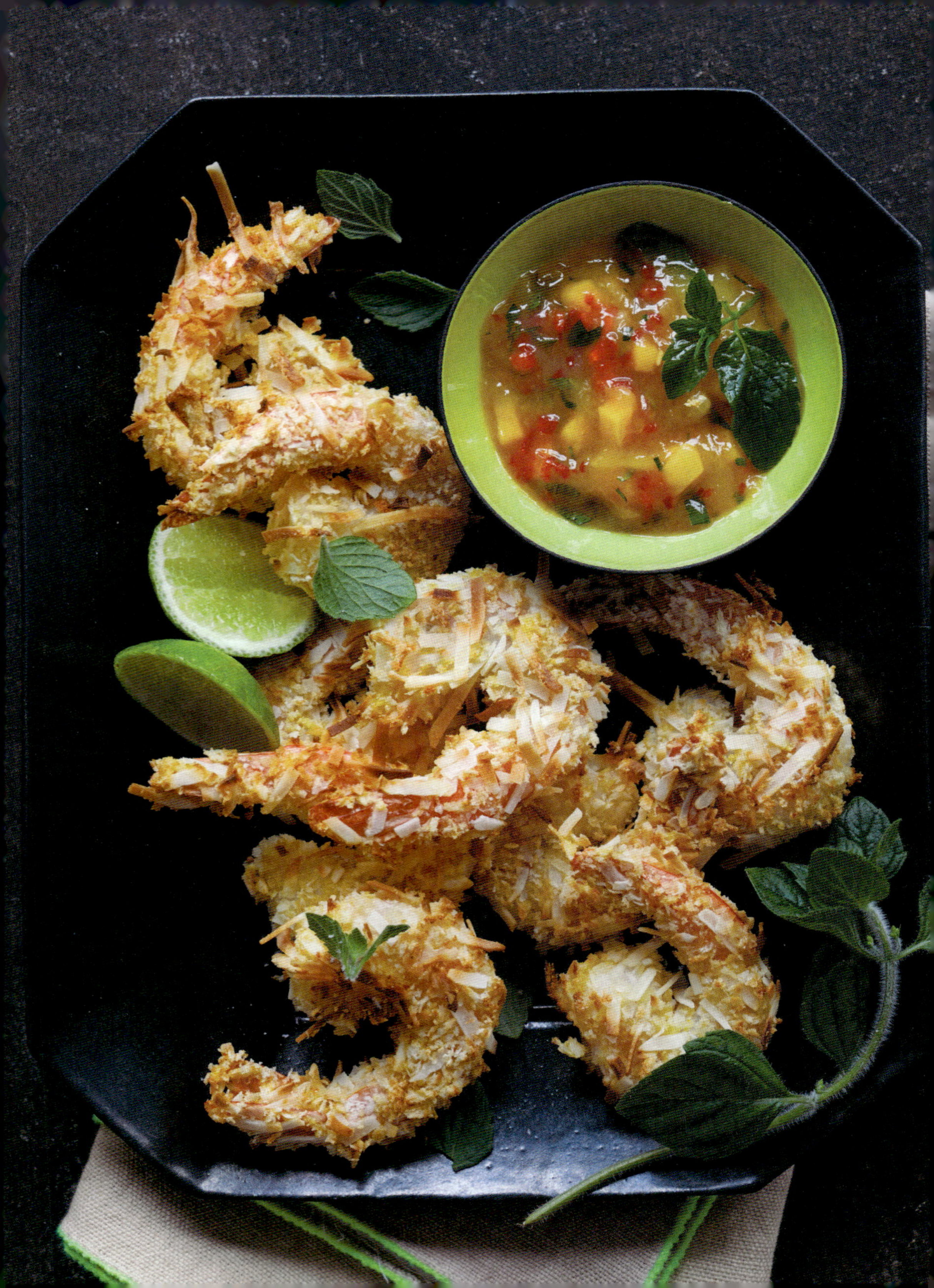

Coconut shrimp with mango dipping sauce

Prep 30 min   Cook 10 min   Serves 6

Cooking these shrimp in an air fryer ensures they'll be crisp and crunchy in no time at all.

Nonstick spray
- 1 mango, pitted, and peeled
- 2 tbsp lime juice
- 1 tsp grated peeled ginger
- 1 tsp kosher salt
- 1½ tbsp chopped mint
- 1 Fresno or jalapeño pepper, seeded and minced
- 3 tbsp cornstarch or all-purpose flour
- 2 large eggs
- ⅓ cup unsweetened shredded coconut
- ⅓ cup panko bread crumbs
- 18 extra-large shrimp (about 1 lb), peeled and deveined, tails left on

Lime wedge

1 To make dipping sauce: Cut up half of mango. Combine with lime juice, ginger, and ¼ tsp salt in a blender and process until smooth. Pour into a small bowl. Dice remaining mango. Add to puree along with mint, pepper, and enough water to make saucy.

2 On a sheet of wax paper, spread cornstarch. In a large shallow bowl, beat eggs. On a separate sheet of wax paper, mix together coconut, panko, and remaining ¾ tsp salt.

3 Dredge shrimp in cornstarch, shaking off excess, then dip into egg, allowing excess to drip off. Press shrimp into coconut mixture until evenly coated on both sides. Place on a wire rack set over baking sheet. Spray shrimp all over with nonstick spray.

4 Depending on air fryer settings, preheat a 6- to 8-qt air fryer to 390°F or 400°F for 3 minutes. Lightly spray fryer basket with nonstick spray. Arrange 9 shrimp in a single layer in basket. Air-fry until shrimp are golden and crispy, 5 to 6 minutes. Transfer to a plate and loosely cover with foil to keep warm. Repeat to fry remaining shrimp. Serve with mango sauce and lime wedges.

Per serving (3 shrimp and 2½ tbsp mango sauce): 143 Cal, 5 g Total Fat, 3 g Sat Fat, 503 mg Sod, 18 g Total Carb, 8 g Sugar, 2 g Fib, 6 g Prot.

Serving idea

As a side, spice up thick slices of pineapple with a dusting of black pepper and ground cinnamon. It's a surprisingly great combination.

Cheese-dusted potato fries

Prep 15 min   Soak 30 min   Cook 30 min   Serves 4

Russet potatoes are the best choice for air fryer fries. Cut them into scant ½-inch-thick sticks to make sure they turn out crispy on the outside and creamy on the inside, just the way we like 'em.

Nonstick spray
- 2 large russet (baking) potatoes, peeled (about 1¼ lb)
- 3 tbsp grated Pecorino Romano or Parmesan
- 1 tbsp salt-free lime seasoning blend (like Mrs. Dash)
- 2 tsp canola oil
- ½ tsp salt

1. Trim ends of potatoes; cut potatoes lengthwise into scant ½-inch slices. Stack slices and cut lengthwise to form scant ½-inch-wide sticks. Put into a large bowl of cold water and let soak 30 minutes. Transfer to a colander to drain. Place potatoes on double layer of paper towels and pat thoroughly dry. Wipe out bowl; set aside.

2. To make seasoning mix, stir together cheese and seasoning blend in cup.

3. Depending on air fryer settings, preheat a 6- to 8-qt to 330°F or 340°F for 3 minutes. Lightly spray fryer basket with nonstick spray. Put potatoes in cleaned bowl and drizzle with oil, tossing until coated evenly. Put potatoes in fryer basket. Air-fry until partially cooked, 13 to 15 minutes, shaking basket a few times so potatoes cook evenly. Wipe bowl clean.

4. Increase air fryer temperature to 390°F or 400°F. Air-fry potatoes until lightly golden, 11 to 13 minutes, tossing once. Transfer fries to cleaned bowl and sprinkle with cheese-seasoning mix; toss until coated evenly. Return fries to basket. Air-fry until golden and crispy, 3 to 5 minutes longer. Sprinkle evenly with salt. Transfer potatoes to a serving bowl and sprinkle with any remaining seasoning mix.

Per serving (½ potato): 181 Cal, 4 g Total Fat, 1 g Sat Fat, 375 mg Sod, 33 g Total Carb, 1 g Sugar, 2 g Fib, 5 g Prot.

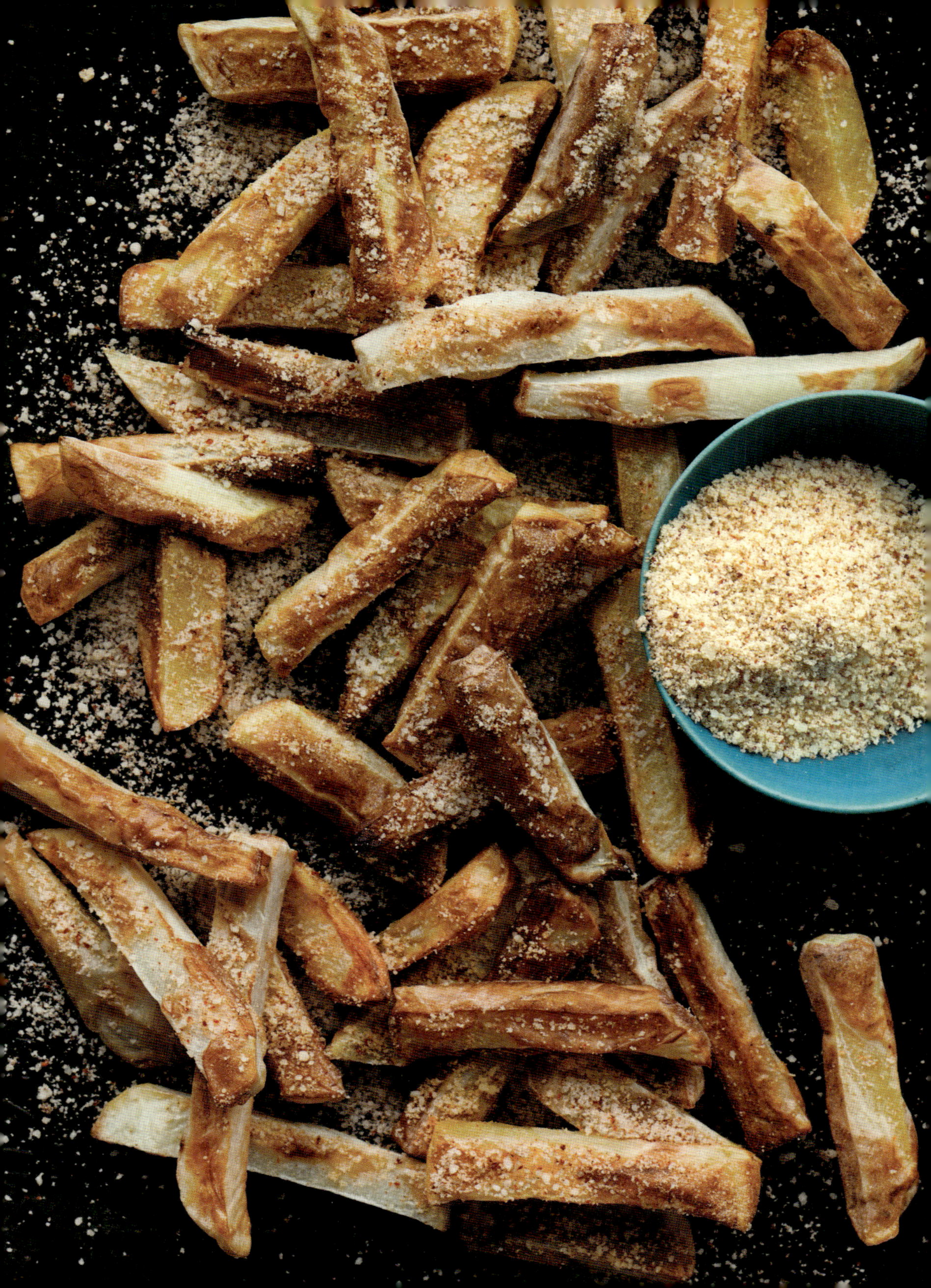

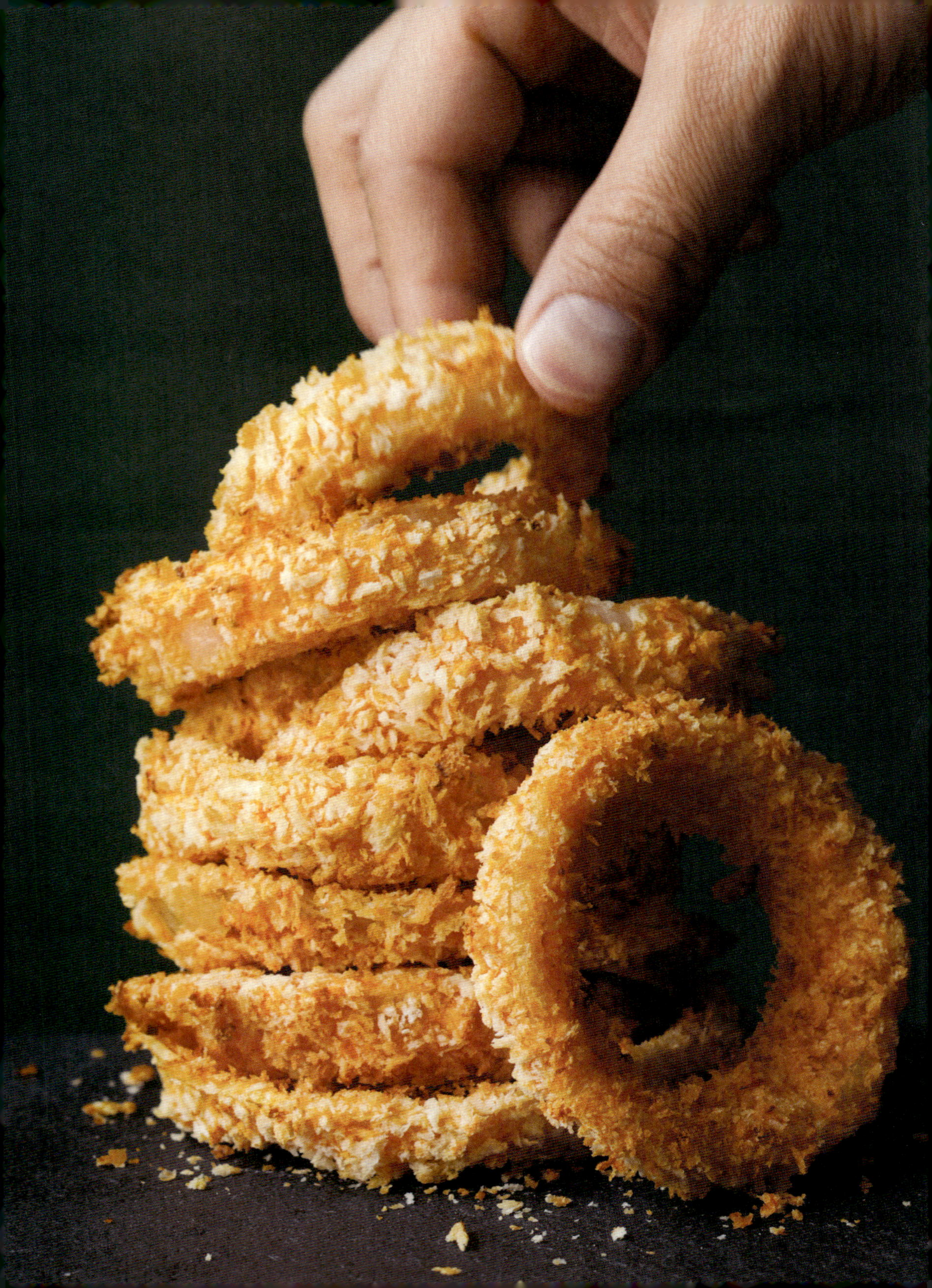

Crispy buttermilk onion rings

Prep 20 min   Cook 20 min   Serves 4

Wonderfully crisp and crunchy onion rings are an all-time fave with burgers. These stay crispy for up to an hour, so you have plenty of time to fire up the grill.

Nonstick spray
- ¼ cup cornstarch
- 1 large egg
- ½ cup low-fat buttermilk
- ⅓ cup all-purpose flour
- 1 tsp hot pepper sauce or to taste
- ¾ tsp salt
- ½ tsp paprika
- 1 cup panko bread crumbs
- 2 (½-lb) sweet onions, such as Vidalia, Texas Sweet or Maui, cut into ½-inch slices

1 On a sheet of wax paper, spread cornstarch. In a medium bowl, beat egg. Whisk in buttermilk, flour, hot sauce, salt, and paprika until smooth. On a separate sheet of wax paper, spread panko.

2 Separate onion slices into rings, selecting 20 largest rings (reserve remaining rings for another use). Coat onion rings, 5 at a time, with cornstarch, using a fork to turn. Using another fork, dip coated rings into batter, letting excess batter drip off. Coat onion rings with panko, turning with a clean fork. Place on baking sheet in a single layer. Repeat to coat remaining onion rings.

3 Depending on air fryer settings, preheat a 6- to 8-qt air fryer to 360°F or 370°F for 3 minutes. Lightly spray basket with nonstick spray. Place 10 rings in basket. Spray onions again and air-fry 5 minutes. Turn rings over and spray. Air-fry until crispy, 5 minutes longer. Repeat with remaining onion rings.

Per serving (5 onion rings): 251 Cal, 4 g Total Fat, 1 g Sat Fat, 708 mg Sod, 45 g Total Carb, 7 g Sugar, 3 g Fib, 8 g Prot.

Recipes by SmartPoints® value

Green

2 SmartPoints
Cherry tomato and basil–topped spaghetti squash, 190
Creamy tomato soup with crab, 105
Mexican chicken soup, 119
Old-fashioned chicken noodle soup, 66
Vietnamese lemongrass chicken soup, 120

3 SmartPoints
Chicken tikka masala, 154
Classic Italian meatballs, 85
Indian fish curry, 144
Korean beef stew, 182
Mushroom, tomato, and thyme chicken, 61
Portobello mushroom and eggplant chili, 28

4 SmartPoints
Beet borscht with beef and cabbage, 198
Cauliflower, potato, and bacon bisque, 197
Coconut shrimp with mango dipping sauce, 209
Garlicky shrimp with charred fennel, 102
Hot-and-sour soup with shiitakes and tofu, 147
Indian-spiced potatoes with cauliflower, 51
Italian vegetable-bean stew, 32
San Francisco fisherman's stew, 101
Sausage, chicken, and shrimp stew, 140
Spiced-up rotisserie-style chicken, 174
Teriyaki pork tenderloin, 136

5 SmartPoints
Basque chicken with chorizo and peppers, 153
Beef carnitas tacos, 128
Brown rice, kale, and sweet potato pilaf, 193
Butternut squash and chickpea chili, 24
Chicken with celery root and apple, 58
Classic chicken cacciatore, 150
Double-mushroom and prosciutto soup, 94
Farro and double-mushroom pot, 39
Five-spice pork stew, 139
Italian-style pot roast, 77
Jamaican jerk chicken, 123
Lamb tagine with lemon and olives, 161
Meatballs in chipotle chile sauce, 124
Nonna's bolognese sauce, 185
Pork in green chile sauce, 143
Roman-style chicken cacciatore, 178
Spicy turkey meatballs, 73
Tex-Mex red chile pork tacos, 186

6 SmartPoints
Apple-stuffed French toast casserole, 21
Bouillabaisse, 162
Cheese and chorizo tortilla casserole, 10
Cheese-dusted potato fries, 210
Chicken tacos with pineapple slaw, 111
Colombian beef and potato empanadas, 202
Crispy buttermilk onion rings, 213
Hearty beef-barley stew, 81
Pork chops with braised cabbage, 90
Provençal-style beef stew, 157
Risotto-style barley and peas, 40
Rosemary-garlic pork roast, 89
Scalloped potatoes with thyme, 55
Smoky beef brisket, 181
Soft polenta with pecorino and mushrooms, 169
Szechuan chicken and broccoli, 115
Tomato, basil, and ricotta frittata, 17

7 SmartPoints
Beef 'n' bean chili, 82
Beef soup with lemongrass and coconut, 132
Braciole with spicy tomato sauce, 78
Cajun chicken-sausage jambalaya, 177
Cauliflower paprikash, 166
Chicken and white bean chili, 69
Cornmeal-crusted fish fingers, 206
Just-like-banana-bread overnight oats, 2
Lamb-ricotta meatballs and sauce, 98
Louisiana jambalaya, 65
Marrakesh-style pork, 135
Moroccan chicken, 112
Parmesan-stuffed artichokes, 97
Piled-high chicken nachos, 62
Rice-and-bean stuffed peppers, 31
Ricotta-and-spinach stuffed cabbage, 44
Sicilian-style pork and fennel ragu, 93
Simply delicious lasagna, 86
Southern-style fried chicken, 201
Summer tomato sauce with pasta, 48
Super-easy three-bean chili, 27

Super-simple chicken parmesan, 202
Turkey–bell pepper meatloaf, 70

8 SmartPoints
Artichoke and bell pepper paella, 52
Carne guisada with charred tortillas, 158
Egg casserole with hash browns and peppers, 13
Italian sausage and mozzarella strata, 18
Low-and-slow sloppy joes, 74
Mojo-style steak tacos, 127
Multigrain hot cereal with mango, 6
North African lentil–chickpea tagine, 36
Parmesan, pasta, and pea frittata, 14
Pumpkin and spice oatmeal, 5
Thai curry with noodles, 116
Tortellini with garlicky tomato sauce, 43

9 SmartPoints
Cheese grits with greens and eggs, 9
Korean food truck tacos, 131
Spaghetti with caramelized onions, 47
Thai coconut-curry chicken, 108
Tomato-eggplant puttanesca, 35
Vegetable bolognese, 165

10 SmartPoints
Risotto with asparagus and chives, 194

12 SmartPoints
Lamb, apricot, and chickpea tagine, 189

Blue

0 SmartPoints
Super-easy three-bean chili, 27
Vietnamese lemongrass chicken soup, 120

1 SmartPoints
Hot-and-sour soup with shiitakes and tofu, 147
Indian fish curry, 144
Mexican chicken soup, 119
North African lentil–chickpea tagine, 36
Old-fashioned chicken noodle soup, 66
Portobello mushroom and eggplant chili, 28

2 SmartPoints
Cherry tomato and basil–topped spaghetti squash, 190
Creamy tomato soup with crab, 105
Italian vegetable-bean stew, 32
San Francisco fisherman's stew, 101
Sausage, chicken, and shrimp stew, 140

3 SmartPoints
Basque chicken with chorizo and peppers, 153
Butternut squash and chickpea chili, 24
Chicken and white bean chili, 69
Chicken tacos with pineapple slaw, 111
Chicken tikka masala, 154
Classic Italian meatballs, 85
Coconut shrimp with mango dipping sauce, 209
Garlicky shrimp with charred fennel, 102
Korean beef stew, 182
Moroccan chicken, 112
Mushroom, tomato, and thyme chicken, 61
Szechuan chicken and broccoli, 115
Tomato, basil, and ricotta frittata, 17

4 SmartPoints
Beet borscht with beef and cabbage, 198
Bouillabaisse, 162
Cauliflower, potato, and bacon bisque, 197
Cheese and chorizo tortilla casserole, 10
Indian-spiced potatoes with cauliflower, 51
Lamb tagine with lemon and olives, 161
Parmesan, pasta, and pea frittata, 14
Southern-style fried chicken, 201
Spiced-up rotisserie-style chicken, 174
Teriyaki pork tenderloin, 136

5 SmartPoints
Apple-stuffed French toast casserole, 21
Beef carnitas tacos, 128
Beef 'n' bean chili, 82
Brown rice, kale, and sweet potato pilaf, 193
Chicken with celery root and apple, 58
Classic chicken cacciatore, 150
Cornmeal-crusted fish fingers, 206
Double-mushroom and prosciutto soup, 94
Farro and double-mushroom pot, 39
Five-spice pork stew, 139
Italian-style pot roast, 77
Jamaican jerk chicken, 123

Recipes by SmartPoints value 215

Meatballs in chipotle chile sauce, 124
Nonna's bolognese sauce, 185
Piled-high chicken nachos, 62
Pork in green chile sauce, 143
Rice-and-bean stuffed peppers, 31
Risotto-style barley and peas, 40
Roman-style chicken cacciatore, 178
Spicy turkey meatballs, 73
Super-simple chicken parmesan, 202
Tex-Mex red chile pork tacos, 186

6 SmartPoints
Cajun chicken-sausage jambalaya, 177
Cheese-dusted potato fries, 210
Colombian beef and potato empanadas, 202
Crispy buttermilk onion rings, 213
Egg casserole with hash browns and peppers, 13
Hearty beef-barley stew, 81
Italian sausage and mozzarella strata, 18
Pork chops with braised cabbage, 90
Provençal-style beef stew, 157
Ricotta-and-spinach stuffed cabbage, 44
Rosemary-garlic pork roast, 89
Scalloped potatoes with thyme, 55
Smoky beef brisket, 181
Soft polenta with pecorino and mushrooms, 169
Thai coconut-curry chicken, 108
Tomato, basil, and ricotta frittata, 17
Tomato-eggplant puttanesca, 35

7 SmartPoints
Artichoke and bell pepper paella, 52
Beef soup with lemongrass and coconut, 132
Braciole with spicy tomato sauce, 78
Cauliflower paprikash, 166
Cheese grits with greens and eggs, 9
Just-like-banana-bread overnight oats, 2
Lamb-ricotta meatballs and sauce, 98
Louisiana jambalaya, 65
Marrakesh-style pork, 135
Parmesan-stuffed artichokes, 97
Sicilian-style pork and fennel ragu, 93
Simply delicious lasagna, 86
Summer tomato sauce with pasta, 48
Turkey–bell pepper meatloaf, 70

8 SmartPoints
Carne guisada with charred tortillas, 158

Lamb, apricot, and chickpea tagine, 189
Low-and-slow sloppy joes, 74
Mojo-style steak tacos, 127
Multigrain hot cereal with mango, 6
Pumpkin and spice oatmeal, 5
Thai curry with noodles, 116
Tortellini with garlicky tomato sauce, 43

9 SmartPoints
Korean food truck tacos, 131
Spaghetti with caramelized onions, 47
Vegetable bolognese, 165

10 SmartPoints
Risotto with asparagus and chives, 194

Purple

0 SmartPoints
Super-easy three-bean chili, 27
Tomato-eggplant puttanesca, 35
Vietnamese lemongrass chicken soup, 120

1 SmartPoints
Brown rice, kale, and sweet potato pilaf, 193
Cheese-dusted potato fries, 210
Creamy tomato soup with crab, 105
Hot-and-sour soup with shiitakes and tofu, 147
Indian fish curry, 144
Indian-spiced potatoes with cauliflower, 51
Italian vegetable-bean stew, 32
Mexican chicken soup, 119
North African lentil-chickpea tagine, 36
Old-fashioned chicken noodle soup, 66
Portobello mushroom and eggplant chili, 28

2 SmartPoints
Cajun chicken-sausage jambalaya, 177
Cherry tomato and basil–topped spaghetti squash, 190
Farro and double-mushroom pot, 39
Parmesan, pasta, and pea frittata, 14
Risotto-style barley and peas, 40
San Francisco fisherman's stew, 101

Sausage, chicken, and shrimp stew, 140
Tomato, basil, and ricotta frittata, 17

3 SmartPoints
Basque chicken with chorizo and peppers, 153
Butternut squash and chickpea chili, 24
Cauliflower, potato, and bacon bisque, 197
Chicken and white bean chili, 69
Chicken tacos with pineapple slaw, 111
Chicken tikka masala, 154
Classic Italian meatballs, 85
Coconut shrimp with mango dipping sauce, 209
Garlicky shrimp with charred fennel, 102
Korean beef stew, 182
Moroccan chicken, 112
Multigrain hot cereal with mango, 6
Mushroom, tomato, and thyme chicken, 61
Scalloped potatoes with thyme, 55
Szechuan chicken and broccoli, 115

4 SmartPoints
Beet borscht with beef and cabbage, 198
Bouillabaisse, 162
Cheese and chorizo tortilla casserole, 10
Hearty beef-barley stew, 81
Just-like-banana-bread overnight oats, 2
Lamb tagine with lemon and olives, 161
Rosemary-garlic pork roast, 89
Southern-style fried chicken, 201
Spiced-up rotisserie-style chicken, 174
Thai coconut-curry chicken, 108
Teriyaki pork tenderloin, 136

5 SmartPoints
Apple-stuffed French toast casserole, 21
Beef carnitas tacos, 128
Beef 'n' bean chili, 82
Chicken with celery root and apple, 58
Classic chicken cacciatore, 150
Cornmeal-crusted fish fingers, 206
Double-mushroom and prosciutto soup, 94
Egg casserole with hash browns and peppers, 13
Five-spice pork stew, 139
Italian-style pot roast, 77
Jamaican jerk chicken, 123
Lamb, apricot, and chickpea tagine, 189
Meatballs in chipotle chile sauce, 124
Nonna's bolognese sauce, 185

Piled-high chicken nachos, 62
Pork in green chile sauce, 143
Pumpkin and spice oatmeal, 5
Rice-and-bean stuffed peppers, 31
Roman-style chicken cacciatore, 178
Spicy turkey meatballs, 73
Super-simple chicken parmesan, 202
Tex-Mex red chile pork tacos, 186

6 SmartPoints
Colombian beef and potato empanadas, 202
Crispy buttermilk onion rings, 213
Italian sausage and mozzarella strata, 18
Pork chops with braised cabbage, 90
Provençal-style beef stew, 157
Ricotta-and-spinach stuffed cabbage, 44
Smoky beef brisket, 181
Soft polenta with pecorino and mushrooms, 169

7 SmartPoints
Artichoke and bell pepper paella, 52
Beef soup with lemongrass and coconut, 132
Braciole with spicy tomato sauce, 78
Cauliflower paprikash, 166
Cheese grits with greens and eggs, 9
Lamb-ricotta meatballs and sauce, 98
Louisiana jambalaya, 65
Marrakesh-style pork, 135
Parmesan-stuffed artichokes, 97
Sicilian-style pork and fennel ragu, 93
Simply delicious lasagna, 86
Summer tomato sauce with pasta, 48
Turkey–bell pepper meatloaf, 70

8 SmartPoints
Carne guisada with charred tortillas, 158
Low-and-slow sloppy joes, 74
Mojo-style steak tacos, 127
Thai curry with noodles, 116
Tortellini with garlicky tomato sauce, 43

9 SmartPoints
Korean food truck tacos, 131
Spaghetti with caramelized onions, 47
Vegetable bolognese, 165

10 SmartPoints
Risotto with asparagus and chives, 194

Index

A

Air fryer, vi
   basics for cooking with, xiv
   Cheese-dusted potato fries, 210
   Coconut shrimp with mango dipping sauce, 209
   Colombian beef and potato empanadas, 205
   Cornmeal-crusted fish fingers, 206
   Crispy buttermilk onion rings, 213
   FAQs, xiv
   Southern-style fried chicken, 201
   Super-simple chicken parmesan, 202
Almond milk: Multigrain hot cereal with mango, 6
Almonds: Moroccan chicken, 112
Apples
   Apple-stuffed French toast casserole, 21
   Chicken with celery root and apple, 58
   Pork chops with braised cabbage, 90
Applesauce, 173
Apricots
   Lamb, apricot, and chickpea tagine, 189
   Marrakesh-style pork, 135
Arrabbiata sauce: Braciole with spicy tomato sauce, 78
Artichokes
   Artichoke and bell pepper paella, 52
   Parmesan-stuffed artichokes, 97
Asparagus: Risotto with asparagus and chives, 194
Avocado
   Beef carnitas tacos, 128
   Piled-high chicken nachos, 62

B

Bacon
   Cauliflower, potato, and bacon bisque, 197
   Cheese grits with greens and eggs, 9
Bananas
   Just-like-banana-bread overnight oats, 2
Barbecue sauce: Smoky beef brisket, 181
Basil
   Cherry tomato and basil-topped spaghetti squash, 190
   Classic Italian meatballs, 85
   Egg casserole with hash browns and peppers, 13
   Nonna's bolognese sauce, 185
   Sicilian-style pork and fennel ragu, 93
   Simply delicious lasagna, 86
   Spicy turkey meatballs, 73
   Summer tomato sauce with pasta, 48
   Super-simple chicken parmesan, 202
   Tomato, basil, and ricotta frittata, 17
Basque chicken with chorizo and peppers, 153
Beans. *See* Black beans; Cannellini beans; Green beans; Pinto beans; Red kidney beans
Beef. *See also* Ground beef
   Beef carnitas tacos, 128
   Beef soup with lemongrass and coconut, 132
   Beet borscht with beef and cabbage, 198
   Braciole with spicy tomato sauce, 78
   Carne guisada with charred tortillas, 158
   Colombian beef and potato empanadas, 205
   Italian-style pot roast, 77
   Korean beef stew, 182
   Korean food truck tacos, 128
   Mojo-style steak tacos, 127
   Provençal-style beef stew, 157
   Smoky beef brisket, 181
Beef broth
   Beet borscht with beef and cabbage, 198
   Double mushroom and prosciutto soup, 94
   Hearty beef-barley stew, 81
   Nonna's bolognese sauce, 185
Beer
   Beef carnitas tacos, 128
   Mojo-style steak tacos, 127
   Smoky beef brisket, 181
Beet borscht with beef and cabbage, 198
Bell peppers
   Artichoke and bell pepper paella, 52
   Basque chicken with chorizo and peppers, 153
   Beef 'n' bean chili, 82
   Butternut squash and chickpea chili, 24
   Cajun chicken-sausage jambalaya, 177
   Carne guisada with charred tortillas, 158

Cauliflower paprikash, 166
Cheese and chorizo tortilla casserole, 10
Classic chicken cacciatore, 160
Egg casserole with hash browns and peppers, 13
Garlicky shrimp with charred fennel, 102
Italian vegetable-bean stew, 32
Louisiana jambalaya, 65
Old-fashioned chicken noodle soup, 66
Pork in green chile sauce, 143
Portobello mushroom and eggplant chili, 28
Rice-and-bean stuffed peppers, 31
Sausage, chicken, and shrimp stew, 140
Szechuan chicken and broccoli, 115
Thai coconut curry chicken, 108
Thai curry with noodles, 116
Tomato-eggplant puttanesca, 35
Turkey-bell pepper meat loaf, 70

Black beans
Portobello mushroom and eggplant chili, 28
Super-easy three-bean chili, 27

Bok choy: Korean beef stew, 182
Bouillabaisse, 162
Braciole with spicy tomato sauce, 78

Bread crumbs
Braciole with spicy tomato sauce, 78
Coconut shrimp with mango dipping sauce, 209
Crispy buttermilk onion rings, 213
Lamb-ricotta meatballs and sauce, 98
Meatballs in chipotle chile sauce, 124
Parmesan-stuffed artichokes, 97
Spicy turkey meatballs, 73
Super-simple chicken parmesan, 202
Turkey–bell pepper meat loaf, 70

Breakfast and brunch
Apple-stuffed French toast casserole, 21
Cheese and chorizo tortilla casserole, 10
Cheese grits with greens and eggs, 9
Egg casserole with hash browns and peppers, 13
Italian sausage and mozzarella strata, 18
Just-like-banana-bread overnight oats, 2
Multigrain hot cereal with mango, 6
Parmesan, pasta, and pea frittata, 14
Pumpkin and spice oatmeal, 5
Tomato, basil, and ricotta frittata, 17

Broccoli
Five-spice pork stew, 139
Szechuan chicken and broccoli, 115

Broth. See Beef broth; Chicken broth; Seafood stock; Vegetable broth

Buttermilk
Crispy buttermilk onion rings, 213
Southern-style fried chicken, 201

Butternut squash
Butternut squash and chickpea chili, 24
Farro and double-mushroom pot, 39
Lamb tagine with lemon and olives, 161
Moroccan chicken, 112
North African lentil-chickpea tagine, 36

C

Cabbage
Beet borscht with beef and cabbage, 198
Chicken tacos with pineapple slaw, 111
Hot-and-sour soup with shiitakes and tofu, 147
Pork chops with braised cabbage, 90
Ricotta and spinach stuffed cabbage, 44
Cajun chicken-sausage jambalaya, 177

Campari tomatoes: Garlicky shrimp with charred fennel, 102

Canadian bacon: Parmesan, pasta, and pea frittata, 14

Cannellini beans
Chicken and white bean chili, 69
Super-easy three-bean chili, 27
Carne guisada with charred tortillas, 158

Carrots
Beef soup with lemongrass and coconut, 132
Beet borscht with beef and

Index 219

cabbage, 198
Chicken with celery root and apple, 58
Five-spice pork stew, 139
Indian fish curry, 144
Italian vegetable-bean stew, 32
Korean beef stew, 182
Korean food truck tacos, 131
Mexican chicken soup, 119
Old-fashioned chicken noodle soup, 66
Roman-style chicken cacciatore, 178
Thai coconut curry chicken, 108

Cauliflower
Cauliflower, potato, and bacon bisque, 197
Cauliflower paprikash, 166
Italian-spiced potatoes with cauliflower, 51
Thai coconut curry chicken, 108

Celery
Butternut squash and chickpea chili, 24
Cajun chicken-sausage jambalaya, 177
Cauliflower, potato, and bacon bisque, 197
Chicken with celery root and apple, 58
Louisiana jambalaya, 65
Nonna's bolognese sauce, 185

Cheddar cheese
Beef 'n' bean chili, 82
Carne guisada with charred tortillas, 158
Cauliflower, potato, and bacon bisque, 197
Cheese grits with greens and eggs, 9

Piled-high chicken nachos, 62
Cheese. *See* Cheddar cheese; Mozzarella cheese; Parmesan cheese; Pecorino-Romano cheese; Ricotta cheese
Cheese and chorizo tortilla casserole, 10
Cheese-dusted potato fries, 210
Cheese grits with greens and eggs, 9
Cherry peppers: Spiced-up rotisserie-style chicken, 174
Cherry tomatoes
Cheese grits with greens and eggs, 9
Cherry tomato and basil-topped spaghetti squash, 190
Mojo-style steak tacos, 127
Tomato, basil, and ricotta frittata, 17

Chicken breasts
Basque chicken with chorizo and peppers, 153
Cajun chicken-sausage jambalaya, 177
Chicken and white bean chili, 69
Chicken tacos with pineapple slaw, 111
Mexican chicken soup, 119
Old-fashioned chicken noodle soup, 66
Piled-high chicken nachos, 62
Sausage, chicken, and shrimp stew, 140
Southern-style fried chicken, 201
Super-simple chicken parmesan, 202
Szechuan chicken and broccoli, 115

Thai coconut curry chicken, 108
Vietnamese lemongrass chicken soup, 120
Chicken broth, 172
Cajun chicken-sausage jambalaya, 177
Cauliflower, potato, and bacon bisque, 197
Chicken and white bean chili, 69
Chicken with celery root and apple, 58
Five-spice pork stew, 139
Louisiana jambalaya, 65
Meatballs in chipotle chile sauce, 124
Mexican chicken soup, 119
Old-fashioned chicken noodle soup, 66
Pork in green chile sauce, 143
Roman-style chicken cacciatore, 178
Rosemary-garlic pork roast, 89
San Francisco fisherman's stew, 101
Sausage, chicken, and shrimp stew, 140
Spiced-up rotisserie-style chicken, 174
Szechuan chicken and broccoli, 115
Teriyaki pork tenderloin, 136
Vietnamese lemongrass chicken soup, 120

Chicken thighs
Chicken tikka masala, 154
Chicken with celery root and apple, 58
Classic chicken cacciatore, 160
Jamaican jerk chicken, 123
Louisiana jambalaya, 65

Moroccan chicken, 112
Mushroom, tomato, and thyme chicken, 61
Roman-style chicken cacciatore, 178
Thai curry with noodles, 116

Chicken, whole
Spiced-up rotisserie-style chicken, 174

Chickpeas
Butternut squash and chickpea chili, 24
Lamb, apricot, and chickpea tagine, 189
Moroccan chicken, 112
North African lentil-chickpea tagine, 36
Tomato-eggplant puttanesca, 35

Chile pepper: Indian fish curry, 144

Chili
Beef 'n' bean chili, 82
Butternut squash and chickpea chili, 24
Chicken and white bean chili, 69
Portobello mushroom and eggplant chili, 28
Super-easy three-bean chili, 27

Chipotles en adobo: Meatballs in chipotle chile sauce, 124

Chives: Risotto with asparagus and chives, 194

Chorizo
Basque chicken with chorizo and peppers, 153
Cheese and chorizo tortilla casserole, 10

Cinnamon-raisin bread: Apple-stuffed French toast casserole, 21

Classic chicken cacciatore, 150

Classic Italian meatballs, 85

Coconut
Coconut shrimp with mango dipping sauce, 209
Multigrain hot cereal with mango, 6

Coconut milk
Beef soup with lemongrass and coconut, 132
Thai coconut curry chicken, 108
Thai curry with noodles, 116

Coconut shrimp with mango dipping sauce, 209

Colombian beef and potato empanadas, 205

Cooked foods, storage times for, xvi

Corn
Hot-and-sour soup with shiitakes and tofu, 147
Piled-high chicken nachos, 62
Super-easy three-bean chili, 27

Cornflake crumbs: Southern-style fried chicken, 201

Cornmeal-crusted fish fingers, 206

Couscous: Lamb, apricot, and chickpea tagine, 189

Crab: Creamy tomato soup with crab, 105

Cranberries: Pork chops with braised cabbage, 90

Creamy tomato soup with crab, 105

Crispy buttermilk onion rings, 213

Cucumbers: Korean food truck tacos, 131

Curry: Indian fish curry, 144

D

Dairy free recipes, xviii

Defrosting
cold water method for, xvii
microwave method for, xvii
refrigerator method for, xvii

Double mushroom and prosciutto soup, 94

E

Egg casserole with hash browns and peppers, 13

Egg noodles: Old-fashioned chicken noodle soup, 66

Eggplant
Portobello mushroom and eggplant chili, 28
Tomato-eggplant puttanesca, 35

Eggs
Apple-stuffed French toast casserole, 21
Cheese and chorizo tortilla casserole, 10
Cheese grits with greens and eggs, 9
Classic Italian meatballs, 85
Egg casserole with hash browns and peppers, 13
Hot-and-sour soup with shiitakes and tofu, 147
Italian sausage and mozzarella strata, 18
Parmesan, pasta, and pea frittata, 14
Soft-cooked and hard-cooked eggs, 173
Tomato, basil, and ricotta frittata, 17

F

Farro and double-mushroom pot, 39
Fennel
    Garlicky shrimp with charred fennel, 102
    Sicilian-style pork and fennel ragu, 93
Fettuccine: Tomato-eggplant puttanesca, 35
Fish and seafood, xix
    Bouillabaisse, 162
    Coconut shrimp with mango dipping sauce, 209
    Cornmeal-crusted fish fingers, 206
    Creamy tomato soup with crab, 105
    Garlicky shrimp with charred fennel, 102
    Indian fish curry, 144
    San Francisco fisherman's stew, 101
    Sausage, chicken, and shrimp stew, 140
Five-spice pork stew, 139
Frittata
    Parmesan, pasta, and pea frittata, 14
    Tomato, basil, and ricotta frittata, 17

G

Garlicky shrimp with charred fennel, 102
Gluten free recipes, xviii
Grape tomatoes
    Egg casserole with hash browns and peppers, 13
    Roman-style chicken cacciatore, 178
Greek yogurt. See also Yogurt

Butternut squash and chickpea chili, 24
Cauliflower paprikash, 166
Chicken tikka masala, 154
North African lentil-chickpea tagine, 36
Portobello mushroom and eggplant chili, 28
Green beans
    Italian vegetable-bean stew, 32
    Thai curry with noodles, 116
Grits: Cheese grits with greens and eggs, 9
Ground beef
    Classic Italian meatballs, 85
    Nonna's bolognese sauce, 185
    Simply delicious lasagna, 86

H

Habanero peppers: Jamaican jerk chicken, 123
Halibut
    Indian fish curry, 144
    San Francisco fisherman's stew, 101
Hearty beef-barley stew, 81
Honey
    Multigrain hot cereal with mango, 6
    Pumpkin and Spice Oatmeal, 5
Hot-and-sour soup with shiitakes and tofu, 147
Hummus, 173

I

Indian-spiced potatoes with cauliflower, 4
Ingredients, choosing, xix
Instant pot, vi
    Applesauce, 173
    Beet borscht with beef

and cabbage, 198
Brown rice, kale, and sweet potato pilaf, 183
Cajun chicken-sausage jambalaya, 177
Cauliflower, potato, and bacon bisque, 197
Cherry tomato and basil–topped spaghetti squash, 190
Chicken stock, 172
Converting slow cooker recipes for, xiii
FAQ's, xiii
Hummus, 173
Korean beef stew, 182
Lamb, apricot, and chickpea tagine, 189
Nonna's bolognese sauce, 185
Plain yogurt, 172
Risotto with asparagus and chives, 194
Roman-style chicken cacciatore, 178
Smoky beef brisket, 181
Soft-cooked and hard-cooked eggs, 173
Spiced-up rotisserie-style chicken, 174
Tex-Mex red chile pork tacos, 186
White rice, 172
Italian fish curry, 144
Italian frying peppers (Cubanelles)
    Egg casserole with hash browns and peppers, 13
    Italian sausage and mozzarella strata, 18
Italian sausage and mozzarella strata, 18
Italian-style pot roast, 77

Italian vegetable-bean stew, 32

J

Jalapeño pepper
    Carne guisada with charred tortillas, 158
    Coconut shrimp with mango dipping sauce, 209
    Italian-spiced potatoes with cauliflower, 51
    Pork in green chile sauce, 143
Jamaican jerk chicken, 123
Jambalaya: Cajun chicken-sausage jambalaya, 177
Just-like-banana-bread overnight oats, 2

K

Kale
    Brown rice, kale, and sweet potato pilaf, 193
    Cheese grits with greens and eggs, 9
Korean beef stew, 182
Korean food truck tacos, 131

L

Lamb
    Lamb, apricot, and chickpea tagine, 189
    Lamb-ricotta meatballs and sauce, 98
    Lamb tagine with lemon and olives, 161
Lean meats, xix
Leeks
    Bouillabaisse, 162
    Old-fashioned chicken noodle soup, 66
    Risotto with asparagus and chives, 194
Leftovers, xvi

Lemongrass
    Beef soup with lemongrass and coconut, 132
    Vietnamese lemongrass chicken soup, 120
Lentils: North African lentil-chickpea tagine, 36
Lettuce. *See* Romaine lettuce
Louisiana jambalaya, 65
Low-and-slow sloppy joes, 74

M

Mangoes
    Coconut shrimp with mango dipping sauce, 209
    Multigrain hot cereal with mango, 6
Marinara sauce
    Sicilian-style pork and fennel ragu, 93
    Super-simple chicken parmesan, 202
    Tortellini with garlicky tomato sauce, 43
Marrakesh-style pork, 135
Meals for 2
    Basque chicken with chorizo and peppers, 153
    Bouillabaisse, 162
    Carne guisada with charred tortillas, 158
    Cauliflower paprikash, 166
    Chicken tikka masala, 154
    Classic chicken cacciatore, 150
    Lamb tagine with lemon and olives, 161
    Provençal-style beef stew, 157
    Soft polenta with pecorino and mushrooms, 169
    Vegetable bolognese, 165
Meatballs
    Classic Italian meatballs, 85

    Lamb-ricotta meatballs and sauce, 98
    Meatballs in chipotle chile sauce, 124
    Spicy turkey meatballs, 73
Meat loaf: Turkey–bell pepper meat loaf, 70
Mexican chicken soup, 119
Mixed vegetables: Artichoke and bell pepper paella, 52
Mojo-style steak tacos, 127
Moroccan chicken, 112
Mozzarella cheese
    Egg casserole with hash browns and peppers, 13
    Italian sausage and mozzarella strata, 18
    Parmesan, pasta, and pea frittata, 14
    Simply delicious lasagna, 86
    Super-simple chicken parmesan, 202
    Tortellini with garlicky tomato sauce, 43
Multigrain hot cereal with mango, 6
Mushrooms
    Cauliflower paprikash, 166
    Classic chicken cacciatore, 160
    Double mushroom and prosciutto soup, 94
    Farro and double-mushroom pot, 39
    Hot-and-sour soup with shiitakes and tofu, 147
    Italian-style pot roast, 77
    Italian vegetable-bean stew, 32
    Mushroom, tomato, and thyme chicken, 61
    Portobello mushroom and eggplant chili, 28

Provençal-style beef stew, 157
Roman-style chicken cacciatore, 178
Simply delicious lasagna, 86
Soft polenta with pecorino and mushrooms, 169
Vegetable bolognese, 165

N

Nonna's bolognese sauce, 185
North African lentil-chickpea tagine, 36
Nuts. *See* Almonds; Peanuts; Pine nuts

O

Oats
Just-like-banana-bread overnight oats, 2
Multigrain hot cereal with mango, 6
Pumpkin and Spice Oatmeal, 5
Okra: Sausage, chicken, and shrimp stew, 140
Old-fashioned chicken noodle soup, 66
Olives
Classic chicken cacciatore, 160
Garlicky shrimp with charred fennel, 102
Lamb tagine with lemon and olives, 161
Tomato-eggplant puttanesca, 35
Onions
Spaghetti with caramelized onions, 47
Crispy buttermilk onion rings, 213
Orange zest
Bouillabaisse, 162

Provençal-style beef stew, 157

P

Parmesan cheese
Spaghetti with caramelized onions, 47
Cheese-dusted potato fries, 210
Cherry Tomato and basil-topped spaghetti squash, 190
Double mushroom and prosciutto soup, 94
Farro and double-mushroom pot, 39
Italian sausage and mozzarella strata, 18
Nonna's bolognese sauce, 185
Parmesan, pasta, and pea frittata, 14
Parmesan-stuffed artichokes, 97
Ricotta and spinach stuffed cabbage, 44
Risotto-style barley and peas, 40
Scalloped potatoes with thyme, 55
Sicilian-style pork and fennel ragu, 93
Simply delicious lasagna, 86
Super-simple chicken parmesan, 202
Vegetable bolognese, 165
Peanut butter
Thai coconut curry chicken, 108
Thai curry with noodles, 116
Peanuts
North African lentil-chickpea tagine, 36
Thai coconut curry chicken, 108

Pearl barley
Hearty beef-barley stew, 81
Multigrain hot cereal with mango, 6
Pearl onions: Mushroom, tomato, and thyme chicken, 61
Pears: Korean beef stew, 182
Peas
Lamb tagine with lemon and olives, 161
Parmesan, pasta, and pea frittata, 14
Risotto-style barley and peas, 40
Pecorino-Romano cheese
Braciole with spicy tomato sauce, 78
Cheese-dusted potato fries, 210
Egg casserole with hash browns and peppers, 13
Italian vegetable-bean stew, 32
Rice-and-bean stuffed peppers, 31
Risotto with asparagus and chives, 194
Soft polenta with pecorino and mushrooms, 169
Penne: Summer tomato sauce with pasta, 48
Peppercorns: Szechuan chicken and broccoli, 115
Peppers. *See* Bell peppers; Cherry peppers; Chile peppers; Habanero peppers; Italian frying peppers (cubanelles); Jalapeño peppers; Poblano peppers; Serrano peppers
Piled-high chicken nachos, 62
Pineapple: Chicken tacos with

pineapple slaw, 111
Pine nuts: Parmesan-stuffed artichokes, 97
Pinto beans: Super-easy three-bean chili, 27
Plum tomatoes
   Beef 'n' bean chili, 82
   Colombian beef and potato empanadas, 205
   Piled-high chicken nachos, 62
   Summer tomato sauce with pasta, 48
Poblano peppers
   Carne guisada with charred tortillas, 158
   Cheese and chorizo tortilla casserole, 10
   Chicken tacos with pineapple slaw, 111
   Mexican chicken soup, 119
   Pork in green chile sauce, 143
Pork
   Five-spice pork stew, 139
   Marrakesh-style pork, 135
   Pork chops with braised cabbage, 90
   Pork in green chile sauce, 143
   Rosemary-garlic pork roast, 89
   Sicilian-style pork and fennel ragu, 93
   Teriyaki pork tenderloin, 136
   Tex-Mex red chile pork tacos, 186
Portobello mushroom and eggplant chili, 28
Potatoes
   Beef soup with lemongrass and coconut, 132
   Cauliflower, potato, and bacon bisque, 197
   Cheese-dusted potato fries, 210

Colombian beef and potato empanadas, 205
Creamy tomato soup with crab, 105
Egg casserole with hash browns and peppers, 13
Italian-spiced potatoes with cauliflower, 51
Italian vegetable-bean stew, 32
Rosemary-garlic pork roast, 89
Scalloped potatoes with thyme, 55
Thai coconut curry chicken, 108
Tomato, basil, and ricotta frittata, 17
Prep ahead, 47, 86, 165, 177
Produce, xix
Prosciutto
   Double mushroom and prosciutto soup, 94
   Parmesan-stuffed artichokes, 97
Provençal-style beef stew, 157
Pumpkin and spice oatmeal, 5

Q

Quinoa: Multigrain hot cereal with mango, 6

R

Radishes
   Korean food truck tacos, 131
   Tex-Mex red chile pork tacos, 186
Ragu: Sicilian-style pork and fennel ragu, 93
Recipes, information about, xviii–xix
Red kidney beans

Beef 'n' bean chili, 82
Italian vegetable-bean stew, 32
Rice-and-bean stuffed peppers, 31
Red onions
   Cheese and chorizo tortilla casserole, 10
   Italian-style pot roast, 77
   Marrakesh-style pork, 135
   Tomato, basil, and ricotta frittata, 17
Red snapper: Bouillabaisse, 162
Red wine
   Braciole with spicy tomato sauce, 78
   Classic chicken cacciatore, 160
   Provençal-style beef stew, 157
Roman-style chicken cacciatore, 178
Rice
   Brown rice, kale, and sweet potato pilaf, 193
   Cajun chicken-sausage jambalaya, 177
   Cauliflower paprikash, 166
   Louisiana jambalaya, 65
   Rice-and-bean stuffed peppers, 31
   Risotto with asparagus and chives, 194
   White rice, 172
Rice noodles
   Thai curry with noodles, 116
   Vietnamese lemongrass chicken soup, 120
Ricotta cheese
   Lamb-ricotta meatballs and sauce, 98
   Ricotta and spinach stuffed cabbage, 44

Simply delicious lasagna, 86
Tomato, basil, and ricotta frittata, 17
Risotto-style barley and peas, 40
Risotto with asparagus and chives, 194
Romaine lettuce: Tex-Mex red chile pork tacos, 186
Roman-style chicken cacciatore, 178
Rosemary-garlic pork roast, 89

S

Salmon: Indian fish curry, 144
Salsa
Beef carnitas tacos, 128
Piled-high chicken nachos, 62
Sandwiches: Low-and-slow sloppy joes, 74
San Francisco fisherman's stew, 101
Sausage, chicken, and shrimp stew, 140
Scallions: Vietnamese lemongrass chicken soup, 120
Scalloped potatoes with thyme, 55
Seafood stock: Bouillabaisse, 162
Serrano pepper: Thai curry with noodles, 116
Sesame seeds: Five-spice pork stew, 139
Shrimp
Bouillabaisse, 162
Coconut shrimp with mango dipping sauce, 209
San Francisco fisherman's stew, 101
Sausage, chicken, and shrimp stew, 140
Sicilian-style pork and fennel

ragu, 93
Simply delicious lasagna, 86
Slow cooker
basics with, ix
converting recipes for the Instant Pot, xiii
easy care of, viii
FAQs, xi
fitness test for, ix
keys to success, viii
manual, viii
programmable, viii
programmable cook-and-carry, viii
tailoring recipes for, x
SmartPoints values, xix
recipes by, 215–216
Smoky beef brisket, 181
Soft-cooked and hard-cooked eggs, 173
Soft polenta with pecorino and mushrooms, 169
Soups
Beef soup with lemongrass and coconut, 132
Beet borscht with beef and cabbage, 198
Cauliflower, potato, and bacon bisque, 197
Creamy tomato soup with crab, 105
Double mushroom and prosciutto soup, 94
Hot-and-sour soup with shiitakes and tofu, 147
Mexican chicken soup, 119
Old-fashioned chicken noodle soup, 66
Vietnamese lemongrass chicken soup, 120
Sour cream
Beef 'n' bean chili, 82

Beet borscht with beef and cabbage, 198
Chicken and white bean chili, 69
Southern-style fried chicken, 201
Soy crumbles: Butternut squash and chickpea chili, 24
Spaghetti
Spaghetti with caramelized onions, 47
Parmesan, pasta, and pea frittata, 14
Vegetable bolognese, 165
Spaghetti squash: Cherry tomato and basil–topped spaghetti squash, 190
Spaghetti with caramelized onions, 47
Spiced-up rotisserie-style chicken, 174
Spicy turkey meatballs, 73
Spinach
Hearty beef-barley stew, 81
Ricotta and spinach stuffed cabbage, 44
Simply delicious lasagna, 86
Tortellini with garlicky tomato sauce, 43
Squash. See Butternut squash; Spaghetti squash
Stew
Bouillabaisse, 162
Five-spice pork stew, 139
Hearty beef-barley stew, 81
Italian vegetable-bean stew, 32
Korean beef stew, 182
Lamb, apricot, and chickpea tagine, 189
Provençal-style beef stew, 157
San Francisco fisherman's stew, 101

226   100 Slow Cooker & Instant Pot® Recipes

Sausage, chicken, and shrimp stew, 140
Stir-fry vegetables; Five-spice pork stew, 139
Storage times for cooked foods, xvi
Summer tomato sauce with pasta, 48
Sun-dried tomatoes:
Parmesan, pasta, and pea frittata, 14
Super-easy three-bean chili, 27
Super-simple chicken parmesan, 202
Sweet potatoes
Brown rice, kale, and sweet potato pilaf, 193
Thai coconut curry chicken, 108
Szechuan chicken and broccoli, 116

T
Tacos
Beef carnitas tacos, 128
Chicken tacos with pineapple slaw, 111
Korean food truck tacos, 131
Mojo-style steak tacos, 127
Tex-Mex red chile pork tacos, 186
Teriyaki pork tenderloin, 136
Tex-Mex red-chile pork tacos, 186
Thai coconut curry chicken, 108
Thai curry with noodles, 116
Thyme: Scalloped potatoes with thyme, 55
Tofu: Hot-and-sour soup with shiitakes and tofu, 147
Tomatillos: Pork in green chile sauce, 143

Tomatoes. *See also* Cherry tomatoes; Campari tomatoes; Grape tomatoes; Plum tomatoes; Sun-dried tomatoes
Basque chicken with chorizo and peppers, 153
Beef 'n' bean chili, 82
Bouillabaisse, 162
Butternut squash and chickpea chili, 24
Cajun chicken-sausage jambalaya, 177
Carne guisada with charred tortillas, 158
Cauliflower paprikash, 166
Cheese and chorizo tortilla casserole, 10
Chicken tikka masala, 154
Classic chicken cacciatore, 160
Classic Italian meatballs, 85
Creamy tomato soup with crab, 105
Farro and double-mushroom pot, 39
Indian fish curry, 144
Italian-style pot roast, 77
Italian vegetable-bean stew, 32
Lamb-ricotta meatballs and sauce, 98
Lamb tagine with lemon and olives, 161
Louisiana jambalaya, 65
Low-and-slow sloppy joes, 74
Meatballs in chipotle chile sauce, 124
Mexican chicken soup, 119
Moroccan chicken, 112
Mushroom, tomato, and thyme chicken, 61
Nonna's bolognese sauce, 185

North African lentil-chickpea tagine, 36
Portobello mushroom and eggplant chili, 28
Provençal-style beef stew, 157
Rice and bean–stuffed peppers, 31
Ricotta and spinach–stuffed cabbage, 44
San Francisco fisherman's stew, 101
Sausage, chicken, and shrimp stew, 140
Simply delicious lasagna, 86
Spicy turkey meatballs, 73
Super-easy three-bean chili, 27
Super-simple chicken parmesan, 202
Tomato, basil, and ricotta frittata, 17
Tomato-eggplant puttanesca, 35
Vegetable bolognese, 165
Tortellini with garlicky tomato sauce, 43
Tortilla chips: Piled-high chicken nachos, 62
Tortillas
Beef carnitas tacos, 128
Carne guisada with charred tortillas, 158
Cheese and chorizo tortilla casserole, 10
Chicken tacos with pineapple slaw, 111
Korean food truck tacos, 131
Mojo-style steak tacos, 127
Turkey bacon: Cauliflower, potato, and bacon bisque, 197
Turkey–bell pepper meat loaf, 70
Turkey, ground
Low-and-slow sloppy joes, 74

Index 227

Meatballs in chipotle chile sauce, 124
Spicy turkey meatballs, 73
Turkey–bell pepper meat loaf, 70
Turkey kielbasa: Cajun chicken-sausage jambalaya, 177
Turkey sausage
    Italian sausage and mozzarella strata, 18
    Louisiana jambalaya, 65
    Sausage, chicken, and shrimp stew, 140

V

Vegan recipes, xviii
Vegetable bolognese, 165
Vegetable broth
    Artichoke and bell pepper paella, 52
    Brown rice, kale, and sweet potato pilaf, 193
    Butternut squash and chickpea chili, 24
    Creamy tomato soup with crab, 105
    Farro and double-mushroom pot, 39
    Hot-and-sour soup with shiitakes and tofu, 147
    Italian vegetable-bean stew, 32
    North African lentil-chickpea tagine, 36
    Risotto-style barley and peas, 40
    Soft polenta with pecorino and mushrooms, 169
    Tomato-eggplant puttanesca, 35
Vegetarian mains
    Artichoke and bell pepper paella, 52
    Butternut squash and chickpea chili, 24
    Spaghetti with caramelized onions, 47
    Farro and double-mushroom pot, 39
    Indian-spiced potatoes with cauliflower, 4
    Italian vegetable-bean stew, 32
    North African lentil-chickpea tagine, 36
    Portobello mushroom and eggplant chili, 28
    Rice and bean–stuffed peppers, 31
    Ricotta and spinach–stuffed cabbage, 44
    Risotto-style barley and peas, 40
    Scalloped potatoes with thyme, 55
    Summer tomato sauce with pasta, 48
    Super-easy three-bean chili, 27
    Tomato-eggplant puttanesca, 35
    Tortellini with garlicky tomato sauce, 43
Vegetarian recipes, xviii
Vietnamese lemongrass chicken soup, 120

W

Weight Watchers, ii
    life on, vi
White rice, 172
White wine
    Bouillabaisse, 162
    Risotto-style barley and peas, 40
    Risotto with asparagus and chives, 194
    Sicilian-style pork and fennel ragu, 93
Whole-grain bread
    Egg casserole with hash browns and peppers, 13
    Italian sausage and mozzarella strata, 18
Whole grains, xix
Whole wheat hamburger buns
    Low-and-slow sloppy joes, 74
Wine. *See* Red wine; White wine

Y

Yogurt, 172. *See also* Greek yogurt
    Cornmeal-crusted fish fingers, 206
    Italian-spiced potatoes with cauliflower, 51
plain, 172

Z

ZeroPoint foods, xix
Zucchini
    Meatballs in chipotle chile sauce, 124
    Tortellini with garlicky tomato sauce, 43